THE HARVARD CLASSICS

The Five-Foot Shelf of Books

Antoinette on the way to her execution
From the painting by François Flameng

Marie Antoinette on the way to her execution

From the painting by François Flameng

THE HARVARD CLASSICS
EDITED BY CHARLES W. ELIOT, LL.D.

Edmund Burke

On Taste
On the Sublime and Beautiful
Reflections on the French Revolution
A Letter to a Noble Lord

With *Introduction* and *Notes*
Volume 24

P. F. Collier & Son Corporation
NEW YORK

CONTENTS

	PAGE
PREFACE	7

ON TASTE

INTRODUCTORY DISCOURSE 11

THE SUBLIME AND BEAUTIFUL

PART I.

SECTION I.—NOVELTY 29

SECT. II.—PAIN AND PLEASURE 30

SECT. III.—THE DIFFERENCE BETWEEN THE REMOVAL OF PAIN, AND POSITIVE PLEASURE 31

SECT. IV.—OF DELIGHT AND PLEASURE AS OPPOSED TO EACH OTHER 33

SECT. V.—JOY AND GRIEF 34

SECT. VI.—OF THE PASSIONS WHICH BELONG TO SELF-PRESERVATION 35

SECT. VII.—OF THE SUBLIME 35

SECT. VIII.—OF THE PASSIONS WHICH BELONG TO SOCIETY . 36

SECT. IX.—THE FINAL CAUSE OF THE DIFFERENCE BETWEEN THE PASSIONS BELONGING TO SELF-PRESERVATION AND THOSE WHICH REGARD THE SOCIETY OF THE SEXES 37

SECT. X.—OF BEAUTY 38

SECT. XI.—SOCIETY AND SOLITUDE 39

SECT. XII.—SYMPATHY, IMITATION, AND AMBITION . . . 39

SECT. XIII.—SYMPATHY 39

SECT. XIV.—THE EFFECTS OF SYMPATHY IN THE DISTRESSES OF OTHERS 40

SECT. XV.—OF THE EFFECTS OF TRAGEDY 42

SECT. XVI.—IMITATION 43

SECT. XVII.—AMBITION 44

SECT. XVIII.—THE RECAPITULATION 45

SECT. XIX.—THE CONCLUSION 46

I

PAGE

PART II.

Section I.—Of the Passion Caused by the Sublime . . . 49
Sect. II.—Terror 49
Sect. III.—Obscurity 50
Sect. IV.—Of the Difference Between Clearness and Obscurity with Regard to the Passions 51
Sect. [IV.]—The Same Subject Continued 52
Sect. V.—Power 55
Sect. VI.—Privation 60
Sect. VII.—Vastness 61
Sect. VIII.—Infinity 62
Sect. IX.—Succession and Uniformity 63
Sect. X.—Magnitude in Building 64
Sect. XI.—Infinity in Pleasing Objects 65
Sect. XII.—Difficulty 65
Sect. XIII.—Magnificence 66
Sect. XIV.—Light 67
Sect. XV.—Light in Building 68
Sect. XVI.—Colour Considered as Productive of the Sublime 69
Sect. XVII.—Sound and Loudness 69
Sect. XVIII.—Suddenness 70
Sect. XIX.—Intermitting 70
Sect. XX.—The Cries of Animals 71
Sect. XXI.—Smell and Taste. Bitters and Stenches . . . 71
Sect. XXII.—Feeling. Pain 73

PART III.

Section I.—Of Beauty 74
Sect. II.—Proportion not the Cause of Beauty in Vegetables 75
Sect. III.—Proportion not the Cause of Beauty in Animals 77
Sect. IV.—Proportion not the Cause of Beauty in the Human Species 78
Sect. V.—Proportion Further Considered 83
Sect. VI.—Fitness not the Cause of Beauty 85
Sect. VII.—The Real Effects of Fitness 87

PAGE

SECT. VIII.—THE RECAPITULATION 89

SECT. IX.—PERFECTION NOT THE CAUSE OF BEAUTY 90

SECT. X.—HOW FAR THE IDEA OF BEAUTY MAY BE APPLIED TO
THE QUALITIES OF THE MIND 90

SECT. XI.—HOW FAR THE IDEA OF BEAUTY MAY BE APPLIED
TO VIRTUE 91

SECT. XII.—THE REAL CAUSE OF BEAUTY 92

SECT. XIII.—BEAUTIFUL OBJECTS SMALL 92

SECT. XIV.—SMOOTHNESS 93

SECT. XV.—GRADUAL VARIATION 94

SECT. XVI.—DELICACY 95

SECT. XVII.—BEAUTY IN COLOUR 95

SECT. XVIII.—RECAPITULATION 96

SECT. XIX.—THE PHYSIOGNOMY 96

SECT. XX.—THE EYE 97

SECT. XXI.—UGLINESS 97

SECT. XXII.—GRACE 98

SECT. XXIII.—ELEGANCE AND SPECIOUSNESS 98

SECT. XXIV.—THE BEAUTIFUL IN FEELING 98

SECT. XXV.—THE BEAUTIFUL IN SOUNDS 100

SECT. XXVI.—TASTE AND SMELL 101

SECT. XXVII.—THE SUBLIME AND BEAUTIFUL COMPARED . . 101

PART IV.

SECTION I.—OF THE EFFICIENT CAUSE OF THE SUBLIME AND
BEAUTIFUL 103

SECT. II.—ASSOCIATION 104

SECT. III.—CAUSE OF PAIN AND FEAR 105

SECT. IV.—CONTINUED 106

SECT. V.—HOW THE SUBLIME IS PRODUCED 107

SECT. VI.—HOW PAIN CAN BE A CAUSE OF DELIGHT . . . 107

SECT. VII.—EXERCISE NECESSARY FOR THE FINER ORGANS . . 108

SECT. VIII.—WHY THINGS NOT DANGEROUS PRODUCE A PASSION
LIKE TERROR 109

SECT. IX.—WHY VISUAL OBJECTS OF GREAT DIMENSIONS ARE
SUBLIME 109

SECT. X.—UNITY, WHY REQUISITE TO VASTNESS 110

CONTENTS

PAGE

SECT. XI.—THE ARTIFICIAL INFINITE 111

SECT. XII.—THE VIBRATIONS MUST BE SIMILAR 112

SECT. XIII.—THE EFFECTS OF SUCCESSION IN VISUAL OBJECTS
EXPLAINED 112

SECT. XIV.—LOCKE'S OPINION CONCERNING DARKNESS CON-
SIDERED 114

SECT. XV.—DARKNESS TERRIBLE IN ITS OWN NATURE . . . 115

SECT. XVI.—WHY DARKNESS IS TERRIBLE 116

SECT. XVII.—THE EFFECTS OF BLACKNESS 117

SECT. XVIII.—THE EFFECTS OF BLACKNESS MODERATED . . . 119

SECT. XIX.—THE PHYSICAL CAUSE OF LOVE 119

SECT. XX.—WHY SMOOTHNESS IS BEAUTIFUL 120

SECT. XXI.—SWEETNESS, ITS NATURE 121

SECT. XXII.—SWEETNESS RELAXING 123

SECT. XXIII.—VARIATION, WHY BEAUTIFUL 124

SECT. XXIV.—CONCERNING SMALLNESS 125

SECT. XXV.—OF COLOUR 127

PART V.

SECTION I.—OF WORDS 129

SECT. II.—THE COMMON EFFECTS OF POETRY, NOT BY RAISING
IDEAS OF THINGS 129

SECT. III.—GENERAL WORDS BEFORE IDEAS 131

SECT. IV.—THE EFFECT OF WORDS 132

SECT. V.—EXAMPLES THAT WORDS MAY AFFECT WITHOUT
RAISING IMAGES 133

SECT. VI.—POETRY NOT STRICTLY AN IMITATIVE ART . . . 137

SECT. VII.—HOW WORDS INFLUENCE THE PASSIONS . . . 137

REFLECTIONS ON THE REVOLUTION IN FRANCE . . 143

A LETTER FROM THE RIGHT HON. EDMUND BURKE
TO A NOBLE LORD 381

GENERAL INTRODUCTION

EDMUND BURKE was born in Dublin in January, 1729, the son of an attorney. His father was Protestant, his mother Catholic; and though the son followed his father's religion, he was always tolerant of the other faith. He was educated at Trinity College, Dublin, where he took his B.A. in 1748, coming to London two years later to study law. But his tastes were more literary than legal, and on giving up law, against his father's wish, before he was called to the bar, he was forced to resort to his pen for a livelihood.

The first of his productions to gain notice was his "Vindication of Natural Society, by a late noble writer," an ironical imitation of the style and arguments of Bolingbroke, carried out with great skill. This pamphlet already showed Burke as a defender of the established order of things. In the same year, 1756, appeared his famous "Philosophical Inquiry into the Origin of our Ideas of the Sublime and Beautiful."

For five years, from 1759 to 1764, Burke's time was largely occupied by his duties as secretary to William Gerard Hamilton, practically his only publications being in the "Annual Register," with which he was connected for many years; yet in this period he found time to form intimacies with the famous group containing, among others, Garrick, Sir Joshua Reynolds, and Dr. Johnson. During the short administration of Lord Rockingham, Burke acted as that nobleman's private secretary, and in January, 1766, he became a member of the House of Commons. Almost at once he came into prominence as a speaker, displaying in the debates on American affairs, which then occupied the House, much independence and a disposition toward a wise expediency rather than a harsh insistence on theoretical sovereignty in dealing with the colonists.

In 1768 Burke bought an estate in Buckinghamshire, for which he was never able to pay in full; and during most of his life he was in financial difficulties. During the Grafton ministry his chief publication was his "Thoughts on the Present Discontents," in which he opposed the reviving influence of the court, and championed the interests of the people. American affairs continued to engage the attention of Parliament, and throughout the struggle with the colonies Burke's voice was constantly raised on behalf of a policy of conciliation. With the aid of his disciple, C. J. Fox, he forced the retirement of Lord North, and when the Whigs came into power in 1782 he was made paymaster of the forces. Aristocratic jealousy, and the difficulties of his own temperament, kept him out of a cabinet position then and later.

The next great issue on which Burke employed his oratorical talents was the impeachment of Warren Hastings. Beginning in 1787, it dragged on for seven years, Burke closing his colossal labors with a nine days' speech. Though Hastings was acquitted, Burke's fervid indignation in supporting the impeachment, and the impeachment itself, were indications of the growth of the sense of responsibility for the humane treatment of subject peoples.

Meantime, the sympathy expressed in England for the French Revolution in its earlier stages roused Burke to express his opposition in his famous "Reflections." In the debates which followed, Burke became separated from his friends Sheridan and Fox, and finally from his party, and he closed his political career in practical isolation.

On his retirement from Parliament in 1794, the King granted him a pension which Pitt found means to increase, but even this well-earned reward he was not allowed to enjoy without the grudging assaults of enemies. His last days were spent in vigorous support of the war against France; and he died July 8, 1797.

Burke never attained a political office in any degree proportioned to his ability and services, but he succeeded, nevertheless, in affecting profoundly the opinion of his time. Latterly the House of Commons tired of his fervid and imaginative eloquence, unwilling perhaps to make the effort necessary to follow his keen intellectual processes, but he found through his writings a larger audience. "Bacon alone excepted," says Buckle, Burke was "the greatest political thinker who has ever devoted himself to the practise of English politics."

PREFACE

I HAVE endeavoured to make this edition something more full and satisfactory than the first. I have sought with the utmost care, and read with equal attention, everything which has appeared in public against my opinions; I have taken advantage of the candid liberty of my friends; and if by these means I have been better enabled to discover the imperfections of the work, the indulgence it has received, imperfect as it was, furnished me with a new motive to spare no reasonable pains for its improvement. Though I have not found sufficient reason, or what appeared to me sufficient, for making any material change in my theory, I have found it necessary in many places to explain, illustrate, and enforce it. I have prefixed an introductory discourse concerning Taste: it is a matter curious in itself; and it leads naturally enough to the principal inquiry. This, with the other explanations, has made the work considerably larger; and by increasing its bulk, has, I am afraid, added to its faults; so that, notwithstanding all my attention, it may stand in need of a yet greater share of indulgence than it required at its first appearance.

They who are accustomed to studies of this nature will expect, and they will allow too for many faults. They know that many of the objects of our inquiry are in themselves obscure and intricate; and that many others have been rendered so by affected refinements or false learning; they know that there are many impediments in the subject, in the prejudices of others, and even in our own, that render it a matter of no small difficulty to show in a clear light the genuine face of nature. They know that, whilst the mind is intent on the general scheme of things, some particular parts must be neglected; that we must often submit the style to the matter, and frequently give up the praise of elegance, satisfied with being clear.

The characters of nature are legible, it is true; but they are not plain enough to enable those who run, to read them. We must make use of a cautious, I had almost said a timorous, method of proceeding. We must not attempt to fly, when we can scarcely pretend to creep. In considering any complex matter, we ought to examine every distinct ingredient in the composition, one by one; and reduce everything to the utmost simplicity; since the condition of our nature binds us to a strict law and very narrow

7

limits. We ought afterwards to re-examine the principles by the effect of the composition, as well as the composition by that of the principles. We ought to compare our subject with things of a similar nature, and even with things of a contrary nature; for discoveries may be, and often are, made by the contrast, which would escape us on the single view. The greater number of the comparisons we make, the more general and the more certain our knowledge is like to prove, as built upon a more extensive and perfect induction.

If an inquiry thus carefully conducted should fail at last of discovering the truth, it may answer an end perhaps as useful, in discovering to us the weakness of our own understanding. If it does not make us knowing, it may make us modest. If it does not preserve us from error, it may at least from the spirit of error; and may make us cautious of pronouncing with positiveness or with haste, when so much labour may end in so much uncertainty.

I could wish that, in examining this theory, the same method were pursued which I endeavoured to observe in forming it. The objections, in my opinion, ought to be proposed, either to the several principles as they are distinctly considered, or to the justness of the conclusion which is drawn from them. But it is common to pass over both the premises and conclusion in silence, and to produce, as an objection, some poetical passage which does not seem easily accounted for upon the principles I endeavour to establish. This manner of proceeding I should think very improper. The task would be infinite, if we could establish no principle until we had previously unravelled the complex texture of every image or description to be found in poets and orators. And though we should never be able to reconcile the effect of such images to our principles, this can never overturn the theory itself, whilst it is founded on certain and indisputable facts. A theory founded on experiment, and not assumed, is always good for so much as it explains. Our inability to push it indefinitely is no argument at all against it. This inability may be owing to our ignorance of some necessary *mediums;* to a want of proper application; to many other causes besides a defect in the principles we employ. In reality, the subject requires a much closer attention than we dare claim from our manner of treating it.

If it should not appear on the face of the work, I must caution the reader against imagining that I intended a full dissertation on the Sublime and Beautiful. My inquiry went no farther than to the origin of these ideas. If the qualities which I have ranged under the head of the Sublime be all found consistent with each other, and all different from those which I place under the head of Beauty; and if those which compose the class of the Beautiful have the same consistency with themselves, and the same opposition to those which are classed under the denomination of Sublime, I am in little pain whether anybody chooses to follow the name I give them or not, provided he allows that what I dispose under different heads are in reality different things in nature. The use I make of the words may be blamed, as too confined or too extended; my meaning cannot well be misunderstood.

To conclude: whatever progress may be made towards the discovery of truth in this matter, I do not repent the pains I have taken in it. The use of such inquiries may be very considerable. Whatever turns the soul inward on itself, tends to concentre its forces, and to fit it for greater and stronger flights of science. By looking into physical causes our minds are opened and enlarged; and in this pursuit, whether we take or whether we lose our game, the chase is certainly of service. Cicero, true as he was to the academic philosophy, and consequently led to reject the certainty of physical, as of every other kind of knowledge, yet freely confesses its great importance to the human understanding; *"Est animorum ingeniorumque nostrorum naturale quoddam quasi pabulum consideratio contemplatioque naturæ."* If we can direct the lights we derive from such exalted speculations, upon the humbler field of the imagination, whilst we investigate the springs, and trace the courses of our passions, we may not only communicate to the taste a sort of philosophical solidity, but we may reflect back on the severer sciences some of the graces and elegancies of taste, without which the greatest proficiency in those sciences will always have the appearance of something illiberal.

ON TASTE

INTRODUCTORY DISCOURSE

O N A superficial view, we may seem to differ very widely from each other in our reasonings, and no less in our pleasures: but notwithstanding this difference, which I think to be rather apparent than real, it is probable that the standard both of reason and taste is the same in all human creatures. For if there were not some principles of judgment as well as of sentiment common to all mankind, no hold could possibly be taken either on their reason or their passions, sufficient to maintain the ordinary correspondence of life. It appears indeed to be generally acknowledged, that with regard to truth and falsehood there is something fixed. We find people in their disputes continually appealing to certain tests and standards, which are allowed on all sides, and are supposed to be established in our common nature. But there is not the same obvious concurrence in any uniform or settled principles which relate to taste. It is even commonly supposed that this delicate and aërial faculty, which seems too volatile to endure even the chains of a definition, cannot be properly tried by any test, nor regulated by any standard. There is so continual a call for the exercise of the reasoning faculty, and it is so much strengthened by perpetual contention, that certain maxims of right reason seem to be tacitly settled amongst the most ignorant. The learned have improved on this rude science, and reduced those maxims into a system. If taste has not been so happily cultivated, it was not that the subject was barren, but that the labourers were few or negligent; for, to say the truth, there are not the same interesting motives to impel us to fix the one, which urge us to ascertain the other. And, after all, if men differ in their opinion concerning such matters, their difference is not attended with the same important consequences; else I make no doubt but that the logic of taste, if I may be allowed the expression, might very possibly be as well digested, and we might come to discuss matters of this nature with as much certainty, as those which seem more immediately within the province of mere reason. And indeed, it is very necessary, at the entrance into such an inquiry as our present, to make this point as clear as possible; for if taste has no fixed principles, if the imagination is not affected according to some invariable and certain laws, our labour is likely to be employed to very little purpose; as it must be judged a useless, if not an absurd undertaking, to lay down rules for caprice, and to set up for a legislator of whims and fancies.

The term taste, like all other figurative terms, is not extremely accurate; the thing which we understand by it is far from a simple and determinate idea in the minds of most men, and it is therefore liable to uncertainty and confusion. I have no great opinion of a definition, the celebrated remedy for the cure of this disorder. For, when we define, we seem in danger of circumscribing nature within the bounds of our own notions, which we often take up by hazard, or embrace on trust, or form out of a limited and partial consideration of the object before us; instead of extending our ideas to take in all that nature comprehends, according to her manner of combining. We are limited in our inquiry by the strict laws to which we have submitted at our setting out.

—*Circa vilem patulumque morabimur orbem,*
Unde pudor proferre pedem vetat aut operis lex.

A definition may be very exact, and yet go but a very little way towards informing us of the nature of the thing defined; but let the virtue of a definition be what it will, in the order of things, it seems rather to follow than to precede our inquiry, of which it ought to be considered as the result. It must be acknowledged, that the methods of disquisition and teaching may be sometimes different, and on very good reason undoubtedly; but, for my part, I am convinced that the method of teaching which approaches most nearly to the method of investigation is incomparably the best; since, not content with serving up a few barren and lifeless truths, it leads to the stock on which they grew; it tends to set the reader himself in the track of invention, and to direct him into those paths in which the author has made his own discoveries, if he should be so happy as to have made any that are valuable.

But to cut off all pretence for cavilling, I mean by the word Taste no more than that faculty or those faculties of the mind, which are affected with, or which form a judgment of, the works of imagination and the elegant arts. This is, I think, the most general idea of that word, and what is the least connected with any particular theory. And my point in this inquiry is, to find whether there are any principles, on which the imagination is affected, so common to all, so grounded and certain, as to supply the means of reasoning satisfactorily about them. And such principles of taste I fancy there are; however paradoxical it may seem to those, who on a superficial view imagine, that there is so great a diversity of tastes, both in kind and degree, that nothing can be more indeterminate.

All the natural powers in man, which I know, that are conversant about external objects, are the senses; the imagination; and the judgment. And first with regard to the senses. We do and we must suppose, that as the conformation of their organs is nearly or altogether the same in all men, so the manner of perceiving external objects is in all men the same, or with little difference. We are satisfied that what appears to be light to one eye, appears light to another; that what seems sweet to one palate, is sweet to another; that what is dark and bitter to this man, is likewise dark and bitter to that; and we conclude in the same manner of great and little, hard and soft, hot and cold, rough and smooth, and indeed of all the natural qualities and affections of bodies. If we suffer ourselves to imagine, that their senses present to different men different images of things, this sceptical proceeding will make every sort of reasoning on every subject vain and frivolous, even that sceptical reasoning itself which had persuaded us to entertain a doubt concerning the agreement of our perceptions. But as there will be little doubt that bodies present similar images to the whole species, it must necessarily be allowed, that the pleasures and the pains which every object excites in one man, it must raise in all mankind, whilst it operates naturally, simply, and by its proper powers only; for if we deny this, we must imagine that the same cause, operating in the same manner, and on subjects of the same kind, will produce different effects; which would be highly absurd. Let us first consider this point in the sense of taste, and the rather, as the faculty in question has taken its name from that sense. All men are agreed to call vinegar sour, honey sweet, and aloes bitter; and as they are all agreed in finding these qualities in those objects, they do not in the least differ concerning their effects with regard to pleasure and pain. They all concur in calling sweetness pleasant, and sourness and bitterness unpleasant. Here there is no diversity in their sentiments; and that there is not, appears fully from the consent of all men in the metaphors which are taken from the sense of taste. A sour temper, bitter expressions, bitter curses, a bitter fate, are terms well and strongly understood by all. And we are altogether as well understood when we say, a sweet disposition, a sweet person, a sweet condition, and the like. It is confessed, that custom and some other causes have made many deviations from the natural pleasures or pains which belong to these several tastes: but then the power of distinguishing between the natural and the acquired relish remains to the very last. A man frequently comes to prefer the taste of tobacco to that of sugar, and the flavour of vinegar to that of milk; but this makes no confusion in tastes, whilst he is sensible that the tobacco and vinegar are not sweet, and whilst he knows that habit alone has reconciled his palate to these alien pleasures. Even with such a person we may speak, and with sufficient precision, concerning tastes. But should any man be found who declares, that to him tobacco has a taste like sugar, and that he cannot distinguish between milk and vinegar; or that tobacco and vinegar are sweet, milk bitter, and sugar sour; we immediately conclude that the organs of this man are out of order, and that his palate is utterly vitiated. We are as far from conferring with such a person upon tastes, as from reasoning concerning the relations of quantity with one who should deny that all the parts together were equal to the whole. We do not call a man of this kind wrong in his notions, but absolutely mad. Exceptions of this sort, in either way, do not at all impeach our general rule, nor make us conclude that men have various principles concerning the relations of quantity or the taste of things. So that when it is said, taste cannot be disputed, it can only mean, that no one can strictly answer what pleasure or pain some particular man may find from the taste of some particular thing. This indeed cannot be disputed; but we may dispute, and with sufficient clearness too, concerning the things which are naturally pleasing or disagreeable to the sense. But when we talk of any peculiar or acquired relish, then we must know the habits, the prejudices, or the distempers of this particular man, and we must draw our conclusion from those.

This agreement of mankind is not confined to the taste solely. The principle of pleasure derived from sight is the same in all. Light is more pleasing than darkness. Summer, when the earth is clad in green, when the heavens are serene and bright, is more agreeable than winter, when everything makes a different appearance. I never remember that anything beautiful, whether a man, a beast, a bird, or a plant, was ever shown, though it were to a hundred people, that they did not all immediately agree that it was beautiful, though some might have thought that it fell short of their expectation, or that other things were still finer. I believe no man thinks a goose to be more beautiful than a swan, or imagines that what they call a Friesland hen excels a peacock. It must be observed, too, that the pleasures of the sight are not near so complicated, and confused, and altered by unnatural habits and associations, as the pleasures of the taste are; because the pleasures of the sight more commonly acquiesce in themselves; and are not so often altered by considerations which are independent of the sight itself. But things do not spontaneously present themselves to the palate as they do to the sight; they are generally applied to it, either as food or as medicine; and, from the qualities which they possess for nutritive or medicinal purposes, they often form the palate by degrees, and by force of these associations. Thus opium is pleasing to Turks, on account of the agreeable delirium it produces. Tobacco is the delight of Dutchmen, as it diffuses a torpor and pleasing stupefaction. Fermented spirits please our common people, because they banish care, and all consideration of future or present evils. All of these would lie absolutely neglected if their properties had originally gone no further than the taste; but all these together, with tea and coffee, and some other things, have passed from the apothecary's shop to our tables, and were taken for health long before they were thought of for pleasure. The effect of the drug has made us use it frequently; and frequent use, combined with the agreeable effect, has made the taste itself at last agreeable. But this does not in the least perplex our reasoning; because we distinguish to the last the acquired from the natural relish. In describing the taste of an unknown fruit, you would scarcely say that it had a sweet and pleasant flavour like tobacco, opium, or garlic, although you spoke to those who were in the constant use of these drugs, and had great pleasure in them. There is in all men a sufficient remembrance of the original natural causes of pleasure, to enable them to bring all things offered to their senses to that standard, and to regulate their feelings and opinions by it. Suppose one who had so vitiated his palate as to take more pleasure in the taste of opium than in that of butter or honey, to be presented with a bolus of squills; there is hardly any doubt but that he would prefer the butter or honey to this nauseous morsel, or to any bitter drug to which he had not been accustomed; which proves that his palate was naturally like that of other men in all things, that it is still like the palate of other men in many things, and only vitiated in some particular points. For in judging of any new thing, even of a taste similar to that which he has been formed by habit to like, he finds his palate affected in a natural manner, and on the common principles. Thus the pleasure of all the senses, of the sight, and even of the taste, that most ambiguous of the senses, is the same in all, high and low, learned and unlearned.

Besides the ideas, with their annexed pains and pleasures, which are presented by the sense; the mind of man possesses a sort of creative power of its own; either in representing at pleasure the images of things in the order and manner in which they were received by the senses, or in combining those images in a new manner, and according to a different order. This power is called imagination; and to this belongs whatever is called wit, fancy, invention, and the like. But it must be observed, that this power of the imagination is incapable of producing anything absolutely new; it can only vary the disposition of those ideas which it has received from the senses. Now the imagination is the most extensive province of pleasure and pain, as it is the region of our fears and our hopes, and of all our passions that are connected with them; and whatever is calculated to affect the imagination with these commanding ideas, by force of any original natural impression, must have the same power pretty equally over all men. For since the imagination is only the representation of the senses, it can only be pleased or displeased with the images, from the same principle on which the sense is pleased or displeased with the realities; and consequently there must be just as close an agreement in the imaginations as in the senses of men. A little attention will convince us that this must of necessity be the case.

But in the imagination, besides the pain or pleasure arising from the properties of the natural object, a pleasure is perceived from the resemblance which the imitation has to the original: the imagination, I conceive, can have no pleasure but what results from one or other of these causes. And these causes operate pretty uniformly upon all men, because they operate by principles in nature, and which are not derived from any particular habits or advantages. Mr. Locke very justly and finely observes of wit, that it is chiefly conversant in tracing resemblances: he remarks, at the same time, that the business of judgment is rather in finding differences. It may perhaps appear, on this supposition, that there is no material distinction between the wit and the judgment, as they both seem to result from different operations of the same faculty of *comparing*. But in reality, whether they are or are not dependent on the same power of the mind, they differ so very materially in many respects, that a perfect union of wit and judgment is one of the rarest things in the world. When two distinct objects are unlike to each other, it is only what we expect; things are in their common way; and therefore they make no impression on the imagination: but when two distinct objects have a resemblance, we are struck, we attend to them, and we are pleased. The mind of man has naturally a far greater alacrity and satisfaction in tracing resemblances than in searching for differences: because by making resemblances we produce *new images;* we unite, we create, we enlarge our stock; but in making distinctions we offer no food at all to the imagination; the task itself is more severe and irksome, and what pleasure we derive from it is something of a negative and indirect nature. A piece of news is told me in the morning; this, merely as a piece of news, as a fact added to my stock, gives me some pleasure. In the evening I find there was nothing in it. What do I gain by this, but the dissatisfaction to find that I have been imposed upon? Hence it is that men are much more naturally inclined to belief than to incredulity. And it is upon this principle, that the most ignorant and barbarous nations have frequently excelled in similitudes, comparisons, metaphors, and allegories, who have been weak and backward in distinguishing and sorting their ideas. And it is for a reason of this kind, that Homer and the Oriental writers, though very fond of similitudes, and though they often strike out such as are truly admirable, seldom take care to have them exact; that is, they are taken with the general resemblance, they paint it strongly, and they take no notice of the difference which may be found between the things compared.

Now, as the pleasure of resemblance is that which principally flatters the imagination, all men are nearly equal in this point, as far as their knowledge of the things represented or compared extends. The principle of this knowledge is very much accidental, as it depends upon experience and observation, and not on the strength or weakness of any natural faculty; and it is from this difference in knowledge, that what we commonly, though with no great exactness, call a difference in taste proceeds. A man to whom sculpture is new, sees a barber's block, or some ordinary piece of statuary, he is immediately struck and pleased, because he sees something like a human figure; and, entirely taken up with this likeness, he does not at all attend to its defects. No person, I believe, at the first time of seeing a piece of imitation ever did. Some time after, we suppose that this novice lights upon a more artificial work of the same nature; he now begins to look with contempt on what he admired at first; not that he admired it even then for its unlikeness to a man, but for that general, though inaccurate, resemblance which it bore to the human figure. What he admired at different times in these so different figures, is strictly the same; and though his knowledge is improved, his taste is not altered. Hitherto his mistake was from a want of knowledge in art; and this arose from his inexperience; but he may be still deficient from a want of knowledge in nature. For it is possible that the man in question may stop here, and that the masterpiece of a great hand may please him no more than the middling performance of a vulgar artist: and this not for want of better or higher relish, but because all men do not observe with sufficient accuracy on the human figure to enable them to judge properly of an imitation of it. And that the critical taste does not depend upon a superior principle in men, but upon superior knowledge, may appear from several instances. The story of the ancient painter and the shoemaker is very well known. The shoemaker set the painter right with regard to some mistakes he had made in the shoe of one of his figures, and which the painter, who had not made such accurate observations on shoes, and was content with a general resemblance, had never observed. But this was no impeachment to the taste of the painter; it only showed some want of knowledge in the art of making shoes. Let us imagine, that an anatomist had come into the painter's working-room. His piece is in general well done, the figure in question in a good attitude, and the parts well adjusted to their various movements; yet the anatomist, critical in his art, may observe the swell of some muscle not quite just in the peculiar action of the figure. Here the anatomist observes what the painter had not observed; and he passes by what the shoemaker had remarked. But a want of the last critical knowledge in anatomy no more reflected on the natural good taste of the painter or of any common observer of his piece, than the want of an exact knowledge in the formation of a shoe. A fine piece of a decollated head of St. John the Baptist was shown to a Turkish emperor; he praised many things, but he observed one defect; he observed that the skin did not shrink from the wounded part of the neck. The sultan on this occasion, though his observation was very just, discovered no more natural taste than the painter who executed this piece, or than a thousand European connoisseurs, who probably never would have made the same observation. His Turkish Majesty had indeed been well acquainted with that terrible spectacle, which the others could only have represented in their imagination. On the subject of their dislike there is a difference between all these people, arising from the different kinds and degrees of their knowledge; but there is something in common to the painter, the shoemaker, the anatomist, and the

Turkish emperor, the pleasure arising from a natural object, so far as each perceives it justly imitated; the satisfaction in seeing an agreeable figure; the sympathy proceeding from a striking and affecting incident. So far as taste is natural, it is nearly common to all.

In poetry, and other pieces of imagination, the same parity may be observed. It is true, that one man is charmed with Don Bellianis, and reads Virgil coldly; whilst another is transported with the Eneid, and leaves Don Bellianis to children. These two men seem to have a taste very different from each other; but in fact they differ very little. In both these pieces, which inspire such opposite sentiments, a tale exciting admiration is told; both are full of action, both are passionate; in both are voyages, battles, triumphs, and continual changes of fortune. The admirer of Don Bellianis perhaps does not understand the refined language of the Eneid, who, if it was degraded into the style of the Pilgrim's Progress, might feel it in all its energy, on the same principle which made him an admirer of Don Bellianis.

In his favourite author he is not shocked with the continual breaches of probability, the confusion of times, the offences against manners, the trampling upon geography; for he knows nothing of geography and chronology, and he has never examined the grounds of probability. He perhaps reads of a shipwreck on the coast of Bohemia; wholly taken up with so interesting an event, and only solicitous for the fate of his hero, he is not in the least troubled at this extravagant blunder. For why should he be shocked at a shipwreck on the coast of Bohemia, who does not know but that Bohemia may be an island in the Atlantic ocean? and after all, what reflection is this on the natural good taste of the person here supposed?

So far then as taste belongs to the imagination, its principle is the same in all men; there is no difference in the manner of their being affected, nor in the causes of the affection; but in the *degree* there is a difference, which arises from two causes principally; either from a greater degree of natural sensibility, or from a closer and longer attention to the object. To illustrate this by the procedure of the senses, in which the same difference is found, let us suppose a

very smooth marble table to be set before two men; they both perceive it to be smooth; and they are both pleased with it because of
this quality. So far they agree. But suppose another, and after that
another table, the latter still smoother than the former, to be set
before them. It is now very probable that these men, who are so
agreed upon what is smooth, and in the pleasure from thence, will
disagree when they come to settle which table has the advantage in
point of polish. Here is indeed the great difference between tastes,
when men come to compare the excess or diminution of things which
are judged by degree and not by measure. Nor is it easy, when such
a difference arises, to settle the point, if the excess or diminution be
not glaring. If we differ in opinion about two quantities, we can
have recourse to a common measure, which may decide the question
with the utmost exactness; and this, I take it, is what gives mathematical knowledge a greater certainty than any other. But in things
whose excess is not judged by greater or smaller, as smoothness and
roughness, hardness and softness, darkness and light, the shades of
colours, all these are very easily distinguished when the difference is
any way considerable, but not when it is minute, for want of some
common measures, which perhaps may never come to be discovered.
In these nice cases, supposing the acuteness of the sense equal, the
greater attention and habit in such things will have the advantage.
In the question about the tables, the marble-polisher will unquestionably determine the most accurately. But notwithstanding this
want of a common measure for settling many disputes relative to
the senses, and their representative the imagination, we find that the
principles are the same in all, and that there is no disagreement until
we come to examine into the pre-eminence or difference of things,
which brings us within the province of the judgment.

So long as we are conversant with the sensible qualities of things,
hardly any more than the imagination seems concerned; little more
also than the imagination seems concerned when the passions are
represented, because by the force of natural sympathy they are felt
in all men without any recourse to reasoning, and their justness
recognized in every breast. Love, grief, fear, anger, joy, all these
passions have, in their turns, affected every mind; and they do not
affect it in an arbitrary or casual manner, but upon certain, natural,

and uniform principles. But as many of the works of imagination are not confined to the representation of sensible objects, nor to efforts upon the passions, but extend themselves to the manners, the characters, the actions, and designs of men, their relations, their virtues, and vices, they come within the province of the judgment, which is improved by attention, and by the habit of reasoning. All these make a very considerable part of what are considered as the objects of taste; and Horace sends us to the schools of philosophy and the world for our instruction in them. Whatever certainty is to be acquired in morality and the science of life; just the same degree of certainty have we in what relates to them in the works of imitation. Indeed it is for the most part in our skill in manners, and in the observances of time and place, and of decency in general, which is only to be learned in those schools to which Horace recommends us, that what is called taste, by way of distinction, consists; and which is in reality no other than a more refined judgment. On the whole it appears to me, that what is called taste, in its most general acceptation, is not a simple idea, but is partly made up of a perception of the primary pleasures of sense, of the secondary pleasures of the imagination, and of the conclusions of the reasoning faculty, concerning the various relations of these, and concerning the human passions, manners, and actions. All this is requisite to form taste, and the ground-work of all these is the same in the human mind; for as the senses are the great originals of all our ideas, and consequently of all our pleasures, if they are not uncertain and arbitrary, the whole ground-work of taste is common to all, and therefore there is a sufficient foundation for a conclusive reasoning on these matters.

Whilst we consider taste merely according to its nature and species, we shall find its principles entirely uniform; but the degree in which these principles prevail in the several individuals of mankind, is altogether as different as the principles themselves are similar. For sensibility and judgment, which are the qualities that compose what we commonly call a *taste,* vary exceedingly in various people. From a defect in the former of these qualities arises a want of taste; a weakness in the latter constitutes a wrong or a bad one. There are some men formed with feelings so blunt, with tempers so cold and phlegmatic, that they can hardly be said to be awake during the whole course of their lives. Upon such persons the most striking objects make but a faint and obscure impression. There are others so continually in the agitation of gross and merely sensual pleasures, or so occupied in the low drudgery of avarice, or so heated in the chase of honours and distinction, that their minds, which had been used continually to the storms of these violent and tempestuous passions, can hardly be put in motion by the delicate and refined play of the imagination. These men, though from a different cause, become as stupid and insensible as the former; but whenever either of these happen to be struck with any natural elegance or greatness, or with these qualities in any work of art, they are moved upon the same principle.

The cause of a wrong taste is a defect of judgment. And this may arise from a natural weakness of understanding, (in whatever the strength of that faculty may consist,) or, which is much more commonly the case, it may arise from a want of proper and well-directed exercise, which alone can make it strong and ready. Besides that ignorance, inattention, prejudice, rashness, levity, obstinacy, in short, all those passions, and all those vices, which pervert the judgment in other matters, prejudice it no less in this its more refined and elegant province. These causes produce different opinions upon everything which is an object of the understanding, without inducing us to suppose that there are no settled principles of reason. And indeed, on the whole, one may observe that there is rather less difference upon matters of taste among mankind, than upon most of those which depend upon the naked reason; and that men are far better agreed on the excellency of a description in Virgil, than on the truth or falsehood of a theory of Aristotle.

A rectitude of judgment in the arts, which may be called a good taste, does in a great measure depend upon sensibility; because, if the mind has no bent to the pleasures of the imagination, it will never apply itself sufficiently to works of that species to acquire a competent knowledge in them. But, though a degree of sensibility is requisite to form a good judgment, yet a good judgment does not necessarily arise from a quick sensibility of pleasure; it frequently happens that a very poor judge, merely by force of a greater complexional sensibility, is more affected by a very poor piece, than the best judge by the most perfect; for as everything new, extraordinary, grand, or passionate, is well calculated to affect such a person, and that the faults do not affect him, his pleasure is more pure and un-mixed; and as it is merely a pleasure of the imagination, it is much higher than any which is derived from a rectitude of the judgment; the judgment is for the greater part employed in throwing stum-bling-blocks in the way of the imagination, in dissipating the scenes of its enchantment, and in tying us down to the disagreeable yoke of our reason: for almost the only pleasure that men have in judging better than others, consists in a sort of conscious pride and superior-ity, which arises from thinking rightly; but then, this is an indirect pleasure, a pleasure which does not immediately result from the ob-ject which is under contemplation. In the morning of our days, when the senses are unworn and tender, when the whole man is awake in every part, and the gloss of novelty fresh upon all the objects that surround us, how lively at that time are our sensations, but how false and inaccurate the judgments we form of things? I despair of ever receiving the same degree of pleasure from the most excellent performances of genius, which I felt at that age from pieces which my present judgment regards as trifling and contempt-ible. Every trivial cause of pleasure is apt to affect the man of too sanguine a complexion: his appetite is too keen to suffer his taste to be delicate; and he is in all respects what Ovid says of himself in love,

> *Molle meum levibus cor est violabile telis,*
> *Et semper causa est, cur ego semper amem.*

One of this character can never be a refined judge; never what the comic poet calls *elegans formarum spectator*. The excellence and force of a composition must always be imperfectly estimated from its effect on the minds of any, except we know the temper and character of those minds. The most powerful effects of poetry and music have been displayed, and perhaps are still displayed, where these arts are but in a very low and imperfect state. The rude hearer is affected by the principles which operate in these arts even in their rudest condition; and he is not skilful enough to perceive the defects. But as the arts advance towards their perfection, the science of criticism advances with equal pace, and the pleasure of judges is frequently interrupted by the faults which are discovered in the most finished compositions.

Before I leave this subject I cannot help taking notice of an opinion which many persons entertain, as if the taste were a separate faculty of the mind, and distinct from the judgment and imagination; a species of instinct, by which we are struck naturally, and at the first glance, without any previous reasoning, with the excellencies, or the defects, of a composition. So far as the imagination and the passions are concerned, I believe it true, that the reason is little consulted; but where disposition, where decorum, where congruity are concerned, in short, wherever the best taste differs from the worst, I am convinced that the understanding operates, and nothing else; and its operation is in reality far from being always sudden, or, when it is sudden, it is often far from being right. Men of the best taste, by consideration, come frequently to change these early and precipitate judgments, which the mind, from its aversion to neutrality and doubt, loves to form on the spot. It is known that the taste (whatever it is) is improved exactly as we improve our judgment, by extending our knowledge, by a steady attention to our object, and by frequent exercise. They who have not taken these methods, if their taste decides quickly, it is always uncertainly; and their quickness is owing to their presumption and rashness, and not to any sudden irradiation, that in a moment dispels all darkness from their minds. But they who have cultivated that species of knowledge which makes the object of taste, by degrees, and habitually, attain not only a soundness, but a readiness of judgment, as men do by the same methods on all other occasions. At first they are obliged to spell, but at least they read with ease and with celerity; but this celerity of its operation is no proof that the taste is a distinct faculty. Nobody, I believe, has attended the course of a discussion, which turned upon matters within the sphere of mere naked reason, but must have observed the extreme readiness with which the whole process of the argument is carried on, the grounds discovered, the objections raised and answered, and the conclusions drawn from premises, with a quickness altogether as great as the taste can be supposed to work with; and yet where nothing but plain reason either is or can be suspected to operate. To multiply principles for every different appearance, is useless, and unphilosophical too in a high degree.

This matter might be pursued much further; but it is not the extent of the subject which must prescribe our bounds, for what subject does not branch out to infinity? It is the nature of our particular scheme, and the single point of view in which we consider it, which ought to put a stop to our researches.

A PHILOSOPHICAL INQUIRY

INTO THE ORIGIN OF OUR IDEAS

OF

THE SUBLIME AND BEAUTIFUL

WITH SEVERAL OTHER ADDITIONS

INTRODUCTORY NOTE

BURKE's eminence in the field of æsthetic theory is not comparable to the distinction he achieved as a statesman, orator, and political thinker; yet it is probable that, in England especially, his political writings have unduly overshadowed his contributions to the theory of the beautiful.

His "Philosophical Inquiry into the Origin of our Ideas of the Sublime and Beautiful: with an Introductory Discourse concerning Taste" was published in its first form in 1756, and in its enlarged form in 1757; but it is understood that it was composed some years earlier. "It was a vigorous enlargement of the principle," says Morley, "which Addison had not long before timidly illustrated, that critics of art seek its principles in the wrong place, so long as they limit their search to poems, pictures, engravings, statues, and buildings, instead of first arranging the sentiments and faculties in man to which art makes its appeal. Addison's treatment was slight and merely literary; Burke dealt boldly with his subject on the basis of the most scientific psychology that was then within his reach. To approach it on the psychological side at all, was to make a distinct and remarkable advance in the method of the inquiry which he had taken in hand."

The influence of the treatise outside of England was considerable and important. Lessing undertook to translate it, and many instances have been pointed out in which his "Laocoön" is indebted to Burke; so that Burke ranks among the sources of that fertilising contribution to the mind of the great German thinker which he was always eager to acknowledge.

THE SUBLIME AND BEAUTIFUL

PART I

Section i.—Novelty

THE first and the simplest emotion which we discover in the human mind, is Curiosity. By curiosity, I mean whatever desire we have for, or whatever pleasure we take in, novelty. We see children perpetually running from place to place, to hunt out something new: they catch with great eagerness, and with very little choice, at whatever comes before them; their attention is engaged by everything, because everything has, in that stage of life, the charm of novelty to recommend it. But as those things, which engage us merely by their novelty, cannot attach us for any length of time, curiosity is the most superficial of all the affections; it changes its object perpetually, it has an appetite which is very sharp, but very easily satisfied; and it has always an appearance of giddiness, restlessness, and anxiety. Curiosity, from its nature, is a very active principle; it quickly runs over the greatest part of its objects, and soon exhausts the variety which is commonly to be met with in nature; the same things make frequent returns, and they return with less and less of any agreeable effect. In short, the occurrences of life, by the time we come to know it a little, would be incapable of affecting the mind with any other sensations than those of loathing and weariness, if many things were not adapted to affect the mind by means of other powers besides novelty in them, and of other passions besides curiosity in ourselves. These powers and passions shall be considered in their place. But whatever these powers are, or upon what principle soever they affect the mind, it is absolutely necessary that they should not be exerted in those things which a daily and vulgar use have brought into a stale unaffecting familiarity. Some degree of novelty must be one of the materials in every instrument which works upon the mind; and curiosity blends itself more or less with all our passions.

SECT. II.—PAIN AND PLEASURE

It seems then necessary towards moving the passions of people advanced in life to any considerable degree, that the objects designed for that purpose, besides their being in some measure new, should be capable of exciting pain or pleasure from other causes. Pain and pleasure are simple ideas, incapable of definition. People are not liable to be mistaken in their feelings, but they are very frequently wrong in the names they give them, and in their reasonings about them. Many are of the opinion, that pain arises necessarily from the removal of some pleasure; as they think pleasure does from the ceasing or diminution of some pain. For my part, I am rather inclined to imagine, that pain and pleasure, in their most simple and natural manner of affecting, are each of a positive nature, and by no means necessarily dependent on each other for their existence. The human mind is often, and I think it is for the most part, in a state neither of pain nor pleasure, which I call a state of indifference. When I am carried from this state into a state of actual pleasure, it does not appear necessary that I should pass through the medium of any sort of pain. If in such a state of indifference, or ease, or tranquillity, or call it what you please, you were to be suddenly entertained with a concert of music; or suppose some object of a fine shape, and bright, lively colours, to be presented before you; or imagine your smell is gratified with the fragrance of a rose; or if without any previous thirst you were to drink of some pleasant kind of wine, or to taste of some sweetmeat without being hungry; in all the several senses, of hearing, smelling and tasting, you undoubtedly find a pleasure; yet if I inquire into the state of your mind previous to these gratifications, you will hardly tell me that they found you in any kind of pain; or, having satisfied these several senses with their several pleasures, will you say that any pain has succeeded, though the pleasure is absolutely over? Suppose on the other hand, a man in the same state of indifference, to receive a violent blow, or to drink of some bitter potion, or to have his ears wounded with some harsh and grating sound; here is no removal of pleasure; and yet here is felt in every sense which is affected, a pain very distinguishable. It may be said, perhaps, that the pain in these cases had its rise from the removal of the pleasure which the man enjoyed before, though that pleasure was of so low a degree as to be perceived only by the removal. But this seems to me a subtilty that is not discoverable in nature. For if, previous to the pain, I do not feel any actual pleasure, I have no reason to judge that any such thing exists; since pleasure is only pleasure as it is felt. The same may be said of pain, and with equal reason. I can never persuade myself that pleasure and pain are mere relations, which can only exist as they are contrasted; but I think I can discern clearly that there are positive pains and pleasures, which do not at all depend upon each other. Nothing is more certain to my own feelings than this. There is nothing which I can distinguish in my mind with more clearness than the three states, of indifference, of pleasure, and of pain. Every one of these I can perceive without any sort of idea of its relation to anything else. Caius is afflicted with a fit of the colic; this man is actually in pain; stretch Caius upon the rack, he will feel a much greater pain: but does this pain of the rack arise from the removal of any pleasure? or is the fit of the colic a pleasure or a pain, just as we are pleased to consider it?

SECT. III.—THE DIFFERENCE BETWEEN THE REMOVAL OF PAIN, AND POSITIVE PLEASURE

WE shall carry this proposition yet a step farther. We shall venture to propose, that pain and pleasure are not only not necessarily dependent for their existence on their mutual diminution or removal, but that, in reality, the diminution or ceasing of pleasure does not operate like positive pain; and that the removal or diminution of pain, in its effect, has very little resemblance to positive pleasure.[1] The former of these propositions will, I believe, be much more readily allowed than the latter; because it is very evident that pleasure, when it has run its career, sets us down very nearly where it found us. Pleasure of every kind quickly satisfies; and when it

[1] Mr. Locke [Essay on the Human Understanding, l. ii. c. 20, sect. 16] thinks that the removal or lessening of a pain is considered and operates as a pleasure, and the loss or diminishing of pleasure as a pain. It is this opinion which we consider here.

is over, we relapse into indifference, or rather we fall into a soft tranquillity, which is tinged with the agreeable colour of the former sensation. I own it is not at first view so apparent, that the removal of a great pain does not resemble positive pleasure; but let us recollect in what state we have found our minds upon escaping some imminent danger, or on being released from the severity of some cruel pain. We have on such occasions found, if I am not much mistaken, the temper of our minds in a tenor very remote from that which attends the presence of positive pleasure; we have found them in a state of much sobriety, impressed with a sense of awe, in a sort of tranquillity shadowed with horror. The fashion of the countenance and the gesture of the body on such occasions is so correspondent to this state of mind, that any person, a stranger to the cause of the appearance, would rather judge us under some consternation, than in the enjoyment of anything like positive pleasure.

> Ὡς δ' ὅτ' ἂν ἄνδρ' ἄτη πυκινὴ λάβῃ, ὅστ' ἐνὶ πάτρῃ
> Φῶτα κατακτείνας, ἄλλων ἐξίκετο δῆμον,
> Ἀνδρὸς ἐς ἀφνειοῦ, θάμβος δ' ἔχει εἰσορόωντας.
>
> Iliad. Ω. 480.

As when a wretch, who, conscious of his crime,
Pursued for murder from his native clime,
Just gains some frontier, breathless, pale, amazed;
All gaze, all wonder!

This striking appearance of the man whom Homer supposes to have just escaped an imminent danger, the sort of mixed passion of terror and surprise, with which he affects the spectators, paints very strongly the manner in which we find ourselves affected upon occasions any way similar. For when we have suffered from any violent emotion, the mind naturally continues in something like the same condition, after the cause which first produced it has ceased to operate. The tossing of the sea remains after the storm; and when this remain of horror has entirely subsided, all the passion, which the accident raised, subsides along with it; and the mind returns to its usual state of indifference. In short, pleasure (I mean anything either in the inward sensation, or in the outward appearance, like pleasure from a positive cause) has never, I imagine, its origin from the removal of pain or danger.

SECT. IV.—OF DELIGHT AND PLEASURE AS OPPOSED TO EACH OTHER

BUT shall we therefore say, that the removal of pain or its diminution is always simply painful? or affirm that the cessation or the lessening of pleasure is always attended itself with a pleasure? By no means. What I advance is no more than this; first, that there are pleasures and pains of a positive and independent nature; and, secondly, that the feeling which results from the ceasing or diminution of pain does not bear a sufficient resemblance to positive pleasure, to have it considered as of the same nature, or to entitle it to be known by the same name; and, thirdly, that upon the same principle the removal or qualification of pleasure has no resemblance to positive pain. It is certain that the former feeling (the removal or moderation of pain) has something in it far from distressing or disagreeable in its nature. This feeling, in many cases so agreeable, but in all so different from positive pleasure, has no name which I know; but that hinders not its being a very real one, and very different from all others. It is most certain that every species of satisfaction or pleasure, how different soever in its manner of affecting, is of a positive nature in the mind of him who feels it. The affection is undoubtedly positive; but the cause may be, as in this case it certainly is, a sort of *Privation*. And it is very reasonable that we should distinguish by some term two things so distinct in nature, as a pleasure that is such simply, and without any relation, from that pleasure which cannot exist without a relation, and that too a relation to pain. Very extraordinary it would be, if these affections, so distinguishable in their causes, so different in their effects, should be confounded with each other, because vulgar use has ranged them under the same general title. Whenever I have occasion to speak of this species of relative pleasure, I call it *Delight;* and I shall take the best care I can to use that word in no other sense. I am satisfied the word is not commonly used in this appropriated signification; but I thought it better to take up a word already known, and to limit its signification, than to introduce a new one, which would not perhaps incorporate so well with the language. I should never have presumed the least alteration in our words, if the nature of the language, framed for the purposes of business rather than those of philosophy, and the nature of my subject, that leads me out of the common track of discourse, did not in a manner necessitate me to it. I shall make use of this liberty with all possible caution. As I make use of the word *Delight* to express the sensation which accompanies the removal of pain or danger; so when I speak of positive pleasure, I shall for the most part call it simply *Pleasure*.

SECT. V.—JOY AND GRIEF

It must be observed that the cessation of pleasure affects the mind three ways. If it simply ceases, after having continued a proper time, the effect is *indifference;* if it be abruptly broken off, there ensues an uneasy sense called *disappointment;* if the object be so totally lost that there is no chance of enjoying it again, a passion arises in the mind, which is called *grief*. Now there is none of these, not even grief, which is the most violent, that I think has any resemblance to positive pain. The person who grieves, suffers his passion to grow upon him; he indulges it, he loves it: but this never happens in the case of actual pain, which no man ever willingly endured for any considerable time. That grief should be willingly endured, though far from a simply pleasing sensation, is not so difficult to be understood. It is the nature of grief to keep its object perpetually in its eye, to present it in its most pleasurable views, to repeat all the circumstances that attend it, even to the last minuteness; to go back to every particular enjoyment, to dwell upon each, and to find a thousand new perfections in all, that were not sufficiently understood before; in grief, the *pleasure* is still uppermost; and the affliction we suffer has no resemblance to absolute pain, which is always odious, and which we endeavor to shake off as soon as possible. The Odyssey of Homer, which abounds with so many natural and affecting images, has none more striking than those which Menelaus raises of the calamitous fate of his friends, and his own manner of feeling it. He owns, indeed, that he often gives himself some intermission from such melancholy reflections; but he observes, too, that, melancholy as they are, they give him pleasure.

> 'Αλλ' ἔμπης πάντας μὲν ὀδυρόμενος καὶ ἀχεύων,
> Πολλάκις ἐν μεγάροισι καθήμενος ἡμετέροισιν,
> Ἄλλοτε μέν τε γόῳ φρένα τέρπομαι, ἄλλοτε δ' αὖτε
> Παύομαι· αἰψηρὸς δὲ κόρος κρυεροῖο γόοιο.

Hom. Od. Δ. 100.

> Still in short intervals of *pleasing woe,*
> Regardful of the friendly dues I owe,
> I to the glorious dead, for ever dear,
> *Indulge* the tribute of a *grateful* tear.

On the other hand, when we recover our health, when we escape an imminent danger, is it with joy that we are affected? The sense on these occasions is far from that smooth and voluptuous satisfaction which the assured prospect of pleasure bestows. The delight which arises from the modifications of pain confesses the stock from whence it sprung, in its solid, strong, and severe nature.

SECT. VI.—OF THE PASSIONS WHICH BELONG TO SELF-PRESERVATION

MOST of the ideas which are capable of making a powerful impression on the mind, whether simply of Pain or Pleasure, or of the modifications of those, may be reduced very nearly to these two heads, *self-preservation* and *society;* to the ends of one or the other of which all our passions are calculated to answer. The passions which concern self-preservation, turn mostly on *pain* or *danger.* The ideas of *pain, sickness,* and *death,* fill the mind with strong emotions of horror; but *life* and *health,* though they put us in a capacity of being affected with pleasure, make no such impression by the simple enjoyment. The passions therefore which are conversant about the preservation of the individual turn chiefly on *pain* and *danger,* and they are the most powerful of all the passions.

SECT. VII.—OF THE SUBLIME

WHATEVER is fitted in any sort to excite the ideas of pain and danger, that is to say, whatever is in any sort terrible, or is conversant about terrible objects, or operates in a manner analogous to terror, is a source of the *sublime;* that is, it is productive of the strongest emotion which the mind is capable of feeling. I say the strongest emotion, because I am satisfied the ideas of pain are much more powerful than those which enter on the part of pleasure. Without all doubt, the torments which we may be made to suffer are much greater in their effect on the body and mind, than any pleasures which the most learned voluptuary could suggest, or than the liveliest imagination, and the most sound and exquisitely sensible body, could enjoy. Nay, I am in great doubt whether any man could be found, who would earn a life of the most perfect satisfaction, at the price of ending it in the torments, which justice inflicted in a few hours on the late unfortunate regicide in France. But as pain is stronger in its operation than pleasure, so death is in general a much more affecting idea than pain; because there are very few pains, however exquisite, which are not preferred to death: nay, what generally makes pain itself, if I may say so, more painful, is, that it is considered as an emissary of this king of terrors. When danger or pain press too nearly, they are incapable of giving any delight, and are simply terrible; but at certain distances, and with certain modifications, they may be, and they are, delightful, as we every day experience. The cause of this I shall endeavour to investigate hereafter.

SECT. VIII.—OF THE PASSIONS WHICH BELONG TO SOCIETY

THE other head under which I class our passions, is that of *society,* which may be divided into two sorts. I. The society of the *sexes,* which answers the purposes of propagation; and next, that more *general society,* which we have with men and with other animals, and which we may in some sort be said to have even with the inanimate world. The passions belonging to the preservation of the individual turn wholly on pain and danger: those which belong to *generation* have their origin in gratifications and *pleasures;* the pleasure most directly belonging to this purpose is of a lively character, rapturous and violent, and confessedly the highest pleasure of sense; yet the absence of this so great an enjoyment scarce amounts to an uneasiness; and, except at particular times, I do not think it affects at all. When men describe in what manner they are affected by pain and danger, they do not dwell on the pleasure of health and the comfort of security, and then lament the *loss* of these satisfactions: the whole turns upon the actual pains and horrors which they endure. But if you listen to the complaints of a forsaken lover, you observe that he insists largely on the pleasures which he enjoyed, or hoped to enjoy, and on the perfection of the object of his desires; it is the *loss* which is always uppermost in his mind. The violent effects produced by love, which has sometimes been even wrought up to madness, is no objection to the rule which we seek to establish. When men have suffered their imaginations to be long affected with any idea, it so wholly engrosses them as to shut out by degrees almost every other, and to break down every partition of the mind which would confine it. Any idea is sufficient for the purpose, as is evident from the infinite variety of causes, which give rise to madness: but this at most can only prove, that the passion of love is capable of producing very extraordinary effects, not that its extraordinary emotions have any connexion with positive pain.

SECT. IX.—THE FINAL CAUSE OF THE DIFFERENCE BETWEEN THE PASSIONS BELONGING TO SELF-PRESERVATION, AND THOSE WHICH REGARD THE SOCIETY OF THE SEXES

THE final cause of the difference in character between the passions which regard self-preservation, and those which are directed to the multiplication of the species, will illustrate the foregoing remarks yet further; and it is, I imagine, worthy of observation even upon its own account. As the performance of our duties of every kind depends upon life, and the performing them with vigour and efficacy depends upon health, we are very strongly affected with whatever threatens the destruction of either: but as we are not made to acquiesce in life and health, the simple enjoyment of them is not attended with any real pleasure, lest, satisfied with that, we should give ourselves over to indolence and inaction. On the other hand, the generation of mankind is a great purpose, and it is requisite that men should be animated to the pursuit of it by some great incentive. It is therefore attended with a very high pleasure; but as it is by no means designed to be our constant business, it is not fit that the absence of this pleasure should be attended with any considerable pain. The difference between men and brutes, in this point, seems to be remarkable. Men are at all times pretty equally disposed to the pleasures of love, because they are to be guided by reason in the time and manner of indulging them. Had any great pain arisen from the want of this satisfaction, reason, I am afraid, would find great difficulties in the performance of its office. But brutes, who obey laws, in the execution of which their own reason has but little share, have their stated seasons; at such times it is not improbable that the sensation from the want is very troublesome, because the end must be then answered, or be missed in many, perhaps for ever; as the inclination returns only with its season.

SECT. X.—OF BEAUTY

THE passion which belongs to generation, merely as such, is lust only. This is evident in brutes, whose passions are more unmixed, and which pursue their purposes more directly than ours. The only distinction they observe with regard to their mates, is that of sex. It is true, that they stick severally to their own species in preference to all others. But this preference, I imagine, does not arise from any sense of beauty which they find in their species, as Mr. Addison supposes, but from a law of some other kind, to which they are subject; and this we may fairly conclude, from their apparent want of choice amongst those objects to which the barriers of their species have confined them. But man, who is a creature adapted to a greater variety and intricacy of relation, connects with the general passion the idea of some *social* qualities, which direct and heighten the appetite which he has in common with all other animals; and as he is not designed like them to live at large, it is fit that he should have something to create a preference, and fix his choice; and this in general should be some sensible quality; as no other can so quickly, so powerfully, or so surely produce its effect. The object therefore of this mixed passion, which we call love, is the *beauty* of the *sex*. Men are carried to the sex in general, as it is the sex, and by the common law of nature; but they are attached to particulars by personal *beauty*. I call beauty a social quality; for where women and men, and not only they, but when other animals give us a sense of joy and pleasure in beholding them, (and there are many that do so,) they inspire us with sentiments of tenderness and affection towards their persons; we like to have them near us, and we enter willingly into a kind of relation with them, unless we should have strong reasons to the contrary. But to what end, in many cases, this was designed, I am unable to discover; for I see no greater reason for a connexion between man and several animals who are attired in so engaging a manner, than between him and some others who entirely want this attraction, or possess it in a far weaker degree. But it is probable, that Providence did not make even this distinction, but with a view to some great end; though we cannot perceive distinctly what it is, as his wisdom is not our wisdom, nor our ways his ways.

SECT. XI.—SOCIETY AND SOLITUDE

THE second branch of the social passions is that which administers to *society in general*. With regard to this, I observe, that society, merely as society, without any particular heightenings, gives us no positive pleasure in the enjoyment; but absolute and entire *solitude,* that is, the total and perpetual exclusion from all society, is as great a positive pain as can almost be conceived. Therefore in the balance between the pleasure of general *society* and the pain of absolute solitude, *pain* is the predominant idea. But the pleasure of any particular social enjoyment outweighs very considerably the uneasiness caused by the want of that particular enjoyment; so that the strongest sensations relative to the habitudes of *particular society* are sensations of pleasure. Good company, lively conversation, and the endearments of friendship, fill the mind with great pleasure; a temporary solitude, on the other hand, is itself agreeable. This may perhaps prove that we are creatures designed for contemplation as well as action; since solitude as well as society has its pleasures; as from the former observation we may discern, that an entire life of solitude contradicts the purposes of our being, since death itself is scarcely an idea of more terror.

SECT. XII.—SYMPATHY, IMITATION, AND AMBITION

UNDER this denomination of society, the passions are of a complicated kind, and branch out into a variety of forms, agreeably to that variety of ends they are to serve in the great chain of society. The three principal links in this chain are *sympathy, imitation, and ambition*.

SECT. XIII.—SYMPATHY

IT is by the first of these passions that we enter into the concerns of others; that we are moved as they are moved, and are never

suffered to be indifferent spectators of almost anything which men
can do or suffer. For sympathy must be considered as a sort of
substitution, by which we are put into the place of another man,
and affected in many respects as he is affected; so that this passion
may either partake of the nature of those which regard self-preservation, and turning upon pain may be a source of the sublime or it
may turn upon ideas of pleasure; and then whatever has been said
of the social affections, whether they regard society in general, or
only some particular modes of it, may be applicable here. It is by
this principle chiefly that poetry, painting, and other affecting arts,
transfuse their passions from one breast to another, and are often
capable of grafting a delight on wretchedness, misery, and death
itself. It is a common observation, that objects which in the reality
would shock, are in tragical, and such like representations, the
source of a very high species of pleasure. This, taken as a fact, has
been the cause of much reasoning. The satisfaction has been commonly attributed, first, to the comfort we receive in considering
that so melancholy a story is no more than a fiction; and, next, to
the contemplation of our own freedom from the evils which we see
represented. I am afraid it is a practice much too common in inquiries of this nature, to attribute the cause of feelings which merely
arise from the mechanical structure of our bodies, or from the natural frame and constitution of our minds, to certain conclusions of
the reasoning faculty on the objects presented to us; for I should
imagine, that the influence of reason in producing our passions is
nothing near so extensive as it is commonly believed.

SECT. XIV.—THE EFFECTS OF SYMPATHY IN THE DISTRESSES OF OTHERS

To examine this point concerning the effect of tragedy in a
proper manner, we must previously consider how we are affected by
the feelings of our fellow-creatures in circumstances of real distress. I am convinced we have a degree of delight, and that no
small one, in the real misfortunes and pains of others; for let the
affection be what it will in appearance, if it does not make us shun
such objects, if on the contrary it induces us to approach them, if
it makes us dwell upon them, in this case I conceive we must have
a delight or pleasure of some species or other in contemplating

objects of this kind. Do we not read the authentic histories of scenes of this nature with as much pleasure as romances or poems, where the incidents are fictitious? The prosperity of no empire, nor the grandeur of no king, can so agreeably affect in the reading, as the ruin of the state of Macedon, and the distress of its unhappy prince. Such a catastrophe touches us in history as much as the destruction of Troy does in fable. Our delight, in cases of this kind, is very greatly heightened, if the sufferer be some excellent person who sinks under an unworthy fortune. Scipio and Cato are both virtuous characters; but we are more deeply affected by the violent death of the one, and the ruin of the great cause he adhered to, than with the deserved triumphs and uninterrupted prosperity of the other; for terror is a passion which always produces delight when it does not press too closely; and pity is a passion accompanied with pleasure, because it arises from love and social affection. Whenever we are formed by nature to any active purpose, the passion which animates us to it is attended with delight, or a pleasure of some kind, let the subject-matter be what it will; and as our Creator has designed that we should be united by the bond of sympathy, he has strengthened that bond by a proportionable delight; and there most where our sympathy is most wanted,—in the distresses of others. If this passion was simply painful, we would shun with the greatest care all persons and places that could excite such a passion; as some, who are so far gone in indolence as not to endure any strong impression, actually do. But the case is widely different with the greater part of mankind; there is no spectacle we so eagerly pursue, as that of some uncommon and grievous calamity; so that whether the misfortune is before our eyes, or whether they are turned back to it in history, it always touches with delight. This is not an unmixed delight, but blended with no small uneasiness. The delight we have in such things, hinders us from shunning scenes of misery; and the pain we feel prompts us to relieve ourselves in relieving those who suffer; and all this antecedent to any reasoning, by an instinct that works us to its own purposes without our concurrence.

SECT. XV.—OF THE EFFECTS OF TRAGEDY

It is thus in real calamities. In imitated distresses the only difference is the pleasure resulting from the effects of imitation; for it is never so perfect, but we can perceive it is imitation, and on that principle are somewhat pleased with it. And indeed in some cases we derive as much or more pleasure from that source than from the thing itself. But then I imagine we shall be much mistaken, if we attribute any considerable part of our satisfaction in tragedy to the consideration that tragedy is a deceit, and its representations no realities. The nearer it approaches the reality, and the farther it removes us from all idea of fiction, the more perfect is its power. But be its power of what kind it will, it never approaches to what it represents. Choose a day on which to represent the most sublime and affecting tragedy we have; appoint the most favourite actors; spare no cost upon the scenes and decorations, unite the greatest efforts of poetry, painting, and music; and when you have collected your audience, just at the moment when their minds are erect with expectation, let it be reported that a state criminal of high rank is on the point of being executed in the adjoining square; in a moment the emptiness of the theatre would demonstrate the comparative weakness of the imitative arts, and proclaim the triumph of the real sympathy. I believe that this notion of our having a simple pain in the reality, yet a delight in the representation, arises from hence, that we do not sufficiently distinguish what we would by no means choose to do, from what we should be eager enough to see if it was once done. The delight in seeing things, which, so far from doing, our heartiest wishes would be to see redressed. This noble capital, the pride of England and of Europe, I believe no man is so strangely wicked as to desire to see destroyed by a conflagration or an earthquake, though he should be removed himself to the greatest distance from the danger. But suppose such a fatal accident to have happened, what numbers from all parts would crowd to behold the ruins, and amongst many who would have been content never to have seen London in its glory! Nor is it, either in real or fictitious distresses, our immunity from them which produces our delight; in my own mind I can discover nothing like it. I apprehend that this mistake is owing to a sort of sophism, by which we are frequently imposed upon; it arises from our not distinguishing between what is indeed a necessary condition to our doing or suffering anything in general, and what is the *cause* of some particular act. If a man kills me with a sword, it is a necessary condition to this that we should have been both of us alive before the fact; and yet it would be absurd to say, that our being both living creatures was the cause of his crime and of my death. So it is certain, that it is absolutely necessary my life should be out of any imminent hazard, before I can take a delight in the sufferings of others, real or imaginary, or indeed in anything else from any cause whatsoever. But then it is a sophism to argue from thence, that this immunity is the cause of my delight either on these or on any occasions. No one can distinguish such a cause of satisfaction in his own mind, I believe; nay, when we do not suffer any very acute pain, nor are exposed to any imminent danger of our lives, we can feel for others, whilst we suffer ourselves; and often then most when we are softened by affliction; we see with pity even distresses which we would accept in the place of our own.

SECT. XVI.—IMITATION

THE second passion belonging to society is imitation, or, if you will, a desire of imitating, and consequently a pleasure in it. This passion arises from much the same cause with sympathy. For as sympathy makes us take a concern in whatever men feel, so this affection prompts us to copy whatever they do; and consequently we have a pleasure in imitating, and in whatever belongs to imitation, merely as it is such, without any intervention of the reasoning faculty, but solely from our natural constitution, which Providence has framed in such a manner as to find either pleasure or delight, according to the nature of the object, in whatever regards the purposes of our being. It is by imitation far more than by precept, that we learn everything; and what we learn thus, we acquire not only more effectually, but more pleasantly. This forms our manners, our opinions, our lives. It is one of the strongest links of society; it is a species of mutual compliance, which all men yield to each other, without constraint to themselves, and which is extremely flattering to all. Herein it is that painting and many other agreeable arts have laid one of the principal foundations of their power. And since, by its influence on our manners and our passions, it is of such great consequence, I shall here venture to lay down a rule, which may inform us with a good degree of certainty when we are to attribute the power of the arts to imitation, or to our pleasure in the skill of the imitator merely, and when to sympathy, or some other cause in conjunction with it. When the object represented in poetry or painting is such as we could have no desire of seeing in the reality, then I may be sure that its power in poetry or painting is owing to the power of imitation, and to no cause operating in the thing itself. So it is with most of the pieces which the painters call still-life. In these a cottage, a dunghill, the meanest and most ordinary utensils of the kitchen, are capable of giving us pleasure. But when the object of the painting or poem is such as we should run to see if real, let it affect us with what odd sort of sense it will, we may rely upon it, that the power of the poem or picture is more owing to the nature of the thing itself than to the mere effect of imitation, or to a consideration of the skill of the imitator, however excellent. Aristotle has spoken so much and so boldly upon the force of imitation in his Poetics, that it makes any further discourse upon this subject the less necessary.

SECT. XVII.—AMBITION

ALTHOUGH imitation is one of the great instruments used by Providence in bringing our nature towards its perfection, yet if men gave themselves up to imitation entirely, and each followed the other, and so on in an eternal circle, it is easy to see that there never could be any improvement amongst them. Men must remain as brutes do, the same at the end that they are at this day, and that they were in the beginning of the world. To prevent this, God has planted in man a sense of ambition, and a satisfaction arising from the contemplation of his excelling his fellows in something deemed valuable amongst them. It is this passion that drives men to all the ways we see in use of signalizing themselves, and that tends to make whatever excites in a man the idea of this distinction so very pleasant. It has been so strong as to make very miserable men take comfort, that they were supreme in misery; and certain it is, that, where we cannot distinguish ourselves by something excellent, we begin to take a complacency in some singular infirmities, follies, or defects of one kind or other. It is on this principle that flattery is so prevalent; for flattery is no more than what raises in a man's mind an idea of a preference which he has not. Now, whatever, either on good or upon bad grounds, tends to raise a man in his own opinion, produces a sort of swelling and triumph, that is extremely grateful to the human mind; and this swelling is never more perceived, nor operates with more force, than when without danger we are conversant with terrible objects; the mind always claiming to itself some part of the dignity and importance of the things which it contemplates. Hence proceeds what Longinus has observed of that glorying sense of inward greatness, that always fills the reader of such passages in poets and orators as are sublime; it is what every man must have felt in himself upon such occasions.

SECT. XVIII.—THE RECAPITULATION

To draw the whole of what has been said into a few distinct points:—The passions which belong to self-preservation turn on pain and danger; they are simply painful when their causes immediately affect us; they are delightful when we have an idea of pain and danger, without being actually in such circumstances; this delight I have not called pleasure, because it turns on pain, and because it is different enough from any idea of positive pleasure. Whatever excites this delight, I call *sublime*. The passions belonging to self-preservation are the strongest of all the passions.

The second head to which the passions are referred with relation to their final cause, is society. There are two sorts of societies. The first is, the society of sex. The passion belonging to this is called love, and it contains a mixture of lust; its object is the beauty of women. The other is the great society with man and all other animals. The passion subservient to this is called likewise love, but it has no mixture of lust, and its object is beauty; which is a name I shall apply to all such qualities in things as induce in us a sense of affection and tenderness, or some other passion the most nearly resembling these. The passion of love has its rise in positive pleasure;

it is, like all things which grow out of pleasure, capable of being mixed with a mode of uneasiness, that is, when an idea of its object is excited in the mind with an idea at the same time of having irretrievably lost it. This mixed sense of pleasure I have not called *pain,* because it turns upon actual pleasure, and because it is, both in its cause and in most of its effects, of a nature altogether different.

Next to the general passion we have for society, to a choice in which we are directed by the pleasure we have in the object, the particular passion under this head called sympathy has the greatest extent. The nature of this passion is, to put us in the place of another in whatever circumstance he is in, and to affect us in a like manner; so that this passion may, as the occasion requires, turn either on pain or pleasure; but with the modifications mentioned in some cases in sect. 11. As to imitation and preference, nothing more need be said.

SECT. XIX.—THE CONCLUSION

I BELIEVED that an attempt to range and methodize some of our most leading passions would be a good preparative to such an inquiry as we are going to make in the ensuing discourse. The passions I have mentioned are almost the only ones which it can be necessary to consider in our present design; though the variety of the passions is great, and worthy in every branch of that variety, of an attentive investigation. The more accurately we search into the human mind, the stronger traces we everywhere find of his wisdom who made it. If a discourse on the use of the parts of the body may be considered as an hymn to the Creator; the use of the passions, which are the organs of the mind, cannot be barren of praise to him, nor unproductive to ourselves of that noble and uncommon union of science and admiration, which a contemplation of the works of infinite wisdom alone can afford to a rational mind: whilst, referring to him whatever we find of right or good or fair in ourselves, discovering his strength and wisdom even in our own weakness and imperfection, honouring them where we discover them clearly, and adoring their profundity where we are lost in our search, we may be inquisitive without impertinence, and elevated without pride; we may be admitted, if I may dare to say so, into the counsels of the Almighty by a consideration of his works. The elevation of the mind ought to be the principal end of all our studies; which if they do not in some measure effect, they are of very little service to us. But, beside this great purpose, a consideration of the rationale of our passions seems to me very necessary for all who would affect them upon solid and sure principles. It is not enough to know them in general: to affect them after a delicate manner, or to judge properly of any work designed to affect them, we should know the exact boundaries of their several jurisdictions; we should pursue them through all their variety of operations, and pierce into the inmost, and what might appear inaccessible, parts of our nature,

Quod latet arcand non enarrabile fibrâ.

Without all this it is possible for a man, after a confused manner, sometimes to satisfy his own mind of the truth of his work; but he can never have a certain determinate rule to go by, nor can he ever make his propositions sufficiently clear to others. Poets, and orators, and painters, and those who cultivate other branches of the liberal arts, have, without this critical knowledge, succeeded well in their several provinces, and will succeed: as among artificers there are many machines made and even invented without any exact knowledge of the principles they are governed by. It is, I own, not uncommon to be wrong in theory, and right in practice; and we are happy that it is so. Men often act right from their feelings, who afterwards reason but ill on them from principle: but as it is impossible to avoid an attempt at such reasoning, and equally impossible to prevent its having some influence on our practice, surely it is worth taking some pains to have it just, and founded on the basis of sure experience. We might expect that the artists themselves would have been our surest guides; but the artists have been too much occupied in the practice: the philosophers have done little; and what they have done, was mostly with a view to their own schemes and systems: and as for those called critics, they have generally sought the rule of the arts in the wrong place; they sought it among poems, pictures, engravings, statues, and buildings. But art can never give the rules that make an art. This is, I believe, the

reason why artists in general, and poets principally, have been confined in so narrow a circle: they have been rather imitators of one
another than of nature; and this with so faithful an uniformity, and
to so remote an antiquity, that it is hard to say who gave the
first model. Critics follow them, and therefore can do little as
guides. I can judge but poorly of anything, whilst I measure it by
no other standard than itself. The true standard of the arts is in
every man's power; and an easy observation of the most common,
sometimes of the meanest, things in nature, will give the truest
lights, where the greatest sagacity and industry, that slights such
observation, must leave us in the dark, or, what is worse, amuse and
mislead us by false lights. In an inquiry it is almost everything to be
once in a right road. I am satisfied I have done but little by these
observations considered in themselves; and I never should have
taken the pains to digest them, much less should I have ever ventured to publish them, if I was not convinced that nothing tends
more to the corruption of science than to suffer it to stagnate. These
waters must be troubled, before they can exert their virtues. A
man who works beyond the surface of things, though he may be
wrong himself, yet he clears the way for others, and may chance
to make even his errors subservient to the cause of truth. In the
following parts I shall inquire what things they are that cause
in us the affections of the sublime and beautiful, as in this I have
considered the affections themselves. I only desire one favour,—that
no part of this discourse may be judged of by itself, and independently of the rest; for I am sensible I have not disposed my materials
to abide the test of a captious controversy, but of a sober and even
forgiving examination, that they are not armed at all points for
battle, but dressed to visit those who are willing to give a peaceful
entrance to truth.

PART II

THE passion caused by the great and sublime in *nature,* when those causes operate most powerfully, is astonishment; and astonishment is that state of the soul, in which all its motions are suspended, with some degree of horror.[1] In this case the mind is so entirely filled with its object, that it cannot entertain any other, nor by consequence reason on that object which employs it. Hence arises the great power of the sublime, that, far from being produced by them, it anticipates our reasonings, and hurries us on by an irresistible force. Astonishment, as I have said, is the effect of the sublime in its highest degree; the inferior effects are admiration, reverence, and respect.

SECT. II.—TERROR

No passion so effectually robs the mind of all its powers of acting and reasoning as *fear.*[2] For fear being an apprehension of pain or death, it operates in a manner that resembles actual pain. Whatever therefore is terrible, with regard to sight, is sublime too, whether this cause of terror be endued with greatness of dimensions or not; for it is impossible to look on anything as trifling, or contemptible, that may be dangerous. There are many animals, who though far from being large, are yet capable of raising ideas of the sublime, because they are considered as objects of terror. As serpents and poisonous animals of almost all kinds. And to things of great dimensions, if we annex an adventitious idea of terror, they become without comparison greater. A level plain of a vast extent on land, is certainly no mean idea; the prospect of such a plain may be as extensive as a prospect of the ocean: but can it ever fill the mind with anything so great as the ocean itself? This is owing to several causes; but it is owing to none more than this, that the ocean is an

[1] Part I. sect. 3, 4, 7.   [2] Part IV. sect. 3–6.

49

object of no small terror. Indeed, terror is in all cases whatsover, either more openly or latently, the ruling principle of the sublime. Several languages bear a strong testimony to the affinity of these ideas. They frequently use the same word, to signify indifferently the modes of astonishment or admiration, and those of terror. Θάμβος is in Greek, either fear or wonder; δεινος is terrible or respectable; αἰδέω, to reverence or to fear. *Vereor* in Latin, is what αἰδέω is in Greek. The Romans used the verb *stupeo,* a term which strongly marks the state of an astonished mind, to express the effect either of simple fear or of astonishment; the word *attonitus* (thunder-struck) is equally expressive of the alliance of these ideas; and do not the French *étonnement,* and the English *astonishment* and *amazement,* point out as clearly the kindred emotions which attend fear and wonder? They who have a more general knowledge of languages, could produce, I make no doubt, many other and equally striking examples.

SECT. III.—OBSCURITY

To make anything very terrible, obscurity[1] seems in general to be necessary. When we know the full extent of any danger, when we can accustom our eyes to it, a great deal of the apprehension vanishes. Every one will be sensible of this, who considers how greatly night adds to our dread, in all cases of danger, and how much the notions of ghosts and goblins, of which none can form clear ideas, affect minds which give credit to the popular tales concerning such sorts of beings. Those despotic governments, which are founded on the passions of men, and principally upon the passion of fear, keep their chief as much as may be from the public eye. The policy has been the same in many cases of religion. Almost all the heathen temples were dark. Even in the barbarous temples of the Americans at this day, they keep their idol in a dark part of the hut, which is consecrated to his worship. For this purpose too the Druids performed all their ceremonies in the bosom of the darkest woods, and in the shade of the oldest and most spreading oaks. No person seems better to have understood the secret of heightening, or of setting terrible things, if I may use the expression, in their

[1] Part IV. sect. 14–16.

strongest light, by the force of a judicious obscurity, than Milton.
His description of Death in the second book is admirably studied;
it is astonishing with what a gloomy pomp, with what a significant
and expressive uncertainty of strokes and colouring, he has finished
the portrait of the king of terrors:

> —The other shape,
> If shape it might be called that shape had none
> Distinguishable, in member, joint, or limb;
> Or substance might be called that shadow seemed;
> For each seemed either; black he stood as night;
> Fierce as ten furies; terrible as hell;
> And shook a deadly dart. What seemed his head
> The likeness of a kingly crown had on.

In this description all is dark, uncertain, confused, terrible, and
sublime to the last degree.

SECT. IV.—OF THE DIFFERENCE BETWEEN CLEARNESS AND OBSCURITY WITH REGARD TO THE PASSIONS

IT is one thing to make an idea clear, and another to make it
affecting to the imagination. If I make a drawing of a palace, or a
temple, or a landscape, I present a very clear idea of those objects; but
then (allowing for the effect of imitation, which is something) my
picture can at most affect only as the palace, temple, or landscape
would have affected in the reality. On the other hand, the most
lively and spirited verbal description I can give raises a very obscure
and imperfect *idea* of such objects; but then it is in my power to raise
a stronger *emotion* by the description than I could do by the best
painting. This experience constantly evinces. The proper manner
of conveying the *affections* of the mind from one to another, is by
words; there is a great insufficiency in all other methods of communication; and so far is a clearness of imagery from being absolutely necessary to an influence upon the passions, that they may be
considerably operated upon, without presenting any image at all, by
certain sounds adapted to that purpose; of which we have a sufficient proof in the acknowledged and powerful effects of instrumental music. In reality, a great clearness helps but little towards

affecting the passions, as it is in some sort an enemy to all enthusi-
asms whatsoever.

SECT. [IV.]—THE SAME SUBJECT CONTINUED

THERE are two verses in Horace's Art of Poetry, that seem to
contradict this opinion; for which reason I shall take a little more
pains in clearing it up. The verses are,

> *Segnius irritant animos demissa per aures,*
> *Quam quæ sunt oculis subjecta fidelibus.*

On this the Abbé du Bos founds a criticism, wherein he gives
painting the preference to poetry in the article of moving the passions; principally on account of the greater *clearness* of the ideas it
represents. I believe this excellent judge was led into this mistake
(if it be a mistake) by his system; to which he found it more con-
formable than I imagine it will be found by experience. I know
several who admire and love painting, and yet who regard the objects of their admiration in that art with coolness enough in comparison of that warmth with which they are animated by affecting
pieces of poetry or rhetoric. Among the common sort of people, I
never could perceive that painting had much influence on their
passions. It is true, that the best sorts of painting, as well as the
best sorts of poetry, are not much understood in that sphere. But it is
most certain, that their passions are very strongly roused by a fanatic
preacher, or by the ballads of Chevy-chase, or the Children in the
Wood, and by other little popular poems and tales that are current
in that rank of life. I do not know of any paintings, bad or good,
that produce the same effect. So that poetry, with all its obscurity,
has a more general, as well as a more powerful, dominion over the
passions, than the other art. And I think there are reasons in nature, why the obscure idea, when properly conveyed, should be
more affecting than the clear. It is our ignorance of things that
causes all our admiration, and chiefly excites our passions. Knowledge and acquaintance make the most striking causes affect but
little. It is thus with the vulgar; and all men are as the vulgar in
what they do not understand. The ideas of eternity and infinity
are among the most affecting we have; and yet perhaps there is

nothing of which we really understand so little, as of infinity and eternity. We do not anywhere meet a more sublime description than this justly celebrated one of Milton, wherein he gives the portrait of Satan with a dignity so suitable to the subject:

> —He above the rest
> In shape and gesture proudly eminent
> Stood like a tower; his form had yet not lost
> All her original brightness, nor appeared
> Less than archangel ruined, and th' excess
> Of glory obscured: as when the sun new risen
> Looks through the horizontal misty air
> Shorn of his beams; or from behind the moon
> In dim eclipse disastrous twilight sheds
> On half the nations; and with fear of change
> Perplexes monarchs.—

Here is a very noble picture; and in what does this poetical picture consist? In images of a tower, an archangel, the sun rising through mists, or in an eclipse, the ruin of monarchs, and the revolutions of kingdoms. The mind is hurried out of itself, by a crowd of great and confused images; which affect because they are crowded and confused. For, separate them, and you lose much of the greatness; and join them, and you infallibly lose the clearness. The images raised by poetry are always of this obscure kind; though in general the effects of poetry are by no means to be attributed to the images it raises; which point we shall examine more at large hereafter.[1] But painting, when we have allowed for the pleasure of imitation, can only affect simply by the images it presents; and even in painting, a judicious obscurity in some things contributes to the effect of the picture; because the images in painting are exactly similar to those in nature; and in nature, dark, confused, uncertain images have a greater power on the fancy to form the grander passions, than those have which are more clear and determinate. But where and when this observation may be applied to practice, and how far it shall be extended, will be better deduced from the nature of the subject, and from the occasion, than from any rules that can be given.

[1] Part V.

I am sensible that this idea has met with opposition, and is likely still to be rejected by several. But let it be considered, that hardly anything can strike the mind with its greatness, which does not make some sort of approach towards infinity; which nothing can do whilst we are able to perceive its bounds; but to see an object distinctly, and to perceive its bounds, is one and the same thing. A clear idea is therefore another name for a little idea. There is a passage in the book of Job amazingly sublime, and this sublimity is principally due to the terrible uncertainty of the thing described: *In thoughts from the visions of the night, when deep sleep falleth upon men, fear came upon me, and trembling, which made all my bones to shake. Then a spirit passed before my face; the hair of my flesh stood up. It stood still,* but I could not discern the form thereof: *an image was before mine eyes, there was silence, and I heard a voice,—Shall mortal man be more just than God?* We are first prepared with the utmost solemnity for the vision; we are first terrified, before we are let even into the obscure cause of our emotion; but when this grand cause of terror makes it appearance, what is it? Is it not wrapt up in the shades of its own incomprehensible darkness, more awful, more striking, more terrible, than the liveliest description, than the clearest painting, could possibly represent it? When painters have attempted to give us clear representations of these very fanciful and terrible ideas, they have, I think, almost always failed; insomuch that I have been at a loss, in all the pictures I have seen of hell, to determine whether the painter did not intend something ludicrous. Several painters have handled a subject of this kind, with a view of assembling as many horrid phantoms as their imagination could suggest; but all the designs I have chanced to meet of the temptation of St. Anthony were rather a sort of odd, wild grotesques, than anything capable of producing a serious passion. In all these subjects poetry is very happy. Its apparitions, its chimeras, its harpies, its allegorical figures, are grand and affecting; and though Virgil's Fame and Homer's Discord are obscure, they are magnificent figures. These figures in painting would be clear enough, but I fear they might become ridiculous.

SECT. V.—POWER

BESIDES those things which *directly* suggest the idea of danger, and those which produce a similar effect from a mechanical cause, I know of nothing sublime, which is not some modification of power. And this branch rises, as naturally as the other two branches, from terror, the common stock of everything that is sublime. The idea of power, at first view, seems of the class of those indifferent ones, which may equally belong to pain or to pleasure. But in reality, the affection, arising from the idea of vast power, is extremely remote from that neutral character. For first, we must remember,[1] that the idea of pain, in its highest degree, is much stronger than the highest degree of pleasure; and that it preserves the same superiority through all the subordinate gradations. From hence it is, that where the chances for equal degrees of suffering or enjoyment are in any sort equal, the idea of the suffering must always be prevalent. And indeed the ideas of pain, and, above all, of death, are so very affecting, that whilst we remain in the presence of whatever is supposed to have the power of inflicting either, it is impossible to be perfectly free from terror. Again, we know by experience, that, for the enjoyment of pleasure, no great efforts of power are at all necessary; nay, we know, that such efforts would go a great way towards destroying our satisfaction: for pleasure must be stolen, and not forced upon us; pleasure follows the will; and therefore we are generally affected with it by many things of a force greatly inferior to our own. But pain is always inflicted by a power in some way superior, because we never submit to pain willingly. So that strength, violence, pain, and terror, are ideas that rush in upon the mind together. Look at a man, or any other animal of prodigious strength, and what is your idea before reflection? Is it that this strength will be subservient to you, to your ease, to your pleasure, to your interest in any sense? No; the emotion you feel is, lest this enormous strength should be employed to the purposes of rapine[2] and destruction. That power derives all its sublimity from the terror with which it is generally accompanied, will appear evidently from its effect in the very few cases, in which it may be possible to

---

[1] Part I. sect. 7.   [2] Vide Part III. sect. 21.

strip a considerable degree of strength of its ability to hurt. When you do this, you spoil it of everything sublime, and it immediately becomes contemptible. An ox is a creature of vast strength; but he is an innocent creature, extremely serviceable, and not at all dangerous; for which reason the idea of an ox is by no means grand. A bull is strong too: but his strength is of another kind; often very destructive, seldom (at least amongst us) of any use in our business; the idea of a bull is therefore great, and it has frequently a place in sublime descriptions, and elevating comparisons. Let us look at another strong animal, in the two distinct lights in which we may consider him. The horse in the light of a useful beast, fit for the plough, the road, the draft; in every social, useful light, the horse has nothing sublime: but is it thus that we are affected with him, *whose neck is clothed with thunder, the glory of whose nostrils is terrible, who swalloweth the ground with fierceness and rage, neither believeth that it is the sound of the trumpet?* In this description, the useful character of the horse entirely disappears, and the terrible and sublime blaze out together. We have continually about us animals of a strength that is considerable, but not pernicious. Amongst these we never look for the sublime; it comes upon us in the gloomy forest, and in the howling wilderness, in the form of the lion, the tiger, the panther, or rhinoceros. Whenever strength is only useful, and employed for our benefit or our pleasure, then it is never sublime: for nothing can act agreeably to us, that does not act in conformity to our will; but to act agreeably to our will, it must be subject to us, and therefore can never be the cause of a grand and commanding conception. The description of the wild ass, in Job, is worked up into no small sublimity, merely by insisting on his freedom, and his setting mankind at defiance; otherwise the description of such an animal could have had nothing noble in it. *Who hath loosed* (says he) *the bands of the wild ass? whose house I have made the wilderness, and the barren land his dwellings. He scorneth the multitude of the city, neither regardeth he the voice of the driver. The range of the mountains is his pasture.* The magnificent description of the unicorn and of leviathan, in the same book, is full of the same heightening circumstances: *Will the unicorn be willing to serve thee? canst thou bind the uni-*

corn with his hand in the furrow? wilt thou trust him because his strength is great?—Canst thou draw out leviathan with an hook?— will he make a covenant with thee? wilt thou take him for a servant for ever? shall not one be cast down even at the sight of him? In short, wheresoever we find strength, and in what light soever we look upon power we shall all along observe the sublime the concomitant of terror, and contempt the attendant on a strength that is subservient and innoxious. The race of dogs, in many of their kinds, have generally a competent degree of strength and swiftness; and they exert these and other valuable qualities which they possess, greatly to our convenience and pleasure. Dogs are indeed the most social, affectionate, and amiable animals of the whole brute creation; but love approaches much nearer to contempt than is commonly imagined; and accordingly, though we caress dogs, we borrow from them an appellation of the most despicable kind, when we employ terms of reproach; and this appellation is the common mark of the last vileness and contempt in every language. Wolves have not more strength than several species of dogs; but, on account of their unmanageable fierceness, the idea of a wolf is not despicable; it is not excluded from grand descriptions and similitudes. Thus we are affected by strength, which is *natural* power. The power which arises from institution in kings and commanders, has the same connexion with terror. Sovereigns are frequently addressed with the title of *dread majesty*. And it may be observed, that young persons, little acquainted with the world, and who have not been used to approach men in power, are commonly struck with an awe which takes away the free use of their faculties. *When I prepared my seat in the street,* (says Job,) *the young men saw me, and hid themselves.* Indeed, so natural is this timidity with regard to power, and so strongly does it inhere in our constitution, that very few are able to conquer it, but by mixing much in the business of the great world, or by using no small violence to their natural dispositions. I know some people are of opinion, that no awe, no degree of terror, accompanies the idea of power; and have hazarded to affirm, that we can contemplate the idea of God himself without any such emotion. I purposely avoided, when I first considered this subject, to introduce the idea of that great and tremendous Being, as an example in an argument so light as this; though it frequently occurred to me, not as an objection to, but as a strong confirmation of, my notions in this matter. I hope, in what I am going to say, I shall avoid presumption, where it is almost impossible for any mortal to speak with strict propriety. I say then, that whilst we consider the Godhead merely as he is an object of the understanding, which forms a complex idea of power, wisdom, justice, goodness, all stretched to a degree far exceeding the bounds of our comprehension, whilst we consider the Divinity in this refined and abstracted light, the imagination and passions are little or nothing affected. But because we are bound, by the condition of our nature, to ascend to these pure and intellectual ideas, through the medium of sensible images, and to judge of these divine qualities by their evident acts and exertions, it becomes extremely hard to disentangle our idea of the cause from the effect by which we are led to know it. Thus when we contemplate the Deity, his attributes and their operation, coming united on the mind, form a sort of sensible image, and as such are capable of affecting the imagination. Now, though in a just idea of the Deity perhaps none of his attributes are predominant, yet, to our imagination, his power is by far the most striking. Some reflection, some comparing, is necessary to satisfy us of his wisdom, his justice, and his goodness. To be struck with his power, it is only necessary that we should open our eyes. But whilst we contemplate so vast an object, under the arm, as it were, of almighty power, and invested upon every side with omnipresence, we shrink into the minuteness of our own nature, and are, in a manner, annihilated before him. And though a consideration of his other attributes may relieve, in some measure, our apprehensions; yet no conviction of the justice with which it is exercised, nor the mercy with which it is tempered, can wholly remove the terror that naturally arises from a force which nothing can withstand. If we rejoice, we rejoice with trembling: and even whilst we are receiving benefits, we cannot but shudder at a power which can confer benefits of such mighty importance. When the prophet David contemplated the wonders of wisdom and power which are displayed in the economy of man, he seems to be struck with a sort of divine horror, and cries out, *Fearfully and wonderfully am I made!* An heathen poet has a senti-

ment of a similar nature; Horace looks upon it as the last effort
of philosophical fortitude, to behold without terror and amazement,
this immense and glorious fabric of the universe:

> *Hunc solem, et stellas, et decedentia certis*
> *Tempora momentis, sunt qui formidine nulla*
> *Imbuti spectent.*

Lucretius is a poet not to be suspected of giving way to superstitious terrors; yet when he supposes the whole mechanism of nature
laid open by the master of his philosophy, his transport on this magnificent view, which he has represented in the colours of such bold
and lively poetry, is overcast with a shade of secret dread and
horror:

> *His ibi me rebus quædam divina voluptas*
> *Percipit, atque horror; quod sic Natura, tua vi*
> *Tam manifesta patens, ex omni parte retecta est.*

But the Scripture alone can supply ideas answerable to the majesty
of this subject. In the Scripture, wherever God is represented as
appearing or speaking, everything terrible in nature is called up
to heighten the awe and solemnity of the Divine presence. The
Psalms, and the prophetical books, are crowded with instances of
this kind. *The earth shook,* (says the psalmist,) *the heavens also*
dropped at the presence of the Lord. And, what is remarkable, the
painting preserves the same character, not only when he is supposed
descending to take vengeance upon the wicked, but even when he
exerts the like plenitude of power in acts of beneficence to mankind.
Tremble, thou earth! at the presence of the Lord; at the presence
of the God of Jacob; which turned the rock into standing water, the
flint into a fountain of waters! It were endless to enumerate all
the passages, both in the sacred and profane writers, which establish
the general sentiment of mankind, concerning the inseparable union
of a sacred and reverential awe, with our ideas of the Divinity. Hence
the common maxim, *Primus in orbe deos fecit timor.* This maxim
may be, as I believe it is, false with regard to the origin of religion.
The maker of the maxim saw how inseparable these ideas were,
without considering that the notion of some great power must be
always precedent to our dread of it. But this dread must necessarily

follow the idea of such a power, when it is once excited in the mind. It is on this principle that true religion has, and must have, so large a mixture of salutary fear; and that false religions have generally nothing else but fear to support them. Before the Christian religion had, as it were, humanized the idea of the Divinity, and brought it somewhat nearer to us, there was very little said of the love of God. The followers of Plato have something of it, and only something; the other writers of pagan antiquity, whether poets or philosophers, nothing at all. And they who consider with what infinite attention, by what a disregard of every perishable object, through what long habits of piety and contemplation, it is that any man is able to attain an entire love and devotion to the Deity, will easily perceive, that it is not the first, the most natural and the most striking, effect which proceeds from that idea. Thus we have traced power through its several gradations unto the highest of all, where our imagination is finally lost; and we find terror, quite throughout the progress, its inseparable companion, and growing along with it, as far as we can possibly trace them. Now as power is undoubtedly a capital source of the sublime, this will point out evidently from whence its energy is derived, and to what class of ideas we ought to unite it.

SECT. VI.—PRIVATION

ALL *general* privations are great, because they are all terrible; *Vacuity, Darkness, Solitude,* and *Silence.* With what a fire of imagination, yet with what severity of judgment, has Virgil amassed all these circumstances, where he knows that all the images of a tremendous dignity ought to be united, at the mouth of hell! where, before he unlocks the secrets of the great deep, he seems to be seized with a religious horror, and to retire astonished at the boldness of his own designs:

> *Dii, quibus imperium est animarum, umbræque*—silentes!
> *Et Chaos, et Phlegethon, loca* nocte silentia *late,*
> *Sit mihi fas audita loqui; sit, numine vestro,*
> *Pandere res alta terra et* caligine *mersas.*
> *Ibant* obscuri, sola *sub* nocte, *per* umbram,
> *Perque domos Ditis* vacuas, *et* inania *regna.*

Ye subterraneous gods, whose awful sway
The gliding ghosts and *silent* shades obey;
O Chaos hoar! and Phlegethon profound!
Whose solemn empire stretches wide around;
Give me, ye great, tremendous powers, to tell
Of scenes and wonders in the depth of hell:
Give me your mighty secrets to display
From those *black* realms of darkness to the day.—PITT

Obscure they went through dreary *shades* that led
Along the *waste* dominions of the *dead*.—DRYDEN.

SECT. VII.—VASTNESS

GREATNESS[1] of dimension is a powerful cause of the sublime. This is too evident, and the observation too common, to need any illustration: it is not so common to consider in what ways greatness of dimension, vastness of extent or quantity, has the most striking effect. For certainly, there are ways and modes, wherein the same quantity of extension shall produce greater effects than it is found to do in others. Extension is either in length, height, or depth. Of these the length strikes least; an hundred yards of even ground will never work such an effect as a tower an hundred yards high, or a rock or mountain of that altitude. I am apt to imagine likewise, that height is less grand than depth; and that we are more struck at looking down from a precipice, than looking up at an object of equal height; but of that I am not very positive. A perpendicular has more force in forming the sublime, than an inclined plane; and the effects of a rugged and broken surface seem stronger than where it is smooth and polished. It would carry us out of our way to enter in this place into the cause of these appearances; but certain it is they afford a large and fruitful field of speculation. However, it may not be amiss to add to these remarks upon magnitude, that, as the great extreme of dimension is sublime, so the last extreme of littleness is in some measure sublime likewise: when we attend to the infinite divisibility of matter, when we pursue animal life into these excessively small, and yet organized beings, that escape the nicest inquisition of the sense; when we push our

[1] Part IV. sect. 9.

discoveries yet downward, and consider those creatures so many degrees yet smaller, and the still diminishing scale of existence, in tracing which the imagination is lost as well as the sense; we become amazed and confounded at the wonders of minuteness; nor can we distinguish in its effects this extreme of littleness from the vast itself. For division must be infinite as well as addition; because the idea of a perfect unity can no more be arrived at, than that of a complete whole, to which nothing may be added.

SECT. VIII.—INFINITY

ANOTHER source of the sublime is *infinity;* if it does not rather belong to the last. Infinity has a tendency to fill the mind with that sort of delightful horror, which is the most genuine effect and truest test of the sublime. There are scarce any things which can become the objects of our senses, that are really and in their own nature infinite. But the eye not being able to perceive the bounds of many things, they seem to be infinite, and they produce the same effects as if they were really so. We are deceived in the like manner, if the parts of some large object are so continued to any indefinite number, that the imagination meets no check which may hinder its extending them at pleasure.

Whenever we repeat any idea frequently, the mind, by a sort of mechanism, repeats it long after the first cause has ceased to operate.[1] After whirling about, when we sit down, the objects about us still seem to whirl. After a long succession of noises, as the fall of waters, or the beating of forge-hammers, the hammers beat and the water roars in the imagination long after the first sounds have ceased to affect it; and they die away at last by gradations which are scarcely perceptible. If you hold up a straight pole, with your eye to one end, it will seem extended to a length almost incredible.[2] Place a number of uniform and equi-distant marks on this pole, they will cause the same deception, and seem multiplied without end. The senses, strongly affected in some one manner, cannot quickly change their tenor, or adapt themselves to other things; but they continue in their old channel until the strength of the first mover decays. This is the reason of an appearance very fre-

---

[1] Part IV. sect. 12.   [2] Part IV. sect. 14.

quent in madmen; that they remain whole days and nights, some-times whole years, in the constant repetition of some remark, some complaint, or song; which having struck powerfully on their dis-ordered imagination in the beginning of their phrensy, every repe-tition reinforces it with new strength; and the hurry of their spirits, unrestrained by the curb of reason, continues it to the end of their lives.

SECT. IX.—SUCCESSION AND UNIFORMITY

SUCCESSION and *uniformity* of parts are what constitute the arti-ficial infinite. 1. *Succession;* which is requisite that the parts may be continued so long and in such a direction, as by their frequent im-pulses on the sense to impress the imagination with an idea of their progress beyond their actual limits. 2. *Uniformity;* because if the figures of the parts should be changed, the imagination at every change finds a check; you are presented at every alteration with the termination of one idea, and the beginning of another; by which means it becomes impossible to continue that uninterrupted pro-gression, which alone can stamp on bounded objects the character of infinity.[1] It is in this kind of artificial infinity, I believe, we ought to look for the cause why a rotund has such a noble effect. For in a rotund, whether it be a building or a plantation, you can nowhere fix a boundary; turn which way you will, the same object still seems to continue, and the imagination has no rest. But the parts must be uniform, as well as circularly disposed, to give this figure its full force; because any difference, whether it be in the disposition, or in the figure, or even in the color of the parts, is highly preju-dicial to the idea of infinity, which every change must check and interrupt, at every alteration commencing a new series. On the same principles of succession and uniformity, the grand appear-ance of the ancient heathen temples, which were generally oblong forms, with a range of uniform pillars on every side, will be easily accounted for. From the same cause also may be derived the grand effect of the aisles in many of our own old cathedrals. The form of a cross used in some churches seems to me not so eligible as the

[1] Mr. Addison, in the Spectator, concerning the pleasures of imagination, thinks it is because in the rotund at one glance you see half the building. This I do not imagine to be the real cause.

parallelogram of the ancients; at least, I imagine it is not so proper
for the outside. For, supposing the arms of the cross every way
equal, if you stand in a direction parallel to any of the side walls,
or colonnades, instead of a deception that makes the building more
extended than it is, you are cut off from a considerable part (two-
thirds) of its *actual* length; and to prevent all possibility of progression, the arms of the cross, taking a new direction, make a right
angle with the beam, and thereby wholly turn the imagination from
the repetition of the former idea. Or suppose the spectator placed
where he may take a direct view of such a building, what will be the
consequence? The necessary consequence will be, that a good part of
the basis of each angle formed by the intersection of the arms of the
cross, must be inevitably lost; the whole must of course assume a
broken, unconnected figure; the lights must be unequal, here strong,
and there weak; without that noble gradation which the perspective
always effects on parts disposed uninterruptedly in a right line. Some
or all of these objections will lie against every figure of a cross, in
whatever view you take it. I exemplified them in the Greek cross,
in which these faults appear the most strongly; but they appear in
some degree in all sorts of crosses. Indeed there is nothing more
prejudicial to the grandeur of buildings, than to abound in angles;
a fault obvious in many; and owing to an inordinate thirst for
variety, which, whenever it prevails, is sure to leave very little true
taste.

SECT. X.—MAGNITUDE IN BUILDING

To the sublime in building, greatness of dimension seems requisite; for on a few parts, and those small, the imagination cannot
rise to any idea of infinity. No greatness in the manner can effectually compensate for the want of proper dimensions. There is no
danger of drawing men into extravagant designs by this rule; it
carries its own caution along with it. Because too great a length in
buildings destroys the purpose of greatness, which it was intended to
promote; the perspective will lessen it in height as it gains in length;
and will bring it at last to a point; turning the whole figure into a
sort of triangle, the poorest in its effect of almost any figure that can
be presented to the eye. I have ever observed, that colonnades and

avenues of trees of a moderate length, were, without comparison, far grander, than when they were suffered to run to immense distances. A true artist should put a generous deceit on the spectators, and effect the noblest designs by easy methods. Designs that are vast only by their dimensions, are always the sign of a common and low imagination. No work of art can be great, but as it deceives; to be otherwise is the prerogative of nature only. A good eye will fix the medium betwixt an excessive length or height, (for the same objection lies against both,) and a short or broken quantity; and perhaps it might be ascertained to a tolerable degree of exactness, if it was my purpose to descend far into the particulars of any art.

SECT. XI.—INFINITY IN PLEASING OBJECTS

INFINITY, though of another kind, causes much of our pleasure in agreeable, as well as of our delight in sublime, images. The spring is the pleasantest of the seasons; and the young of most animals, though far from being completely fashioned, afford a more agreeable sensation than the full-grown; because the imagination is entertained with the promise of something more, and does not acquiesce in the present object of the sense. In unfinished sketches of drawing, I have often seen something which pleased me beyond the best finishing; and this I believe proceeds from the cause I have just now assigned.

SECT. XII.—DIFFICULTY

ANOTHER[1] source of greatness is *Difficulty*. When any work seems to have required immense force and labor to effect it, the idea is grand. Stonehenge, neither for disposition nor ornament, has anything admirable; but those huge rude masses of stone, set on end, and piled each on other, turn the mind on the immense force necessary for such a work. Nay, the rudeness of the work increases this cause of grandeur, as it excludes the idea of art and contrivance; for dexterity produces another sort of effect, which is different enough from this.

[1] Part IV. sect. 4–6.

SECT. XIII.—MAGNIFICENCE

Magnificence is likewise a source of the sublime. A great profusion of things, which are splendid or valuable in themselves, is *magnificent*. The starry heaven, though it occurs so very frequently to our view, never fails to excite an idea of grandeur. This cannot be owing to the stars themselves, separately considered. The number is certainly the cause. The apparent disorder augments the grandeur, for the appearance of care is highly contrary to our idea of magnificence. Besides, the stars lie in such apparent confusion, as makes it impossible on ordinary occasions to reckon them. This gives them the advantage of a sort of infinity. In works of art, this kind of grandeur, which consists in multitude, is to be very courteously admitted; because a profusion of excellent things is not to be attained, or with too much difficulty; and because in many cases this splendid confusion would destroy all use, which should be attended to in most of the works of art with the greatest care; besides, it is to be considered, that unless you can produce an appearance of infinity by your disorder, you will have disorder only without magnificence. There are, however, a sort of fireworks, and some other things, that in this way succeed well, and are truly grand. There are also many descriptions in the poets and orators, which owe their sublimity to a richness and profusion of images, in which the mind is so dazzled as to make it impossible to attend to that exact coherence and agreement of the allusions, which we should require on every other occasion. I do not now remember a more striking example of this, than the description which is given of the king's army in the play of Henry the Fourth:

> —All furnished, all in arms,
> All plumed like ostriches that with the wind
> Baited like eagles having lately bathed:
> As full of spirit as the month of May,
> And gorgeous as the sun in Midsummer,
> Wanton as youthful goats, wild as young bulls.
> I saw young Harry with his beaver on
> Rise from the ground like feathered Mercury;
> And vaulted with such ease into his seat,
> As if an angel dropp'd down from the clouds
> To turn and wind a fiery Pegasus.

In that excellent book, so remarkable for the vivacity of its descriptions as well as the solidity and penetration of its sentences, the Wisdom of the Son of Sirach, there is a noble panegyric on the high priest Simon the son of Onias; and it is a very fine example of the point before us:

How was he honoured in the midst of the people, in his coming out of the sanctuary! He was as the morning star in the midst of a cloud, and as the moon at the full; as the sun shining upon the temple of the Most High, and as the rainbow giving light in the bright clouds: and as the flower of roses in the spring of the year, as lilies by the rivers of waters, and as the frankincense tree in summer; as fire and incense in the censer, and as a vessel of gold set with precious stones; as a fair olive tree budding forth fruit, and as a cypress which groweth up to the clouds. When he put on the robe of honour, and was clothed with the perfection of glory, when he went up to the holy altar, he made the garment of holiness honourable. He himself stood by the hearth of the altar, compassed with his brethren round about; as a young cedar in Libanus, and as palm trees compassed they him about. So were all the sons of Aaron in their glory, and the oblations of the Lord in their hands, &c.

SECT. XIV.—LIGHT

HAVING considered extension, so far as it is capable of raising ideas of greatness; *colour* comes next under consideration. All colours depend on *light*. Light therefore ought previously to be examined; and with its opposite, darkness. With regard to light, to make it a cause capable of producing the sublime, it must be attended with some circumstances, besides its bare faculty of showing other objects. Mere light is too common a thing to make a strong impression on the mind, and without a strong impression nothing can be sublime. But such a light as that of the sun, immediately exerted on the eye, as it overpowers the sense, is a very great idea. Light of an inferior strength to this, if it moves with great celerity, has the same power; for lightning is certainly productive of grandeur, which it owes chiefly to the extreme velocity of its motion. A quick transition from light to darkness, or from darkness to light, has yet a greater effect.

But darkness is more productive of sublime ideas than light. Our great poet was convinced of this; and indeed so full was he of this idea, so entirely possessed with the power of a well-managed darkness, that in describing the appearance of the Deity, amidst that profusion of magnificent images, which the grandeur of his subject provokes him to pour out upon every side, he is far from forgetting the obscurity which surrounds the most incomprehensible of all beings, but

> —With majesty of *darkness* round
> Circles his throne.—

And what is no less remarkable, our author had the secret of preserving this idea, even when he seemed to depart the farthest from it, when he describes the light and glory which flows from the Divine presence; a light which by its very excess is converted into a species of darkness.

> *Dark* with excessive *light* thy skirts appear.

Here is an idea not only poetical in a high degree, but strictly and philosophically just. Extreme light, by overcoming the organs of sight, obliterates all objects, so as in its effect exactly to resemble darkness. After looking for some time at the sun, two black spots, the impression which it leaves, seem to dance before our eyes. Thus are two ideas as opposite as can be imagined reconciled in the extremes of both; and both, in spite of their opposite nature, brought to concur in producing the sublime. And this is not the only instance wherein the opposite extremes operate equally in favour of the sublime, which in all things abhors mediocrity.

SECT. XV.—LIGHT IN BUILDING

As the management of light is a matter of importance in architecture, it is worth inquiring, how far this remark is applicable to building. I think then, that all edifices calculated to produce an idea of the sublime, ought rather to be dark and gloomy, and this for two reasons; the first is, that darkness itself on other occasions is known by experience to have a greater effect on the passions than light. The second is, that to make an object very striking, we should make it as different as possible from the objects with which we have been immediately conversant; when therefore you enter a building, you cannot pass into a greater light than you had in the open air; to go into one some few degrees less luminous, can make only a trifling change; but to make the transition thoroughly striking, you ought to pass from the greatest light, to as much darkness as is consistent with the uses of architecture. At night the contrary rule will hold, but for the very same reason; and the more highly a room is then illuminated, the grander will the passion be.

SECT. XVI.—COLOUR CONSIDERED AS PRODUCTIVE OF THE SUBLIME

AMONG colours, such as are soft or cheerful (except perhaps a strong red which is cheerful) are unfit to produce grand images. An immense mountain covered with a shining green turf, is nothing, in this respect, to one dark and gloomy; the cloudy sky is more grand than the blue; and night more sublime and solemn than day. Therefore in historical painting, a gay or gaudy drapery can never have a happy effect: and in buildings, when the highest degree of the sublime is intended, the materials and ornaments ought neither to be white, nor green, nor yellow, nor blue, nor a pale red, nor violet, nor spotted, but of sad and fuscous colours, as black, or brown, or deep purple, and the like. Much of gilding, mosaics, painting, or statues, contribute but little to the sublime. This rule need not be put in practice, except where an uniform degree of the most striking sublimity is to be produced, and that in every particular; for it ought to be observed, that this melancholy kind of greatness, though it be certainly the highest, ought not to be studied in all sorts of edifices, where yet grandeur must be studied: in such cases the sublimity must be drawn from the other sources; with a strict caution however against anything light and riant; as nothing so effectually deadens the whole taste of the sublime.

SECT. XVII.—SOUND AND LOUDNESS

THE eye is not the only organ of sensation by which a sublime passion may be produced. Sounds have a great power in these as in most other passions. I do not mean words, because words do not affect simply by their sounds, but by means altogether different. Excessive loudness alone is sufficient to overpower the soul, to suspend its action, and to fill it with terror. The noise of vast cataracts, raging storms, thunder, or artillery, awakes a great and awful sensation in the mind, though we can observe no nicety or artifice in those sorts of music. The shouting of multitudes has a similar effect; and, by the sole strength of the sound, so amazes and confounds the imagination, that, in this staggering and hurry of the mind, the best-established tempers can scarcely forbear being borne down, and joining in the common cry, and common resolution of the crowd.

SECT. XVIII.—SUDDENNESS

A SUDDEN beginning or sudden cessation of sound of any considerable force, has the same power. The attention is roused by this; and the faculties driven forward, as it were, on their guard. Whatever, either in sights or sounds, makes the transition from one extreme to the other easy, causes no terror, and consequently can be no cause of greatness. In everything sudden and unexpected, we are apt to start; that is, we have a perception of danger, and our nature rouses us to guard against it. It may be observed that a single sound of some strength, though but of short duration, if repeated after intervals, has a grand effect. Few things are more awful than the striking of a great clock, when the silence of the night prevents the attention from being too much dissipated. The same may be said of a single stroke on a drum, repeated with pauses; and of the successive firing of cannon at a distance. All the effects mentioned in this section have causes very nearly alike.

SECT. XIX.—INTERMITTING

A LOW, tremulous, intermitting sound, though it seems in some respects opposite to that just mentioned, is productive of the sublime. It is worth while to examine this a little. The fact itself must be determined by every man's own experience and reflection. I have already observed,[1] that night increases our terror, more perhaps than anything else; it is our nature, when we do not know what may happen to us, to fear the worst that can happen; and hence it is, that uncertainty is so terrible, that we often seek to be rid of it, at the hazard of certain mischief. Now, some low, confused, uncertain

[1] Sect. 3.

sounds, leave us in the same fearful anxiety concerning their causes, that no light, or an uncertain light, does concerning the objects that surround us.

> Quale per incertam lunam sub luce maligna
> Est iter in sylvis.—

> —A faint shadow of uncertain light,
> Like as a lamp, whose life doth fade away;
> Or as the moon clothed with cloudy night
> Doth show to him who walks in fear and great affright.
>
> SPENSER.

But light now appearing and now leaving us, and so off and on, is even more terrible than total darkness: and a sort of uncertain sounds are, when the necessary dispositions concur, more alarming than a total silence.

SECT. XX.—THE CRIES OF ANIMALS

SUCH sounds as imitate the natural inarticulate voices of men, or any animals in pain or danger, are capable of conveying great ideas; unless it be the well-known voice of some creature, on which we are used to look with contempt. The angry tones of wild beasts are equally capable of causing a great and awful sensation.

> Hinc exaudiri gemitus iræque leonum
> Vincla recusantum, et sera sub nocte rudentum;
> Setigerique sues, atque in præsepibus ursi
> Sævire; et formæ magnorum ululare luporum.

It might seem that these modulations of sound carry some connexion with the nature of the things they represent, and are not merely arbitrary; because the natural cries of all animals, even of those animals with whom we have not been acquainted, never fail to make themselves sufficiently understood; this cannot be said of language. The modifications of sound, which may be productive of the sublime, are almost infinite. Those I have mentioned are only a few instances to show on what principles they are all built.

SECT. XXI.—SMELL AND TASTE. BITTERS AND STENCHES

Smells and Tastes have some share too in ideas of greatness; but it is a small one, weak in its nature, and confined in its operations.

I shall only observe, that no smells or tastes can produce a grand sensation, except excessive bitters, and intolerable stenches. It is true, that these affections of the smell and taste, when they are in their full force, and lean directly upon the sensory, are simply painful, and accompanied with no sort of delight; but when they are moderated, as in a description or narrative, they become sources of the sublime, as genuine as any other, and upon the very same principle of a moderated pain. "A cup of bitterness;" "to drain the bitter cup of fortune;" "the bitter apples of Sodom;" these are all ideas suitable to a sublime description. Nor is this passage of Virgil without sublimity, where the stench of the vapour in Albunea conspires so happily with the sacred horror and gloominess of that prophetic forest:

> At rex sollicitus monstris oracula Fauni
> Fatidici genitoris adit, lucosque sub alta
> Consulit Albunea, nemorum quæ maxima sacro
> Fonte sonat; sævamque exhalat opaca Mephitim.

In the sixth book, and in a very sublime description, the poisonous exhalation of Acheron is not forgotten, nor does it all disagree with the other images amongst which it is introduced:

> Spelunca alta fuit, vastoque immanis hiatu,
> Scrupea, tuta lacu nigro, nemorumque tenebris;
> Quam super haud ullæ poterant impune volantes
> Tendere iter pennis: talis sese halitus atris
> Faucibus effundens supera ad convexa ferebat.

I have added these examples, because some friends, for whose judgment I have great deference, were of opinion that if the sentiment stood nakedly by itself, it would be subject, at first view, to burlesque and ridicule; but this I imagine would principally arise from considering the bitterness and stench in company with mean and contemptible ideas, with which it must be owned they are often united; such an union degrades the sublime in all other instances as well as in those. But it is one of the tests by which the sublimity of an image is to be tried, not whether it becomes mean when associated with mean ideas; but whether, when united with images of an allowed grandeur, the whole composition is supported with dignity. Things which are terrible are always great; but when things possess disagreeable qualities, or such as have indeed some degree of danger, but of a danger easily overcome, they are merely *odious;* as toads and spiders.

SECT. XXII.—FEELING. PAIN

OF *feeling,* little more can be said than that the idea of bodily pain, in all the modes and degrees of labour, pain, anguish, torment, is productive of the sublime; and nothing else in this sense can produce it. I need not give here any fresh instances, as those given in the former sections abundantly illustrate a remark that, in reality, wants only an attention to nature, to be made by everybody.

Having thus run through the causes of the sublime with reference to all the senses, my first observation (sect. 7) will be found very nearly true; that the sublime is an idea belonging to self-preservation; that it is therefore one of the most affecting we have; that its strongest emotion is an emotion of distress; and that no pleasure[1] from a positive cause belongs to it. Numberless examples, besides those mentioned, might be brought in support of these truths, and many perhaps useful consequences drawn from them—

Sed fugit interea, fugit irrevocabile tempus,
Singula dum capti circumvectamur amore.

[1] Vide Part I. sect. 6.

PART III

Section I.—Of Beauty

IT IS my design to consider beauty as distinguished from the sublime; and, in the course of the inquiry, to examine how far it is consistent with it. But previous to this, we must take a short review of the opinions already entertained of this quality; which I think are hardly to be reduced to any fixed principles; because men are used to talk of beauty in a figurative manner, that is to say, in a manner extremely uncertain, and indeterminate. By beauty I mean that quality or those qualities in bodies, by which they cause love, or some passion similar to it. I confine this definition to the merely sensible qualities of things, for the sake of preserving the utmost simplicity in a subject, which must always distract us whenever we take in those various causes of sympathy which attach us to any persons or things from secondary considerations, and not from the direct force which they have merely on being viewed. I likewise distinguish love (by which I mean that satisfaction which arises to the mind upon contemplating anything beautiful, of whatsoever nature it may be) from desire or lust; which is an energy of the mind, that hurries us on to the possession of certain objects, that do not affect us as they are beautiful, but by means altogether different. We shall have a strong desire for a woman of no remarkable beauty; whilst the greatest beauty in men, or in other animals, though it causes love, yet excites nothing at all of desire. Which shows that beauty, and the passion caused by beauty, which I call love, is different from desire, though desire may sometimes operate along with it; but it is to this latter that we must attribute those violent and tempestuous passions, and the consequent emotions of the body, which attend what is called love in some of its ordinary acceptations, and not to the effects of beauty merely as it is such.

SECT. II.—PROPORTION NOT THE CAUSE OF BEAUTY IN VEGETABLES

BEAUTY hath usually been said to consist in certain proportions of parts. On considering the matter, I have great reason to doubt, whether beauty be at all an idea belonging to proportion. Proportion relates almost wholly to convenience, as every idea of order seems to do; and it must therefore be considered as a creature of the understanding, rather than a primary cause acting on the senses and imagination. It is not by the force of long attention and inquiry that we find any object to be beautiful; beauty demands no assistance from our reasoning; even the will is unconcerned; the appearance of beauty as effectually causes some degree of love in us, as the application of ice or fire produces the ideas of heat or cold. To gain something like a satisfactory conclusion in this point, it were well to examine, what proportion is; since several who make use of that word do not always seem to understand very clearly the force of the term, nor to have very distinct ideas concerning the thing itself. Proportion is the measure of relative quantity. Since all quantity is divisible, it is evident that every distinct part, into which any quantity is divided, must bear some relation to the other parts, or to the whole. These relations give an origin to the idea of proportion. They are discovered by mensuration, and they are the objects of mathematical inquiry. But whether any part of any determinate quantity be a fourth, or a fifth, or a sixth, or a moiety of the whole; or whether it be of equal length with any other part, or double its length, or but one half, is a matter merely indifferent to the mind; it stands neuter in the question; and it is from this absolute indifference and tranquillity of the mind, that mathematical speculations derive some of their most considerable advantages; because there is nothing to interest the imagination; because the judgment sits free and unbiassed to examine the point. All proportions, every arrangement of quantity, is alike to the understanding, because the same truths result to it from all; from greater, from lesser, from equality and inequality. But surely beauty is no idea belonging to mensuration; nor has it anything to do with calculation and geometry. If it had, we might then point out some certain measures which we could demonstrate to be beautiful, either as simply considered, or as relating to others; and we could call in those natural objects, for whose beauty we have no voucher but the sense, to this happy standard, and confirm the voice of our passions by the determination of our reason. But since we have not this help, let us see whether proportion can in any sense be considered as the cause of beauty, as hath been so generally, and by some so confidently, affirmed. If proportion be one of the constituents of beauty, it must derive that power either from some natural properties inherent in certain measures, which operate mechanically; from the operation of custom; or from the fitness which some measures have to answer some particular ends of conveniency. Our business therefore is to inquire, whether the parts of those objects, which are found beautiful in the vegetable or animal kingdoms, are constantly so formed according to such certain measures, as may serve to satisfy us that their beauty results from those measures, on the principle of a natural mechanical cause; or from custom; or, in fine, from their fitness for any determinate purposes. I intend to examine this point under each of these heads in their order. But before I proceed further, I hope it will not be thought amiss, if I lay down the rules which governed me in this inquiry, and which have misled me in it, if I have gone astray. 1. If two bodies produce the same or a similar effect on the mind, and on examination they are found to agree in some of their properties, and to differ in others; the common effect is to be attributed to the properties in which they agree, and not to those in which they differ. 2. Not to account for the effect of a natural object from the effect of an artificial object. 3. Not to account for the effect of any natural object from a conclusion of our reason concerning its uses, if a natural cause may be assigned. 4. Not to admit any determinate quantity, or any relation of quantity, as the cause of a certain effect, if the effect is produced by different or opposite measures and relations; or if these measures and relations may exist, and yet the effect may not be produced. These are the rules which I have chiefly followed, whilst I examined into the power of proportion considered as a natural cause; and these, if he thinks them just, I request the reader to carry with him throughout the following discussion; whilst we inquire in the first place, in what things we find this quality of beauty; next, to see whether in these we can find any assignable proportions, in such a manner as ought to convince us that our idea of beauty results from them. We shall consider this pleasing power, as it appears in vegetables, in the inferior animals, and in man. Turning our eyes to the vegetable creation, we find nothing there so beautiful as flowers; but flowers are almost of every sort of shape, and of every sort of disposition; they are turned and fashioned into an infinite variety of forms; and from these forms botanists have given them their names, which are almost as various. What proportion do we discover between the stalks and the leaves of flowers, or between the leaves and the pistils? How does the slender stalk of the rose agree with the bulky head under which it bends? But the rose is a beautiful flower; and can we undertake to say that it does not owe a great deal of its beauty even to that disproportion: the rose is a large flower, yet it grows upon a small shrub; the flower of the apple is very small, and grows upon a large tree; yet the rose and the apple blossom are both beautiful, and the plants that bear them are most engagingly attired, notwithstanding this disproportion. What by general consent is allowed to be a more beautiful object than an orange-tree, flourishing at once with its leaves, its blossoms, and its fruit? but it is in vain that we search here for any proportion between the height, the breadth, or anything else concerning the dimensions of the whole, or concerning the relation of the particular parts to each other. I grant that we may observe, in many flowers, something of a regular figure, and of a methodical disposition of the leaves. The rose has such a figure and such a disposition of its petals; but in an oblique view, when this figure is in a good measure lost, and the order of the leaves confounded, it yet retains its beauty; the rose is even more beautiful before it is full blown; in the bud, before this exact figure is formed; and this is not the only instance wherein method and exactness, the soul of proportion, are found rather prejudicial than serviceable to the cause of beauty.

SECT. III.—PROPORTION NOT THE CAUSE OF BEAUTY IN ANIMALS

THAT proportion has but a small share in the formation of beauty, is full as evident among animals. Here the greatest variety of shapes and dispositions of parts are well fitted to excite this idea.

The swan, confessedly a beautiful bird, has a neck longer than the rest of his body, and but a very short tail: is this a beautiful proportion? We must allow that it is. But then what shall we say to the peacock, who has comparatively but a short neck, with a tail longer than the neck and the rest of the body taken together? How many birds are there that vary infinitely from each of these standards, and from every other which you can fix; with proportions different, and often directly opposite to each other! and yet many of these birds are extremely beautiful; when upon considering them we find nothing in any one part that might determine us, *a priori,* to say what the others ought to be, nor indeed to guess anything about them, but what experience might show to be full of disappointment and mistake. And with regard to the colours either of birds or flowers, for there is something similar in the colouring of both, whether they are considered in their extension or gradation, there is nothing of proportion to be observed. Some are of but one single colour, others have all the colours of the rainbow; some are of the primary colours, others are of the mixt; in short, an attentive observer may soon conclude, that there is as little of proportion in the colouring as in the shapes of these objects. Turn next to beasts; examine the head of a beautiful horse; find what proportion that bears to his body, and to his limbs, and what relations these have to each other; and when you have settled these proportions as a standard of beauty, then take a dog or cat, or any other animal, and examine how far the same proportions between their heads and their necks, between those and the body, and so on, are found to hold. I think we may safely say, that they differ in every species, yet that there are individuals, found in a great many species so differing, that have a very striking beauty. Now, if it be allowed that very different and even contrary forms and dispositions are consistent with beauty, it amounts I believe to a concession, that no certain measures, operating from a natural principle, are necessary to produce it; at least so far as the brute species is concerned.

SECT. IV.—PROPORTION NOT THE CAUSE OF BEAUTY IN THE HUMAN SPECIES

THERE are some parts of the human body that are observed to hold certain proportions to each other; but before it can be proved that the efficient cause of beauty lies in these, it must be shown, that wherever these are found exact, the person to whom they belong is beautiful: I mean in the effect produced on the view, either of any member distinctly considered, or of the whole body together. It must be likewise shown, that these parts stand in such a relation to each other, that the comparison between them may be easily made, and that the affection of the mind may naturally result from it. For my part, I have at several times very carefully examined many of those proportions, and found them hold very nearly or altogether alike in many subjects, which were not only very different from one another, but where one has been very beautiful, and the other very remote from beauty. With regard to the parts which are found so proportioned, they are often so remote from each other, in situation, nature, and office, that I cannot see how they admit of any comparison, nor consequently how any effect owing to proportion can result from them. The neck, say they, in beautiful bodies, should measure with the calf of the leg; it should likewise be twice the circumference of the wrist. And an infinity of observations of this kind are to be found in the writings and conversations of many. But what relation has the calf of the leg to the neck; or either of these parts to the wrist? These proportions are certainly to be found in handsome bodies. They are as certainly in ugly ones; as any who will take the pains to try may find. Nay, I do not know but they may be least perfect in some of the most beautiful. You may assign any proportion you please to every part of the human body; and I undertake that a painter shall religiously observe them all, and notwithstanding produce, if he pleases, a very ugly figure. The same painter shall considerably deviate from these proportions, and produce a very beautiful one. And indeed it may be observed in the master-pieces of the ancient and modern statuary, that several of them differ very widely from the proportions of others, in parts very conspicuous and of great consideration; and that they differ no less from the proportions we find in living men, of forms extremely striking and agreeable. And after all, how are the partisans of proportional beauty agreed amongst themselves about the proportions of the human body? Some hold it to be seven heads; some make it eight; whilst others extend it even to ten; a vast difference in such a small number of divisions! Others take other methods of estimating the proportions, and all with equal success. But are these proportions exactly the same in all handsome men? or are they at all the proportions found in beautiful women? Nobody will say that they are; yet both sexes are undoubtedly capable of beauty, and the female of the greatest; which advantage I believe will hardly be attributed to the superior exactness of proportion in the fair sex. Let us rest a moment on this point; and consider how much difference there is between the measures that prevail in many similar parts of the body, in the two sexes of this single species only. If you assign any determinate proportions to the limbs of a man, and if you limit human beauty to these proportions, when you find a woman who differs in the make and measures of almost every part, you must conclude her not to be beautiful, in spite of the suggestions of your imagination; or, in obedience to your imagination, you must renounce your rules; you must lay by the scale and compass, and look out for some other cause of beauty. For if beauty be attached to certain measures which operate from a *principle in nature,* why should similar parts with different measures of proportion be found to have beauty, and this too in the very same species? But to open our view a little, it is worth observing, that almost all animals have parts of very much the same nature, and destined nearly to the same purposes; a head, neck, body, feet, eyes, ears, nose, and mouth; yet Providence to provide in the best manner for their several wants, and to display the riches of his wisdom and goodness in his creation, has worked out of these few and similar organs and members, a diversity hardly short of infinite in their disposition, measures, and relation. But, as we have before observed, amidst this infinite diversity, one particular is common to many species: several of the individuals which compose them are capable of affecting us with a sense of loveliness; and whilst they agree in producing this effect, they differ extremely in the relative measures of those parts which have produced it. These considerations were sufficient to induce me to reject the notion of any particular proportions that operated by nature to produce a pleasing effect; but those who will agree with me with regard to a particular proportion, are strongly prepossessed in favour of one more indefinite. They imagine, that although beauty in general is annexed to no certain measures common to the several kinds of pleasing plants and animals; yet that there is a certain proportion in each species absolutely essential to the beauty of that particular kind. If we consider the animal world in general, we find beauty confined to no certain measures: but as some peculiar measure and relation of parts is what distinguishes each peculiar class of animals, it must of necessity be, that the beautiful in each kind will be found in the measures and proportions of that kind; for otherwise it would deviate from its proper species, and become in some sort monstrous: however, no species is so strictly confined to any certain proportions, that there is not a considerable variation amongst the individuals; and as it has been shown of the human, so it may be shown of the brute kinds, that beauty is found indifferently in all the proportions which each kind can admit, without quitting its common form; and it is this idea of a common form that makes the proportion of parts at all regarded, and not the operation of any natural cause: indeed a little consideration will make it appear, that it is not measure, but manner, that creates all the beauty which belongs to shape. What light do we borrow from these boasted proportions, when we study ornamental design? It seems amazing to me, that artists, if they were as well convinced as they pretend to be, that proportion is a principal cause of beauty, have not by them at all times accurate measurements of all sorts of beautiful animals to help them to proper proportions, when they would contrive anything elegant; especially as they frequently assert that it is from an observation of the beautiful in nature they direct their practice. I know that it has been said long since, and echoed backward and forward from one writer to another a thousand times, that the proportions of building have been taken from those of the human body. To make this forced analogy complete, they represent a man with his arms raised and extended at full length, and then describe a sort of square, as it is formed by passing lines along the extremities of this strange figure. But it appears very clearly to me, that the human figure never supplied the architect with any of his ideas. For, in the first place, men are very rarely seen in this strained posture; it is not natural to them; neither is it at all becoming. Secondly, the view of the human figure so disposed, does not naturally suggest the idea of a square, but rather of a cross; as that large space between the arms and the ground must be filled with something before it can make anybody think of a square. Thirdly, several buildings are by no means of the form of that particular square, which are notwithstanding planned by the best architects, and produce an effect altogether as good, and perhaps a better. And certainly nothing could be more unaccountably whimsical, than for an architect to model his performance by the human figure, since no two things can have less resemblance or analogy, than a man and a house, or temple: do we need to observe, that their purposes are entirely different? What I am apt to suspect is this: that these analogies were devised to give a credit to the work of art, by showing a conformity between them and the noblest works in nature; not that the latter served at all to supply hints for the perfection of the former. And I am the more fully convinced, that the patrons of proportion have transferred their artificial ideas to nature, and not borrowed from thence the proportions they use in works of art; because in any discussion of this subject they always quit as soon as possible the open field of natural beauties, the animal and vegetable kingdoms, and fortify themselves within the artificial lines and angles of architecture. For there is in mankind an unfortunate propensity to make themselves, their views, and their works, the measure of excellence in everything whatsoever. Therefore, having observed that their dwellings were most commodious and firm when they were thrown into regular figures, with parts answerable to each other; they transferred these ideas to their gardens; they turned their trees into pillars, pyramids, and obelisks; they formed their hedges into so many green walls, and fashioned their walks into squares, triangles, and other mathematical figures, with exactness and symmetry; and they thought, if they were not imitating, they were at least improving nature, and teaching her to know her business. But nature has at last escaped from their discipline and their fetters; and our gardens, if nothing else, declare we begin to feel that mathematical ideas are not the true measures of beauty. And surely they are full as little so in the animal as the vegetable world. For is it not extraordinary, that in these fine descriptive pieces, these innumerable odes and elegies, which are in the mouths of all the world, and many of which have been the entertainment of ages, that in these pieces which describe love with such a passionate energy, and represent its object in such an infinite variety of lights, not one word is said of proportion, if it be, what some insist it is, the principal component of beauty; whilst, at the same time, several other qualities are very frequently and warmly mentioned? But if proportion has not this power, it may appear odd how men came originally to be so prepossessed in its favour. It arose, I imagine, from the fondness I have just mentioned, which men bear so remarkably to their own works and notions; it arose from false reasonings on the effects of the customary figure of animals; it arose from the Platonic theory of fitness and aptitude. For which reason, in the next section, I shall consider the effects of custom in the figure of animals; and afterwards the idea of fitness: since, if proportion does not operate by a natural power attending some measures, it must be either by custom, or the idea of utility; there is no other way.

SECT. V.—PROPORTION FURTHER CONSIDERED

If I am not mistaken, a great deal of the prejudice in favour of proportion has arisen, not so much from the observation of any certain measures found in beautiful bodies, as from a wrong idea of the relation which deformity bears to beauty, to which it has been considered as the opposite; on this principle it was concluded, that where the causes of deformity were removed, beauty must naturally and necessarily be introduced. This I believe is a mistake. For *deformity* is opposed not to beauty, but to the *complete common form*. If one of the legs of a man be found shorter than the other, the man is deformed; because there is something wanting to complete the whole idea we form of a man; and this has the same effect in natural faults, as maiming and mutilation produce from accidents. So if the back be humped, the man is deformed; because his back has an unusual figure, and what carries with it the idea of some disease or misfortune. So if a man's neck be considerably longer or shorter than usual, we say he is deformed in that part, because men are not commonly made in that manner. But surely every hour's experience may convince us, that a man may have his legs of an equal length, and resembling each other in all respects, and his neck of a just size, and his back quite straight, without having at the same time the least perceivable beauty. Indeed beauty is so far from belonging to the idea of custom, that in reality what affects us in that manner is extremely rare and uncommon. The beautiful strikes us as much by its novelty as the deformed itself. It is thus in those species of animals with which we are acquainted; and if one of a new species were represented, we should by no means wait until custom had settled an idea of proportion, before we decided concerning its beauty or ugliness: which shows that the general idea of beauty can be no more owing to customary than to natural proportion. Deformity arises from the want of the common proportions; but the necessary result of their existence in any object is not beauty. If we suppose proportion in natural things to be relative to custom and use, the nature of use and custom will show, that beauty, which is a *positive* and powerful quality, cannot result from it. We are so wonderfully formed, that, whilst we are creatures vehemently desirous of novelty, we are as strongly attached to habit and custom. But it is the nature of things which hold us by custom, to affect us very little whilst we are in possession of them, but strongly when they are absent. I remember to have frequented a certain place every day for a long time together; and I may truly say, that so far from finding pleasure in it, I was affected with a sort of weariness and disgust; I came, I went, I returned, without pleasure; yet if by any means I passed by the usual time of my going thither, I was remarkably uneasy, and was not quiet till I had got into my old track. They who use snuff, take it almost without being sensible that they take it, and the acute sense of smell is deadened, so as to feel hardly anything from so sharp a stimulus; yet deprive the snuff-taker of his box, and he is the most uneasy mortal in the world. Indeed so far are use and habit from being causes of pleasure, merely as such, that the effect of constant use is to make all things of whatever kind entirely un-affecting. For as use at last takes off the painful effect of many things, it reduces the pleasurable effect in others in the same man-ner, and brings both to a sort of mediocrity and indifference. Very justly is use called a second nature; and our natural and common state is one of absolute indifference, equally prepared for pain or pleasure. But when we are thrown out of this state, or deprived of anything requisite to maintain us in it; when this chance does not happen by pleasure from some mechanical cause, we are always hurt. It is so with the second nature, custom, in all things which relate to it. Thus the want of the usual proportions in men and other animals is sure to disgust, though their presence is by no means any cause of real pleasure. It is true, that the proportions laid down as causes of beauty in the human body, are frequently found in beautiful ones, because they are generally found in all mankind; but if it can be shown too, that they are found without beauty, and that beauty frequently exists without them, and that this beauty, where it exists, always can be assigned to other less equivocal causes, it will naturally lead us to conclude, that proportion and beauty are not ideas of the same nature. The true opposite to beauty is not disproportion or deformity, but *ugliness:* and as it proceeds from causes opposite to those of positive beauty, we cannot consider it until we come to treat of that. Between beauty and ugliness there is a sort of mediocrity, in which the assigned proportions are most commonly found; but this has no effect upon the passions.

SECT. VI.—FITNESS NOT THE CAUSE OF BEAUTY

It is said that the idea of utility, or of a part's being well adapted to answer its end, is the cause of beauty, or indeed beauty itself. If it were not for this opinion, it had been impossible for the doctrine of proportion to have held its ground very long; the world would be soon weary of hearing of measures which related to nothing, either of a natural principle, or of a fitness to answer some end; the idea which mankind most commonly conceive of proportion, is the suitableness of means to certain ends, and, where this is not the question, very seldom trouble themselves about the effect of different measures of things. Therefore it was necessary for this theory to insist, that not only artificial but natural objects took their beauty from the fitness of the parts for their several purposes. But in framing this theory, I am apprehensive that experience was not sufficiently consulted. For, on that principle, the wedge-like snout of a swine, with its tough cartilage at the end, the little sunk eyes, and the whole make of the head, so well adapted to its offices of digging and rooting, would be extremely beautiful. The great bag hanging to the bill of a pelican, a thing highly useful to this animal, would be likewise as beautiful in our eyes. The hedge-hog, so well secured against all assaults by his prickly hide, and the porcupine with his missile quills, would be then considered as creatures of no small elegance. There are few animals whose parts are better contrived than those of the monkey; he has the hands of a man, joined to the springy limbs of a beast; he is admirably calculated for running, leaping, grappling, and climbing; and yet there are few animals which seem to have less beauty in the eyes of all mankind. I need say little on the trunk of the elephant, of such various usefulness, and which is so far from contributing to his beauty. How well fitted is the wolf for running and leaping! how admirably is the lion armed for battle! but will any one therefore call the elephant, the wolf, and the lion, beautiful animals? I believe nobody will think the form of a man's leg so well adapted to running, as those of a horse, a dog, a deer, and several other creatures; at least they have not that appearance: yet, I believe, a well-fashioned human leg will be allowed to far exceed all these in beauty. If the fitness of parts was what constituted the loveliness of their form, the actual employment of them would undoubtedly much augment it; but this, though it is sometimes so upon another principle, is far from being always the case. A bird on the wing is not so beautiful as when it is perched; nay, there are several of the domestic fowls which are seldom seen to fly, and which are nothing the less beautiful on that account; yet birds are so extremely different in their form from the beast and human kinds, that you cannot, on the principle of fitness, allow them anything agreeable, but in consideration of their parts being designed for quite other purposes. I never in my life chanced to see a peacock fly; and yet before, very long before, I considered any aptitude in his form for the aërial life, I was struck with the extreme beauty which raises that bird above many of the best flying fowls in the world; though, for anything I saw, his way of living was much like that of the swine, which fed in the farm-yard along with him. The same may be said of cocks, hens, and the like; they are of the flying kind in figure; in their manner of moving not very different from men and beasts. To leave these foreign examples; if beauty in our own species was annexed to use, men would be much more lovely than women; and strength and agility would be considered as the only beauties. But to call strength by the name of beauty, to have but one denomination for the qualities of a Venus and Hercules, so totally different in almost all respects, is surely a strange confusion of ideas, or abuse of words. The cause of this confusion, I imagine, proceeds from our frequently perceiving the parts of the human and other animal bodies to be at once very beautiful, and very well adapted to their purposes; and we are deceived by a sophism, which makes us take that for a cause which is only a concomitant: this is the sophism of the fly, who imagined he raised a great dust, because he stood upon the chariot that really raised it. The stomach, the lungs, the liver, as well as other parts, are incomparably well adapted to their purposes; yet they are far from having any beauty. Again, many things are very beautiful, in which it is impossible to discern any idea of use. And I appeal to the first and most natural feelings of mankind, whether on beholding a beautiful eye, or a well-fashioned mouth, or a well-turned leg, any ideas of their being well fitted for seeing, eating, or running, ever present themselves. What idea of use is it that flowers excite, the most beautiful part of the vegetable world? It is true, that the infinitely wise and good Creator has, of his bounty, frequently joined beauty to those things which he has made useful to us: but this does not prove that an idea of use and beauty are the same thing, or that they are any way dependent on each other.

SECT. VII.—THE REAL EFFECTS OF FITNESS

WHEN I excluded proportion and fitness from any share in beauty, I did not by any means intend to say that they were of no value, or that they ought to be disregarded in works of art. Works of art are the proper sphere of their power; and here it is that they have their full effect. Whenever the wisdom of our Creator intended that we should be affected with anything, he did not confide the execution of his design to the languid and precarious operation of our reason; but he endued it with powers and properties that prevent the understanding, and even the will; which, seizing upon the senses and imagination, captivate the soul before the understanding is ready either to join with them, or to oppose them. It is by a long deduction, and much study, that we discover the adorable wisdom of God in his works: when we discover it, the effect is very different, not only in the manner of acquiring it, but in its own nature, from that which strikes us without any preparation from the sublime or the beautiful. How different is the satisfaction of an anatomist, who discovers the use of the muscles and of the skin, the excellent contrivance of the one for the various movements of the body, and the wonderful texture of the other, at once a general covering, and at once a general outlet as well as inlet; how different is this from the affection which possesses an ordinary man at the sight of a delicate, smooth skin, and all the other parts of beauty, which require no investigation to be perceived! In the former case, whilst we look up to the Maker with admiration and praise, the object which causes it may be odious and distasteful; the latter very often so touches us by its power on the imagination, that we examine but little into the artifice of its contrivance; and we have need of a strong effort of our reason to disentangle our minds from the allurements of the object, to a consideration of that wisdom which invented so powerful a machine. The effect of proportion and fitness, at least so far as they proceed from a mere consideration of the work itself, produces approbation, the acquiescence of the understanding, but not love, nor any passion of that species. When we examine the structure of a watch, when we come to know thoroughly the use of every part of it, satisfied as we are with the fitness of the whole, we are far enough from perceiving anything like beauty in the watch-work itself; but let us look on the case, the labour of some curious artist in engraving, with little or no idea of use, we shall have a much livelier idea of beauty than we ever could have had from the watch itself, though the master-piece of Graham. In beauty, as I said, the effect is previous to any knowledge of the use; but to judge of proportion, we must know the end for which any work is designed. According to the end, the proportion varies. Thus there is one proportion of a tower, another of a house; one proportion of a gallery, another of a hall, another of a chamber. To judge of the proportions of these, you must be first acquainted with the purposes for which they were designed. Good sense and experience, acting together, find out what is fit to be done in every work of art. We are

rational creatures, and in all our works we ought to regard their
end and purpose; the gratification of any passion, how innocent
soever, ought only to be of a secondary consideration. Herein is
placed the real power of fitness and proportion; they operate on the
understanding considering them, which *approves* the work and
acquiesces in it. The passions, and the imagination which principally raises them, have here very little to do. When a room appears
in its original nakedness, bare walls and a plain ceiling; let its proportion be ever so excellent, it pleases very little; a cold approbation
is the utmost we can reach; a much worse proportioned room with
elegant mouldings and fine festoons, glasses, and other merely
ornamental furniture, will make the imagination revolt against the
reason; it will please much more than the naked proportion of the
first room, which the understanding has so much approved as admirably fitted for its purposes. What I have here said and before
concerning proportion, is by no means to persuade people absurdly to
neglect the idea of use in the works of art. It is only to show that
these excellent things, beauty and proportion, are not the same; not
that they should either of them be disregarded.

SECT. VIII.—THE RECAPITULATION

On the whole; if such parts in human bodies as are found proportioned, were likewise constantly found beautiful, as they certainly
are not; or if they were so situated, as that a pleasure might flow
from the comparison, which they seldom are; or if any assignable
proportions were found, either in plants or animals, which were
always attended with beauty, which never was the case; or if, where
parts were well adapted to their purposes, they were constantly
beautiful, and when no use appeared, there was no beauty, which
is contrary to all experience; we might conclude, that beauty con-
sisted in proportion or utility. But since, in all respects, the case is
quite otherwise; we may be satisfied that beauty does not depend on
these, let it owe its origin to what else it will.

SECT. IX.—PERFECTION NOT THE CAUSE OF BEAUTY

THERE is another notion current, pretty closely allied to the former; that *Perfection* is the constituent cause of beauty. This opinion has been made to extend much further than to sensible objects. But in these, so far is perfection, considered as such, from being the cause of beauty, that this quality, where it is highest, in the female sex, almost always carries with it an idea of weakness and imperfection. Women are very sensible of this; for which reason, they learn to lisp, to totter in their walk, to counterfeit weakness, and even sickness. In all they are guided by nature. Beauty in distress is much the most affecting beauty. Blushing has little less power; and modesty in general, which is a tacit allowance of imperfection, is itself considered as an amiable quality, and certainly heightens every other that is so. I know it is in everybody's mouth, that we ought to love perfection. This is to me a sufficient proof, that it is not the proper object of love. Who ever said we *ought* to love a fine woman, or even any of these beautiful animals which please us? Here to be affected, there is no need of the concurrence of our will.

SECT. X.—HOW FAR THE IDEA OF BEAUTY MAY BE APPLIED TO THE QUALITIES OF THE MIND

NOR is this remark in general less applicable to the qualities of the mind. Those virtues which cause admiration, and are of the sublimer kind, produce terror rather than love; such as fortitude, justice, wisdom, and the like. Never was any man amiable by force of these qualities. Those which engage our hearts, which impress us with a sense of loveliness, are the softer virtues; easiness of temper, compassion, kindness, and liberality; though certainly those latter are of less immediate and momentous concern to society, and of less dignity. But it is for that reason that they are so amiable. The great virtues turn principally on dangers, punishments, and troubles, and are exercised rather in preventing the worst mischiefs, than in dispensing favours; and are therefore not lovely, though highly venerable. The subordinate turn on reliefs, gratifications, and indulgences; and are therefore more lovely, though inferior in dignity. Those persons who creep into the hearts of most people, who are chosen as the companions of their softer hours, and their reliefs from care and anxiety, are never persons of shining qualities or strong virtues. It is rather the soft green of the soul on which we rest our eyes, that are fatigued with beholding more glaring objects. It is worth observing how we feel ourselves affected in reading the characters of Cæsar and Cato, as they are so finely drawn and contrasted in Sallust. In one the *ignoscendo largiundo;* in the other, *nil largiundo.* In one, the *miseris perfugium;* in the other, *malis perniciem.* In the latter we have much to admire, much to reverence, and perhaps something to fear; we respect him, but we respect him at a distance. The former makes us familiar with him; we love him, and he leads us whither he pleases. To draw things closer to our first and most natural feelings, I will add a remark made upon reading this section by an ingenious friend. The authority of a father, so useful to our well-being, and so justly venerable upon all accounts, hinders us from having that entire love for him that we have for our mothers, where the parental authority is almost melted down into the mother's fondness and indulgence. But we generally have a great love for our grandfathers, in whom this authority is removed a degree from us, and where the weakness of age mellows it into something of a feminine partiality.

SECT. XI.—HOW FAR THE IDEA OF BEAUTY MAY BE APPLIED TO VIRTUE

FROM what has been said in the foregoing section, we may easily see how far the application of beauty to virtue may be made with propriety. The general application of this quality to virtue, has a strong tendency to confound our ideas of things; and it has given rise to an infinite deal of whimsical theory; as the affixing the name of beauty to proportion, congruity, and perfection, as well as to qualities of things yet more remote from our natural ideas of it, and from one another, has tended to confound our ideas of beauty, and left us no standard or rule to judge by, that was not even more uncertain and fallacious than our own fancies. This loose and inaccurate manner of speaking has therefore misled us both in the theory of taste and of morals; and induced us to remove the science of our duties from their proper basis, (our reason, our relations, and our necessities,) to rest it upon foundations altogether visionary and unsubstantial.

SECT. XII.—THE REAL CAUSE OF BEAUTY

HAVING endeavoured to show what beauty is not, it remains that we should examine, at least with equal attention, in what it really consists. Beauty is a thing much too affecting not to depend upon some positive qualities. And, since it is no creature of our reason, since it strikes us without any reference to use, and even where no use at all can be discerned, since the order and method of nature is generally very different from our measures and proportions, we must conclude that beauty is, for the greater part, some quality in bodies acting mechanically upon the human mind by the intervention of the senses. We ought therefore to consider attentively in what manner those sensible qualities are disposed, in such things as by experience we find beautiful, or which excite in us the passion of love, or some correspondent affection.

SECT. XIII.—BEAUTIFUL OBJECTS SMALL

THE most obvious point that presents itself to us in examining any object, is its extent or quantity. And what degree of extent prevails in bodies that are held beautiful, may be gathered from the usual manner of expression concerning it. I am told that, in most languages, the objects of love are spoken of under diminutive epithets. It is so in all languages of which I have any knowledge. In Greek the ωγ and other diminutive terms are almost always the terms of affection and tenderness. These diminutives were commonly added by the Greeks to the names of persons with whom they conversed on terms of friendship and familiarity. Though the Romans were a people of less quick and delicate feelings, yet they naturally slid into the lessening termination upon the same occasions. Anciently in the English language the diminishing *ling* was added to the names of persons and things that were the objects of love. Some we retain still, as *darling,* (or little dear,) and a few others. But, to this day, in ordinary conversation, it is usual to add the endearing name of *little* to everything we love: the French and Italians make

use of these affectionate diminutives even more than we. In the
animal creation, out of our own species, it is the small we are inclined
to be fond of; little birds, and some of the smaller kinds of beasts. A
great beautiful thing is a manner of expression scarcely ever used;
but that of a great ugly thing is very common. There is a wide
difference between admiration and love. The sublime, which is the
cause of the former, always dwells on great objects, and terrible; the
latter on small ones, and pleasing; we submit to what we admire,
but we love what submits to us; in one case we are forced, in the
other we are flattered, into compliance. In short, the ideas of the
sublime and the beautiful stand on foundations so different, that it
is hard, I had almost said impossible, to think of reconciling them
in the same subject, without considerably lessening the effect of the
one or the other upon the passions. So that, attending to their
quantity, beautiful objects are comparatively small.

SECT. XIV.—SMOOTHNESS

THE next property constantly observable in such objects is *smoothness:*[1] a quality so essential to beauty, that I do not now recollect
anything beautiful that is not smooth. In trees and flowers, smooth
leaves are beautiful; smooth slopes of earth in gardens; smooth
streams in the landscape; smooth coats of birds and beasts in animal
beauties; in fine women, smooth skins; and in several sorts of ornamental furniture, smooth and polished surfaces. A very considerable
part of the effect of beauty is owing to this quality; indeed the most
considerable. For, take any beautiful object, and give it a broken
and rugged surface; and however well formed it may be in other
respects, it pleases no longer. Whereas, let it want ever so many
of the other constituents, if it wants not this, it becomes more pleasing than almost all the others without it. This seems to me so evident, that I am a good deal surprised, that none who have handled
the subject have made any mention of the quality of smoothness, in
the enumeration of those that go to the forming of beauty. For indeed any ruggedness, any sudden projection, any sharp angle, is in
the highest degree contrary to that idea.

[1] Part IV. sect. 21.

SECT. XV.—GRADUAL VARIATION

But as perfectly beautiful bodies are not composed of angular parts, so their parts never continue long in the same right line.[1] They vary their direction every moment, and they change under the eye by a deviation continually carrying on, but for whose beginning or end you will find it difficult to ascertain a point. The view of a beautiful bird will illustrate this observation. Here we see the head increasing insensibly to the middle, from whence it lessens gradually until it mixes with the neck; the neck loses itself in a larger swell, which continues to the middle of the body, when the whole decreases again to the tail; the tail takes a new direction; but it soon varies its new course: it blends again with the other parts; and the line is perpetually changing, above, below, upon every side. In this description I have before me the idea of a dove; it agrees very well with most of the conditions of beauty. It is smooth and downy; its parts are (to use that expression) melted into one another; you are presented with no sudden protuberance through the whole, and yet the whole is continually changing. Observe that part of a beautiful woman where she is perhaps the most beautiful, about the neck and breasts; the smoothness; the softness; the easy and insensible swell; the variety of the surface, which is never for the smallest space the same; the deceitful maze, through which the unsteady eye slides giddily, without knowing where to fix or whither it is carried. Is not this a demonstration of that change of surface, continual, and yet hardly perceptible at any point, which forms one of the great constituents of beauty? It gives me no small pleasure to find that I can strengthen my theory in this point, by the opinion of the very ingenious Mr. Hogarth; whose idea of the line of beauty I take in general to be extremely just. But the idea of variation, without attending so accurately to the *manner* of the variation, has led him to consider angular figures as beautiful: these figures, it is true, vary greatly; yet they vary in a sudden and broken manner; and I do not find any natural object which is angular, and at the same time beautiful. Indeed few natural objects are entirely angular. But I think those which approach the most nearly to it are the ugliest. I must add too,

[1] Part IV, sect. 23.

that, so far as I could observe of nature, though the varied line is that alone in which complete beauty is found, yet there is no particular line which is always found in the most completely beautiful, and which is therefore beautiful in preference to all other lines. At least I never could observe it.

SECT. XVI.—DELICACY

An air of robustness and strength is very prejudicial to beauty. An appearance of *delicacy,* and even of fragility, is almost essential to it. Whoever examines the vegetable or animal creation will find this observation to be founded in nature. It is not the oak, the ash, or the elm, or any of the robust trees of the forest, which we consider as beautiful; they are awful and majestic; they inspire a sort of reverence. It is the delicate myrtle, it is the orange, it is the almond, it is the jasmine, it is the vine, which we look on as vegetable beauties. It is the flowery species, so remarkable for its weakness and momentary duration, that gives us the liveliest idea of beauty and elegance. Among animals, the greyhound is more beautiful than the mastiff; and the delicacy of a gennet, a barb, or an Arabian horse, is much more amiable than the strength and stability of some horses of war or carriage. I need here say little of the fair sex, where I believe the point will be easily allowed me. The beauty of women is considerably owing to their weakness or delicacy, and is even enhanced by their timidity, a quality of mind analogous to it. I would not here be understood to say, that weakness betraying very bad health has any share in beauty; but the ill effect of this is not because it is weakness, but because the ill state of health, which produces such weakness, alters the other conditions of beauty; the parts in such a case collapse; the bright color, the *lumen purpureum juventæ,* is gone; and the fine variation is lost in wrinkles, sudden breaks, and right lines.

SECT. XVII.—BEAUTY IN COLOUR

As to the colours usually found in beautiful bodies, it may be somewhat difficult to ascertain them, because, in the several parts of nature, there is an infinite variety. However, even in this variety, we may mark out something on which to settle. First, the colours of beautiful bodies must not be dusky or muddy, but clean and fair. Secondly, they must not be of the strongest kind. Those which seem most appropriated to beauty, are the milder of every sort; light greens; soft blues; weak whites; pink reds; and violets. Thirdly, if the colours be strong and vivid, they are always diversified, and the object is never of one strong colour; there are almost always such a number of them, (as in variegated flowers,) that the strength and glare of each is considerably abated. In a fine complexion, there is not only some variety in the colouring, but the colours: neither the red nor the white are strong and glaring. Besides, they are mixed in such a manner, and with such gradations, that it is impossible to fix the bounds. On the same principle it is, that the dubious colour in the necks and tails of peacocks, and about the heads of drakes, is so very agreeable. In reality, the beauty both of shape and colouring are as nearly related, as we can well suppose it possible for things of such different natures to be.

SECT. XVIII.—RECAPITULATION

On the whole, the qualities of beauty, as they are merely sensible qualities, are the following: First, to be comparatively small. Secondly, to be smooth. Thirdly, to have a variety in the direction of the parts; but, fourthly, to have those parts not angular, but melted as it were into each other. Fifthly, to be of a delicate frame, without any remarkable appearance of strength. Sixthly, to have its colours clear and bright, but not very strong and glaring. Seventhly, or if it should have any glaring colour, to have it diversified with others. These are, I believe, the properties on which beauty depends; properties that operate by nature, and are less liable to be altered by caprice, or confounded by a diversity of tastes, than any other.

SECT. XIX.—THE PHYSIOGNOMY

THE *physiognomy* has a considerable share in beauty, especially in that of our own species. The manners give a certain determination to the countenance; which, being observed to correspond pretty regularly with them, is capable of joining the effect of certain agreeable qualities of the mind to those of the body. So that to form a finished human beauty, and to give it its full influence, the face

must be expressive of such gentle and amiable qualities as correspond
with the softness, smoothness, and delicacy of the outward form.

SECT. XX.—THE EYE

I HAVE hitherto purposely omitted to speak of the *eye,* which has
so great a share in the beauty of the animal creation, as it did not fall
so easily under the foregoing heads, though in fact it is reducible to
the same principles. I think, then, that the beauty of the eye consists,
first, in its *clearness;* what *coloured* eye shall please most, depends
a good deal on particular fancies; but none are pleased with an eye
whose water (to use that term) is dull and muddy.[1] We are pleased
with the eye in this view, on the principle upon which we like
diamonds, clear water, glass, and such like transparent substances.
Secondly, the motion of the eye contributes to its beauty, by continually shifting its direction; but a slow and languid motion is
more beautiful than a brisk one; the latter is enlivening; the former
lovely. Thirdly, with regard to the union of the eye with the neighbouring parts, it is to hold the same rule that is given of other beautiful ones; it is not to make a strong deviation from the line of the
neighbouring parts; nor to verge into any exact geometrical figure.
Besides all this, the eye affects, as it is expressive of some qualities
of the mind, and its principal power generally arises from this; so
that what we have just said of the physiognomy is applicable here.

SECT XXI.—UGLINESS

IT may perhaps appear like a sort of repetition of what we have
before said, to insist here upon the nature of *ugliness;* as I imagine
it to be in all respects the opposite to those qualities which we have
laid down for the constituents of beauty. But though ugliness be
the opposite to beauty, it is not the opposite to proportion and fitness.
For it is possible that a thing may be very ugly with any proportions,
and with a perfect fitness to any uses. Ugliness I imagine likewise
to be consistent enough with an idea of the sublime. But I would
by no means insinuate that ugliness of itself is a sublime idea, unless
united with such qualities as excite a strong terror.

[1] Part IV. sect. 25.

SECT. XXII.—GRACE

Gracefulness is an idea not very different from beauty; it consists of much the same things. Gracefulness is an idea belonging to *posture* and *motion*. In both these, to be graceful, it is requisite that there be no appearance of difficulty; there is required a small inflection of the body; and a composure of the parts in such a manner, as not to encumber each other, not to appear divided by sharp and sudden angles. In this ease, this roundness, this delicacy of attitude and motion, it is that all the magic of grace consists, and what is called its *je ne sçai quoi;* as will be obvious to any observer, who considers attentively the Venus de Medicis, the Antinous, or any statue generally allowed to be graceful in a high degree.

SECT. XXIII.—ELEGANCE AND SPECIOUSNESS

When any body is composed of parts smooth and polished without pressing upon each other, without showing any ruggedness or confusion, and at the same time affecting some *regular shape,* I call it *elegant.* It is closely allied to the beautiful, differing from it only in this *regularity;* which, however, as it makes a very material difference in the affection produced, may very well constitute another species. Under this head I rank those delicate and regular works of art, that imitate no determinate object in nature, as elegant buildings, and pieces of furniture. When any object partakes of the above-mentioned qualities, or of those of beautiful bodies, and is withal of great dimensions, it is full as remote from the idea of mere beauty; I call it *fine* or *specious.*

SECT. XXIV.—THE BEAUTIFUL IN FEELING

The foregoing description of beauty, so far as it is taken in by the eye, may be greatly illustrated by describing the nature of objects, which produce a similar effect through the touch. This I call the beautiful in *Feeling.* It corresponds wonderfully with what causes the same species of pleasure to the sight. There is a chain in all our sensations; they are all but different sorts of feelings calculated to be affected by various sorts of objects, but all to be affected after the same manner. All bodies that are pleasant to the touch, are so by the slightness of the resistance they make. Resistance is either to motion along the surface, or to the pressure of the parts on one another: if the former be slight, we call the body smooth; if the latter, soft. The chief pleasure we receive by feeling, is in the one or the other of these qualities; and if there be a combination of both, our pleasure is greatly increased. This is so plain, that it is rather more fit to illustrate other things, than to be illustrated itself by an example. The next source of pleasure in this sense, as in every other, is the continually presenting somewhat new; and we find that bodies which continually vary their surface, are much the most pleasant or beautiful to the feeling, as any one that pleases may experience. The third property in such objects is, that though the surface continually varies its direction, it never varies it suddenly. The application of anything sudden, even though the impression itself have little or nothing of violence, is disagreeable. The quick application of a finger a little warmer or colder than usual, without notice, makes us start; a slight tap on the shoulder, not expected, has the same effect. Hence it is that angular bodies, bodies that suddenly vary the direction of the outline, afford so little pleasure to the feeling. Every such change is a sort of climbing or falling in miniature; so that squares, triangles, and other angular figures, are neither beautiful to the sight nor feeling. Whoever compares his state of mind, on feeling soft, smooth, variegated, unangular bodies, with that in which he finds himself, on the view of a beautiful object, will perceive a very striking analogy in the effects of both; and which may go a good way towards discovering their common cause. Feeling and sight, in this respect, differ in but a few points. The touch takes in the pleasure of softness, which is not primarily an object of sight; the sight, on the other hand, comprehends colour, which can hardly be made perceptible to the touch; the touch, again, has the advantage in a new idea of pleasure resulting from a moderate degree of warmth; but the eye triumphs in the infinite extent and multiplicity of its objects. But there is such a similitude in the pleasures of these senses, that I am apt to fancy, if it were possible that one might discern colour by feeling, (as it is said some blind men have done,) that the same colours, and the same disposition of colouring, which are found beautiful to the sight, would be found likewise most grateful to the

touch. But, setting aside conjectures, let us pass to the other sense;
of Hearing.

SECT. XXV.—THE BEAUTIFUL IN SOUNDS

In this sense we find an equal aptitude to be affected in a soft and
delicate manner; and how far sweet or beautiful sounds agree with
our descriptions of beauty in other senses, the experience of every one
must decide. Milton has described this species of music in one of
his juvenile poems.[1] I need not say that Milton was perfectly well
versed in that art; and that no man had a finer ear, with a happier
manner of expressing the affections of one sense by metaphors taken
from another. The description is as follows:

> —And ever against eating cares,
> Lap me in *soft* Lydian airs;
> In notes with many a *winding* bout
> Of *linked sweetness long drawn* out;
> With wanton heed, and giddy cunning,
> The *melting* voice through *mazes* running;
> *Untwisting* all the chains that tie
> The hidden soul of harmony.

Let us parallel this with the softness, the winding surface, the unbroken continuance, the easy gradation of the beautiful in other
things; and all the diversities of the several senses, with all their
several affections, will rather help to throw lights from one another
to finish one clear, consistent idea of the whole, than to obscure it by
their intricacy and variety.

To the above-mentioned description I shall add one or two remarks. The first is; that the beautiful in music will not bear that
loudness and strength of sounds, which may be used to raise other
passions; nor notes which are shrill, or harsh, or deep; it agrees best
with such as are clear, even, smooth, and weak. The second is; that
great variety, and quick transitions from one measure or tone to
another, are contrary to the genius of the beautiful in music. Such
transitions[2] often excite mirth, or other sudden and tumultuous passions; but not that sinking, that melting, that languor, which is the
characteristical effect of the beautiful as it regards every sense. The

---

[1] L'Allegro.

[2] I ne'er am merry, when I hear sweet music.—SHAKESPEARE.

passion excited by beauty is in fact nearer to a species of melancholy, than to jollity and mirth. I do not here mean to confine music to any one species of notes, or tones, neither is it an art in which I can say I have any great skill. My sole design in this remark is, to settle a consistent idea of beauty. The infinite variety of the affections of the soul will suggest to a good head, and skilful ear, a variety of such sounds as are fitted to raise them. It can be no prejudice to this, to clear and distinguish some few particulars, that belong to the same class, and are consistent with each other, from the immense crowd of different, and sometimes contradictory, ideas, that rank vulgarly under the standard of beauty. And of these it is my intention to mark such only of the leading points as show the conformity of the sense of Hearing with all the other senses, in the article of their pleasures.

SECT. XXVI.—TASTE AND SMELL

THIS general agreement of the senses is yet more evident on minutely considering those of taste and smell. We metaphorically apply the idea of sweetness to sights and sounds; but as the qualities of bodies, by which they are fitted to excite either pleasure or pain in these senses, are not so obvious as they are in the others, we shall refer an explanation of their analogy, which is a very close one, to that part, wherein we come to consider the common efficient cause of beauty, as it regards all the senses. I do not think anything better fitted to establish a clear and settled idea of visual beauty than this way of examining the similar pleasures of other senses; for one part is sometimes clear in one of the senses, that is more obscure in another; and where there is a clear concurrence of all, we may with more certainty speak of any one of them. By this means, they bear witness to each other; nature is, as it were, scrutinized; and we report nothing of her but what we receive from her own information.

SECT. XXVII.—THE SUBLIME AND BEAUTIFUL COMPARED

ON closing this general view of beauty, it naturally occurs, that we should compare it with the sublime; and in this comparison there appears a remarkable contrast. For sublime objects are vast in their dimensions, beautiful ones comparatively small: beauty should

be smooth and polished; the great, rugged and negligent; beauty
should shun the right line, yet deviate from it insensibly; the great
in many cases loves the right line, and when it deviates it often makes
a strong deviation: beauty should not be obscure; the great ought
to be dark and gloomy: beauty should be light and delicate; the great
ought to be solid, and even massive. They are indeed ideas of a
very different nature, one being founded on pain, the other on
pleasure; and however they may vary afterwards from the direct
nature of their causes, yet these causes keep up an eternal distinction between them, a distinction never to be forgotten by any whose
business it is to affect the passions. In the infinite variety of natural
combinations, we must expect to find the qualities of things the most
remote imaginable from each other united in the same object. We
must expect also to find combinations of the same kind in the works
of art. But when we consider the power of an object upon our passions, we must know that when anything is intended to affect the
mind by the force of some predominant property, the affection produced is like to be the more uniform and perfect, if all the other
properties or qualities of the object be of the same nature, and tending to the same design, as the principal.

> If black and white blend, soften, and unite
> A thousand ways, are there no black and white?

If the qualities of the sublime and beautiful are sometimes found
united, does this prove that they are the same; does it prove that
they are any way allied; does it prove even that they are not opposite
and contradictory? Black and white may soften, may blend; but
they are not therefore the same. Nor, when they are so softened
and blended with each other, or with different colours, is the power
of black as black, or of white as white, so strong as when each stands
uniform and distinguished.

PART IV

SECTION I.—OF THE EFFICIENT CAUSE OF THE SUBLIME AND BEAUTIFUL

WHEN I say I intend to inquire into the efficient cause of
Sublimity and Beauty, I would not be understood to say,
that I can come to the ultimate cause. I do not pretend that
I shall ever be able to explain, why certain affections of the body
produce such a distinct emotion of mind, and no other; or why the
body is at all affected by the mind, or the mind by the body. A little
thought will show this to be impossible. But I conceive, if we can
discover what affections of the mind produce certain emotions of
the body, and what distinct feelings and qualities of body shall produce certain determinate passions in the mind, and no others, I
fancy a great deal will be done; something not unuseful towards a
distinct knowledge of our passions, so far at least as we have them
at present under our consideration. This is all, I believe, we can do.
If we could advance a step farther, difficulties would still remain,
as we should be still equally distant from the first cause. When
Newton first discovered the property of attraction, and settled its
laws, he found it served very well to explain several of the most remarkable phænomena in nature; but yet, with reference to the general system of things, he could consider attraction but as an effect,
whose cause at that time he did not attempt to trace. But when he
afterwards began to account for it by a subtle elastic æther, this great
man (if in so great a man it be not impious to discover anything
like a blemish) seemed to have quitted his usual cautious manner of
philosophizing; since, perhaps, allowing all that has been advanced
on this subject to be sufficiently proved, I think it leaves us with as
many difficulties as it found us. The great chain of causes, which
links one to another, even to the throne of God himself, can never be
unravelled by any industry of ours. When we go but one step
beyond the immediate sensible qualities of things, we go out of our

depth. All we do after is but a faint struggle, that shows we are in an element which does not belong to us. So that when I speak of cause, and efficient cause, I only mean certain affections of the mind, that cause certain changes in the body; or certain powers and properties in bodies, that work a change in the mind. As if I were to explain the motion of a body falling to the ground, I would say it was caused by gravity; and I would endeavour to show after what manner this power operated, without attempting to show why it operated in this manner: or if I were to explain the effects of bodies striking one another by the common laws of percussion, I should not endeavour to explain how motion itself is communicated.

SECT. II.—ASSOCIATION

It is no small bar in the way of our inquiry into the cause of our passions, that the occasions of many of them are given, and that their governing motions are communicated at a time when we have not capacity to reflect on them; at a time of which all sort of memory is worn out of our minds. For besides such things as affect us in various manners, according to their natural powers, there are associations made at that early season, which we find it very hard afterwards to distinguish from natural effects. Not to mention the unaccountable antipathies which we find in many persons, we all find it impossible to remember when a steep became more terrible than a plain; or fire or water more terrible than a clod of earth; though all these are very probably either conclusions from experience, or arising from the premonitions of others; and some of them impressed, in all likelihood, pretty late. But as it must be allowed that many things affect us after a certain manner, not by any natural powers they have for that purpose, but by association; so it would be absurd, on the other hand, to say that all things affect us by association only; since some things must have been originally and naturally agreeable or disagreeable, from which the others derive their associated powers; and it would be, I fancy, to little purpose to look for the cause of our passions in association, until we fail of it in the natural properties of things.

SECT. III.—CAUSE OF PAIN AND FEAR

I HAVE before observed,[1] that whatever is qualified to cause terror is a foundation capable of the sublime; to which I add, that not only these, but many things from which we cannot probably apprehend any danger, have a similar effect, because they operate in a similar manner. I observed too,[2] that whatever produces pleasure, positive and original pleasure, is fit to have beauty ingrafted on it. Therefore, to clear up the nature of these qualities, it may be necessary to explain the nature of pain and pleasure on which they depend. A man who suffers under violent bodily pain, (I suppose the most violent, because the effect may be the more obvious,) I say a man in great pain has his teeth set, his eyebrows are violently contracted, his forehead is wrinkled, his eyes are dragged inwards, and rolled with great vehemence, his hair stands on end, the voice is forced out in short shrieks and groans, and the whole fabric totters. Fear, or terror, which is an apprehension of pain or death, exhibits exactly the same effects, approaching in violence to those just mentioned, in proportion to the nearness of the cause, and the weakness of the subject. This is not only so in the human species; but I have more than once observed in dogs, under an apprehension of punishment, that they have writhed their bodies, and yelped, and howled, as if they had actually felt the blows. From hence I conclude, that pain and fear act upon the same parts of the body, and in the same manner, though somewhat differing in degree; that pain and fear consist in an unnatural tension of the nerves; that this is sometimes accompanied with an unnatural strength, which sometimes suddenly changes into an extraordinary weakness; that these effects often come on alternately, and are sometimes mixed with each other. This is the nature of all convulsive agitations, especially in weaker subjects, which are the most liable to the severest impressions of pain and fear. The only difference between pain and terror is, that things which cause pain operate on the mind by the intervention of the body; whereas things that cause terror generally affect the bodily organs by the operation of the mind suggesting the danger; but both agreeing, either primarily or secondarily, in producing a

[1] Part I. sect. 8.   [2] Part I. sect. 10.

tension, contraction, or violent emotion of the nerves,[1] they agree likewise in everything else. For it appears very clearly to me, from this, as well as from many other examples, that when the body is disposed, by any means whatsoever, to such emotions as it would acquire by the means of a certain passion; it will of itself excite something very like that passion in the mind.

SECT. IV.—CONTINUED

To this purpose Mr. Spon, in his Récherches d' Antiquité, gives us a curious story of the celebrated physiognomist Campanella. This man, it seems, had not only made very accurate observations on human faces, but was very expert in mimicking such as were any way remarkable. When he had a mind to penetrate into the inclinations of those he had to deal with, he composed his face, his gesture, and his whole body, as nearly as he could into the exact similitude of the person he intended to examine; and then carefully observed what turn of mind he seemed to acquire by this change. So that, says my author, he was able to enter into the dispositions and thoughts of people as effectually as if he had been changed into the very men. I have often observed, that on mimicking the looks and gestures of angry, or placid, or frighted, or daring men, I have involuntarily found my mind turned to that passion, whose appearance I endeavoured to imitate; nay, I am convinced it is hard to avoid it, though one strove to separate the passion from its correspondent gestures. Our minds and bodies are so closely and intimately connected, that one is incapable of pain or pleasure without the other. Campanella, of whom we have been speaking, could so abstract his attention from any sufferings of his body, that he was able to endure the rack itself without much pain; and in lesser pains everybody must have observed, that, when we can employ our attention on anything else, the pain has been for a time suspended: on the other hand, if by any means the body is indisposed to perform such gestures, or to be stimulated into such emotions, as any passion usually produces in it, that passion itself never can arise, though its cause should be never

---

[1] I do not here enter into the question debated among physiologists, whether pain be the effect of a contraction, or a tension of the nerves. Either will serve my purpose; for by tension, I mean no more than a violent pulling of the fibres, which compose any muscle or membrane, in whatever way this is done.

so strongly in action; though it should be merely mental, and immediately affecting none of the senses. As an opiate or spirituous liquors, shall suspend the operation of grief, or fear, or anger, in spite of all our efforts to the contrary; and this by inducing in the body a disposition contrary to that which it receives from these passions.

SECT. V.—HOW THE SUBLIME IS PRODUCED

HAVING considered terror as producing an unnatural tension and certain violent emotions of the nerves; it easily follows, from what we have just said, that whatever is fitted to produce such a tension must be productive of a passion similar to terror,[1] and consequently must be a source of the sublime, though it should have no idea of danger connected with it. So that little remains towards showing the cause of the sublime, but to show that the instances we have given of it in the second part relate to such things as are fitted by nature to produce this sort of tension, either by the primary operation of the mind or the body. With regard to such things as effect by the associated idea of danger, there can be no doubt but that they produce terror, and act by some modification of that passion; and that terror, when sufficiently violent, raises the emotions of the body just mentioned, can as little be doubted. But if the sublime is built on terror, or some passion like it, which has pain for its object, it is previously proper to inquire how any species of delight can be derived from a cause so apparently contrary to it. I say *delight*, because, as I have often remarked, it is very evidently different in its cause, and in its own nature, from actual and positive pleasure.

SECT. VI.—HOW PAIN CAN BE A CAUSE OF DELIGHT

PROVIDENCE has so ordered it, that a state of rest and inaction, however it may flatter our indolence, should be productive of many inconveniences; that it should generate such disorders, as may force us to have recourse to some labour, as a thing absolutely requisite to make us pass our lives with tolerable satisfaction; for the nature of rest is to suffer all the parts of our bodies to fall into a relaxation, that not only disables the members from performing their functions,

[1] Part II. sect. 2.

but takes away the vigorous tone of fibre which is requisite for carrying on the natural and necessary secretions. At the same time, that in this languid inactive state, the nerves are more liable to the most horrid convulsions, than when they are sufficiently braced and strengthened. Melancholy, dejection, despair, and often self-murder, is the consequence of the gloomy view we take of things in this relaxed state of body. The best remedy for all these evils is exercise or *labour;* and labour is a surmounting of *difficulties,* an exertion of the contracting power of the muscles; and as such resembles pain, which consists in tension or contraction, in everything but degree. Labour is not only requisite to preserve the coarser organs in a state fit for their functions; but it is equally necessary to those finer and more delicate organs, on which, and by which, the imagination, and perhaps the other mental powers, act. Since it is probable, that not only the inferior parts of the soul, as the passions are called, but the understanding itself, makes use of some fine corporeal instruments in its operation; though what they are, and where they are, may be somewhat hard to settle; but that it does make use of such, appears from hence; that a long exercise of the mental powers induces a remarkable lassitude of the whole body; and, on the other hand, that great bodily labour, or pain, weakens, and sometimes actually destroys, the mental faculties. Now, as a due exercise is essential to the coarse muscular parts of the constitution, and that without this rousing they would become languid and diseased, the very same rule holds with regard to those finer parts we have mentioned; to have them in proper order, they must be shaken and worked to a proper degree.

SECT. VII.—EXERCISE NECESSARY FOR THE FINER ORGANS

As common labour, which is a mode of pain, is the exercise of the grosser, a mode of terror is the exercise of the finer parts of the system; and if a certain mode of pain be of such a nature as to act upon the eye or the ear, as they are the most delicate organs, the affection approaches more nearly to that which has a mental cause. In all these cases, if the pain and terror are so modified as not to be actually noxious; if the pain is not carried to violence, and the terror is not conversant about the present destruction of the person, as these emotions clear the parts, whether fine or gross, of a dangerous and troublesome encumbrance, they are capable of producing delight; not pleasure, but a sort of delightful horror, a sort of tranquillity tinged with terror; which, as it belongs to self-preservation, is one of the strongest of all the passions. Its object is the sublime.[1] Its highest degree I call *astonishment;* the subordinate degrees are awe, reverence, and respect, which, by the very etymology of the words show from what source they are derived, and how they stand distinguished from positive pleasure.

SECT. VIII.—WHY THINGS NOT DANGEROUS PRODUCE A PASSION LIKE TERROR

[2]A MODE of terror or pain is always the cause of the sublime. For terror, or associated danger, the foregoing explication is, I believe, sufficient. It will require something more trouble to show, that such examples as I have given of the sublime in the second part are capable of producing a mode of pain, and of being thus allied to terror, and to be accounted for on the same principles. And first of such objects as are great in their dimensions. I speak of visual objects.

SECT. IX.—WHY VISUAL OBJECTS OF GREAT DIMENSIONS ARE SUBLIME

VISION is performed by having a picture, formed by the rays of light which are reflected from the object, painted in one piece, instantaneously, on the retina, or last nervous part of the eye. Or, according to others, there is but one point of any object painted on the eye in such a manner as to be perceived at once; but by moving the eye, we gather up, with great celerity, the several parts of the object, so as to form one uniform piece. If the former opinion be allowed, it will be considered,[3] that though all the light reflected from a large body should strike the eye in one instant; yet we must suppose that the body itself is formed of a vast number of distinct points, every one of which, or the ray from every one, makes an impression on the retina. So that, though the image of one point should cause but a small tension of this membrane, another and another, and another stroke, must in their progress cause a very great one, until it arrives at last to the highest degree; and the whole

[1] Part II. sect 2.   [2] Part I. sect. 7.   Part II. sect 2.
[3] Part II. sect. 7.

capacity of the eye, vibrating in all its parts, must approach near to the nature of what causes pain, and consequently must produce an idea of the sublime. Again, if we take it, that one point only of an object is distinguishable at once, the matter will amount nearly to the same thing, or rather it will make the origin of the sublime from greatness of dimension yet clearer. For if but one point is observed at once, the eye must traverse the vast space of such bodies with great quickness, and consequently the fine nerves and muscles destined to the motion of that part must be very much strained; and their great sensibility must make them highly affected by this straining. Besides, it signifies just nothing to the effect produced, whether a body has its parts connected and makes its impression at once; or, making but one impression of a point at a time, causes a succession of the same or others so quickly as to make them seem united; as is evident from the common effect of whirling about a lighted torch or piece of wood: which, if done with celerity, seems a circle of fire.

SECT. X.—UNITY WHY REQUISITE TO VASTNESS

It may be objected to this theory, that the eye generally receives an equal number of rays at all times, and that therefore a great object cannot affect it by the number of rays, more than that variety of objects which the eye must always discern whilst it remains open. But to this I answer, that admitting an equal number of rays, or an equal quantity of luminous particles, to strike the eye at all times, yet if these rays frequently vary their nature, now to blue, now to red, and so on, or their manner of termination, as to a number of petty squares, triangles, or the like, at every change, whether of colour or shape, the organ has a sort of relaxation or rest; but this relaxation and labour so often interrupted, is by no means productive of ease; neither has it the effect of vigorous and uniform labour. Whoever has remarked the different effects of some strong exercise, and some little piddling action, will understand why a teasing, fretful employment, which at once wearies and weakens the body, should have nothing great; these sorts of impulses, which are rather teasing than painful, by continually and suddenly altering their tenor and direction, prevent that full tension, that species of uniform labour, which is allied to strong pain, and causes the sublime. The sum total of things of various kinds, though it should equal the number of the uniform parts composing some *one* entire object, is not equal in its effect upon the organs of our bodies. Besides the one already assigned, there is another very strong reason for the difference. The mind in reality hardly ever can attend diligently to more than one thing at a time; if this thing be little, the effect is little, and a number of other little objects cannot engage the attention; the mind is bounded by the bounds of the object; and what is not attended to, and what does not exist, are much the same in effect; but the eye, or the mind, (for in this case there is no difference,) in great, uniform objects, does not readily arrive at their bounds; it has no rest whilst it contemplates them; the image is much the same everywhere. So that everything great by its quantity must necessarily be one, simple and entire.

SECT. XI.—THE ARTIFICIAL INFINITE

WE have observed, that a species of greatness arises from the artificial infinite; and that this infinite consists in an uniform succession of great parts: we observed, too, that the same uniform succession had a like power in sounds. But because the effects of many things are clearer in one of the senses than in another, and that all the senses bear analogy to and illustrate one another, I shall begin with this power in sounds, as the cause of the sublimity from succession is rather more obvious in the sense of hearing. And I shall here, once for all, observe, that an investigation of the natural and mechanical causes of our passions, besides the curiosity of the subject, gives, if they are discovered, a double strength and lustre to any rules we deliver on such matters. When the ear receives any simple sound, it is struck by a single pulse of the air, which makes the eardrum and the other membranous parts vibrate according to the nature and species of the stroke. If the stroke be strong, the organ of hearing suffers a considerable degree of tension. If the stroke be repeated pretty soon after, the repetition causes an expectation of another stroke. And it must be observed, that expectation itself causes a tension. This is apparent in many animals, who, when they prepare for hearing any sound, rouse themselves, and prick up their ears:

so that here the effect of the sounds is considerably augmented by a new auxiliary, the expectation. But though, after a number of strokes, we expect still more, not being able to ascertain the exact time of their arrival, when they arrive, they produce a sort of surprise, which increases this tension yet further. For I have observed, that when at any time I have waited very earnestly for some sound, that returned at intervals, (as the successive firing of cannon,) though I fully expected the return of the sound, when it came it always made me start a little; the ear-drum suffered a convulsion, and the whole body consented with it. The tension of the part thus increasing at every blow, by the united forces of the stroke itself, the expectation, and the surprise, it is worked up to such a pitch as to be capable of the sublime; it is brought just to the verge of pain. Even when the cause has ceased, the organs of hearing being often successively struck in a similar manner, continue to vibrate in that manner for some time longer; this is an additional help to the greatness of the effect.

SECT. XII.—THE VIBRATIONS MUST BE SIMILAR

But if the vibration be not similar at every impression, it can never be carried beyond the number of actual impressions; for move any body, as a pendulum, in one way, and it will continue to oscillate in an arch of the same circle, until the known causes make it rest; but if after first putting it in motion in one direction, you push it into another, it can never reassume the first direction; because it can never move itself, and consequently it can have but the effect of that last motion; whereas, if in the same direction you act upon it several times, it will describe a greater arch, and move a longer time.

SECT. XIII.—THE EFFECTS OF SUCCESSION IN VISUAL OBJECTS EXPLAINED

If we can comprehend clearly how things operate upon one of our senses, there can be very little difficulty in conceiving in what manner they affect the rest. To say a great deal therefore upon the corresponding affections of every sense, would tend rather to fatigue us by an useless repetition, than to throw any new light upon the subject by that ample and diffuse manner of treating it; but as in this discourse we chiefly attach ourselves to the sublime, as it affects the eye, we shall consider particularly why a successive disposition of uniform parts in the same right line should be sublime,[1] and upon what principle this disposition is enabled to make a comparatively small quantity of matter produce a grander effect, than a much larger quantity disposed in another manner. To avoid the perplexity of general notions; let us set before our eyes a colonnade of uniform pillars planted in a right line; let us take our stand in such a manner, that the eye may shoot along this colonnade, for it has its best effect in this view. In our present situation it is plain, that the rays from the first round pillar will cause in the eye a vibration of that species; an image of the pillar itself. The pillar immediately succeeding increases it; that which follows renews and enforces the impression; each in its order as it succeeds, repeats impulse after impulse, and stroke after stroke, until the eye, long exercised in one particular way, cannot lose that object immediately; and, being violently roused by this continued agitation, it presents the mind with a grand or sublime conception. But instead of viewing a rank of uniform pillars, let us suppose that they succeed each other, a round and a square one alternately. In this case the vibration caused by the first round pillar perishes as soon as it is formed: and one of quite another sort (the square) directly occupies its place; which, however, it resigns as quickly to the round one; and thus the eye proceeds, alternately; taking up one image, and laying down another, as long as the building continues. From whence it is obvious, that, at the last pillar, the impression is as far from continuing as it was at the very first; because, in fact, the sensory can receive no distinct impression but from the last; and it can never of itself resume a dissimilar impression: besides, every variation of the object is a rest and relaxation to the organs of sight; and these reliefs prevent that powerful emotion so necessary to produce the sublime. To produce therefore a perfect grandeur in such things as we have been mentioning, there should be a perfect simplicity, an absolute uniformity in disposition, shape, and colouring. Upon this principle of succession and uniformity it may be asked, why a long bare wall should not be a more sublime object than a colonnade; since the succession is no way interrupted; since the eye meets no check; since nothing

[1] Part II. sect. 10.

more uniform can be conceived? A long bare wall is certainly not
so grand an object as a colonnade of the same length and height.
It is not altogether difficult to account for this difference. When we
look at a naked wall, from the evenness of the object, the eye runs
along its whole space, and arrives quickly at its termination; the
eye meets nothing which may interrupt its progress; but then it
meets nothing which may detain it a proper time to produce a very
great and lasting effect. The view of the bare wall, if it be of a
great height and length, is undoubtedly grand; but this is only *one*
idea, and not a *repetition* of *similar* ideas: it is therefore great, not
so much upon the principle of *infinity,* as upon that of *vastness.*
But we are not so powerfully affected with any one impulse, unless
it be one of a prodigious force indeed, as we are with a succession of
similar impulses; because the nerves of the sensory do not (if I may
use the expression) acquire a habit of repeating the same feeling in
such a manner as to continue it longer than its cause is in action;
besides, all the effects which I have attributed to expectation and
surprise in sect. 11, can have no place in a bare wall.

SECT. XIV.—LOCKE'S OPINION CONCERNING DARKNESS CONSIDERED

It is Mr. Locke's opinion, that darkness is not naturally an idea
of terror; and that, though an excessive light is painful to the sense,
the greatest excess of darkness is no ways troublesome. He observes
indeed in another place, that a nurse or an old woman having once
associated the idea of ghosts and goblins with that of darkness, night,
ever after, becomes painful and horrible to the imagination. The
authority of this great man is doubtless as great as that of any man
can be, and it seems to stand in the way of our general principle.[1]
We have considered darkness as a cause of the sublime; and we
have all along considered the sublime as depending on some modification of pain or terror: so that if darkness be no way painful or
terrible to any, who have not had their minds early tainted with
superstitions, it can be no source of the sublime to them. But, with
all deference to such an authority, it seems to me, that an association
of a more general nature, an association which takes in all mankind,
and make darkness terrible; for in utter darkness it is impossible to

[1] Part II. sect. 3.

know in what degree of safety we stand; we are ignorant of the objects that surround us; we may every moment strike against some dangerous obstruction; we may fall down a precipice the first step we take; and if an enemy approach, we know not in what quarter to defend ourselves; in such a case strength is no sure protection; wisdom can only act by guess; the boldest are staggered, and he, who would pray for nothing else towards his defence, is forced to pray for light.

> Ζεῦ πάτερ, ἀλλὰ σὺ ῥῦσαι ὑπ' ἠέρος υἷας Ἀχαιῶν·
> Ποίησον δ' αἴθρην, δὸς δ' ὀφθαλμοῖσιν ἰδέσθαι·
> Ἐν δὲ φάει καὶ ὄλεσσον.—

As to the association of ghosts and goblins; surely it is more natural to think, that darkness, being originally an idea of terror, was chosen as a fit scene for such terrible representations, than that such representations have made darkness terrible. The mind of man very easily slides into an error of the former sort; but it is very hard to imagine, that the effect of an idea so universally terrible in all times, and in all countries, as darkness, could possibly have been owing to a set of idle stories, or to any cause of a nature so trivial, and of an operation so precarious.

SECT. XV.—DARKNESS TERRIBLE IN ITS OWN NATURE

PERHAPS it may appear on inquiry that blackness and darkness are in some degree painful by their natural operation, independent of any associations whatsoever. I must observe, that the ideas of darkness and blackness are much the same; and they differ only in this, that blackness is a more confined idea. Mr. Cheselden has given us a very curious story of a boy, who had been born blind, and continued so until he was thirteen or fourteen years old; he was then couched for a cataract, by which operation he received his sight. Among many remarkable particulars that attended his first perceptions and judgments on visual objects, Cheselden tells us, that the first time the boy saw a black object, it gave him great uneasiness; and that some time after, upon accidentally seeing a negro woman, he was struck with great horror at the sight. The horror, in this case, can scarcely be supposed to arise from any association. The boy appears by the account to have been particularly observing and sensible for one of his age; and therefore it is probable, if the great uneasiness he felt at the first sight of black had arisen from its connexion with any other disagreeable ideas, he would have observed and mentioned it. For an idea, disagreeable only by association, has the cause of its ill effect on the passions evident enough at the first impression; in ordinary cases, it is indeed frequently lost; but this is, because the original association was made very early, and the consequent impression repeated often. In our instance, there was no time for such a habit; and there is no reason to think that the ill effects of black on his imagination were more owing to its connexion with any disagreeable ideas, than that the good effects of more cheerful colours were derived from their connexion with pleasing ones. They had both probably their effects from their natural operation.

SECT. XVI.—WHY DARKNESS IS TERRIBLE

IT may be worth while to examine how darkness can operate in such a manner as to cause pain. It is observable, that still as we recede from the light, nature has so contrived it, that the pupil is enlarged by the retiring of the iris, in proportion to our recess. Now, instead of declining from it but a little, suppose that we withdraw entirely from the light; it is reasonable to think, that the contraction of the radial fibres of the iris is proportionably greater; and that this part may by great darkness come to be so contracted as to strain the nerves that compose it beyond their natural tone; and by this means to produce a painful sensation. Such a tension it seems there certainly is, whilst we are involved in darkness; for in such a state, whilst the eye remains open, there is a continual nisus to receive light; this is manifest from the flashes and luminous appearances which often seem in these circumstances to play before it; and which can be nothing but the effect of spasms, produced by its own efforts in pursuit of its object: several other strong impulses will produce the idea of light in the eye, besides the substance of light itself, as we experience on many occasions. Some, who allow darkness to be a cause of the sublime, would infer, from the dilatation of the pupil, that a relaxation may be productive of the sublime, as well as a convulsion: but they do not, I believe, consider that although the circular ring of the iris be in some sense a sphincter, which may possibly be dilated by a simple relaxation, yet in one respect it differs from most of the other sphincters of the body, that it is furnished with antago- nist muscles, which are the radial fibres of the iris: no sooner does the circular muscle begin to relax, than these fibres, wanting their counterpoise, are forcibly drawn back, and open the pupil to a con- siderable wideness. But though we were not apprized of this, I believe any one will find, if he opens his eyes and makes an effort to see in a dark place, that a very perceivable pain ensues. And I have heard some ladies remark, that after having worked a long time upon a ground of black, their eyes were so pained and weak- ened, they could hardly see. It may perhaps be objected to this theory of the mechanical effect of darkness, that the ill effects of darkness or blackness seem rather mental than corporeal: and I own it is true, that they do so; and so do all those that depend on the affections of the finer parts of our system. The ill effects of bad weather appear often no otherwise, than in a melancholy and dejection of spirits; though without doubt, in this case, the bodily organs suffer first, and the mind through these organs.

SECT. XVII.—THE EFFECTS OF BLACKNESS

BLACKNESS is but a *partial darkness;* and therefore, it derives some of its powers from being mixed and surrounded with coloured bodies. In its own nature, it cannot be considered as a colour. Black bodies, reflecting none or but a few rays, with regard to sight, are but as so many vacant spaces dispersed among the objects we view. When the eye lights on one of these vacuities, after having been kept in some degree of tension by the play of the adjacent colours upon it, it sud- denly falls into a relaxation; out of which it as suddenly recovers by a convulsive spring. To illustrate this: let us consider, that when we in- tend to sit on a chair, and find it much lower than was expected, the shock is very violent; much more violent than could be thought from so slight a fall as the difference between one chair and another can possibly make. If, after descending a flight of stairs, we attempt inad- vertently to take another step in the manner of the former ones, the shock is extremely rude and disagreeable; and by no art can we cause such a shock by the same means when we expect and prepare for it. When I say that this is owing to having the change made contrary to expectation, I do not mean solely, when the *mind* expects. I mean, likewise, that when any organ of sense is for some time affected in some one manner, if it be suddenly affected otherwise, there ensues a convulsive motion; such a convulsion as is caused when anything happens against the expectance of the mind. And though it may appear strange that such a change as produces a relaxation should immediately produce a sudden convulsion; it is yet most certainly so, and so in all the senses. Every one knows that sleep is a relaxation; and that silence, where nothing keeps the organs of hearing in action, is in general fittest to bring on this relaxation; yet when a sort of murmuring sounds dispose a man to sleep, let these sounds cease suddenly, and the person immediately awakes; that is, the parts are braced up suddenly, and he awakes. This I have often experienced myself, and I have heard the same from observing persons. In like manner, if a person in broad day-light were falling asleep, to introduce a sudden darkness would prevent his sleep for that time, though silence and darkness in themselves, and not suddenly introduced, are very favourable to it. This I knew only by conjecture on the analogy of the senses when I first digested these observations; but I have since experienced it. And I have often experienced, and so have a thousand others, that on the first inclining towards sleep, we have been suddenly awakened with a most violent start; and that this start was generally preceded by a sort of dream of our falling down a precipice: whence does this strange motion arise, but from the too sudden relaxation of the body, which by some mechanism in nature restores itself by as quick and vigorous an exertion of the contracting power of the muscles? The dream itself is caused by this relaxation; and it is of too uniform a nature to be attributed to any other cause. The parts relax too suddenly, which is in the nature of falling; and this accident of the body induces this image in the mind. When we are in a confirmed state of health and vigour, as all changes are then less sudden, and less on the extreme, we can seldom complain of this disagreeable sensation.

SECT. XVIII.—THE EFFECTS OF BLACKNESS MODERATED

THOUGH the effects of black be painful originally, we must not think they always continue so. Custom reconciles us to everything. After we have been used to the sight of black objects, the terror abates, and the smoothness and glossiness, or some agreeable accident, of bodies so coloured, softens in some measure the horror and sternness of their original nature; yet the nature of their original impression still continues. Black will always have something melancholy in it, because the sensory will always find the change to it from other colours too violent; or if it occupy the whole compass of the sight, it will then be darkness; and what was said of darkness will be applicable here. I do not purpose to go into all that might be said to illustrate this theory of the effects of light and darkness, neither will I examine all the different effects produced by the various modifications and mixtures of these two causes. If the foregoing observations have any foundation in nature, I conceive them very sufficient to account for all the phenomena that can arise from all the combinations of black with other colours. To enter into every particular, or to answer every objection, would be an endless labour. We have only followed the most leading roads; and we shall observe the same conduct in our inquiry into the cause of beauty.

SECT. XIX.—THE PHYSICAL CAUSE OF LOVE

WHEN we have before us such objects as excite love and complacency, the body is affected, so far as I could observe, much in the following manner: the head reclines something on one side; the eyelids are more closed than usual, and the eyes roll gently with an inclination to the object; the mouth is a little opened, and the breath drawn slowly, with now and then a low sigh; the whole body is composed, and the hands fall idly to the sides. All this is accompanied with an inward sense of melting and languor. These appearances are always proportioned to the degree of beauty in the object, and of sensibility in the observer. And this gradation from the highest pitch of beauty and sensibility, even to the lowest of mediocrity and indifference, and their correspondent effects, ought to be kept in view, else this description will seem exaggerated, which

it certainly is not. But from this description it is almost impossible
not to conclude, that beauty acts by relaxing the solids of the whole
system. There are all the appearances of such a relaxation; and a
relaxation somewhat below the natural tone seems to me to be the
cause of all positive pleasure. Who is a stranger to that manner of
expression so common in all times and in all countries, of being
softened, relaxed, enervated, dissolved, melted away by pleasure?
The universal voice of mankind, faithful to their feelings, concurs in
affirming this uniform and general effect: and although some odd
and particular instance may perhaps be found, wherein there appears
a considerable degree of positive pleasure, without all the characters of relaxation, we must not therefore reject the conclusion we
had drawn from a concurrence of many experiments; but we must
still retain it, subjoining the exceptions which may occur, according
to the judicious rule laid down by Sir Isaac Newton in the third
book of his Optics. Our position will, I conceive, appear confirmed
beyond any reasonable doubt, if we can show that such things as we
have already observed to be the genuine constituents of beauty, have
each of them, separately taken, a natural tendency to relax the fibres.
And if it must be allowed us, that the appearance of the human body,
when all these constituents are united together before the sensory,
further favours this opinion, we may venture, I believe, to conclude,
that the passion called love is produced by this relaxation. By the
same method of reasoning which we have used in the inquiry into
the causes of the sublime, we may likewise conclude, that as a beautiful object presented to the sense, by causing a relaxation of the body,
produces the passion of love in the mind; so if by any means the
passion should first have its origin in the mind, a relaxation of the
outward organs will as certainly ensue in a degree proportioned to
the cause.

SECT. XX.—WHY SMOOTHNESS IS BEAUTIFUL

It is to explain the true cause of visual beauty, that I call in
the assistance of the other senses. If it appears that *smoothness* is a
principal cause of pleasure to the touch, taste, smell, and hearing,
it will be easily admitted a constituent of visual beauty; especially
as we have before shown, that this quality is found almost without

exception in all bodies that are by general consent held beautiful.
There can be no doubt that bodies which are rough and angular,
rouse and vellicate the organs of feeling, causing a sense of pain,
which consists in the violent tension or contraction of the muscular
fibres. On the contrary, the application of smooth bodies relaxes;
gentle stroking with a smooth hand allays violent pains and cramps,
and relaxes the suffering parts from their unnatural tension; and
it has therefore very often no mean effect in removing swellings and
obstructions. The sense of feeling is highly gratified with smooth
bodies. A bed smoothly laid, and soft, that is, where the resistance
is every way inconsiderable, is a great luxury, disposing to an universal relaxation, and inducing beyond anything else that species of
it called sleep.

SECT. XXI.—SWEETNESS, ITS NATURE

Nor is it only in the touch that smooth bodies cause positive
pleasure by relaxation. In the smell and taste, we find all things
agreeable to them, and which are commonly called sweet, to be of a
smooth nature, and that they all evidently tend to relax their respective sensories. Let us first consider the taste. Since it is most easy
to inquire into the property of liquids, and since all things seem to
want a fluid vehicle to make them tasted at all, I intend rather to
consider the liquid than the solid parts of our food. The vehicles of
all tastes are *water* and *oil*. And what determines the taste is some
salt, which affects variously according to its nature, or its manner of
being combined with other things. Water and oil, simply considered, are capable of giving some pleasure to the taste. Water, when
simple, is insipid, inodorous, colourless, and smooth; it is found,
when *not cold,* to be a great resolver of spasms, and lubricator of
the fibres; this power it probably owes to its smoothness. For as
fluidity depends, according to the most general opinion, on the
roundness, smoothness, and weak cohesion, of the component parts
of any body; and as water acts merely as a simple fluid; it follows
that the cause of its fluidity is likewise the cause of its relaxing
quality; namely, the smoothness and slippery texture of its parts.
The other fluid vehicle of taste is *oil*. This too, when simple, is
insipid, inodorous, colourless, and smooth to the touch and taste.

It is smoother than water, and in many cases yet more relaxing. Oil is in some degree pleasant to the eye, the touch, and the taste, insipid as it is. Water is not so grateful; which I do not know on what principle to account for, other than that water is not so soft and smooth. Suppose that to this oil or water were added a certain quantity of a specific salt, which had a power of putting the nervous papillæ of the tongue into a gentle vibratory motion; as suppose, sugar dissolved in it. The smoothness of the oil, and the vibratory power of the salt, cause the sense we call sweetness. In all sweet bodies, sugar, or a substance very little different from sugar, is constantly found. Every species of salt, examined by the microscope, has its own distinct, regular, invariable form. That of nitre is a pointed oblong; that of sea-salt an exact cube; that of sugar a perfect globe. If you have tried how smooth globular bodies, as the marbles with which boys amuse themselves, have affected the touch when they are rolled backward and forward and over one another, you will easily conceive how sweetness, which consists in a salt of such nature, affects the taste; for a single globe, (though somewhat pleasant to the feeling,) yet by the regularity of its form, and the somewhat too sudden deviation of its parts from a right line, is nothing near so pleasant to the touch as several globes, where the hand gently rises to one and falls to another; and this pleasure is greatly increased if the globes are in motion, and sliding over one another; for this soft variety prevents that weariness, which the uniform disposition of the several globes would otherwise produce. Thus in sweet liquors, the parts of the fluid vehicle, though most probably round, are yet so minute, as to conceal the figure of their component parts from the nicest inquisition of the microscope; and consequently, being so excessively minute, they have a sort of flat simplicity to the taste, resembling the effects of plain smooth bodies to the touch; for if a body be composed of round parts excessively small, and packed pretty closely together, the surface will be both to the sight and touch as if it were nearly plain and smooth. It is clear from their unveiling their figure to the microscope, that the particles of sugar are considerably larger than those of water or oil, and consequently, that their effects from their roundness will be more distinct and palpable to the nervous papillæ of that nice organ the tongue: they will induce that sense called sweetness, which in a weak manner we discover in oil, and in a yet weaker, in water; for, insipid as they are, water and oil are in some degree sweet; and it may be observed, that the insipid things of all kinds approach more nearly to the nature of sweetness than to that of any other taste.

SECT. XXII.—SWEETNESS RELAXING

In the other senses we have remarked, that smooth things are relaxing. Now it ought to appear that sweet things, which are the smooth of taste, are relaxing too. It is remarkable, that in some languages, soft and sweet have but one name. *Doux* in French signifies soft as well as sweet. The Latin *Dulcis,* and the Italian *Dolce,* have in many cases the same double signification. That sweet things are generally relaxing, is evident; because all such, especially those which are most oily, taken frequently, or in a large quantity, very much enfeeble the tone of the stomach. Sweet smells, which bear a great affinity to sweet tastes, relax very remarkably. The smell of flowers disposes people to drowsiness; and this relaxing effect is further apparent from the prejudice which people of weak nerves receive from their use. It were worth while to examine, whether tastes of this kind, sweet ones, tastes that are caused by smooth oils and a relaxing salt, are not the original pleasant tastes. For many, which use has rendered such, were not at all agreeable at first. The way to examine this, is to try what nature has originally provided for us, which she has undoubtedly made originally pleasant; and to analyze this provision. *Milk* is the first support of our childhood. The component parts of this are water, oil, and a sort of a very sweet salt, called the sugar of milk. All these when blended have a great *smoothness* to the taste, and a relaxing quality to the skin. The next thing children covet is *fruit,* and of fruits those principally which are sweet; and every one knows that the sweetness of fruit is caused by a subtle oil, and such salt as that mentioned in the last section. Afterwards custom, habit, the desire of novelty, and a thousand other causes, confound, adulterate, and change our palates, so that we can no longer reason with any satisfaction about them. Before we quit this article, we must observe, that as smooth things are, as such, agreeable to the taste, and are found of a relaxing quality; so, on the other hand, things which are found by experience to be of a strengthening quality, and fit to brace the fibres, are almost universally rough and pungent to the taste, and in many cases rough even to the touch. We often apply the quality of sweetness, metaphorically, to visual objects. For the better carrying on this remarkable analogy of the senses, we may here call sweetness the beautiful of the taste.

SECT. XXIII.—VARIATION, WHY BEAUTIFUL

ANOTHER principal property of beautiful objects is, that the line of their parts is continually varying its direction; but it varies it by a very insensible deviation; it never varies it so quickly as to surprise, or by the sharpness of its angle to cause any twitching or convulsion of the optic nerve. Nothing long continued in the same manner, nothing very suddenly varied, can be beautiful; because both are opposite to that agreeable relaxation which is the characteristic effect of beauty. It is thus in all the senses. A motion in a right line is that manner of moving, next to a very gentle descent, in which we meet the least resistance; yet it is not that manner of moving which, next to a descent, wearies us the least. Rest certainly tends to relax; yet there is a species of motion which relaxes more than rest; a gentle oscillatory motion, a rising and falling. Rocking sets children to sleep better than absolute rest; there is indeed scarce anything at that age which gives more pleasure than to be gently lifted up and down; the manner of playing which their nurses use with children, and the weighing and swinging used afterwards by themselves as a favourite amusement, evince this very sufficiently. Most people must have observed the sort of sense they have had on being swiftly drawn in an easy coach on a smooth turf, with gradual ascents and declivities. This will give a better idea of the beautiful, and point out its probable course better, than almost anything else. On the contrary, when one is hurried over a rough, rocky, broken road, the pain felt by these sudden inequalities shows why similar sights, feelings, and sounds are so contrary to beauty: and with regard to the feeling, it is exactly the same in its effect, or very nearly the same, whether, for instance, I move my hand along the surface of a body of a certain shape, or whether such a body is

moved along my hand. But to bring this analogy of the senses home
to the eye: if a body presented to that sense has such a waving surface, that the rays of light reflected from it are in a continual insensible deviation from the strongest to the weakest (which is always
the case in a surface gradually unequal,) it must be exactly similar in
its effects on the eye and touch; upon the one of which it operates
directly, on the other, indirectly. And this body will be beautiful,
if the lines which compose its surface are not continued, even so
varied, in a manner that may weary or dissipate the attention. The
variation itself must be continually varied.

SECT. XXIV.—CONCERNING SMALLNESS

To avoid a sameness which may arise from the too frequent repetition of the same reasonings, and of illustrations of the same nature,
I will not enter very minutely into every particular that regards
beauty, as it is founded on the disposition of its quantity, or its
quantity itself. In speaking of the magnitude of bodies there is great
uncertainty, because the ideas of great and small are terms almost
entirely relative to the species of the objects, which are infinite. It
is true, that having once fixed the species of any object, and the dimensions common in the individuals of that species, we may observe some that exceed, and some that fall short of, the ordinary
standard: those which greatly exceed are, by that excess, provided
the species itself be not very small, rather great and terrible than
beautiful; but as in the animal world, and in a good measure in the
vegetable world likewise, the qualities that constitute beauty may
possibly be united to things of greater dimensions; when they are so
united, they constitute a species something different both from the
sublime and beautiful, which I have before called *fine*: but this
kind, I imagine, has not such a power on the passions either as vast
bodies have which are endued with the correspondent qualities of
the sublime, or as the qualities of beauty have when united in a
small object. The affection produced by large bodies adorned with
the spoils of beauty, is a tension continually relieved; which approaches to the nature of mediocrity. But if I were to say how I find
myself affected upon such occasions, I should say, that the sublime
suffers less by being united to some of the qualities of beauty, than

beauty does by being joined to greatness of quantity, or any other properties of the sublime. There is something so over-ruling in whatever inspires us with awe, in all things which belongs ever so remotely to terror, that nothing else can stand in their presence. There lie the qualities of beauty either dead or unoperative; or at most exerted to mollify the rigour and sternness of the terror, which is the natural concomitant of greatness. Besides the extraordinary great in every species, the opposite to this, the dwarfish and diminutive, ought to be considered. Littleness, merely as such, has nothing contrary to the idea of beauty. The humming-bird, both in shape and colouring, yields to none of the winged species, of which it is the least; and perhaps his beauty is enhanced by his smallness. But there are animals, which, when they are extremely small, are rarely (if ever) beautiful. There is a dwarfish size of men and women, which is almost constantly so gross and massive in comparison of their height, that they present us with a very disagreeable image. But should a man be found not above two or three feet high, supposing such a person to have all the parts of his body of a delicacy suitable to such a size, and otherwise endued with the common qualities of other beautiful bodies, I am pretty well convinced that a person of such a stature might be considered as beautiful; might be the object of love; might give us very pleasing ideas on viewing him. The only thing which could possibly interpose to check our pleasure is, that such creatures, however formed, are unusual, and are often therefore considered as something monstrous. The large and gigantic, though very compatible with the sublime, is contrary to the beautiful. It is impossible to suppose a giant the object of love. When we let our imagination loose in romance, the ideas we naturally annex to that size are those of tyranny, cruelty, injustice, and everything horrid and abominable. We paint the giant ravaging the country, plundering the innocent traveller, and afterwards gorged with his half-living flesh: such are Polyphemus, Cacus, and others, who make so great a figure in romances and heroic poems. The event we attend to with the greatest satisfaction is their defeat and death. I do not remember, in all that multitude of deaths with which the Iliad is filled, that the fall of any man, remarkable for his great stature and strength, touches us with pity; nor does it appear that the author, so well read in human nature, ever intended it should. It is Simoisius, in the soft bloom of youth, torn from his parents, who tremble for a courage so ill suited to his strength; it is another hurried by war from the new embraces of his bride, young, and fair, and a novice to the field, who melts us by his untimely fate. Achilles, in spite of the many qualities of beauty which Homer has bestowed on his outward form, and the many great virtues with which he has adorned his mind, can never make us love him. It may be observed, that Homer has given the Trojans, whose fate he has designed to excite our compassion, infinitely more of the amiable, social virtues than he has distributed among his Greeks. With regard to the Trojans, the passion he chooses to raise is pity; pity is a passion founded on love; and these *lesser,* and if I may say domestic virtues, are certainly the most amiable. But he has made the Greeks far their superiors in the politic and military virtues. The councils of Priam are weak; the arms of Hector comparatively feeble; his courage far below that of Achilles. Yet we love Priam more than Agamemnon, and Hector more than his conqueror Achilles. Admiration is the passion which Homer would excite in favour of the Greeks, and he has done it by bestowing on them the virtues which have little to do with love. This short digression is perhaps not wholly beside our purpose, where our business is to show, that objects of great dimensions are incompatible with beauty, the more incompatible as they are greater; whereas the small, if ever they fail of beauty, this failure is not to be attributed to their size.

SECT. XXV.—OF COLOUR

With regard to colour, the disquisition is almost infinite: but I conceive the principles laid down in the beginning of this part are sufficient to account for the effects of them all, as well as for the agreeable effects of transparent bodies, whether fluid or solid. Suppose I look at a bottle of muddy liquor, of a blue or red colour; the blue or red rays cannot pass clearly to the eye, but are suddenly and unequally stopped by the intervention of little opaque bodies, which without preparation change the idea, and change it too into one disagreeable in its own nature, conformably to the principles laid down in sect. 24. But when the ray passes without such opposition through the glass or liquor, when the glass or liquor is quite transparent, the light is sometimes softened in the passage, which makes it more agreeable even as light; and the liquor reflecting all the rays of its proper colour *evenly,* it has such an effect on the eye, as smooth opaque bodies have on the eye and touch. So that the pleasure here is compounded of the softness of the transmitted, and the evenness of the reflected light. This pleasure may be heightened by the common principles in other things, if the shape of the glass which holds the transparent liquor be so judiciously varied, as to present the colour gradually and interchangeably, weakened and strengthened with all the variety which judgment in affairs of this nature shall suggest. On a review of all that has been said of the effects as well as the causes of both, it will appear, that the sublime and beautiful are built on principles very different, and that their affections are as different: the great has terror for its basis; which, when it is modified, causes that emotion in the mind which I have called astonishment; the beautiful is founded on mere positive pleasure, and excites in the soul that feeling which is called love. Their causes have made the subject of this fourth part.

PART V

Section I.—Of Words

NATURAL objects affect us, by the laws of that connexion which Providence has established between certain motions and configurations of bodies, and certain consequent feelings in our mind. Painting affects us in the same manner, but with the superadded pleasure of imitation. Architecture affects by the laws of nature, and the law of reason: from which latter result the rules of proportion, which make a work to be praised or censured, in the whole or in some part, when the end for which it was designed is or is not properly answered. But as to words; they seem to me to affect us in a manner very different from that in which we are affected by natural objects, or by painting or architecture; yet words have as considerable a share in exciting ideas of beauty and of the sublime as many of those, and sometimes a much greater than any of them: therefore an inquiry into the manner by which they excite such emotions is far from being unnecessary in a discourse of this kind.

SECT. II.—THE COMMON EFFECTS OF POETRY, NOT BY RAISING IDEAS OF THINGS

THE common notion of the power of poetry and eloquence, as well as that of words in ordinary conversation, is that they affect the mind by raising in it ideas of those things for which custom has appointed them to stand. To examine the truth of this notion, it may be requisite to observe, that words may be divided into three sorts. The first are such as represent many simple ideas *united by nature* to form some one determinate composition, as man, horse, tree, castle, &c. These I call *aggregate words*. The second are they that stand for one simple idea of such compositions, and no more; as red, blue, round, square, and the like. These I call *simple abstract* words. The third are those which are formed by an union, an *arbitrary* union, of both the others, and of the various relations between them in greater or less degrees of complexity; as virtue, honour, persuasion, magistrate, and the like. These I call *compound abstract* words. Words, I am sensible, are capable of being classed into more curious distinctions; but these seem to be natural, and enough for our purpose; and they are disposed in that order in which they are commonly taught, and in which the mind gets the ideas they are substituted for. I shall begin with the third sort of words; compound abstracts, such as virtue, honour, persuasion, docility. Of these I am convinced, that whatever power they may have on the passions, they do not derive it from any representation raised in the mind of the things for which they stand. As compositions, they are not real essences, and hardly cause, I think, any real ideas. Nobody, I believe, immediately on hearing the sounds, virtue, liberty, or honour, conceives any precise notions of the particular modes of action and thinking together with the mixt and simple ideas and the several relations of them for which these words are substituted; neither has he any general idea, compounded of them; for if he had, then some of those particular ones, though indistinct perhaps, and confused, might come soon to be perceived. But this, I take it, is hardly ever the case. For, put yourself upon analyzing one of these words, and you must reduce it from one set of general words to another, and then into the simple abstracts and aggregates, in a much longer series than may be at first imagined, before any real idea emerges to light, before you come to discover anything like the first principles of such compositions; and when you have made such a discovery of the original ideas, the effect of the composition is utterly lost. A train of thinking of this sort is much too long to be pursued in the ordinary ways of conversation; nor is it at all necessary that it should. Such words are in reality but mere sounds; but they are sounds which being used on particular occasions, wherein we receive some good, or suffer some evil, or see others affected with good or evil; or which we hear applied to other interesting things or events; and being applied in such a variety of cases, that we know readily by habit to what things they belong, they produce in the mind, whenever they are afterwards mentioned, effects similar to those of their occasions. The sounds being often used without reference to any particular occasion, and carrying still their first impressions, they at last utterly lose their connexion with the particular occasions that gave rise to them; yet the sound, without any annexed notion, continues to operate as before.

SECT. III.—GENERAL WORDS BEFORE IDEAS

MR. LOCKE has somewhere observed, with his usual sagacity, that most general words, those belonging to virtue and vice, good and evil, especially, are taught before the particular modes of action to which they belong are presented to the mind; and with them, the love of the one, and the abhorrence of the other; for the minds of children are so ductile, that a nurse, or any person about a child, by seeming pleased or displeased with anything, or even any word, may give the disposition of the child a similar turn. When, afterwards, the several occurrences in life come to be applied to these words, and that which is pleasant often appears under the name of evil; and what is disagreeable to nature is called good and virtuous; a strange confusion of ideas and affections arises in the minds of many; and an appearance of no small contradiction between their notions and their actions. There are many who love virtue and who detest vice, and this not from hypocrisy or affectation, who notwithstanding very frequently act ill and wickedly in particulars without the least remorse; because these particular occasions never come into view, when the passions on the side of virtue were so warmly affected by certain words heated originally by the breath of others; and for this reason, it is hard to repeat certain sets of words, though owned by themselves unoperative, without being in some degree affected; especially if a warm and affecting tone of voice accompanies them, as suppose,

Wise, valiant, generous, good, and great.

These words, by having no application, ought to be unoperative; but when words commonly sacred to great occasions are used, we are affected by them even without the occasions. When words which have been generally so applied are put together without any rational view, or in such a manner that they do not rightly agree with each other, the style is called bombast. And it requires in several cases much good sense and experience to be guarded against the force of such language; for when propriety is neglected, a greater number of these affecting words may be taken into the service and a greater variety may be indulged in combining them.

SECT. IV.—THE EFFECT OF WORDS

If words have all their possible extent of power, three effects arise in the mind of the hearer. The first is, the *sound;* the second, the *picture,* or representation of the thing signified by the sound; the third is, the *affection* of the soul produced by one or by both of the foregoing. *Compounded abstract* words, of which we have been speaking, (honour, justice, liberty, and the like,) produce the first and the last of these effects, but not the second. *Simple abstracts* are used to signify some one simple idea, without much adverting to others which may chance to attend it, as blue, green, hot, cold, and the like; these are capable of affecting all three of the purposes of words; as the *aggregate* words, man, castle, horse, &c., are in a yet higher degree. But I am of opinion, that the most general effect, even of these words, does not arise from their forming pictures of the several things they would represent in the imagination; because, on a very diligent examination of my own mind, and getting others to consider theirs, I do not find that once in twenty times any such picture is formed, and when it is, there is most commonly a particular effort of the imagination for that purpose. But the aggregate words operate, as I said of the compound-abstracts, not by presenting any image to the mind, but by having from use the same effect on being mentioned, that their original has when it is seen. Suppose we were to read a passage to this effect: "The river Danube rises in a moist and mountainous soil in the heart of Germany, where winding to and fro, it waters several principalities, until, turning into Austria, and leaving the walls of Vienna, it passes into Hungary; there with a vast flood, augmented by the Saave and the Drave, it quits Christendom, and rolling through the barbarous countries which border on Tartary, it enters by many mouths in the Black Sea." In this description many things are mentioned, as

mountains, rivers, cities, the sea, &c. But let anybody examine himself, and see whether he has had impressed on his imagination any
pictures of a river, mountain, watery soil, Germany, &c. Indeed it is
impossible, in the rapidity and quick succession of words in conversation to have ideas both of the sound of the word, and of the
thing represented: besides, some words, expressing real essences, are
so mixed with others of a general and nominal import, that it is impracticable to jump from sense to thought, from particulars to gen-
erals, from things to words, in such a manner as to answer the purposes of life; nor is it necessary that we should.

SECT. V.—EXAMPLES THAT WORDS MAY AFFECT WITHOUT RAISING IMAGES

I FIND it very hard to persuade several that their passions are
affected by words from whence they have no ideas; and yet harder
to convince them, that in the ordinary course of conversation we
are sufficiently understood without raising any images of the things
concerning which we speak. It seems to be an odd subject of dispute
with any man, whether he has ideas in his mind or not. Of this, at
first view, every man, in his own forum, ought to judge without
appeal. But, strange as it may appear, we are often at a loss to know
what ideas we have of things, or whether we have any ideas at all
upon some subjects. It even requires a good deal of attention to be
thoroughly satisfied on this head. Since I wrote these papers, I
found two very striking instances of the possibility there is that a
man may hear words without having any idea of the things which
they represent, and yet afterwards be capable of returning them to
others, combined in a new way, and with great propriety, energy
and instruction. The first instance is that of Mr. Blacklock, a poet
blind from his birth. Few men blessed with the most perfect sight
can describe visual objects with more spirit and justness than this
blind man; which cannot possibly be attributed to his having a
clearer conception of the things he describes than is common to
other persons. Mr. Spence, in an elegant preface which he has written to the works of this poet, reasons very ingeniously, and, I imagine, for the most part, very rightly, upon the cause of this extraordinary phenomenon; but I cannot altogether agree with him, that
some improprieties in language and thought, which occur in these

poems, have arisen from the blind poet's imperfect conception of visual objects, since such improprieties, and much greater, may be found in writers even of a higher class than Mr. Blacklock, and who notwithstanding possessed the faculty of seeing in its full perfection. Here is a poet doubtless as much affected by his own descriptions as any that reads them can be; and yet he is affected with this strong enthusiasm by things of which he neither has nor can possibly have any idea further than that of a bare sound: and why may not those who read his works be affected in the same manner that he was, with as little of any real ideas of the things described? The second instance is of Mr. Saunderson, professor of mathematics in the university of Cambridge. This learned man had acquired great knowledge in natural philosophy, in astronomy, and whatever sciences depend upon mathematical skill. What was the most extraordinary and the most to my purpose, he gave excellent lectures upon light and colours; and this man taught others the theory of these ideas which they had, and which he himself undoubtedly had not. But it is probable that the words red, blue, green, answered to him as well as the ideas of the colours themselves; for the ideas of greater or lesser degrees of refrangibility being applied to these words, and the blind man being instructed in what other respects they were found to agree or to disagree, it was as easy for him to reason upon the words, as if he had been fully master of the ideas. Indeed it must be owned he could make no new discoveries in the way of experiment. He did nothing but what we do every day in common discourse. When I wrote this last sentence, and used the words *every day* and *common discourse,* I had no images in my mind of any succession of time; nor of men in conference with each other; nor do I imagine that the reader will have any such ideas on reading it. Neither when I spoke of red, or blue, and green, as well as refrangibility, had I these several colours or the rays of light passing into a different medium, and there diverted from their course, painted before me in the way of images. I know very well that the mind possesses a faculty of raising such images at pleasure; but then an act of the will is necessary to this; and in ordinary conversation or reading it is very rarely that any image at all is excited in the mind. If I say, "I shall go to Italy next summer," I am well understood. Yet I believe nobody has by this painted in his imagination the exact figure of the speaker passing by land or by water, or both; sometimes on horseback, sometimes in a carriage; with all the particulars of the journey. Still less has he any idea of Italy, the country to which I propose to go; or of the greenness of the fields, the ripening of the fruits, and the warmth of the air, with the change to this from a different season, which are the ideas for which the word *summer* is substituted: but least of all has he any image from the word *next;* for this word stands for the idea of many summers, with the exclusion of all but one: and surely the man who says *next summer,* has no images of such a succession and such an exclusion.

In short, it is not only of those ideas which are commonly called abstract, and of which no image at all can be formed, but even of particular, real beings, that we converse without any idea of them excited in the imagination; as will certainly appear on a diligent examination of our minds. Indeed, so little does poetry depend for its effect on the power of raising sensible images, that I am convinced it would lose a very considerable part of its energy, if this were the necessary result of all description. Because that union of affecting words, which is the most powerful of all poetical instruments, would frequently lose its force, along with its propriety and consistency, if the sensible images were always excited. There is not perhaps in the whole Eneid a more grand and laboured passage than the description of Vulcan's cavern in Etna, and the works that are there carried on. Virgil dwells particularly on the formation of the thunder, which he describes unfinished under the hammers of the Cyclops. But what are the principles of this extraordinary composition?

> *Tres imbris torti radios, tres nubis aquosæ*
> *Addiderant; rutili tres ignis, et alitis austri:*
> *Fulgores nunc terrificos, sonitumque, metumque*
> *Miscebant operi, flammisque sequacibus iras.*

This seems to me admirably sublime; yet if we attend coolly to the kind of sensible images which a combination of ideas of this sort must form, the chimeras of madmen cannot appear more wild and absurd than such a picture. *"Three rays of twisted showers, three of watery clouds, three of fire, and three of the winged south wind; then mixed they in the work terrific lightnings, and sound, and fear, and anger, with pursuing flames."* This strange composition is formed into a gross body; it is hammered by the Cyclops, it is in part polished, and partly continues rough. The truth is, if poetry gives us a noble assemblage of words corresponding to many noble ideas which are connected by circumstances of time or place, or related to each other as cause and effect, or associated in any natural way, they may be moulded together in any form, and perfectly answer their end. The picturesque connexion is not demanded; because no real picture is formed; nor is the effect of the description at all the less upon this account. What is said of Helen by Priam and the old men of his council, is generally thought to give us the highest possible idea of that fatal beauty.

> Οὐ νέμεσις, Τρῶας καὶ ἐϋκνήμιδας Ἀχαιοὺς,
> Τοιῇ δ᾽ ἀμφὶ γυναικὶ πολὺν χρόνον ἄλγεα πάσχειν·
> Αἰνῶς δ᾽ ἀθανάτῃσι θεῇς εἰς ὦπα ἔοικεν.

> They cried, No wonder such celestial charms
> For nine long years have set the world in arms;
> What winning graces! what majestic mien!
> She moves a goddess, and she looks a queen. POPE.

Here is not one word said of the particulars of her beauty; nothing which can in the least help us to any precise idea of her person; but yet we are much more touched by this manner of mentioning her than by those long and laboured descriptions of Helen, whether handed down by tradition, or formed by fancy, which are to be met with in some authors. I am sure it affects me much more than the minute description which Spenser has given of Belphebe; though I own that there are parts in that description, as there are in all the descriptions of that excellent writer, extremely fine and poetical.

The terrible picture which Lucretius has drawn of religion, in order to display the magnanimity of his philosophical hero in opposing her, is thought to be designed with great boldness and spirit.

> *Humana ante oculos foedè cum vita jaceret,*
> *In terris, oppressa gravi sub religione,*

Quæ caput e cœli regionibus ostendebat
Horribili super aspectu mortalibus instans;
Primus Graius homo mortales tollere contra
Est oculos ausus.—

What idea do you derive from so excellent a picture? none at all, most certainly: neither has the poet said a single word which might in the least serve to mark a single limb or feature of the phantom, which he intended to represent in all the horrors imagination can conceive. In reality, poetry and rhetoric do not succeed in exact description so well as painting does; their business is, to affect rather by sympathy than imitation; to display rather the effect of things on the mind of the speaker, or of others, than to present a clear idea of the things themselves. This is their most extensive province, and that in which they succeed the best.

SECT. VI.—POETRY NOT STRICTLY AN IMITATIVE ART

HENCE we may observe that poetry, taken in its most general sense, cannot with strict propriety be called an art of imitation. It is indeed an imitation so far as it describes the manners and passions of men which their words can express; where *animi motus effert interprete lingua.* There it is strictly imitation; and all merely *dramatic* poetry is of this sort. But *descriptive* poetry operates chiefly by *substitution;* by the means of sounds, which by custom have the effect of realities. Nothing is an imitation further than as it resembles some other thing; and words undoubtedly have no sort of resemblance to the ideas, for which they stand.

SECT. VII.—HOW WORDS INFLUENCE THE PASSIONS

Now, as words affect, not by any original power, but by representation, it might be supposed, that their influence over the passions should be but light; yet it is quite otherwise; for we find by experience, that eloquence and poetry are as capable, nay indeed much more capable, of making deep and lively impressions than any other arts, and even than nature itself in very many cases. And this arises chiefly from these three causes. First, that we take an extraordinary part in the passions of others, and that we are easily affected and brought into sympathy by any tokens which are shown of them; and there are no tokens which can express all the circumstances of most passions so fully as words; so that if a person speaks upon any subject, he can not only convey the subject to you, but likewise the manner in which he is himself affected by it. Certain it is, that the influence of most things on our passions is not so much from the things themselves, as from our opinions concerning them; and these again depend very much on the opinions of other men, conveyable for the most part by words only. Secondly, there are many things of a very affecting nature, which can seldom occur in the reality, but the words that represent them often do; and thus they have an opportunity of making a deep impression and taking root in the mind, whilst the idea of the reality was transient; and to some perhaps never really occurred in any shape, to whom it is notwithstanding very affecting, as war, death, famine, &c. Besides, many ideas have never been at all presented to the senses of any men but by words, as God, angels, devils, heaven, and hell, all of which have, however, a great influence over the passions. Thirdly, by words we have it in our power to make such *combinations* as we cannot possibly do otherwise. By this power of combining, we are able, by the addition of well-chosen circumstances, to give a new life and force to the simple object. In painting we may represent any fine figure we please; but we never can give it those enlivening touches which it may receive from words. To represent an angel in a picture, you can only draw a beautiful young man winged: but what painting can furnish out anything so grand as the addition of one word, "the angel of the *Lord*"? It is true, I have here no clear idea; but these words affect the mind more than the sensible image did; which is all I contend for. A picture of Priam dragged to the altar's foot, and there murdered, if it were well executed, would undoubtedly be very moving, but there are very aggravating circumstances, which it could never represent:

Sanguine fœdantem *quos ipse saeraverat* ignes.

As a further instance, let us consider those lines of Milton, where he describes the travels of the fallen angels through their dismal habitation:

> —O'er many a dark and dreary vale
> They passed, and many a region dolorous;
> O'er many a frozen, many a fiery Alp;
> Rocks, caves, lakes, fens, bogs, dens, and shades of death,
> A universe of death.—

Here is displayed the force of union in

> Rocks, caves, lakes, dens, bogs, fens, and shades;

which yet would lose the greatest part of their effect, if they were not the

> Rocks, caves, lakes, dens, bogs, fens, and shades—
> ——of *Death*.

This idea or this affection caused by a word, which nothing but a word could annex to the others, raises a very great degree of the sublime; and this sublime is raised yet higher by what follows, a *"universe of Death."* Here are again two ideas not presentable but by language; and an union of them great and amazing beyond conception; if they may properly be called ideas which present no distinct image to the mind:—but still it will be difficult to conceive how words can move the passions which belong to real objects, without representing these objects clearly. This is difficult to us, because we do not sufficiently distinguish, in our observations upon language, between a clear expression and a strong expression. These are frequently confounded with each other, though they are in reality extremely different. The former regards the understanding, the latter belongs to the passions. The one describes a thing as it is; the latter describes it as it is felt. Now, as there is a moving tone of voice, an impassioned countenance, an agitated gesture, which affect independently of the things about which they are exerted, so there are words, and certain dispositions of words, which being peculiarly devoted to passionate subjects; and always used by those who are under the influence of any passion, touch and move us more than those which far more clearly and distinctly express the subject matter. We yield to sympathy what we refuse to description. The truth is, all verbal description, merely as naked description, though never so exact, conveys so poor and insufficient an idea of the thing described, that it could scarcely have the smallest effect, if the speaker did not call in to his aid those modes of speech that mark a strong and lively feeling in himself. Then, by the contagion of our passions, we catch a fire already kindled in another, which probably might never have been struck out by the object described. Words, by strongly conveying the passions, by those means which we have already mentioned, fully compensate for their weakness in other respects. It may be observed, that very polished languages, and such as are praised for their superior clearness and perspicuity, are generally deficient in strength. The French language has that perfection and that defect, whereas the Oriental tongues, and in general the languages of most unpolished people, have a great force and energy of expression; and this is but natural. Uncultivated people are but ordinary observers of things, and not critical in distinguishing them; but, for that reason, they admire more, and are more affected with what they see, and therefore express themselves in a warmer and more passionate manner. If the affection be well conveyed, it will work its effect without any clear idea, often without any idea at all of the thing which has originally given rise to it.

It might be expected from the fertility of the subject, that I should consider poetry, as it regards the sublime and beautiful, more at large; but it must be observed that in this light it has been often and well handled already. It was not my design to enter into the criticism of the sublime and beautiful in any art, but to attempt to lay down such principles as may tend to ascertain, to distinguish, and to form a sort of standard for them; which purposes I thought might be best effected by an inquiry into the properties of such things in nature, as raise love and astonishment in us; and by showing in what manner they operated to produce these passions. Words were only so far to be considered, as to show upon what principle they were capable of being the representatives of these natural things, and by what powers they were able to affect us often as strongly as the things they represent, and sometimes much more strongly.

REFLECTIONS

ON

THE REVOLUTION IN FRANCE

AND

ON THE PROCEEDINGS IN CERTAIN SOCIETIES
IN LONDON RELATIVE TO THAT EVENT

IN A LETTER

INTENDED TO HAVE BEEN SENT
TO A GENTLEMAN IN PARIS

1790

INTRODUCTORY NOTE

THE characteristic passion of Burke's life was his love of order. In spite of the varying relations held by him toward the different parties in England during his political career, one may easily find the key to his consistency in this central principle. When the King's party sought to increase the royal prerogative, he resisted; when the old Whigs sought to make the government of the country a means to the enrichment of their class, he resisted; and when the sympathizers with the Revolution sought, as Burke thought, to abolish government, he resisted. Liberty he claimed that he loved, but "a liberty connected with order"; and in each of the political movements just mentioned he discerned an attack on either liberty or order. He had a profound veneration for the accumulated wisdom of centuries of experience, and held that the bounds of liberty should be enlarged with great caution and very gradually. That a political system had lasted a long time was to him an argument that it must to a large extent be fit for its purpose, and that therefore it should not be rashly changed.

With such views, Burke was bound to oppose the French Revolution. The sweeping away of the traditions of ages, the erection of new forms of government built on abstract theories, were abhorrent to him; and he threw himself with vehemence into opposition. Much that was hopeful in the Revolution he failed to see; and he could not in his passion discriminate carefully among men and motives. But his treatment of the situation in these "Reflections," written before the Terror had begun to alienate sympathy, shows great insight and prophetic wisdom. This book led the reaction in England and made its author a European figure. In this country to-day, with our traditional sympathy with the great upheaval, it is in the highest degree valuable to see these momentous events through the eyes of a great contemporary conservative.

REFLECTIONS

ON

THE REVOLUTION IN FRANCE

IN A LETTER

INTENDED TO HAVE BEEN SENT
TO A GENTLEMAN IN PARIS

[1790]

IT MAY not be unnecessary to inform the reader, that the following Reflections had their origin in a correspondence between
the Author and a very young gentleman at Paris, who did him
the honour of desiring his opinion upon the important transactions,
which then, and ever since, have so much occupied the attention of
all men. An answer was written some time in the month of October,
1789; but it was kept back upon prudential considerations. That
letter is alluded to in the beginning of the following sheets. It has
been since forwarded to the person to whom it was addressed. The
reasons for the delay in sending it were assigned in a short letter
to the same gentleman. This produced on his part a new and pressing application for the Author's sentiments.

The Author began a second and more full discussion on the subject. This he had some thoughts of publishing early in the last
spring; but, the matter gaining upon him, he found that what he
had undertaken not only far exceeded the measure of a letter, but
that its importance required rather a more detailed consideration
than at that time he had any leisure to bestow upon it. However,
having thrown down his first thoughts in the form of a letter,
and, indeed, when he sat down to write, having intended it for a
private letter, he found it difficult to change the form of address,
when his sentiments had grown into a greater extent, and had re-

ceived another direction. A different plan, he is sensible, might be more favourable to a commodious division and distribution of his matter.

_____

DEAR SIR,

You are pleased to call again, and with some earnestness, for my thoughts on the late proceedings in France. I will not give you reason to imagine that I think my sentiments of such value as to wish myself to be solicited about them. They are of too little consequence to be very anxiously either communicated or withheld. It was from attention to you, and to you only, that I hesitated at the time when you first desired to receive them. In the first letter I had the honour to write to you, and which at length I send, I wrote neither for, nor from, any description of men; nor shall I in this. My errors, if any, are my own. My reputation alone is to answer for them.

You see, Sir, by the long letter I have transmitted to you, that though I do most heartily wish that France may be animated by a spirit of rational liberty, and that I think you bound, in all honest policy, to provide a permanent body in which that spirit may reside, and an effectual organ by which it may act, it is my misfortune to entertain great doubts concerning several material points in your late transactions.

You imagined, when you wrote last, that I might possibly be reckoned among the approvers of certain proceedings in France, from the solemn public seal of sanction they have received from two clubs of gentlemen in London, called the Constitutional Society, and the Revolution Society.

I certainly have the honour to belong to more clubs than one, in which the constitution of this kingdom, and the principles of the glorious Revolution, are held in high reverence and I reckon myself among the most forward in my zeal for maintaining that constitution and those principles in their utmost purity and vigour. It is because I do so that I think it necessary for me that there should be no mistake. Those who cultivate the memory of our Revolution, and those who are attached to the constitution of this kingdom, will take good care how they are involved with persons, who under the pretext of zeal towards the Revolution and constitution too frequently wander from their true principles; and are ready on every occasion to depart from the firm but cautious and deliberate spirit which produced the one, and which presides in the other. Before I proceed to answer the more material particulars in your letter, I shall beg leave to give you such information as I have been able to obtain of the two clubs which have thought proper, as bodies, to interfere in the concerns of France; first assuring you, that I am not, and that I have never been, a member of either of those societies.

The first, calling itself the Constitutional Society, or Society for Constitutional Information, or by some such title, is, I believe, of seven or eight years standing. The institution of this society appears to be of a charitable, and so far of a laudable nature: it was intended for the circulation, at the expense of the members, of many books, which few others would be at the expense of buying; and which might lie on the hands of the booksellers, to the great loss of an useful body of men. Whether the books, so charitably circulated, were ever as charitably read, is more than I know. Possibly several of them have been exported to France; and, like goods not in request here, may with you have found a market. I have heard much talk of the lights to be drawn from books that are sent from hence. What improvements they have had in their passage (as it is said some liquors are meliorated by crossing the sea) I cannot tell: but I never heard a man of common judgment, or the least degree of information, speak a word in praise of the greater part of the publications circulated by that society; nor have their proceedings been accounted, except by some of themselves, as of any serious consequence.

Your National Assembly seems to entertain much the same opinion that I do of this poor charitable club. As a nation, you reserved the whole stock of your eloquent acknowledgments for the Revolution Society; when their fellows in the Constitutional were, in equity, entitled to some share. Since you have selected the Revolution Society as the great object of your national thanks and praises, you will think me excusable in making its late conduct the subject of my observations. The National Assembly of France has given importance to these gentlemen by adopting them: and they return the favour, by acting as a committee in England for extending the principles of the National Assembly. Henceforward we must consider them as a kind of privileged persons; as no inconsiderable members in the diplomatic body. This is one among the revolutions which have given splendour to obscurity, and distinction to undiscerned merit. Until very lately I do not recollect to have heard of this club. I am quite sure that it never occupied a moment of my thoughts; nor, I believe, those of any person out of their own set. I find, upon inquiry, that on the anniversary of the Revolution in 1688, a club of dissenters, but of what denomination I know not, have long had the custom of hearing a sermon in one of their churches; and that afterwards they spent the day cheerfully, as other clubs do, at the tavern. But I never heard that any public measure, or political system, much less that the merits of the constitution of any foreign nation, had been the subject of a formal proceeding at their festivals; until, to my inexpressible surprise, I found them in a sort of public capacity, by a congratulatory address, giving an authoritative sanction to the proceedings of the National Assembly in France.

In the ancient principles and conduct of the club, so far at least as they were declared, I see nothing to which I could take exception. I think it very probable, that for some purpose, new members may have entered among them; and that some truly Christian politicians, who love to dispense benefits, but are careful to conceal the hand which distributes the dole, may have made them the instruments of their pious designs. Whatever I may have reason to suspect concerning private management, I shall speak of nothing as of a certainty but what is public.

For one, I should be sorry to be thought, directly or indirectly, concerned in their proceedings. I certainly take my full share, along with the rest of the world, in my individual and private capacity, in speculating on what has been done, or is doing, on the public stage, in any place ancient or modern; in the republic of Rome, or the republic of Paris; but having no general apostolical mission, being a citizen of a particular state, and being bound up, in a considerable degree, by its public will, I should think it at least improper and irregular for me to open a formal public correspondence with the actual government of a foreign nation, without the express authority of the government under which I live.

I should be still more unwilling to enter into that correspondence under anything like an equivocal description, which to many, unacquainted with our usages, might make the address, in which I joined, appear as the act of persons in some sort of corporate capacity, acknowledged by the laws of this kingdom, and authorized to speak the sense of some part of it. On account of the ambiguity and uncertainty of unauthorized general descriptions, and of the deceit which may be practised under them, and not from mere formality, the House of Commons would reject the most sneaking petition for the most trifling object, under that mode of signature to which you have thrown open the folding doors of your presence chamber, and have ushered into your National Assembly with as much ceremony and parade, and with as great a bustle of applause, as if you had been visited by the whole representative majesty of the whole English nation. If what this society has thought proper to send forth had been a piece of argument, it would have signified little whose argument it was. It would be neither the more nor the less convincing on account of the party it came from. But this is only a vote and resolution. It stands solely on authority; and in this case it is the mere authority of individuals, few of whom appear. Their signatures ought, in my opinion, to have been annexed to their instrument. The world would then have the means of knowing how many they are; who they are; and of what value their opinions may be, from their personal abilities, from their knowledge, their experience, or their lead and authority in this state. To me, who am but a plain man, the proceeding looks a little too refined, and too ingenious; it has too much the air of a political stratagem, adopted for the sake of giving, under a high-sounding name, an importance to the public declarations of this club, which, when the matter came to be closely inspected, they did not altogether so well deserve. It is a policy that has very much the complexion of a fraud.

I flatter myself that I love a manly, moral, regulated liberty as well as any gentleman of that society, be he who he will; and perhaps I have given as good proofs of my attachment to that cause, in the whole course of my public conduct. I think I envy liberty as little as they do, to any other nation. But I cannot stand forward, and give praise or blame to anything which relates to human actions, and human concerns, on a simple view of the object, as it stands stripped of every relation, in all the nakedness and solitude of metaphysical abstraction. Circumstances (which with some gentlemen pass for nothing) give in reality to every political principle its distinguishing colour and discriminating effect. The circumstances are what render every civil and political scheme beneficial or noxious to mankind. Abstractedly speaking, government, as well as liberty, is good; yet could I, in common sense, ten years ago, have felicitated France on her enjoyment of a government (for she then had a government) without inquiry what the nature of that government was, or how it was administered? Can I now congratulate the same nation upon its freedom? Is it because liberty in the abstract may be classed amongst the blessings of mankind, that I am seriously to felicitate a mad-man, who has escaped from the protecting restraint and wholesome darkness of his cell, on his restoration to the enjoyment of light and liberty? Am I to congratulate a highwayman and murderer, who has broke prison, upon the recovery of his natural rights? This would be to act over again the scene of the criminals condemned to the galleys, and their heroic deliverer, the metaphysic knight of the sorrowful countenance.

When I see the spirit of liberty in action, I see a strong principle at work; and this, for a while, is all I can possibly know of it. The wild *gas,* the fixed air, is plainly broke loose: but we ought to suspend our judgment until the first effervescence is a little subsided, till the liquor is cleared, and until we see something deeper than the agitation of a troubled and frothy surface. I must be tolerably sure, before I venture publicly to congratulate men upon a blessing, that they have really received one. Flattery corrupts both the receiver and the giver; and adulation is not of more service to the people than to kings. I should therefore suspend my congratulations on the new liberty of France, until I was informed how it had been combined with government; with public force; with the discipline and obedience of armies; with the collection of an effective and well-distributed revenue; with morality and religion; with the solidity of property; with peace and order; with civil and social manners. All these (in their way) are good things too; and, without them, liberty is not a benefit whilst it lasts, and is not likely to continue long. The effect of liberty to individuals is that they may do what they please: we ought to see what it will please them to do, before we risk congratulations, which may be soon turned into complaints. Prudence would dictate this in the case of separate, insulated, private men; but liberty, when men act in bodies, is *power*. Considerate people, before they declare themselves, will observe the use which is made of *power;* and particularly of so trying a thing as *new* power in *new* persons, of whose principles, tempers, and dispositions they have little or no experience, and in situations, where those who appear the most stirring in the scene may possibly not be the real movers.

All these considerations however were below the transcendental dignity of the Revolution Society. Whilst I continued in the country, from whence I had the honour of writing to you, I had but an imperfect idea of their transactions. On my coming to town, I sent for an account of their proceedings, which had been published by their authority, containing a sermon of Dr. Price, with the Duke de Rochefaucault's and the Archbishop of Aix's letter, and several other documents annexed. The whole of that publication, with the manifest design of connecting the affairs of France with those of England, by drawing us into an imitation of the conduct of the National Assembly, gave me a considerable degree of uneasiness. The effect of that conduct upon the power, credit, prosperity, and tranquillity of France, became every day more evident. The form of constitution to be settled, for its future polity, became more clear. We are now in a condition to discern, with tolerable exactness, the true nature of the object held up to our imitation. If the prudence of reserve and decorum dictates silence in some circumstances, in others prudence of a higher order may justify us in speaking our thoughts. The beginnings of confusion with us in England are at present feeble enough; but, with you, we have seen an infancy, still more feeble, growing by moments into a strength to heap mountains upon mountains, and to wage war with heaven itself. Whenever our neighbour's house is on fire, it cannot be amiss for the engines to play a little on our own. Better to be despised for too anxious apprehensions, than ruined by too confident a security.

Solicitous chiefly for the peace of my own country, but by no means unconcerned for yours, I wish to communicate more largely what was at first intended only for your private satisfaction. I shall still keep your affairs in my eye, and continue to address myself to you. Indulging myself in the freedom of epistolary intercourse, I beg leave to throw out my thoughts, and express my feelings, just as they arise in my mind, with very little attention to formal method. I set out with the proceedings of the Revolution Society; but I shall not confine myself to them. Is it possible I should? It appears to me as if I were in a great crisis, not of the affairs of France alone, but of all Europe, perhaps of more than Europe. All circumstances taken together, the French Revolution is the most astonishing that has hitherto happened in the world. The most wonderful things are brought about in many instances by means the most absurd and ridiculous; in the most ridiculous modes; and, apparently, by the most contemptible instruments. Everything seems out of nature in this strange chaos of levity and ferocity, and of all sorts of crimes jumbled together with all sorts of follies. In viewing this monstrous tragi-comic scene, the most opposite passions necessarily succeed, and sometimes mix with each other in the mind; alternate contempt and indignation; alternate laughter and tears; alternate scorn and horror.

It cannot, however, be denied, that to some this strange scene appeared in quite another point of view. Into them it inspired no other sentiments than those of exultation and rapture. They saw nothing in what has been done in France, but a firm and temperate exertion of freedom; so consistent, on the whole, with morals and with piety as to make it deserving not only of the secular applause of dashing Machiavelian politicians, but to render it a fit theme for all the devout effusions of sacred eloquence.

On the forenoon of the 4th of November last, Doctor Richard Price, a non-conforming minister of eminence, preached at the dissenting meeting-house of the Old Jewry, to his club or society, a very extraordinary miscellaneous sermon, in which there are some good moral and religious sentiments, and not ill expressed, mixed up in a sort of porridge of various political opinions and reflections; but the Revolution in France is the grand ingredient in the cauldron. I consider the address transmitted by the Revolution Society to the National Assembly, through Earl Stanhope, as originating in the principles of the sermon, and as a corollary from them. It was moved by the preacher of that discourse. It was passed by those who came reeking from the effect of the sermon, without any censure or qualification, expressed or implied. If, however, any of the gentlemen concerned shall wish to separate the sermon from the resolution, they know how to acknowledge the one, and to disavow the other. They may do it: I cannot.

For my part, I looked on that sermon as the public declaration of a man much connected with literary caballers, and intriguing philosophers; with political theologians, and theological politicians, both at home and abroad. I know they set him up as a sort of oracle; because, with the best intentions in the world, he naturally *philippizes,* and chants his prophetic song in exact unison with their designs.

That sermon is in a strain which I believe has not been heard in this kingdom, in any of the pulpits which are tolerated or encouraged in it, since the year 1648; when a predecessor of Dr. Price, the Rev. Hugh Peters, made the vault of the king's own chapel at St. James's ring with the honour and privilege of the saints, who, with the "high praises of God in their mouths, and a *two*-edged sword in their hands, were to execute judgment on the heathen and punishments upon the *people;* to bind their *kings* with chains, and their *nobles* with fetters of iron."[1] Few harangues from the pulpit, except in the days of your league in France, or in the days of our solemn league and covenant in England, have ever breathed less of the spirit of moderation than this lecture in the Old Jewry. Supposing, however, that something like moderation were visible in this political sermon; yet politics and the pulpit are terms that have little agreement. No sound ought to be heard in the church but the healing voice of Christian charity. The cause of civil liberty and civil government gains as little as that of religion by this confusion of duties. Those who quit their proper character, to assume

[1] Psalm cxlix.

what does not belong to them, are, for the greater part, ignorant both of the character they leave, and of the character they assume. Wholly unacquainted with the world in which they are so fond of meddling, and inexperienced in all its affairs, on which they pronounce with so much confidence, they have nothing of politics but the passions they excite. Surely the church is a place where one day's truce ought to be allowed to the dissensions and animosities of mankind.

This pulpit style, revived after so long a discontinuance, had to me the air of novelty, and of a novelty not wholly without danger. I do not charge this danger equally to every part of the discourse. The hint given to a noble and reverend lay-divine, who is supposed high in office in one of our universities,[2] and other lay-divines "of *rank* and literature," may be proper and seasonable, though somewhat new. If the noble *Seekers* should find nothing to satisfy their pious fancies in the old staple of the national church, or in all the rich variety to be found in the well-assorted warehouses of the dissenting congregations, Dr. Price advises them to improve upon nonconformity; and to set up, each of them, a separate meeting-house upon his own particular principles.[3] It is somewhat remarkable that this reverend divine should be so earnest for setting up new churches, and so perfectly indifferent concerning the doctrine which may be taught in them. His zeal is of a curious character. It is not for the propagation of his own opinions, but of any opinions. It is not for the diffusion of truth, but for the spreading of contradiction. Let the noble teachers but dissent, it is no matter from whom or from what. This great point once secured, it is taken for granted their religion will be rational and manly. I doubt whether religion would reap all the benefits which the calculating divine computes from this "great company of great preachers." It would certainly be a valuable addition of nondescripts to the ample collection of known classes, genera and species, which at present beautify the *hortus siccus* of dissent. A sermon from a noble duke,

[2] Discourse on the Love of our Country, Nov. 4th, 1789, by Dr. Richard Price, 3rd edition, p. 17 and 18.

[3] "Those who dislike that mode of worship which is prescribed by public authority, ought, if they can find *no* worship *out* of the church which they approve, *to set up a separate worship for themselves;* and by doing this, and giving an example of a rational and manly worship, men of *weight* from their *rank* and literature may do the greatest service to society and the world."—P. 18, Dr. Price's Sermon.

or a noble marquis, or a noble earl, or baron bold, would certainly increase and diversify the amusements of this town, which begins to grow satiated with the uniform round of its vapid dissipations. I should only stipulate that these new *Mess-Johns* in robes and coronets should keep some sort of bounds in the democratic and levelling principles which are expected from their titled pulpits. The new evangelists will, I dare say, disappoint the hopes that are conceived of them. They will not become, literally as well as figuratively, polemic divines, nor be disposed so to drill their congregations, that they may, as in former blessed times, preach their doctrines to regiments of dragoons and corps of infantry and artillery. Such arrangements, however favourable to the cause of compulsory freedom, civil and religious, may not be equally conducive to the national tranquillity. These few restrictions I hope are no great stretches of intolerance, no very violent exertions of despotism.

But I may say of our preacher, *"utinam nugis tota illa dedisset tempora sævitiæ."*—All things in this his fulminating bull are not of so innoxious a tendency. His doctrines affect our constitution in its vital parts. He tells the Revolution Society in this political sermon, that his Majesty "is almost the *only* lawful king in the world, because the *only* one who owes his crown to the *choice of his people."* As to the kings of *the world,* all of whom (except one) this archpontiff of the *rights of men,* with all the plenitude, and with more than the boldness, of the papal deposing power in its meridian fervour of the twelfth century, puts into one sweeping clause of ban and anathema, and proclaims usurpers by circles of longitude and latitude, over the whole globe, it behoves them to consider how they admit into their territories these apostolic missionaries, who are to tell their subjects they are not lawful kings. That is their concern. It is ours, as a domestic interest of some moment, seriously to consider the solidity of the *only* principle upon which these gentlemen acknowledge a king of Great Britain to be entitled to their allegiance.

This doctrine, as applied to the prince now on the British throne, either is nonsense, and therefore neither true nor false, or it affirms a most unfounded, dangerous, illegal, and unconstitutional position. According to this spiritual doctor of politics, if his Majesty does not owe his crown to the choice of his people, he is no *lawful king*. Now nothing can be more untrue than that the crown of this kingdom is so held by his Majesty. Therefore if you follow their rule, the king of Great Britain, who most certainly does not owe his high office to any form of popular election, is in no respect better than the rest of the gang of usurpers, who reign, or rather rob, all over the face of this our miserable world, without any sort of right or title to the allegiance of their people. The policy of this general doctrine, so qualified, is evident enough. The propagators of this political gospel are in hopes that their abstract principle (their principle that a popular choice is necessary to the legal existence of the sovereign magistracy) would be overlooked, whilst the king of Great Britain was not affected by it. In the mean time the ears of their congregations would be gradually habituated to it, as if it were a first principle admitted without dispute. For the present it would only operate as a theory, pickled in the preserving juices of pulpit eloquence, and laid by for future use. *Condo et compono quæ mox depromere possim*. By this policy, whilst our government is soothed with a reservation in its favour, to which it has no claim, the security, which it has in common with all governments, so far as opinion is security, is taken away.

Thus these politicians proceed, whilst little notice is taken of their doctrines; but when they come to be examined upon the plain meaning of their words, and the direct tendency of their doctrines, then equivocations and slippery constructions come into play. When they say the king owes his crown to the choice of his people, and is therefore the only lawful sovereign in the world, they will perhaps tell us they mean to say no more than that some of the king's predecessors have been called to the throne by some sort of choice; and therefore he owes his crown to the choice of his people. Thus, by a miserable subterfuge, they hope to render their proposition safe, by rendering it nugatory. They are welcome to the asylum they seek for their offence, since they take refuge in their folly. For, if you admit this interpretation, how does their idea of election differ from our idea of inheritance?

And how does the settlement of the crown in the Brunswick line derived from James the First come to legalize our monarchy, rather than that of any of the neighbouring countries? At some time or other, to be sure, all the beginners of dynasties were chosen by those who called them to govern. There is ground enough for the opinion that all the kingdoms of Europe were, at a remote period, elective, with more or fewer limitations in the objects of choice. But whatever kings might have been here, or elsewhere, a thousand years ago, or in whatever manner the ruling dynasties of England or France may have begun, the king of Great Britain is, at this day, king by a fixed rule of succession, according to the laws of his country; and whilst the legal conditions of the compact of sovereignty are performed by him, (as they are performed,) he holds his crown in contempt of the choice of the Revolution Society, who have not a single vote for a king amongst them, either individually or collectively; though I make no doubt they would soon erect themselves into an electoral college, if things were ripe to give effect to their claim. His Majesty's heirs and successors, each in his time and order, will come to the crown with the same contempt of their choice with which his Majesty has succeeded to that he wears.

Whatever may be the success of evasion in explaining away the gross error of *fact*, which supposes that his Majesty (though he holds it in concurrence with the wishes) owes his crown to the choice of his people, yet nothing can evade their full explicit declaration concerning the principle of a right in the people to choose; which right is directly maintained, and tenaciously adhered to. All the oblique insinuations concerning election bottom in this proposition, and are referable to it. Lest the foundation of the king's exclusive legal title should pass for a mere rant of adulatory freedom, the political divine proceeds dogmatically to assert,[4] that, by the principles of the Revolution, the people of England have acquired three fundamental rights, all which, with him, compose one system, and lie together in one short sentence; namely, that we have acquired a right

1. "To choose our own governors."
2. "To cashier them for misconduct."
3. "To frame a government for ourselves."

This new, and hitherto unheard-of, bill of rights, though made in

[4] P. 34. Discourse on the Love of our Country, by Dr. Price.

the name of the whole people, belongs to those gentlemen and their faction only. The body of the people of England have no share in it. They utterly disclaim it. They will resist the practical assertion of it with their lives and fortunes. They are bound to do so by the laws of their country, made at the time of that very Revolution which is appealed to in favour of the fictitious rights claimed by the Society which abuses its name.

These gentlemen of the Old Jewry, in all their reasonings on the Revolution of 1688, have a Revolution which happened in England about forty years before, and the late French Revolution, so much before their eyes, and in their hearts, that they are constantly confounding all the three together. It is necessary that we should separate what they confound. We must recall their erring fancies to the *acts* of the Revolution which we revere, for the discovery of its true *principles*. If the *principles* of the Revolution of 1688 are anywhere to be found, it is in the statute called the *Declaration of Right*. In that most wise, sober, and considerate declaration, drawn up by great lawyers and great statesmen, and not by warm and inexperienced enthusiasts, not one word is said, nor one suggestion made, of a general right "to choose our own *governors;* to cashier them for misconduct; and to *form* a government for *ourselves."*

This Declaration of Right (the act of the 1st of William and Mary, sess. 2, ch. 2) is the corner-stone of our constitution, as reinforced, explained, improved, and in its fundamental principles for ever settled. It is called "An Act for declaring the rights and liberties of the subject, and for *settling* the *succession* of the crown." You will observe, that these rights and this succession are declared in one body, and bound indissolubly together.

A few years after this period, a second opportunity offered for asserting a right of election to the crown. On the prospect of a total failure of issue from King William, and from the Princess, afterwards Queen Anne, the consideration of the settlement of the crown, and of a further security for the liberties of the people, again came before the legislature. Did they this second time make any provision for legalizing the crown on the spurious revolution principles of the Old Jewry? No. They followed the principles which prevailed in the Declaration of Right; indicating with more precision the persons who were to inherit in the Protestant line. This act also incorporated, by the same policy, our liberties, and an hereditary succession in the same act. Instead of a right to choose our own governors, they declared that the *succession* in that line (the Protestant line drawn from James the First) was absolutely necessary "for the peace, quiet, and security of the realm," and that it was equally urgent on them "to maintain a *certainty in the succession* thereof, to which the subjects may safely have recourse for their protection." Both these acts, in which are heard the unerring, unambiguous oracles of revolution policy, instead of countenancing the delusive, gipsy predictions of a "right to choose our governors," prove to a demonstration how totally adverse the wisdom of the nation was from turning a case of necessity into a rule of law.

Unquestionably there was at the Revolution, in the person of King William, a small and a temporary deviation from the strict order of a regular hereditary succession; but it is against all genuine principles of jurisprudence to draw a principle from a law made in a special case, and regarding an individual person. *Privilegium non transit in exemplum.* If ever there was a time favourable for establishing the principle, that a king of popular choice was the only legal king, without all doubt it was at the Revolution. Its not being done at that time is a proof that the nation was of opinion it ought not to be done at any time. There is no person so completely ignorant of our history as not to know, that the majority in parliament of both parties were so little disposed to anything resembling that principle, that at first they were determined to place the vacant crown, not on the head of the Prince of Orange, but on that of his wife Mary, daughter of King James, the eldest born of the issue of that king, which they acknowledged as undoubtedly his. It would be to repeat a very trite story, to recall to your memory all those circumstances which demonstrated that their accepting King William was not properly a *choice;* but to all those who did not wish, in effect, to recall King James, or to deluge their country in blood, and again to bring their religion, laws, and liberties into the peril they had just escaped, it was an act of *necessity,* in the strictest moral sense in which necessity can be taken.

In the very act, in which for a time, and in a single case, parliament departed from the strict order of inheritance, in favour of a prince, who, though not next, was however very near, in the line of succession, it is curious to observe how Lord Somers, who drew the bill called the Declaration of Right, has comported himself on that delicate occasion. It is curious to observe with what address this temporary solution of continuity is kept from the eye; whilst all that could be found in this act of necessity to countenance the idea of an hereditary succession is brought forward, and fostered, and made the most of, by this great man, and by the legislature who followed him. Quitting the dry, imperative style of an act of parliament, he makes the Lords and Commons fall to a pious, legislative ejaculation, and declare, that they consider it "as a marvellous providence, and merciful goodness of God to this nation, to preserve their said Majesties' *royal* persons, most happily to reign over us *on the throne of their ancestors,* for which, from the bottom of their hearts, they return their humblest thanks and praises."—The legislature plainly had in view the act of recognition of the first of Queen Elizabeth, chap. 3rd, and of that of James the First, chap. 1st, both acts strongly declaratory of the inheritable nature of the crown, and in many parts they follow, with a nearly literal precision, the words and even the form of thanksgiving which is found in these old declaratory statutes.

The two Houses, in the act of King William, did not thank God that they had found a fair opportunity to assert a right to choose their own governors, much less to make an election the *only lawful* title to the crown. Their having been in a condition to avoid the very appearance of it, as much as possible, was by them considered as a providential escape. They threw a politic, well-wrought veil over every circumstance tending to weaken the rights, which in the meliorated order of succession they meant to perpetuate; or which might furnish a precedent for any future departure from what they had then settled for ever. Accordingly, that they might not relax the nerves of their monarchy, and that they might preserve a close conformity to the practice of their ancestors, as it appeared in the declaratory statutes of Queen Mary[5] and Queen Elizabeth, in the

---

[5] 1st Mary, sess. 3. ch. 1.

next clause they vest, by recognition, in their Majesties, *all* the legal prerogatives of the crown, declaring, "that in them they are most *fully,* rightfully, and *entirely* invested, incorporated, united, and annexed." In the clause which follows, for preventing questions, by reason of any pretended titles to the crown, they declare, (observing also in this the traditionary language, along with the traditionary policy of the nation, and repeating as from a rubric the language of the preceding acts of Elizabeth and James,) that on the preserving "a *certainty* in the SUCCESSION thereof, the unity, peace, and tranquillity of this nation doth, under God, wholly depend."

They knew that a doubtful title of succession would but too much resemble an election; and that an election would be utterly destructive of the "unity, peace, and tranquillity of this nation," which they thought to be considerations of some moment. To provide for these objects, and therefore to exclude for ever the Old Jewry doctrine of "a right to choose our own governors," they follow with a clause containing a most solemn pledge, taken from the preceding act of Queen Elizabeth, as solemn a pledge as ever was or can be given in favour of an hereditary succession, and as solemn a renunciation as could be made of the principles by this Society imputed to them. "The Lords spiritual and temporal, and Commons, do, in the name of all the people aforesaid, most humbly and faithfully submit *themselves, their heirs and posterities for ever;* and do faithfully promise that they will stand to maintain, and defend their said Majesties, and also the *limitation of the crown,* herein specified and contained, to the utmost of their powers," &c. &c.

So far is it from being true, that we acquired a right by the Revolution to elect our kings, that if we had possessed it before, the English nation did at that time most solemnly renounce and abdicate it, for themselves, and for all their posterity for ever. These gentlemen may value themselves as much as they please on their Whig principles; but I never desire to be thought a better Whig than Lord Somers; or to understand the principles of the Revolution better than those by whom it was brought about; or to read in the Declaration of Right any mysteries unknown to those whose penetrating style has engraved in our ordinances, and in our hearts, the words and spirit of that immortal law.

It is true, that, aided with the powers derived from force and opportunity, the nation was at that time, in some sense, free to take what course it pleased for filling the throne; but only free to do so upon the same grounds on which they might have wholly abolished their monarchy, and every other part of their constitution. However, they did not think such bold changes within their commission. It is indeed difficult, perhaps impossible, to give limits to the mere *abstract* competence of the supreme power, such as was exercised by parliament at that time; but the limits of a *moral* competence, subjecting, even in powers more indisputably sovereign, occasional will to permanent reason, and to the steady maxims of faith, justice, and fixed fundamental policy, are perfectly intelligible, and perfectly binding upon those who exercise any authority, under any name, or under any title, in the state. The House of Lords, for instance, is not morally competent to dissolve the House of Commons; no, nor even to dissolve itself, nor to abdicate, if it would, its portion in the legislature of the kingdom. Though a king may abdicate for his own person, he cannot abdicate for the monarchy. By as strong, or by a stronger reason, the House of Commons cannot renounce its share of authority. The engagement and pact of society, which generally goes by the name of the constitution, forbids such invasion and such surrender. The constituent parts of a state are obliged to hold their public faith with each other, and with all those who derive any serious interest under their engagements, as much as the whole state is bound to keep its faith with separate communities. Otherwise competence and power would soon be confounded, and no law be left but the will of a prevailing force. On this principle the succession of the crown has always been what it now is, an hereditary succession by law: in the old line it was a succession by the common law; in the new by the statute law, operating on the principles of the common law, not changing the substance, but regulating the mode, and describing the persons. Both these descriptions of law are of the same force, and are derived from an equal authority, emanating from the common agreement and original compact of the state, *communi sponsione reipublicæ,* and as such are equally binding on king and people too, as long as the terms are observed, and they continue the same body politic.

It is far from impossible to reconcile, if we do not suffer ourselves to be entangled in the mazes of metaphysic sophistry, the use both of a fixed rule and an occasional deviation; the sacredness of an hereditary principle of succession in our government, with a power of change in its application in cases of extreme emergency. Even in that extremity, (if we take the measure of our rights by our exercise of them at the Revolution,) the change is to be confined to the peccant part only; to the part which produced the necessary deviation; and even then it is to be effected without a decomposition of the whole civil and political mass, for the purpose of originating a new civil order out of the first elements of society.

A state without the means of some change is without the means of its conservation. Without such means it might even risk the loss of that part of the constitution which it wished the most religiously to preserve. The two principles of conservation and correction operated strongly at the two critical periods of the Restoration and Revolution, when England found itself without a king. At both those periods the nation had lost the bond of union in their ancient edifice; they did not, however, dissolve the whole fabric. On the contrary, in both cases they regenerated the deficient part of the old constitution through the parts which were not impaired. They kept these old parts exactly as they were, that the part recovered might be suited to them. They acted by the ancient organized states in the shape of their old organization, and not by the organic *moleculæ* of a disbanded people. At no time, perhaps, did the sovereign legislature manifest a more tender regard to that fundamental principle of British constitutional policy, than at the time of the Revolution, when it deviated from the direct line of hereditary succession. The crown was carried somewhat out of the line in which it had before moved; but the new line was derived from the same stock. It was still a line of hereditary descent; still an hereditary descent in the same blood, though an hereditary descent qualified with Protestantism. When the legislature altered the direction, but kept the principle, they showed that they held it inviolable.

On this principle, the law of inheritance had admitted some amendment in the old time, and long before the era of the Revolution. Some time after the conquest, great questions arose upon the legal principles of hereditary descent. It became a matter of doubt, whether the heir *per capita* or the heir *per stirpes* was to succeed; but whether the heir *per capita* gave way when the heirdom *per stirpes* took place, or the Catholic heir when the Protestant was preferred, the inheritable principle survived with a sort of immortality through all transmigrations—*multosque per annos stat fortuna domus, et avi numerantur avorum*. This is the spirit of our constitution, not only in its settled course, but in all its revolutions. Whoever came in, or, however he came in, whether he obtained the crown by law, or by force, the hereditary succession was either continued or adopted. The gentlemen of the Society for Revolutions see nothing in that of 1688 but the deviation from the constitution; and they take the deviation from the principle for the principle. They have little regard to the obvious consequences of their doctrine, though they must see, that it leaves positive authority in very few of the positive institutions of this country. When such an unwarrantable maxim is once established, that no throne is lawful but the elective, no one act of the princes who preceded this era of fictitious election can be valid. Do these theorists mean to imitate some of their predecessors, who dragged the bodies of our ancient sovereigns out of the quiet of their tombs? Do they mean to attaint and disable backwards all the kings that have reigned before the Revolution, and consequently to stain the throne of England with the blot of a continual usurpation? Do they mean to invalidate, annul, or to call into question, together with the titles of the whole line of our kings, that great body of our statute law which passed under those whom they treat as usurpers? to annul laws of inestimable value to our liberties—of as great value at least as any which have passed at or since the period of the Revolution? If kings, who did not owe their crown to the choice of their people, had no title to make laws, what will become of the statute *de tallagio non concedendo?*—of the *petition of right?*—of the act of *habeas corpus?* Do these new doctors of the rights of men presume to assert, that King James the Second, who came to the crown as next of blood, according to the rules of a then unqualified succession, was not to all intents and purposes a lawful king of England, before he had done any of those acts which were justly construed into an abdication of his crown? If he was not, much trouble in parliament might have been saved at the period these gentlemen commemorate. But King James was a bad king with a good title, and not an usurper. The princes who succeeded according to the act of parliament which settled the crown on the Electress Sophia and on her descendants, being Protestants, came in as much by a title of inheritance as King James did. He came in according to the law, as it stood at his accession to the crown; and the princes of the House of Brunswick came to the inheritance of the crown, not by election, but by the law as it stood at their several accessions of Protestant descent and inheritance, as I hope I have shown sufficiently.

The law, by which this royal family is specifically destined to the succession, is the act of the 12th and 13th of King William. The terms of this act bind "us and our *heirs,* and our *posterity,* to them, their *heirs,* and their *posterity,*" being Protestants, to the end of time, in the same words as the Declaration of Right had bound us to the heirs of King William and Queen Mary. It therefore secures both an hereditary crown and an hereditary allegiance. On what ground, except the constitutional policy of forming an establishment to secure that kind of succession which is to preclude a choice of the people for ever, could the legislature have fastidiously rejected the fair and abundant choice which our country presented to them, and searched in strange lands for a foreign princess, from whose womb the line of our future rulers were to derive their title to govern millions of men through a series of ages?

The Princess Sophia was named in the act of settlement of the 12th and 13th of King William, for a *stock* and root of *inheritance* to our kings, and not for her merits as a temporary administratrix of a power, which she might not, and in fact did not, herself ever exercise. She was adopted for one reason, and for one only, because, says the act, "the most excellent Princess Sophia, Electress and Duchess Dowager of Hanover, is *daughter* of the most excellent Princess Elizabeth, late Queen of Bohemia, *daughter* of our late *sovereign lord* King James the First, of happy memory, and is hereby declared to be the next in *succession* in the Protestant line," &c., &c.; "and the crown shall continue to the *heirs* of her body, being Protestants." This limitation was made by parliament, that through the

Princess Sophia an inheritable line not only was to be continued in future, but (what they thought very material) that through her it was to be connected with the old stock of inheritance in King James the First; in order that the monarchy might preserve an unbroken unity through all ages, and might be preserved (with safety to our religion) in the old approved mode by descent, in which, if our liberties had been once endangered, they had often, through all storms and struggles of prerogative and privilege, been preserved. They did well. No experience has taught us, that in any other course or method than that of an *hereditary crown* our liberties can be regularly perpetuated and preserved sacred as our *hereditary right*. An irregular, convulsive movement may be necessary to throw off an irregular, convulsive disease. But the course of succession is the healthy habit of the British constitution. Was it that the legislature wanted, at the act for the limitation of the crown in the Hanoverian line, drawn through the female descendants of James the First, a due sense of the inconveniences of having two or three, or possibly more, foreigners in succession to the British throne? No!—they had a due sense of the evils which might happen from such foreign rule, and more than a due sense of them. But a more decisive proof cannot be given of the full conviction of the British nation, that the principles of the Revolution did not authorize them to elect kings at their pleasure, and without any attention to the ancient fundamental principles of our government, than their continuing to adopt a plan of hereditary Protestant succession in the old line, with all the dangers and all the inconveniences of its being a foreign line full before their eyes, and operating with the utmost force upon their minds.

A few years ago I should be ashamed to overload a matter, so capable of supporting itself, by the then unnecessary support of any argument; but this seditious, unconstitutional doctrine is now publicly taught, avowed, and printed. The dislike I feel to revolutions, the signals for which have so often been given from pulpits; the spirit of change that is gone abroad; the total contempt which prevails with you, and may come to prevail with us, of all ancient institutions, when set in opposition to a present sense of convenience, or to the bent of a present inclination: all these considerations make it not unadvisable, in my opinion, to call back our attention to the true principles of our own domestic laws; that, you, my French friend, should begin to know, and that we should continue to cherish them. We ought not, on either side of the water, to suffer ourselves to be imposed upon by the counterfeit wares which some persons, by a double fraud, export to you in illicit bottoms, as raw commodities of British growth, though wholly alien to our soil, in order afterwards to smuggle them back again into this country, manufactured after the newest Paris fashion of an improved liberty.

The people of England will not ape the fashions they have never tried, nor go back to those which they have found mischievous on trial. They look upon the legal hereditary succession of their crown as among their rights, not as among their wrongs; as a benefit, not as a grievance; as a security for their liberty, not as a badge of servitude. They look on the frame of their commonwealth, *such as it stands,* to be of inestimable value; and they conceive the undisturbed succession of the crown to be a pledge of the stability and perpetuity of all the other members of our constitution.

I shall beg leave, before I go any further, to take notice of some paltry artifices, which the abettors of election, as the only lawful title to the crown, are ready to employ, in order to render the support of the just principles of our constitution a task somewhat invidious. These sophisters substitute a fictitious cause, and feigned personages, in whose favour they suppose you engaged, whenever you defend the inheritable nature of the crown. It is common with them to dispute as if they were in a conflict with some of those exploded fanatics of slavery, who formerly maintained, what I believe no creature now maintains, "that the crown is held by divine hereditary and indefeasible right."—These old fanatics of single arbitrary power dogmatized as if hereditary royalty was the only lawful government in the world, just as our new fanatics of popular arbitrary power maintain that a popular election is the sole lawful source of authority. The old prerogative enthusiasts, it is true, did speculate foolishly, and perhaps impiously too, as if monarchy had more of a divine sanction than any other mode of government; and as if a right to govern by inheritance were in strictness *indefeasible* in every person, who should be found in the succession to a throne, and under every circumstance, which no civil or political right can be. But an absurd opinion concerning the king's hereditary right to the crown does not prejudice one that is rational, and bottomed upon solid principles of law and policy. If all the absurd theories of lawyers and divines were to vitiate the objects in which they are conversant, we should have no law and no religion left in the world. But an absurd theory on one side of a question forms no justification for alleging a false fact, or promulgating mischievous maxims, on the other.

The second claim of the Revolution Society is "a right of cashiering their governors for *misconduct*." Perhaps the apprehensions our ancestors entertained of forming such a precedent as that "of cashiering for misconduct," was the cause that the declaration of the act, which implied the abdication of King James, was, if it had any fault, rather too guarded, and too circumstantial.[6] But all this guard, and all this accumulation of circumstances, serves to show the spirit of caution which predominated in the national councils in a situation in which men irritated by oppression, and elevated by a triumph over it, are apt to abandon themselves to violent and extreme courses: it shows the anxiety of the great men who influenced the conduct of affairs at that great event to make the Revolution a parent of settlement, and not a nursery of future revolutions.

No government could stand a moment, if it could be blown down with anything so loose and indefinite as an opinion of *"misconduct."* They who led at the Revolution grounded the virtual abdication of King James upon no such light and uncertain principle. They charged him with nothing less than a design, confirmed by a multitude of illegal overt acts, to *subvert the Protestant church and state,* and their *fundamental,* unquestionable laws and liberties: they charged him with having broken the *original contract* between king and people. This was more than *misconduct.* A grave and overruling necessity obliged them to take the step they took, and took with infinite reluctance, as under that most rigorous of all

---

[6] "That King James the Second, having endeavoured to *subvert the constitution* of the kingdom by breaking the *original contract* between King and people, and, by the advice of Jesuits, and other wicked persons, having violated the *fundamental* laws, and *having withdrawn himself out of the kingdom,* hath *abdicated* the government, and the throne is thereby *vacant.*"

laws. Their trust for the future preservation of the constitution was not in future revolutions. The grand policy of all their regulations was to render it almost impracticable for any future sovereign to compel the states of the kingdom to have again recourse to those violent remedies. They left the crown what, in the eye and estimation of law, it had never been, perfectly irresponsible. In order to lighten the crown still further, they aggravated responsibility on ministers of state. By the statute of the 1st of King William, sess. 2nd, called *"the act for declaring the rights and liberties of the subject, and for settling the succession to the crown,"* they enacted, that the ministers should serve the crown on the terms of that declaration. They secured soon after the *frequent meetings of parliament,* by which the whole government would be under the constant inspection and active control of the popular representative and of the magnates of the kingdom. In the next great constitutional act, that of the 12th and 13th of King William, for the further limitation of the crown, and *better* securing the rights and liberties of the subject, they provided, "that no pardon under the great seal of England should be pleadable to an impeachment by the Commons in parliament." The rule laid down for government in the Declaration of Right, the constant inspection of parliament, the practical claim of impeachment, they thought infinitely a better security not only for their constitutional liberty, but against the vices of administration, than the reservation of a right so difficult in the practice, so uncertain in the issue, and often so mischievous in the consequences, as that of "cashiering their governors."

Dr. Price, in his sermon,[7] condemns very properly the practice of gross, adulatory addresses to kings. Instead of this fulsome style, he proposes that his Majesty should be told, on occasions of congratulation, that "he is to consider himself as more properly the servant than the sovereign of his people." For a compliment, this new form of address does not seem to be very soothing. Those who are servants in name, as well as in effect, do not like to be told of their situation, their duty, and their obligations. The slave, in the old play, tells his master, *"Hæc commemoratio est quasi exprobatio."* It is not pleasant as compliment; it is not wholesome as instruc-

[7] P. 22–24.

tion. After all, if the king were to bring himself to echo this new kind of address, to adopt it in terms, and even to take the appellation of Servant of the People as his royal style, how either he or we should be much mended by it, I cannot imagine. I have seen very assuming letters, signed, Your most obedient, humble servant. The proudest denomination that ever was endured on earth took a title of still greater humility than that which is now proposed for sovereigns by the Apostle of Liberty. Kings and nations were trampled upon by the foot of one calling himself "the Servant of Servants;" and mandates for deposing sovereigns were sealed with the signet of "the Fisherman."

I should have considered all this as no more than a sort of flippant, vain discourse, in which, as in an unsavoury fume, several persons suffer the spirit of liberty to evaporate, if it were not plainly in support of the idea, and a part of the scheme, of "cashiering kings for misconduct." In that light it is worth some observation.

Kings, in one sense, are undoubtedly the servants of the people, because their power has no other rational end than that of the general advantage; but it is not true that they are, in the ordinary sense, (by our constitution at least,) anything like servants; the essence of whose situation is to obey the commands of some other, and to be removable at pleasure. But the king of Great Britain obeys no other person; all other persons are individually, and collectively too, under him, and owe to him a legal obedience. The law, which knows neither to flatter nor to insult, calls this high magistrate, not our servant, as this humble divine calls him, but *"our sovereign Lord the king;"* and we, on our parts, have learned to speak only the primitive language of the law, and not the confused jargon of their Babylonian pulpits.

As he is not to obey us, but as we are to obey the law in him, our constitution has made no sort of provision towards rendering him, as a servant, in any degree responsible. Our constitution knows nothing of a magistrate like the *Justicia* of Arragon; nor of any court legally appointed, nor of any process legally settled, for submitting the king to the responsibility belonging to all servants. In this he is not distinguished from the Commons and the Lords; who, in their several public capacities, can never be called to an account for their conduct; although the Revolution Society chooses to assert, in direct opposition to one of the wisest and most beautiful parts of our constitution, that "a king is no more than the first servant of the public, created by it, *and responsible to it.*"

Ill would our ancestors at the Revolution have deserved their fame for wisdom, if they had found no security for their freedom, but in rendering their government feeble in its operations, and precarious in its tenure; if they had been able to contrive no better remedy against arbitrary power than civil confusion. Let these gentlemen state who that *representative* public is to whom they will affirm the king, as a servant, to be responsible. It will then be time enough for me to produce to them the positive statute law which affirms that he is not.

The ceremony of cashiering kings, of which these gentlemen talk so much at their ease, can rarely, if ever, be performed without force. It then becomes a case of war, and not of constitution. Laws are commanded to hold their tongues amongst arms; and tribunals fall to the ground with the peace they are no longer able to uphold. The Revolution of 1688 was obtained by a just war, in the only case in which any war, and much more a civil war, can be just. "Justa bella quibus *necessaria.*" The question of dethroning, or, if these gentlemen like the phrase better, "cashiering kings," will always be, as it has always been, an extraordinary question of state, and wholly out of the law; a question (like all other questions of state) of dispositions, and of means, and of probable consequences, rather than of positive rights. As it was not made for common abuses, so it is not to be agitated by common minds. The speculative line of demarcation, where obedience ought to end, and resistance must begin, is faint, obscure, and not easily definable. It is not a single act, or a single event, which determines it. Governments must be abused and deranged indeed, before it can be thought of; and the prospect of the future must be as bad as the experience of the past. When things are in that lamentable condition, the nature of the disease is to indicate the remedy to those whom nature has qualified to administer in extremities this critical, ambiguous, bitter potion to a distempered state. Times, and occasions, and provocations, will teach their own lessons. The wise will determine from the gravity of the case; the irritable, from sensibility to oppression; the high-minded, from disdain and indignation at abusive power in unworthy hands; the brave and bold, from the love of honourable danger in a generous cause: but, with or without right, a revolution will be the very last resource of the thinking and the good.

The third head of right, asserted by the pulpit of the Old Jewry, namely, the "right to form a government for ourselves," has, at least, as little countenance from anything done at the Revolution, either in precedent or principle, as the two first of their claims. The Revolution was made to preserve our *ancient,* indisputable laws and liberties, and that *ancient* constitution of government which is our only security for law and liberty. If you are desirous of knowing the spirit of our constitution, and the policy which predominated in that great period which has secured it to this hour, pray look for both in our histories, in our records, in our acts of parliament, and journals of parliament, and not in the sermons of the Old Jewry, and the after-dinner toasts of the Revolution Society. In the former you will find other ideas and another language. Such a claim is as ill-suited to our temper and wishes as it is unsupported by any appearance of authority. The very idea of the fabrication of a new government is enough to fill us with disgust and horror. We wished at the period of the Revolution, and do now wish, to derive all we possess as *an inheritance from our forefathers.* Upon that body and stock of inheritance we have taken care not to inoculate any scion alien to the nature of the original plant. All the reformations we have hitherto made have proceeded upon the principle of reverence to antiquity; and I hope, nay I am persuaded, that all those which possibly may be made hereafter, will be carefully formed upon analogical precedent, authority, and example.

Our oldest reformation is that of Magna Charta. You will see that Sir Edward Coke, that great oracle of our law, and indeed all the great men who follow him, to Blackstone,[8] are industrious to prove the pedigree of our liberties. They endeavour to prove, that the ancient charter, the Magna Charta of King John, was connected with another positive charter from Henry I., and that both the one and the other were nothing more than a re-affirmance of the still

[8] See Blackstone's Magna Charta, printed at Oxford, 1759.

more ancient standing law of the kingdom. In the matter of fact, for the greater part, these authors appear to be in the right; perhaps not always; but if the lawyers mistake in some particulars, it proves my position still the more strongly; because it demonstrates the powerful prepossession towards antiquity, with which the minds of all our lawyers and legislators, and of all the people whom they wish to influence, have been always filled; and the stationary policy of this kingdom in considering their most sacred rights and franchises as an *inheritance.*

In the famous law of the 3rd of Charles I., called the *Petition of Right,* the parliament says to the king, "Your subjects have *inherited* this freedom," claiming their franchises not on abstract principles "as the rights of men," but as the rights of Englishmen, and as a patrimony derived from their forefathers. Selden, and the other profoundly learned men, who drew this Petition of Right, were as well acquainted, at least, with all the general theories concerning the "rights of men," as any of the discoursers in our pulpits, or on your tribune; full as well as Dr. Price, or as the Abbé Sieyès. But, for reasons worthy of that practical wisdom which superseded their theoretic science, they preferred this positive, recorded, *hereditary* title to all which can be dear to the man and the citizen, to that vague speculative right, which exposed their sure inheritance to be scrambled for and torn to pieces by every wild, litigious spirit.

The same policy pervades all the laws which have since been made for the preservation of our liberties. In the 1st of William and Mary, in the famous statute, called the Declaration of Right, the two Houses utter not a syllable of "a right to frame a government for themselves." You will see, that their whole care was to secure the religion, laws, and liberties, that had been long possessed, and had been lately endangered. "Taking[9] into their most serious consideration the *best* means for making such an establishment, that their religion, laws, and liberties might not be in danger of being again subverted," they auspicate all their proceedings, by stating as some of those *best* means, "in the *first place*" to do "as their *ancestors in like cases have usually* done for vindicating their *ancient* rights and liberties, to *declare;*"—and then they pray the king and

[9] 1 W. and M.

queen, "that it may be *declared* and enacted, that *all and singular* the rights and liberties *asserted and declared,* are the true *ancient* and indubitable rights and liberties of the people of this kingdom."

You will observe, that from Magna Charta to the Declaration of Right, it has been the uniform policy of our constitution to claim and assert our liberties, as an *entailed inheritance* derived to us from our forefathers, and to be transmitted to our posterity; as an estate specially belonging to the people of this kingdom, without any reference whatever to any other more general or prior right. By this means our constitution preserves a unity in so great a diversity of its parts. We have an inheritable crown; an inheritable peerage; and a House of Commons and a people inheriting privileges, franchises, and liberties, from a long line of ancestors.

This policy appears to me to be the result of profound reflection; or rather the happy effect of following nature, which is wisdom without reflection, and above it. A spirit of innovation is generally the result of a selfish temper, and confined views. People will not look forward to posterity, who never look backward to their ancestors. Besides, the people of England well know, that the idea of inheritance furnishes a sure principle of conservation, and a sure principle of transmission; without at all excluding a principle of improvement. It leaves acquisition free; but it secures what it acquires. Whatever advantages are obtained by a state proceeding on these maxims, are locked fast as in a sort of family settlement; grasped as in a kind of mortmain for ever. By a constitutional policy, working after the pattern of nature, we receive, we hold, we transmit our government and our privileges, in the same manner in which we enjoy and transmit our property and our lives. The institutions of policy, the goods of fortune, the gifts of providence, are handed down to us, and from us, in the same course and order. Our political system is placed in a just correspondence and symmetry with the order of the world, and with the mode of existence decreed to a permanent body composed of transitory parts; wherein, by the disposition of a stupendous wisdom, moulding together the great mysterious incorporation of the human race, the whole, at one time, is never old, or middle-aged, or young, but, in a condition of unchangeable constancy, moves on through the varied tenor of perpetual decay, fall, renovation, and progression. Thus, by preserving the method of nature in the conduct of the state, in what we improve, we are never wholly new; in what we retain, we are never wholly obsolete. By adhering in this manner and on those principles to our forefathers, we are guided not by the superstition of antiquarians, but by the spirit of philosophic analogy. In this choice of inheritance we have given to our frame of polity the image of a relation in blood; binding up the constitution of our country with our dearest domestic ties; adopting our fundamental laws into the bosom of our family affections; keeping inseparable, and cherishing with the warmth of all their combined and mutually reflected charities, our state, our hearths, our sepulchres, and our altars.

Through the same plan of a conformity to nature in our artificial institutions, and by calling in the aid of her unerring and powerful instincts, to fortify the fallible and feeble contrivances of our reason, we have derived several other, and those no small benefits, from considering our liberties in the light of an inheritance. Always acting as if in the presence of canonized forefathers, the spirit of freedom, leading in itself to misrule and excess, is tempered with an awful gravity. This idea of a liberal descent inspires us with a sense of habitual native dignity, which prevents that upstart insolence almost inevitably adhering to and disgracing those who are the first acquirers of any distinction. By this means our liberty becomes a noble freedom. It carries an imposing and majestic aspect. It has a pedigree and illustrating ancestors. It has its bearings and its ensigns armorial. It has its gallery of portraits; its monumental inscriptions; its records, evidences, and titles. We procure reverence to our civil institutions on the principle upon which nature teaches us to revere individual men; on account of their age, and on account of those from whom they are descended. All your sophisters cannot produce anything better adapted to preserve a rational and manly freedom than the course that we have pursued, who have chosen our nature rather than our speculations, our breasts rather than our inventions, for the great conservatories and magazines of our rights and privileges.

You might, if you pleased, have profited of our example, and have given to your recovered freedom a correspondent dignity. Your privileges, though discontinued, were not lost to memory. Your constitution, it is true, whilst you were out of possession, suffered waste and dilapidation; but you possessed in some parts the walls, and, in all, the foundations, of a noble and venerable castle. You might have repaired those walls; you might have built on those old foundations. Your constitution was suspended before it was perfected; but you had the elements of a constitution very nearly as good as could be wished. In your old states you possessed that variety of parts corresponding with the various descriptions of which your community was happily composed; you had all that combination, and all that opposition of interests, you had that action and counteraction, which, in the natural and in the political world, from the reciprocal struggle of discordant powers, draws out the harmony of the universe. These opposed and conflicting interests, which you considered as so great a blemish in your old and in our present constitution, interpose a salutary check to all precipitate resolutions. They render deliberation a matter not of choice, but of necessity; they make all change a subject of *compromise,* which naturally begets moderation; they produce *temperaments* preventing the sore evil of harsh, crude, unqualified reformations; and rendering all the headlong exertions of arbitrary power, in the few or in the many for ever impracticable. Through that diversity of members and interests, general liberty had as many securities as there were separate views in the several orders; whilst by pressing down the whole by the weight of a real monarchy, the separate parts would have been prevented from warping, and starting from their allotted places.

You had all these advantages in your ancient states; but you chose to act as if you had never been moulded into civil society, and had everything to begin anew. You began ill, because you began by despising everything that belonged to you. You set up your trade without a capital. If the last generations of your country appeared without much lustre in your eyes, you might have passed them by, and derived your claims from a more early race of ancestors. Under a pious predilection for those ancestors, your imaginations would have realized in them a standard of virtue and wisdom, beyond the vulgar practice of the hour; and you would have risen with the example to whose imitation you aspired. Respecting your forefathers, you would have been taught to respect yourselves. You would not have chosen to consider the French as a people of yesterday, as a nation of low-born servile wretches until the emancipating year of 1789. In order to furnish, at the expense of your honour, an excuse to your apologists here for several enormities of yours, you would not have been content to be represented as a gang of Maroon slaves, suddenly broke loose from the house of bondage, and therefore to be pardoned for your abuse of the liberty to which you were not accustomed, and ill fitted. Would it not, my worthy friend, have been wiser to have you thought, what I, for one, always thought you, a generous and gallant nation, long misled to your disadvantage by your high and romantic sentiments of fidelity, honour, and loyalty; that events had been unfavourable to you, but that you were not enslaved through any illiberal or servile disposition; that in your most devoted submission, you were actuated by a principle of public spirit, and that it was your country you worshipped, in the person of your king? Had you made it to be understood, that in the delusion of this amiable error you had gone further than your wise ancestors; that you were resolved to resume your ancient privileges, whilst you preserved the spirit of your ancient and your recent loyalty and honour; or if, diffident of yourselves, and not clearly discerning the almost obliterated constitution of your ancestors, you had looked to your neighbours in this land, who had kept alive the ancient principles and models of the old common law of Europe meliorated and adapted to its present state—by following wise examples you would have given new examples of wisdom to the world. You would have rendered the cause of liberty venerable in the eyes of every worthy mind in every nation. You would have shamed despotism from the earth, by showing that freedom was not only reconcilable, but, as when well disciplined it is, auxiliary to law. You would have had an unoppressive but a productive revenue. You would have had a flourishing commerce to feed it. You would have had a free constitution; a potent monarchy; a disciplined army; a reformed and venerated clergy; a mitigated but spirited nobility, to lead your virtue, not to overlay it; you would have had a liberal order of commons, to emulate and to recruit that nobility; you would have had a protected, satisfied, laborious, and obedient people, taught to seek and to recognise the happiness that is to be found by virtue in all conditions; in which consists the true moral equality of mankind, and not in that monstrous fiction, which, by inspiring false ideas and vain expectations into men destined to travel in the obscure walk of laborious life, serves only to aggravate and embitter that real inequality, which it never can remove; and which the order of civil life establishes as much for the benefit of those whom it must leave in an humble state, as those whom it is able to exalt to a condition more splendid, but not more happy. You had a smooth and easy career of felicity and glory laid open to you, beyond anything recorded in the history of the world; but you have shown that difficulty is good for man.

Compute your gains: see what is got by those extravagant and presumptuous speculations which have taught your leaders to despise all their predecessors, and all their contemporaries, and even to despise themselves, until the moment in which they became truly despicable. By following those false lights, France has bought undisguised calamities at a higher price than any nation has purchased the most unequivocal blessings! France has bought poverty by crime! France has not sacrificed her virtue to her interest, but she has abandoned her interest, that she might prostitute her virtue. All other nations have begun the fabric of a new government, or the reformation of an old, by establishing originally, or by enforcing with greater exactness, some rites or other of religion. All other people have laid the foundations of civil freedom in severer manners, and a system of a more austere and masculine morality. France, when she let loose the reins of regal authority, doubled the license of a ferocious dissoluteness in manners, and of an insolent irreligion in opinions and practices; and has extended through all ranks of life, as if she were communicating some privilege, or laying open some secluded benefit, all the unhappy corruptions that usually were the disease of wealth and power. This is one of the new principles of equality in France.

France, by the perfidy of her leaders, has utterly disgraced the tone of lenient council in the cabinets of princes, and disarmed it of its most potent topics. She has sanctified the dark, suspicious maxims of tyrannous distrust; and taught kings to tremble at (what will hereafter be called) the delusive plausibilities of moral politicians. Sovereigns will consider those, who advise them to place an unlimited confidence in their people, as subverters of their thrones; as traitors who aim at their destruction, by leading their easy good-nature, under specious pretences, to admit combinations of bold and faithless men into a participation of their power. This alone (if there were nothing else) is an irreparable calamity to you and to mankind. Remember that your parliament of Paris told your king, that, in calling the states together, he had nothing to fear but the prodigal excess of their zeal in providing for the support of the throne. It is right that these men should hide their heads. It is right that they should bear their part in the ruin which their counsel has brought on their sovereign and their country. Such sanguine declarations tend to lull authority asleep; to encourage it rashly to engage in perilous adventures of untried policy; to neglect those provisions, preparations, and precautions, which distinguish benevolence from imbecility; and without which no man can answer for the salutary effect of any abstract plan of government or of freedom. For want of these, they have seen the medicine of the state corrupted into its poison. They have seen the French rebel against a mild and lawful monarch, with more fury, outrage, and insult, than ever any people has been known to rise against the most illegal usurper, or the most sanguinary tyrant. Their resistance was made to concession; their revolt was from protection; their blow was aimed at a hand holding out graces, favours, and immunities.

This was unnatural. The rest is in order. They have found their punishment in their success. Laws overturned; tribunals subverted; industry without vigour; commerce expiring; the revenue unpaid, yet the people impoverished; a church pillaged, and a state not relieved; civil and military anarchy made the constitution of the kingdom; everything human and divine sacrificed to the idol of public credit, and national bankruptcy the consequence; and, to crown all, the paper securities of new, precarious, tottering power, the discredited paper securities of impoverished fraud and beggared rapine, held out as a currency for the support of an empire, in lieu of the two great recognised species that represent the lasting, conventional credit of mankind, which disappeared and hid themselves in the earth from whence they came, when the principle of property, whose creatures and representatives they are, was systematically subverted.

Were all these dreadful things necessary? Were they the inevitable results of the desperate struggle of determined patriots, compelled to wade through blood and tumult, to the quiet shore of a tranquil and prosperous liberty? No! nothing like it. The fresh ruins of France, which shock our feelings wherever we can turn our eyes, are not the devastation of civil war; they are the sad but instructive monuments of rash and ignorant counsel in time of profound peace. They are the display of inconsiderate and presumptuous, because unresisted and irresistible, authority. The persons who have thus squandered away the precious treasure of their crimes, the persons who have made this prodigal and wild waste of public evils, (the last stake reserved for the ultimate ransom of the state,) have met in their progress with little, or rather with no opposition at all. Their whole march was more like a triumphal procession, than the progress of a war. Their pioneers have gone before them, and demolished and laid everything level at their feet. Not one drop of *their* blood have they shed in the cause of the country they have ruined. They have made no sacrifices to their projects of greater consequence than their shoe-buckles, whilst they were imprisoning their king, murdering their fellow-citizens, and bathing in tears, and plunging in poverty and distress, thousands of worthy men and worthy families. Their cruelty has not even been the base result of fear. It has been the effect of their sense of perfect safety, in authorizing treasons, robberies, rapes, assassinations, slaughters, and burnings, throughout their harassed land. But the cause of all was plain from the beginning.

This unforced choice, this fond election of evil, would appear perfectly unaccountable, if we did not consider the composition of the National Assembly: I do not mean its formal constitution, which, as it now stands, is exceptionable enough, but the materials of which, in a great measure, it is composed, which is of ten thousand times greater consequence than all the formalities in the world. If we were to know nothing of this assembly but by its title and function, no colours could paint to the imagination anything more venerable. In that light the mind of an inquirer, subdued by such an awful image as that of the virtue and wisdom of a whole people collected into a focus, would pause and hesitate in condemning things even of the very worst aspect. Instead of blameable, they would appear only mysterious. But no name, no power, no function, no artificial institution whatsoever, can make the men of whom any system of authority is composed any other than God, and nature, and education, and their habits of life have made them. Capacities beyond these the people have not to give. Virtue and wisdom may be the objects of their choice; but their choice confers neither the one nor the other on those upon whom they lay their ordaining hands. They have not the engagement of nature, they have not the promise of revelation, for any such powers.

After I had read over the list of the persons and descriptions elected into the *Tiers État,* nothing which they afterwards did could appear astonishing. Among them, indeed, I saw some of known rank; some of shining talents; but of any practical experience in the state, not one man was to be found. The best were only men of theory. But whatever the distinguished few may have been, it is the substance and mass of the body which constitutes its character, and must finally determine its direction. In all bodies, those who will lead, must also, in a considerable degree, follow. They must conform their propositions to the taste, talent, and disposition, of those whom they wish to conduct: therefore, if an assembly is viciously or feebly composed in a very great part of it, nothing but such a supreme degree of virtue as very rarely appears in the world, and for that reason cannot enter into calculation, will prevent the men of talent disseminated through it from becoming only the expert instruments of absurd projects! If, what is the more likely event, instead of that unusual degree of virtue, they should be actuated by sinister ambition, and a lust of meretricious glory, then the feeble part of the assembly, to whom at first they conform, becomes in its turn the dupe and instrument of their designs. In this political traffic, the leaders will be obliged to bow to the ignorance of their followers, and the followers to become subservient to the worst designs of their leaders.

To secure any degree of sobriety in the propositions made by the leaders in any public assembly, they ought to respect, in some

degree perhaps to fear, those whom they conduct. To be led any
otherwise than blindly, the followers must be qualified, if not for
actors, at least for judges; they must also be judges of natural weight
and authority. Nothing can secure a steady and moderate conduct
in such assemblies, but that the body of them should be respectably
composed, in point of condition in life, or permanent property, of
education, and of such habits as enlarge and liberalize the under
standing.

In the calling of the states-general of France, the first thing that
struck me, was a great departure from the ancient course. I found
the representation for the third estate composed of six hundred persons. They were equal in number to the representatives of both the
other orders. If the orders were to act separately, the number would
not, beyond the consideration of the expense, be of much moment.
But when it became apparent that the three orders were to be melted
down into one, the policy and necessary effect of this numerous representation became obvious. A very small desertion from either of
the other two orders must throw the power of both into the hands
of the third. In fact, the whole power of the state was soon resolved
into that body. Its due composition became therefore of infinitely
the greater importance.

Judge, Sir, of my surprise, when I found that a very great proportion of the assembly (a majority, I believe, of the members who
attended) was composed of practitioners in the law. It was composed, not of distinguished magistrates, who had given pledges to
their country of their science, prudence, and integrity; not of leading
advocates, the glory of the bar; not of renowned professors in universities;—but for the far greater part, as it must in such a number,
of the inferior, unlearned, mechanical, merely instrumental members
of the profession. There were distinguished exceptions; but the general composition was of obscure provincial advocates, of stewards of
petty local jurisdictions, country attornies, notaries, and the whole
train of the ministers of municipal litigation, the fomenters and conductors of the petty war of village vexation. From the moment I
read the list, I saw distinctly, and very nearly as it has happened,
all that was to follow.

The degree of estimation in which any profession is held becomes the standard of the estimation in which the professors hold themselves. Whatever the personal merits of many individual lawyers might have been, and in many it was undoubtedly very considerable, in that military kingdom no part of the profession had been much regarded, except the highest of all, who often united to their professional offices great family splendour, and were invested with great power and authority. These certainly were highly respected, and even with no small degree of awe. The next rank was not much esteemed; the mechanical part was in a very low degree of repute.

Whenever the supreme authority is vested in a body so composed, it must evidently produce the consequences of supreme authority placed in the hands of men not taught habitually to respect themselves; who had no previous fortune in character at stake; who could not be expected to bear with moderation, or to conduct with discretion, a power, which they themselves, more than any others, must be surprised to find in their hands. Who could flatter himself that these men, suddenly, and, as it were, by enchantment, snatched from the humblest rank of subordination, would not be intoxicated with their unprepared greatness? Who could conceive that men, who are habitually meddling, daring, subtle, active, of litigious dispositions and unquiet minds, would easily fall back into their old condition of obscure contention, and laborious, low, and unprofitable chicane? Who could doubt but that, at any expense to the state, of which they understood nothing, they must pursue their private interests which they understood but too well? It was not an event depending on chance, or contingency. It was inevitable; it was necessary; it was planted in the nature of things. They must *join* (if their capacity did not permit them to *lead*) in any project which could procure to them a *litigious constitution;* which could lay open to them those innumerable lucrative jobs, which follow in the train of all great convulsions and revolutions in the state, and particularly in all great and violent permutations of property. Was it to be expected that they would attend to the stability of property, whose existence had always depended upon whatever rendered property questionable, ambiguous, and insecure? Their objects would be enlarged with their elevation, but their disposition and habits, and mode of accomplishing their designs, must remain the same.

Well! but these men were to be tempered and restrained by other descriptions, of more sober and more enlarged understandings. Were they then to be awed by the super-eminent authority and awful dignity of a handful of country clowns, who have seats in that assembly, some of whom are said not to be able to read and write? and by not a greater number of traders, who, though somewhat more instructed, and more conspicuous in the order of society, had never known anything beyond their counting-house. No! both these descriptions were more formed to be overborne and swayed by the intrigues and artifices of lawyers, than to become their counterpoise. With such a dangerous disproportion, the whole must needs be governed by them. To the faculty of law was joined a pretty considerable proportion of the faculty of medicine. This faculty had not, any more than that of the law, possessed in France its just estimation. Its professors, therefore, must have the qualities of men not habituated to sentiments of dignity. But supposing they had ranked as they ought to do, and as with us they do actually, the sides of sick beds are not the academies for forming statesmen and legislators. Then came the dealers in stocks and funds, who must be eager, at any expense, to change their ideal paper wealth for the more solid substance of land. To these were joined men of other descriptions, from whom as little knowledge of, or attention to, the interests of a great state was to be expected, and as little regard to the stability of any institution; men formed to be instruments, not controls. Such in general was the composition of the *Tiers État* in the National Assembly; in which was scarcely to be perceived the slightest traces of what we call the natural landed interest of the country.

We know that the British House of Commons, without shutting its doors to any merit in any class, is, by the sure operation of adequate causes, filled with everything illustrious in rank, in descent, in hereditary and in acquired opulence, in cultivated talents, in military, civil, naval, and politic distinction, that the country can afford. But supposing, what hardly can be supposed as a case, that the House of Commons should be composed in the same manner with the *Tiers État* in France, would this dominion of chicane be borne with patience, or even conceived without horror? God forbid I should insinuate anything derogatory to that profession, which is another priesthood, administrating the rights of sacred justice. But whilst I revere men in the functions which belong to them, and would do as much as one man can do to prevent their exclusion from any, I cannot, to flatter them, give the lie to nature. They are good and useful in the composition; they must be mischievous if they preponderate so as virtually to become the whole. Their very excellence in their peculiar functions may be far from a qualification for others. It cannot escape observation, that when men are too much confined to professional and faculty habits, and as it were inveterate in the recurrent employment of that narrow circle, they are rather disabled than qualified for whatever depends on the knowledge of mankind, on experience in mixed affairs, on a comprehensive, connected view of the various, complicated, external and internal interests, which go to the formation of that multifarious thing called a state.

After all, if the House of Commons were to have a wholly professional and faculty composition, what is the power of the House of Commons, circumscribed and shut in by the immovable barriers of laws, usages, positive rules of doctrine and practice, counterpoised by the House of Lords, and every moment of its existence at the discretion of the crown to continue, prorogue, or dissolve us? The power of the House of Commons, direct or indirect, is indeed great; and long may it be able to preserve its greatness, and the spirit belonging to true greatness, at the full; and it will do so, as long as it can keep the breakers of law in India from becoming the makers of law for England. The power, however, of the House of Commons, when least diminished, is as a drop of water in the ocean, compared to that residing in a settled majority of your National Assembly. That assembly, since the destruction of the orders, has no fundamental law, no strict convention, no respected usage to restrain it. Instead of finding themselves obliged to conform to a fixed constitution, they have a power to make a constitution which shall conform to their designs. Nothing in heaven or upon earth can serve as a control on them. What ought to be the heads, the hearts, the dispositions, that are qualified, or that dare, not only to make laws under a fixed constitution, but at one heat to strike out a totally new constitution for a great kingdom, and in every part of it, from the monarch on the throne to the vestry of a parish? But—*"fools rush in where angels fear to tread."* In such a state of unbounded power for undefined and undefinable purposes, the evil of a moral and almost physical inaptitude of the man to the function must be the greatest we can conceive to happen in the management of human affairs.

Having considered the composition of the third estate as it stood in its original frame, I took a view of the representatives of the clergy. There too it appeared, that full as little regard was had to the general security of property, or to the aptitude of the deputies for the public purposes, in the principles of their election. That election was so contrived, as to send a very large proportion of mere country curates to the great and arduous work of new-modelling a state; men who never had seen the state so much as in a picture; men who knew nothing of the world beyond the bounds of an obscure village; who immersed in hopeless poverty, could regard all property, whether secular or ecclesiastical, with no other eye than that of envy; among whom must be many who, for the smallest hope of the meanest dividend in plunder, would readily join in any attempts upon a body of wealth, in which they could hardly look to have any share, except in a general scramble. Instead of balancing the power of the active chicaners in the other assembly, these curates must necessarily become the active coadjutors, or at best the passive instruments, of those by whom they had been habitually guided in their petty village concerns. They too could hardly be the most conscientious of their kind, who presuming upon their incompetent understanding, could intrigue for a trust which led them from their natural relation to their flocks, and their natural spheres of action, to undertake the regeneration of kingdoms. This preponderating weight, being added to the force of the body of chicane in the *Tiers État,* completed that momentum of ignorance, rashness, presumption, and lust of plunder, which nothing has been able to resist.

To observing men it must have appeared from the beginning, that the majority of the Third Estate, in conjunction with such a deputation from the clergy as I have described, whilst it pursued the destruction of the nobility, would inevitably become subservient to the worst designs of individuals in that class. In the spoil and humiliation of their own order these individuals would possess a sure fund for the pay of their new followers. To squander away the objects which made the happiness of their fellows, would be to them no sacrifice at all. Turbulent, discontented men of quality, in proportion as they are puffed up with personal pride and arrogance, generally despise their own order. One of the first symptoms they discover of a selfish and mischievous ambition, is a profligate disregard of a dignity which they partake with others. To be attached to the subdivision, to love the little platoon we belong to in society, is the first principle (the germ as it were) of public affections. It is the first link in the series by which we proceed towards a love to our country, and to mankind. The interest of that portion of social arrangement is a trust in the hands of all those who compose it; and as none but bad men would justify it in abuse, none but traitors would barter it away for their own personal advantage.

There were in the time of our civil troubles in England (I do not know whether you have any such in your assembly in France) several persons, like the then Earl of Holland, who by themselves or their families had brought an odium on the throne, by the prodigal dispensation of its bounties towards them, who afterwards joined in the rebellions arising from the discontents of which they were themselves the cause; men who helped to subvert that throne to which they owed, some of them, their existence, others all that power which they employed to ruin their benefactor. If any bounds are set to the rapacious demands of that sort of people, or that others are permitted to partake in the objects they would engross, revenge and envy soon fill up the craving void that is left in their avarice. Confounded by the complication of distempered passions, their reason is disturbed; their views become vast and perplexed; to others inexplicable; to themselves uncertain. They find, on all sides, bounds to their unprincipled ambition in any fixed order of things. Both in the fog and haze of confusion all is enlarged, and appears without any limit.

When men of rank sacrifice all ideas of dignity to an ambition without a distinct object, and work with low instruments and for low ends, the whole composition becomes low and base. Does not

something like this now appear in France? Does it not produce
something ignoble and inglorious? a kind of meanness in all the
prevalent policy? a tendency in all that is done to lower along with
individuals all the dignity and importance of the state? Other revolutions have been conducted by persons, who, whilst they attempted
or affected changes in the commonwealth, sanctified their ambition
by advancing the dignity of the people whose peace they troubled.
They had long views. They aimed at the rule, not at the destruction,
of their country. They were men of great civil, and great military
talents, and if the terror, the ornament of their age. They were not
like Jew brokers, contending with each other who could best remedy
with fraudulent circulation and depreciated paper the wretchedness
and ruin brought on their country by their degenerate councils. The
compliment made to one of the great bad men of the old stamp
(Cromwell) by his kinsman, a favourite poet of that time, shows
what it was he proposed, and what indeed to a great degree he
accomplished, in the success of his ambition:

> "Still as *you* rise, the *state,* exalted too,
> Finds no distemper whilst 'tis changed by *you;*
> Changed like the world's great scene, when without noise
> The rising sun night's *vulgar* lights destroys."

These disturbers were not so much like men usurping power,
as asserting their natural place in society. Their rising was to illu-
minate and beautify the world. Their conquest over their competitors was by outshining them. The hand that, like a destroying angel,
smote the country, communicated to it the force and energy under
which it suffered. I do not say, (God forbid)–I do not say, that
the virtues of such men were to be taken as a balance to their crimes;
but they were some corrective to their effects. Such was, as I said,
our Cromwell. Such were your whole race of Guises, Condés, and
Colignis. Such the Richelieus, who in more quiet times acted in the
spirit of a civil war. Such, as better men, and in a less dubious cause,
were your Henry the Fourth and your Sully, though nursed in civil
confusions, and not wholly without some of their taint. It is a thing
to be wondered at, to see how very soon France, when she had a

moment to respire, recovered and emerged from the longest and most dreadful civil war that ever was known in any nation. Why? Because among all their massacres, they had not slain the *mind* in their country. A conscious dignity, a noble pride, a generous sense of glory and emulation, was not extinguished. On the contrary, it was kindled and inflamed. The organs also of the state, however shattered, existed. All the prizes of honour and virtue, all the rewards, all the distinctions remained. But your present confusion, like a palsy, has attacked the fountain of life itself. Every person in your country, in a situation to be actuated by a principle of honour, is disgraced and degraded, and can entertain no sensation of life, except in a mortified and humiliated indignation. But this generation will quickly pass away. The next generation of the nobility will resemble the artificers and clowns, and money-jobbers, usurers, and Jews, who will be always their fellows, sometimes their masters.

Believe me, Sir, those who attempt to level, never equalise. In all societies, consisting of various descriptions of citizens, some description must be uppermost. The levellers therefore only change and pervert the natural order of things; they load the edifice of society, by setting up in the air what the solidity of the structure requires to be on the ground. The association of tailors and carpenters, of which the republic (of Paris, for instance) is composed, cannot be equal to the situation, into which, by the worst of usurpations, an usurpation on the prerogatives of nature, you attempt to force them.

The Chancellor of France at the opening of the states, said, in a tone of oratorical flourish, that all occupations were honourable. If he meant only, that no honest employment was disgraceful, he would not have gone beyond the truth. But in asserting that anything is honourable, we imply some distinction in its favour. The occupation of a hair-dresser, or of a working tallow-chandler, cannot be a matter of honour to any person—to say nothing of a number of other more servile employments. Such descriptions of men ought not to suffer oppression from the state; but the state suffers oppression, if such as they, either individually or collectively are permitted to rule. In this you think you are combating prejudice, but you are at war with nature.[10]

I do not, my dear Sir, conceive you to be of that sophistical, captious spirit, or of that uncandid dulness, as to require, for every general observation or sentiment, an explicit detail of the correctives and exceptions, which reason will presume to be included in all the general propositions which come from reasonable men. You do not imagine, that I wish to confine power, authority, and distinction to blood, and names, and titles. No, Sir. There is no qualification for government but virtue and wisdom, actual or presumptive. Wherever they are actually found, they have, in whatever state, condition, profession, or trade, the passport of Heaven to human place and honour. Woe to the country which would madly and impiously reject the service of the talents and virtues, civil, military, or religious, that are given to grace and to serve it; and would condemn to obscurity everything formed to diffuse lustre and glory around a state! Woe to that country too, that, passing into the opposite extreme, considers a low education, a mean contracted view of things, a sordid, mercenary occupation, as a preferable title to command! Everything ought to be open; but not indifferently to every man. No rotation; no appointment by lot; no mode of election operating in the spirit of sortition, or rotation, can be generally good in a government conversant in extensive objects. Because they have no tendency, direct or indirect, to select the man with a view to the duty, or to accommodate the one to the other. I do not hesitate to say, that the road to eminence and power, from obscure condition, ought not to be made too easy, nor a thing too much of course. If rare merit be the rarest

---

[10] Ecclesiasticus, chap. xxxviii. verses 24, 25. "The wisdom of a learned man cometh by opportunity of leisure; and he that hath little business shall become wise."—"How can he get wisdom that holdeth the plough, and that glorieth in the goad; that driveth oxen; and is occupied in their labours; and whose talk is of bullocks?"

Ver. 27. "So every carpenter and work-master that laboureth night and day," &c.

Ver. 33. "They shall not be sought for in public counsel, nor sit high in the congregation: They shall not sit on the judge's seat, nor understand the sentence of judgment; they cannot declare justice and judgment, and they shall not be found where parables are spoken."

Ver. 34. "But they will maintain the state of the world."

I do not determine whether this book be canonical, as the Gallican church (till lately) has considered it, or apocryphal, as here it is taken. I am sure it contains a great deal of sense and truth.

of all rare things, it ought to pass through some sort of probation. The temple of honour ought to be seated on an eminence. If it be opened through virtue, let it be remembered too, that virtue is never tried but by some difficulty and some struggle.

Nothing is a due and adequate representation of a state, that does not represent its ability, as well as its property. But as ability is a vigorous and active principle, and as property is sluggish, inert, and timid, it never can be safe from the invasions of ability, unless it be, out of all proportion, predominant in the representation. It must be represented too in great masses of accumulation, or it is not rightly protected. The characteristic essence of property, formed out of the combined principles of its acquisition and conservation, is to be *unequal*. The great masses therefore which excite envy, and tempt rapacity, must be put out of the possibility of danger. Then they form a natural rampart about the lesser properties in all their gradations. The same quantity of property, which is by the natural course of things divided among many, has not the same operation. Its defensive power is weakened as it is diffused. In this diffusion each man's portion is less than what, in the eagerness of his desires, he may flatter himself to obtain by dissipating the accumulations of others. The plunder of the few would indeed give but a share inconceivably small in the distribution to the many. But the many are not capable of making this calculation; and those who lead them to rapine never intend this distribution.

The power of perpetuating our property in our families is one of the most valuable and interesting circumstances belonging to it, and that which tends the most to the perpetuation of society itself. It makes our weakness subservient to our virtue; it grafts benevolence even upon avarice. The possessors of family wealth, and of the distinction which attends hereditary possession, (as most concerned in it) are the natural securities for this transmission. With us the House of Peers is formed upon this principle. It is wholly composed of hereditary property and hereditary distinction; and made therefore the third of the legislature; and, in the last event, the sole judge of all property in all its subdivisions. The House of Commons too, though not necessarily, yet in fact, is always so composed, in the far greater part. Let those large proprietors be what they will, and they have their chance of being amongst the best, they are, at the very worst, the ballast in the vessel of the commonwealth. For though hereditary wealth, and the rank which goes with it, are too much idolized by creeping sycophants, and the blind, abject admirers of power, they are too rashly slighted in shallow speculations of the petulant, assuming, short-sighted coxcombs of philosophy. Some decent, regulated pre-eminence, some preference (not exclusive appropriation) given to birth, is neither unnatural, nor unjust, nor impolitic.

It is said, that twenty-four millions ought to prevail over two hundred thousand. True; if the constitution of a kingdom be a problem of arithmetic. This sort of discourse does well enough with the lamp-post for its second: to men who *may* reason calmly, it is ridiculous. The will of the many, and their interest, must very often differ; and great will be the difference when they make an evil choice. A government of five hundred country attornies and obscure curates is not good for twenty-four millions of men, though it were chosen by eight and forty millions; nor is it the better for being guided by a dozen of persons of quality, who have betrayed their trust in order to obtain that power. At present, you seem in everything to have strayed out of the high road of nature. The property of France does not govern it. Of course property is destroyed, and rational liberty has no existence. All you have got for the present is a paper circulation, and a stock-jobbing constitution: and, as to the future, do you seriously think that the territory of France, upon the republican system of eighty-three independent municipalities, (to say nothing of the parts that compose them) can ever be governed as one body, or can ever be set in motion by the impulse of one mind? When the National Assembly has completed its work, it will have accomplished its ruin. These commonwealths will not long bear a state of subjection to the republic of Paris. They will not bear that this one body should monopolize the captivity of the king, and the dominion over the assembly calling itself National. Each will keep its own portion of the spoil of the church to itself; and it will not suffer either that spoil, or the more just fruits of their industry, or the natural produce of their soil, to be sent to swell the insolence, or pamper the luxury, of the mechanics of Paris. In this they will see none of the equality, under the pretence of which they have been tempted to throw off their allegiance to their sovereign, as well as the ancient constitution of their country. There can be no capital city in such a constitution as they have lately made. They have forgot, that when they framed democratic governments, they had virtually dismembered their country. The person, whom they persevere in calling king, has not power left to him by the hundredth part sufficient to hold together this collection of republics. The republic of Paris will endeavour indeed to complete the debauchery of the army, and illegally to perpetuate the assembly, without resort to its constituents, as the means of continuing its despotism. It will make efforts, by becoming the heart of a boundless paper circulation, to draw everything to itself; but in vain. All this policy in the end will appear as feeble as it is now violent.

If this be your actual situation, compared to the situation to which you were called, as it were by the voice of God and man, I cannot find it in my heart to congratulate you on the choice you have made, or the success which has attended your endeavours. I can as little recommend to any other nation a conduct grounded on such principles, and productive of such effects. That I must leave to those who can see farther into your affairs than I am able to do, and who best know how far your actions are favourable to their designs. The gentlemen of the Revolution Society, who were so early in their congratulations, appear to be strongly of opinion that there is some scheme of politics relative to this country in which your proceedings may, in some way, be useful. For your Dr. Price, who seems to have speculated himself into no small degree of fervour upon this subject, addresses his auditory in the following very remarkable words: "I cannot conclude without recalling *particularly* to your recollection a consideration which I have *more than once alluded to,* and which probably your thoughts have *been all along anticipating;* a consideration with which my *mind is impressed more than I can express.* I mean the consideration of the *favourableness of the present times to all exertions in the cause of liberty.*"

It is plain that the mind of this *political* Preacher was at the time big with some extraordinary design; and it is very probable that the thoughts of his audience, who understood him better than I do, did all along run before him in his reflection, and in the whole train of consequences to which it led.

Before I read that sermon, I really thought I had lived in a free country; and it was an error I cherished, because it gave me a greater liking to the country I lived in. I was indeed, aware, that a jealous, ever-waking vigilance, to guard the treasure of our liberty, not only from invasion, but from decay and corruption, was our best wisdom, and our first duty. However, I considered that treasure rather as a possession to be secured, than as a prize to be contended for. I did not discern how the present time came to be so very favourable to all *exertions* in the cause of freedom. The present time differs from any other only by the circumstance of what is doing in France. If the example of that nation is to have an influence on this, I can easily conceive why some of their proceedings which have an unpleasant aspect, and are not quite reconcilable to humanity, generosity, good faith, and justice, are palliated with so much milky goodnature towards the actors, and borne with so much heroic fortitude towards the sufferers. It is certainly not prudent to discredit the authority of an example we mean to follow. But allowing this, we are led to a very natural question;—What is that cause of liberty, and what are those exertions in its favour, to which the example of France is so singularly auspicious? Is our monarchy to be annihilated, with all the laws, all the tribunals, and all the ancient corporations of the kingdom? Is every land-mark of the country to be done away in favour of a geometrical and arithmetical constitution? Is the House of Lords to be voted useless? Is episcopacy to be abolished? Are the church lands to be sold to Jews and jobbers; or given to bribe new-invented municipal republics into a participation in sacrilege? Are all the taxes to be voted grievances, and the revenue reduced to a patriotic contribution, or patriotic presents? Are silver shoe-buckles to be substituted in the place of the land tax and the malt tax, for the support of the naval strength of this kingdom? Are all orders, ranks, and distinctions to be confounded, that out of universal anarchy, joined to national bankruptcy, three or four thousand democracies should be formed into eighty-three, and that they may all, by some sort of unknown attractive power, be organized into one? For this great end is the army to be seduced from its discipline and its fidelity, first by every kind of debauchery, and then by the terrible precedent of a donative in the increase of pay? Are the curates to be seduced from their bishops, by holding out to them the delusive hope of a dole out of the spoils of their own order? Are the citizens of London to be drawn from their allegiance by feeding them at the expense of their fellow-subjects? Is a compulsory paper currency to be substituted in the place of the legal coin of this kingdom? Is what remains of the plundered stock of public revenue to be employed in the wild project of maintaining two armies to watch over and to fight with each other? If these are the ends and means of the Revolution Society, I admit that they are well assorted; and France may furnish them for both with precedents in point.

I see that your example is held out to shame us. I know that we are supposed a dull, sluggish race, rendered passive by finding our situation tolerable, and prevented by a mediocrity of freedom from ever attaining to its full perfection. Your leaders in France began by affecting to admire, almost to adore, the British constitution; but as they advanced, they came to look upon it with a sovereign contempt. The friends of your National Assembly amongst us have full as mean an opinion of what was formerly thought the glory of their country. The Revolution Society has discovered that the English nation is not free. They are convinced that the inequality in our representation is a "defect in our constitution *so gross and palpable, as to make it excellent chiefly in form and theory.*[11]" That a representation in the legislature of a kingdom is not only the basis of all constitutional liberty in it, but of *"all legitimate government;* that without it a *government* is nothing but an *usurpation;"*—that "when the representation is *partial,* the kingdom possesses liberty only *partially;* and if extremely partial, it gives only a *semblance;* and if not only extremely partial, but corruptly chosen, it becomes a *nuisance."* Dr. Price considers this inadequacy of representation as our *fundamental grievance;* and though, as to the corruption of this semblance of representation, he hopes it is not yet arrived to its full perfection of depravity, he fears that "nothing will be done towards gaining for us this *essential blessing,* until some *great abuse of power*

[11] Discourse on the Love of our Country, 3rd edit. p. 39.

again provokes our resentment, or some *great calamity* again alarms our fears, or perhaps till the acquisition of a *pure and equal representation by other countries,* whilst we are *mocked* with the *shadow,* kindles our shame." To this he subjoins a note in these words: "A representation chosen chiefly by the Treasury, and a *few* thousands of the *dregs* of the people, who are generally paid for their votes."

You will smile here at the consistency of those democratists, who, when they are not on their guard, treat the humbler part of the community with the greatest contempt, whilst, at the same time, they pretend to make them the depositories of all power. It would require a long discourse to point out to you the many fallacies that lurk in the generality and equivocal nature of the terms "inadequate representation." I shall only say here, in justice to that old-fashioned constitution, under which we have long prospered, that our representation has been found perfectly adequate to all the purposes for which a representation of the people can be desired or devised. I defy the enemies of our constitution to show the contrary. To detail the particulars in which it is found so well to promote its ends, would demand a treatise on our practical constitution. I state here the doctrine of the Revolutionists, only that you and others may see what an opinion these gentlemen entertain of the constitution of their country, and why they seem to think that some great abuse of power, or some great calamity, as giving a chance for the blessing of a constitution according to their ideas, would be much palliated to their feelings; you see *why they* are so much enamoured of your fair and equal representation, which being once obtained, the same effects might follow. You see they consider our House of Commons as only "a semblance," "a form," "a theory," "a shadow," "a mockery," perhaps "a nuisance."

These gentlemen value themselves on being systematic; and not without reason. They must therefore look on this gross and palpable defect of representation, this fundamental grievance, (so they call it,) as a thing not only vicious in itself, but as rendering our whole government absolutely *illegitimate,* and not at all better than a downright *usurpation.* Another revolution, to get rid of this illegitimate and usurped government, would of course be perfectly justifiable, if not absolutely necessary. Indeed their principle, if you observe it with any attention, goes much further than to an alteration in the election of the House of Commons; for, if popular representation, or choice, is necessary to the *legitimacy* of all government, the House of Lords is, at one stroke, bastardized and corrupted in blood. That House is no representative of the people at all, even in "semblance or in form." The case of the crown is altogether as bad. In vain the crown may endeavour to screen itself against these gentlemen by the authority of the establishment made on the Revolution. The Revolution which is resorted to for a title, on their system, wants a title itself. The Revolution is built, according to their theory, upon a basis not more solid than our present formalities, as it was made by a House of Lords, not representing any one but themselves; and by a House of Commons exactly such as the present, that is, as they term it, by a mere "shadow and mockery" of representation.

Something they must destroy, or they seem to themselves to exist for no purpose. One set is for destroying the civil power through the ecclesiastical; another, for demolishing the ecclesiastic through the civil. They are aware that the worst consequences might happen to the public in accomplishing this double ruin of church and state; but they are so heated with their theories, that they give more than hints, that this ruin, with all the mischiefs that must lead to it and attend it, and which to themselves appear quite certain, would not be unacceptable to them, or very remote from their wishes. A man amongst them of great authority, and certainly of great talents, speaking of a supposed alliance between church and state says, "perhaps *we must wait for the fall of the civil powers* before this most unnatural alliance be broken. Calamitous no doubt will that time be. But what convulsion in the political world ought to be a subject of lamentation, if it be attended with so desirable an effect?" You see with what a steady eye these gentlemen are prepared to view the greatest calamities which can befall their country.

It is no wonder therefore, that with these ideas of everything in their constitution and government at home, either in church or state, as illegitimate and usurped, or at best as a vain mockery, they look abroad with an eager and passionate enthusiasm. Whilst they are possessed by these notions, it is vain to talk to them of the practice of their ancestors, the fundamental laws of their country, the fixed form of a constitution, whose merits are confirmed by the solid test of long experience, and an increasing public strength and national prosperity. They despise experience as the wisdom of unlettered men; and as for the rest, they have wrought under-ground a mine that will blow up, at one grand explosion, all examples of antiquity, all precedents, charters, and acts of parliament. They have "the rights of men." Against these there can be no prescription; against these no agreement is binding: these admit no temperament, and no compromise: anything withheld from their full demand is so much of fraud and injustice. Against these their rights of men let no government look for security in the length of its continuance, or in the justice and lenity of its administration. The objections of these speculatists, if its forms do not quadrate with their theories, are as valid against such an old and beneficent government, as against the most violent tyranny, or the greenest usurpation. They are always at issue with governments, not on a question of abuse, but a question of competency, and a question of title. I have nothing to say to the clumsy subtilty of their political metaphysics. Let them be their amusement in the schools.—*"Illa se jactat in aula—Æolus, et clauso ventorum carcere regnet."*—But let them not break prison to burst like a Levanter, to sweep the earth with their hurricane, and to break up the fountains of the great deep to overwhelm us.

Far am I from denying in theory, full as far is my heart from withholding in practice, (if I were of power to give or to withhold,) the *real* rights of men. In denying their false claims of right, I do not mean to injure those which are real, and are such as their pretended rights would totally destroy. If civil society be made for the advantage of man, all the advantages for which it is made become his right. It is an institution of beneficence; and law itself is only beneficence acting by a rule. Men have a right to live by that rule; they have a right to do justice, as between their fellows, whether their fellows are in public function or in ordinary occupation. They have a right to the fruits of their industry; and to the means of making their industry fruitful. They have a right to the acquisitions of their parents; to the nourishment and improvement of their offspring; to instruction in life, and to consolation in death. Whatever each man can separately do, without trespassing upon others, he has a right to do for himself; and he has a right to a fair portion of all which society, with all its combinations of skill and force, can do in his favour. In this partnership all men have equal rights; but not to equal things. He that has but five shillings in the partnership, has as good a right to it, as he that has five hundred pounds has to his larger proportion. But he has not a right to an equal dividend in the product of the joint stock; and as to the share of power, authority, and direction which each individual ought to have in the management of the state, that I must deny to be amongst the direct original rights of man in civil society; for I have in my contemplation the civil social man, and no other. It is a thing to be settled by convention.

If civil society be the offspring of convention, that convention must be its law. That convention must limit and modify all the descriptions of constitution which are formed under it. Every sort of legislative, judicial, or executory power are its creatures. They can have no being in any other state of things; and how can any man claim under the conventions of civil society, rights which do not so much as suppose its existence? rights which are absolutely repugnant to it? One of the first motives to civil society, and which becomes one of its fundamental rules, is, *that no man should be judge in his own cause*. By this each person has at once divested himself of the first fundamental right of uncovenanted man, that is, to judge for himself, and to assert his own cause. He abdicates all right to be his own governor. He inclusively, in a great measure, abandons the right of self-defence, the first law of nature. Men cannot enjoy the rights of an uncivil and of a civil state together. That he may obtain justice, he gives up his right of determining what it is in points the most essential to him. That he may secure some liberty, he makes a surrender in trust of the whole of it.

Government is not made in virtue of natural rights, which may and do exist in total independence of it; and exist in much greater clearness, and in a much greater degree of abstract perfection: but their abstract perfection is their practical defect. By having a right to everything they want everything. Government is a contrivance of human wisdom to provide for human *wants*. Men have a right that these wants should be provided for by this wisdom. Among these wants is to be reckoned the want, out of civil society, of a sufficient restraint upon their passions. Society requires not only that the passions of individuals should be subjected, but that even in the mass and body, as well as in the individuals, the inclinations of men should frequently be thwarted, their will controlled, and their passions brought into subjection. This can only be done *by a power out of themselves;* and not, in the exercise of its function, subject to that will and to those passions which it is its office to bridle and subdue. In this sense the restraints on men, as well as their liberties, are to be reckoned among their rights. But as the liberties and the restrictions vary with times and circumstances, and admit of infinite modifications, they cannot be settled upon any abstract rule; and nothing is so foolish as to discuss them upon that principle.

The moment you abate anything from the full rights of men, each to govern himself, and suffer any artificial, positive limitation upon those rights, from that moment the whole organization of government becomes a consideration of convenience. This it is which makes the constitution of a state, and the due distribution of its powers, a matter of the most delicate and complicated skill. It requires a deep knowledge of human nature and human necessities, and of the things which facilitate or obstruct the various ends, which are to be pursued by the mechanism of civil institutions. The state is to have recruits to its strength, and remedies to its distempers. What is the use of discussing a man's abstract right to food or medicine? The question is upon the method of procuring and administering them. In that deliberation I shall always advise to call in the aid of the farmer and the physician, rather than the professor of metaphysics.

The science of constructing a commonwealth, or renovating it, or reforming it, is, like every other experimental science, not to be taught *à priori.* Nor is it a short experience that can instruct us in that practical science: because the real effects of moral causes are not always immediate; but that which in the first instance is prejudicial may be excellent in its remoter operation; and its excellence may arise even from the ill effects it produces in the beginning. The reverse also happens: and very plausible schemes, with very pleasing commencements, have often shameful and lamentable conclusions.

In states there are often some obscure and almost latent causes, things which appear at first view of little moment, on which a very great part of its prosperity or adversity may most essentially depend. The science of government being therefore so practical in itself, and intended for such practical purposes, a matter which requires experience, and even more experience than any person can gain in his whole life, however sagacious and observing he may be, it is with infinite caution that any man ought to venture upon pulling down an edifice, which has answered in any tolerable degree for ages the common purposes of society, or on building it up again, without having models and patterns of approved utility before his eyes.

These metaphysic rights entering into common life, like rays of light which pierce into a dense medium, are, by the laws of nature, refracted from their straight line. Indeed in the gross and complicated mass of human passions and concerns, the primitive rights of men undergo such a variety of refractions and reflections, that it becomes absurd to talk of them as if they continued in the simplicity of their original direction. The nature of man is intricate; the objects of society are of the greatest possible complexity: and therefore no simple disposition or direction of power can be suitable either to man's nature, or to the quality of his affairs. When I hear the simplicity of contrivance aimed at and boasted of in any new political constitutions, I am at no loss to decide that the artificers are grossly ignorant of their trade, or totally negligent of their duty. The simple governments are fundamentally defective, to say no worse of them. If you were to contemplate society in but one point of view, all these simple modes of polity are infinitely captivating. In effect each would answer its single end much more perfectly than the more complex is able to attain all its complex purposes. But it is better that the whole should be imperfectly and anomalously answered, than that, while some parts are provided for with great exactness, others might be totally neglected, or perhaps materially injured, by the over-care of a favourite member.

The pretended rights of these theorists are all extremes: and in proportion as they are metaphysically true, they are morally and politically false. The rights of men are in a sort of *middle,* incapable of definition, but not impossible to be discerned. The rights of men in governments are their advantages; and these are often in balances between differences of good; in compromises sometimes between good and evil, and sometimes between evil and evil. Political reason is a computing principle; adding, subtracting, multiplying, and dividing, morally and not metaphysically, or mathematically, true moral denominations.

By these theorists the right of the people is almost always sophistically confounded with their power. The body of the community, whenever it can come to act, can meet with no effectual resistance; but till power and right are the same, the whole body of them has no right inconsistent with virtue, and the first of all virtues, prudence. Men have no right to what is not reasonable, and to what is not for their benefit; for though a pleasant writer said, *Liceat perire poetis,* when one of them, in cold blood, is said to have leaped into the flames of a volcanic revolution, *Ardentem frigidus Ætnam insiluit,* I consider such a frolic rather as an unjustifiable poetic license, than as one of the franchises of Parnassus; and whether he was a poet, or divine, or politician, that chose to exercise this kind of right, I think that more wise, because more charitable, thoughts would urge me rather to save the man than to preserve his brazen slippers as the monuments of his folly.

The kind of anniversary sermons to which a great part of what I write refers, if men are not shamed out of their present course, in commemorating the fact, will cheat many out of the principles, and deprive them of the benefits, of the revolution they commemorate. I confess to you, Sir, I never liked this continual talk of resistance, and revolution, or the practice of making the extreme medicine of the constitution its daily bread. It renders the habit of society dangerously valetudinary: it is taking periodical doses of mercury sublimate, and swallowing down repeated provocatives of cantharides to our love of liberty.

This distemper of remedy, grown habitual, relaxes and wears out, by a vulgar and prostituted use, the spring of that spirit which is to be exerted on great occasions. It was in the most patient period of Roman servitude that themes of tyrannicide made the ordinary exercise of boys at school—*cum perimit sævos classis numerosa tyrannos.* In the ordinary state of things, it produces in a country like ours the worst effects, even on the cause of that liberty which it abuses with the dissoluteness of an extravagant speculation. Almost all the high-bred republicans of my time have, after a short space, become the most decided, thorough-paced courtiers; they soon left the business of a tedious, moderate, but practical resistance, to those of us whom, in the pride and intoxication of their theories, they have slighted as not much better than Tories. Hypocrisy, of course, delights in the most sublime speculations; for, never intending to go beyond speculation, it costs nothing to have it magnificent. But even in cases where rather levity than fraud was to be suspected in these ranting speculations, the issue has been much the same. These professors, finding their extreme principles not applicable to cases which call only for a qualified, or, as I may say, civil and legal resistance, in such cases employ no resistance at all. It is with them a war or a revolution, or it is nothing. Finding their schemes of politics not adapted to the state of the world in which they live, they often come to think lightly of all public principle; and are ready, on their part, to abandon for a very trivial interest what they find of very trivial value. Some indeed are of more steady and persevering natures; but these are eager politicians out of parliament, who have little to tempt them to abandon their favourite projects. They have some change in the church or state, or both, constantly in their view. When that is the case, they are always bad citizens, and perfectly unsure connexions. For, considering their speculative designs as of infinite value, and the actual arrangement of the state as of no estimation, they are at best indifferent about it. They see no merit in the good, and no fault in the vicious, management of public affairs; they rather rejoice in the latter, as more propitious to revolution. They see no merit or demerit in any man, or any action, or any political principle, any further than as they may forward or retard their design of change: they therefore take up, one day, the most violent and stretched prerogative, and another time the wildest democratic ideas of freedom, and pass from one to the other without any sort or regard to cause, to person, or to party.

In France you are now in the crisis of a revolution, and in the transit from one form of government to another—you cannot see that character of men exactly in the same situation in which we see it in this country. With us it is militant; with you it is triumphant; and you know how it can act when its power is commensurate to its will. I would not be supposed to confine those observations to any description of men, or to comprehend all men of any description within them—No! far from it. I am as incapable of that injustice, as I am of keeping terms with those who profess principles of extremities; and who, under the name of religion, teach little else than wild and dangerous politics. The worst of these politics of revolution is this: they temper and harden the breast, in order to prepare it for the desperate strokes which are sometimes used in extreme occasions. But as these occasions may never arrive, the mind receives a gratuitous taint; and the moral sentiments suffer not a little, when no political purpose is served by the depravation. This sort of people are so taken up with their theories about the rights of man, that they have totally forgotten his nature. Without opening one new avenue to the understanding, they have succeeded in stopping up those that lead to the heart. They have perverted in themselves, and in those that attend to them, all the well-placed sympathies of the human breast.

This famous sermon of the Old Jewry breathes nothing but this spirit through all the political part. Plots, massacres, assassinations, seem to some people a trivial price for obtaining a revolution. Cheap, bloodless reformation, a guiltless liberty, appear flat and vapid to their taste. There must be a great change of scene; there must be a magnificent stage effect; there must be a grand spectacle to rouse the imagination, grown torpid with the lazy enjoyment of sixty years' security and the still unanimating repose of public prosperity. The preacher found them all in the French Revolution. This inspires a juvenile warmth through his whole frame. His enthusiasm kindles as he advances; and when he arrives at his peroration it is in a full blaze. Then viewing, from the Pisgah of his pulpit, the free, moral, happy, flourishing and glorious state of France, as in a bird's-eye landscape of a promised land, he breaks out into the following rapture:

"What an eventful period is this! I am *thankful* that I have lived to it; I could almost say, *Lord, now lettest thou thy servant depart in peace, for mine eyes have seen thy salvation.*—I have lived to see a diffusion of knowledge, which has undermined superstition and error.—I have lived to see *the rights of men* better understood than ever; and nations panting for liberty which seemed to have lost the idea of it.—I have lived to see *Thirty Millions of People,* indignant and resolute, spurning at slavery, and demanding liberty with an irresistible voice. *Their king led in triumph and an arbitrary monarch surrendering himself to his subjects.*[12]"

Before I proceed further, I have to remark, that Dr. Price seems rather to overvalue the great acquisitions of light which he has obtained and diffused in this age. The last century appears to me to have been quite as much enlightened. It had, though in a different place, a triumph as memorable as that of Dr. Price; and some of the great preachers of that period partook of it as eagerly as he has done in the triumph of France. On the trial of the Rev. Hugh Peters for high treason, it was deposed, that when King Charles was brought to London for his trial, the Apostle of Liberty in that day conducted the *triumph*. "I saw," says the witness, "his Majesty in the coach with six horses, and Peters riding before the king, *triumphing*." Dr. Price, when he talks as if he had made a discovery, only follows a precedent; for, after the commencement of the king's trial, this precursor, the same Dr. Peters, concluding a long prayer at the Royal Chapel at Whitehall, (he had very triumphantly chosen his place) said, "I have prayed and preached these twenty years; and now I may say with old Simeon, *Lord, now lettest thou thy servant depart in peace, for mine eyes have seen thy salvation.*[13]" Peters had not the fruits of his prayer; for he neither departed so soon as he wished, nor in peace. He became (what I heartily hope none of his followers may be in this country) himself a sacrifice to the triumph which he led as pontiff.

They dealt at the Restoration, perhaps, too hardly with this poor good man. But we owe it to his memory and his sufferings, that he had as much illumination, and as much zeal, and had as effectually

---

[12] Another of these reverend gentlemen, who was witness to some of the spectacles which Paris has lately exhibited, expresses himself thus:—"*A king dragged in submissive triumph by his conquering subjects,* is one of those appearances of grandeur which seldom rise in the prospect of human affairs, and which, during the remainder of my life, I shall think of with wonder and gratification." These gentlemen agree marvellously in their feelings.   [13] State Trials, vol. ii. p. 360, p. 363.

undermined all *the superstition and error* which might impede the great business he was engaged in, as any who follow and repeat after him, in this age, which would assume to itself an exclusive title to the knowledge of the rights of men, and all the glorious consequences of that knowledge.

After this sally of the preacher of the Old Jewry, which differs only in place and time, but agrees perfectly with the spirit and letter of the rapture of 1648, the Revolution Society, the fabricators of governments, the heroic band of cashierers of monarchs, electors of sovereigns, and leaders of kings in triumph, strutting with a proud consciousness of the diffusion of knowledge, of which every member had obtained so large a share in the donative, were in haste to make a general diffusion of the knowledge they had thus gratuitously received. To make this bountiful communication, they adjourned from the church in the Old Jewry to the London Tavern; where the same Dr. Price, in whom the fumes of his oracular tripod were not entirely evaporated, moved and carried the resolution, or address of congratulation transmitted by Lord Stanhope to the National Assembly of France.

I find a preacher of the gospel profaning the beautiful and prophetic ejaculation, commonly called *"nunc dimittis,"* made on the first presentation of our Saviour in the Temple, and applying it, with an inhuman and unnatural rapture, to the most horrid, atrocious, and afflicting spectacle that perhaps ever was exhibited to the pity and indignation of mankind. This *"leading in triumph,"* a thing in its best form unmanly and irreligious, which fills our preacher with such unhallowed transports, must shock, I believe, the moral taste of every well-born mind. Several English were the stupefied and indignant spectators of that triumph. It was (unless we have been strangely deceived) a spectacle more resembling a procession of American savages, entering into Onondaga, after some of their murders called victories, and leading into hovels hung round with scalps, their captives, overpowered with the scoffs and buffets of women as ferocious as themselves, much more than it resembled the triumphal pomp of a civilized, martial nation—if a civilized nation, or any men who had a sense of generosity, were capable of a personal triumph over the fallen and afflicted.

This, my dear Sir, was not the triumph of France. I must believe that, as a nation, it overwhelmed you with shame and horror. I must believe that the National Assembly find themselves in a state of the greatest humiliation in not being able to punish the authors of this triumph, or the actors in it; and that they are in a situation in which any inquiry they may make upon the subject must be destitute even of the appearance of liberty or impartiality. The apology of that assembly is found in their situation; but when we approve what they *must* bear, it is in us the degenerate choice of a vitiated mind.

With a compelled appearance of deliberation, they vote under the dominion of a stern necessity. They sit in the heart, as it were, of a foreign republic: they have their residence in a city whose constitution has emanated neither from the charter of their king, nor from their legislative power. There they are surrounded by an army not raised either by the authority of their crown, or by their command; and which, if they should order to dissolve itself, would instantly dissolve them. There they sit, after a gang of assassins had driven away some hundreds of the members; whilst those who held the same moderate principles, with more patience or better hope, continued every day exposed to outrageous insults and murderous threats. There a majority, sometimes real, sometimes pretended, captive itself, compels a captive king to issue as royal edicts, at third hand, the polluted nonsense of their most licentious and giddy coffeehouses. It is notorious, that all their measures are decided before they are debated. It is beyond doubt, that under the terror of the bayonet, and the lamp-post, and the torch to their houses, they are obliged to adopt all the crude and desperate measures suggested by clubs composed of a monstrous medley of all conditions, tongues, and nations. Among these are found persons, in comparison of whom Catiline would be thought scrupulous, and Cethegus a man of sobriety and moderation. Nor is it in these clubs alone that the public measures are deformed into monsters. They undergo a previous distortion in academies, intended as so many seminaries for these clubs, which are set up in all the places of public resort. In these meetings of all sorts, every counsel, in proportion as it is daring, and violent, and perfidious, is taken for the mark of superior genius. Humanity and compassion are ridiculed as the fruits of superstition and ignorance. Tenderness to individuals is considered as treason to the public. Liberty is always to be estimated perfect as property is rendered insecure. Amidst assassination, massacre, and confiscation, perpetrated or meditated, they are forming plans for the good order of future society. Embracing in their arms the carcases of base criminals, and promoting their relations on the title of their offences, they drive hundreds of virtuous persons to the same end, by forcing them to subsist by beggary or by crime.

The assembly, their organ, acts before them the farce of deliberation with as little decency as liberty. They act like the comedians of a fair before a riotous audience; they act amidst the tumultuous cries of a mixed mob of ferocious men, and of women lost to shame, who, according to their insolent fancies, direct, control, applaud, explode them; and sometimes mix and take their seats amongst them; domineering over them with a strange mixture of servile petulance and proud, presumptuous authority. As they have inverted order in all things, the gallery is in the place of the house. This assembly, which overthrows kings and kingdoms, has not even the physiognomy and aspect of a grave legislative body—*nec color imperii, nec frons ulla senatûs*. They have a power given to them, like that of the evil principle, to subvert and destroy; but none to construct, except such machines as may be fitted for further subversion and further destruction.

Who is it that admires, and from the heart is attached to, national representative assemblies, but must turn with horror and disgust from such a profane burlesque, and abominable perversion of that sacred institute? Lovers of monarchy, lovers of republics, must alike abhor it. The members of your assembly must themselves groan under the tyranny of which they have all the shame, none of the direction, and little of the profit. I am sure many of the members who compose even the majority of that body must feel as I do, notwithstanding the applauses of the Revolution Society. Miserable king! miserable assembly! How must that assembly be silently scandalized with those of their members, who could call a day which seemed to blot the sun out of heaven, *"un beau jour!"*[14] How must they be inwardly indignant at hearing others, who thought fit to

[14] 6th of October, 1789.

declare to them, "that the vessel of the state would fly forward in her course towards regeneration with more speed than ever," from the stiff gale of treason and murder, which preceded our preacher's triumph! What must they have felt, whilst, with outward patience, and inward indignation, they heard of the slaughter of innocent gentlemen in their houses, that "the blood spilled was not the most pure!" What must they have felt, when they were besieged by complaints of disorders which shook their country to its foundations, at being compelled coolly to tell the complainants, that they were under the protection of the law, and that they would address the king (the captive king) to cause the laws to be enforced for their protection; when the enslaved ministers of that captive king had formally notified to them, that there were neither law, nor authority, nor power left to protect! What must they have felt at being obliged, as a felicitation on the present new year, to request their captive king to forget the stormy period of the last, on account of the great good which *he* was likely to produce to his people; to the complete attainment of which good they adjourned the practical demonstrations of their loyalty, assuring him of their obedience, when he should no longer possess any authority to command!

This address was made with much good nature and affection, to be sure. But among the revolutions in France must be reckoned a considerable revolution in their ideas of politeness. In England we are said to learn manners at second-hand from your side of the water, and that we dress our behaviour in the frippery of France. If so, we are still in the old cut; and have not so far conformed to the new Parisian mode of good breeding, as to think it quite in the most refined strain of delicate compliment (whether in condolence or congratulation) to say, to the most humiliated creature that crawls upon the earth, that great public benefits are derived from the murder of his servants, the attempted assassination of himself and of his wife, and the mortification, disgrace, and degradation, that he has personally suffered. It is a topic of consolation which our ordinary of Newgate would be too humane to use to a criminal at the foot of the gallows. I should have thought that the hangman of Paris, now that he is liberalized by the vote of the National Assembly, and is allowed his rank and arms in the herald's college of the rights of men, would be too generous, too gallant a man, too full of the sense of his new dignity, to employ that cutting consolation to any of the persons whom the *leze nation* might bring under the administration of his *executive powers*.

A man is fallen indeed, when he is thus flattered. The anodyne draught of oblivion, thus drugged, is well calculated to preserve a galling wakefulness, and to feed the living ulcer of a corroding memory. Thus to administer the opiate potion of amnesty, powdered with all the ingredients of scorn and contempt, is to hold to his lips, instead of "the balm of hurt minds," the cup of human misery full to the brim, and to force him to drink it to the dregs.

Yielding to reasons, at least as forcible as those which were so delicately urged in the compliment on the new year, the king of France will probably endeavour to forget these events and that compliment. But history, who keeps a durable record of all our acts, and exercises her awful censure over the proceedings of all sorts of sovereigns, will not forget either those events, or the era of this liberal refinement in the intercourse of mankind. History will record, that on the morning of the 6th of October, 1789, the king and queen of France, after a day of confusion, alarm, dismay, and slaughter, lay down, under the pledged security of public faith, to indulge nature in a few hours of respite, and troubled, melancholy repose. From this sleep the queen was first startled by the voice of the sentinel at her door, who cried out to her to save herself by flight—that this was the last proof of fidelity he could give—that they were upon him, and he was dead. Instantly he was cut down. A band of cruel ruffians and assassins, reeking with his blood, rushed into the chamber of the queen, and pierced with a hundred strokes of bayonets and poniards the bed, from whence this persecuted woman had but just time to fly almost naked, and, through ways unknown to the murderers, had escaped to seek refuge at the feet of a king and husband, not secure of his own life for a moment.

This king, to say no more of him, and this queen, and their infant children, (who once would have been the pride and hope of a great and generous people,) were then forced to abandon the sanctuary of the most splendid palace in the world, which they left swimming in blood, polluted by massacre, and strewed with scattered limbs and mutilated carcases. Thence they were conducted into the capital of their kingdom.

Two had been selected from the unprovoked, unresisted, promiscuous slaughter, which was made of the gentlemen of birth and family who composed the king's body guard. These two gentlemen, with all the parade of an execution of justice, were cruelly and publicly dragged to the block, and beheaded in the great court of the palace. Their heads were stuck upon spears, and led the procession; whilst the royal captives who followed in the train were slowly moved along, amidst the horrid yells, and shrilling screams, and frantic dances, and infamous contumelies, and all the unutterable abominations of the furies of hell, in the abused shape of the vilest of women.

After they had been made to taste, drop by drop, more than the bitterness of death, in the slow torture of a journey of twelve miles, protracted to six hours, they were, under a guard, composed of those very soldiers who had thus conducted them through this famous triumph, lodged in one of the old palaces of Paris, now converted into a bastile for kings.

Is this a triumph to be consecrated at altars? to be commemorated with grateful thanksgiving? to be offered to the divine humanity with fervent prayer and enthusiastic ejaculation?—These Theban and Thracian orgies, acted in France, and applauded only in the Old Jewry, I assure you, kindle prophetic enthusiasm in the minds but of very few people in this kingdom: although a saint and apostle, who may have revelations of his own, and who has so completely vanquished all the mean superstitions of the heart, may incline to think it pious and decorous to compare it with the entrance into the world of the Prince of Peace, proclaimed in a holy temple by a venerable sage, and not long before not worse announced by the voice of angels to the quiet innocence of shepherds.

At first I was at a loss to account for this fit of unguarded transport. I knew, indeed, that the sufferings of monarchs make a delicious repast to some sort of palates. There were reflections which might serve to keep this appetite within some bounds of temperance. But when I took one circumstance into my consideration, I was obliged to confess, that much allowance ought to be made for the society, and that the temptation was too strong for common discretion; I mean, the circumstance of the *Io Pæan* of the triumph, the animating cry which called "for *all* the BISHOPS to be hanged on the lamp-posts,[15]" might well have brought forth a burst of enthusiasm on the foreseen consequences of this happy day. I allow to so much enthusiasm some little deviation from prudence. I allow this prophet to break forth into hymns of joy and thanksgiving on an event which appears like the precursor of the Millenium, and the projected fifth monarchy, in the destruction of all church establishments.

There was, however, (as in all human affairs there is) in the midst of this joy, something to exercise the patience of these worthy gentlemen, and to try the long-suffering of their faith. The actual murder of the king and queen, and their child, was wanting to the other auspicious circumstances of this *"beautiful day."* The actual murder of the bishops, though called for by so many holy ejaculations, was also wanting. A group of regicide and sacrilegious slaughter, was indeed boldly sketched, but it was only sketched. It unhappily was left unfinished, in this great history-piece of the massacre of innocents. What hardy pencil of a great master, from the school of the rights of men, will finish it, is to be seen hereafter. The age has not yet the complete benefit of that diffusion of knowledge that has undermined superstition and error; and the king of France wants another object or two to consign to oblivion, in consideration of all the good which is to arise from his own sufferings, and the patriotic crimes of an enlightened age.[16]

15 Tous les Evêques à la lanterne.

16 It is proper here to refer to a letter written upon this subject by an eye-witness. That eye-witness was one of the most honest, intelligent, and eloquent members of the National Assembly, one of the most active and zealous reformers of the state. He was obliged to secede from the assembly; and he afterwards became a voluntary exile, on account of the horrors of this pious triumph, and the dispositions of men, who, profiting of crimes, if not causing them, have taken the lead in public affairs.

Extract of M. de Lally Tollendal's Second Letter to a Friend

"Parlons du parti que j'ai pris; il est bien justifié dans ma conscience.—Ni cette ville coupable, ni cette assemblée plus coupable encore, ne meritoient que je me justifie; mais j'ai à cœur que vous, et les personnes qui pensent comme vous, ne me condamnent pas.—Ma santé, je vous jure, me rendoit mes fonctions impossibles; mais même en les mettant de côté il a été au-dessus de mes forces de supporter plus long-tems l'horreur que me causoit ce sang,—ces têtes cette reine *presque égorgée*,—ce roi, —amené *sclave*,—entrantà Paris, au milieu de ses assassins, et précédé des têtes de ses malheureux grades—ces perfides janissaires, ces assassins, ces femmes cannibales,

Although this work of our new light and knowledge did not go to the length that in all probability it was intended it should be carried, yet I must think that such treatment of any human creatures must be shocking to any but those who are made for accomplishing revolutions. But I cannot stop here. Influenced by the inborn feelings of my nature, and not being illuminated by a single ray of this new-sprung modern light, I confess to you, Sir, that the exalted rank of the persons suffering, and particularly the sex, the beauty, and the amiable qualities of the descendant of so many kings and emperors, with the tender age of royal infants, insensible only through infancy and innocence of the cruel outrages to which their parents were exposed, instead of being a subject of exultation, adds not a little to my sensibility on that most melancholy occasion.

I hear that the august person, who was the principal object of our preacher's triumph, though he supported himself, felt much on that

ce cri de TOUS LES EVEQUES A LA LANTERNE, dans le moment où le roi entre sa capitale avec deux évêques de son conseil dans sa voiture—un *coup de fusil,* que j'ai vu tirer dans un *des carosses de la reine.* M. Bailly appellant cela *un beau jour,*—¬ assemblée ayant déclaré froidement le matin, qu'il n'étoit pas de sa dignité d'aller toute entière environner le roi—M. Mirabeau disant impunément dans cette assemblée que le vaisseau de l'état, loins d'être arrêté dans sa course, s'élanceroit avec plus de rapidité que jamais vers sa régénération—M. Barnave, riant avec lui, quand des flots de sang coulaient autour de nous—le vertueux Mounier* échappant par miracle à vingt assassins, qui avoient voulu faire de sa tête un trophée de plus: Voilà ce qui me fit jurer de ne plus mettre le pied *dans cette caverne d' Antropophages* [the National Assembly] où je n'avois plus de force d'élever la voix, où depuis six semaines je l'avois élevée en vain.

"Moi, Mounier, et tous les honnêtes gens, ont pensé que le dernier effort à faire pour le bien étoit d'en sortir. Aucune idée de crainte ne s'est approchée de moi. Je rougirois de m'en défendre. J'avois encore reçû sur la route de la part de ce peuple, moins coupable que ceux qui l'ont enivré de fureur, des acclamations, et des applaudissemens, dont d'autres auroient été flattés, et qui m'ont fait frémir. C'est à l'indignation, c'est à l'horreur, c'est aux convulsions physiques, que le seul aspect du sang me fait éprouver que j'ai cédé. On brave une seul mort; on la brave plusieurs fois, quand elle peut être utile. Mais aucune puissance sous le Ciel, mais aucune opinion publique, ou privée n'ont le droit de me condamner à souffrir inutilement mille supplices par minute, et à perir de désespoir, de rage, au milieu des *triomphes,* du crime que je n'ai pu arrêter. Ils me proscriront, ils confisqueront mes biens. Je labourerai la terre, et je ne les verrai plus.—Voilà ma justification. Vous pourrez la lire, la montrer, la laisser copier; tant pis pour ceux qui ne la comprendront pas; ce ne sera alors moi qui auroit eu tort de la leur donner."

This military man had not so good nerves as the peaceable gentleman of the Old Jewry.—See Mons. Mounier's narrative of these transactions; a man also of honour, and virtue, and talents, and therefore a fugitive.

*N. B. Mr. Mounier was then speaker of the National Assembly. He has since been obliged to live in exile, though one of the firmest asserters of liberty.

shameful occasion. As a man, it became him to feel for his wife and his children, and the faithful guards of his person, that were massacred in cold blood about him; as a prince, it became him to feel for the strange and frightful transformation of his civilized subjects, and to be more grieved for them than solicitous for himself. It derogates little from his fortitude, while it adds infinitely to the honour of his humanity. I am very sorry to say it, very sorry indeed, that such personages are in a situation in which it is not becoming in us to praise the virtues of the great.

I hear, and I rejoice to hear, that the great lady, the other object of the triumph, has borne that day, (one is interested that beings made for suffering should suffer well) and that she bears all the succeeding days, that she bears the imprisonment of her husband, and her own captivity, and the exile of her friends, and the insulting adulation of addresses, and the whole weight of her accumulated wrongs, with a serene patience, in a manner suited to her rank and race, and becoming the offspring of a sovereign distinguished for her piety and her courage: that, like her, she has lofty sentiments; that she feels with the dignity of a Roman matron; that in the last extremity she will save herself from the last disgrace; and that, if she must fall, she will fall by no ignoble hand.

It is now sixteen or seventeen years since I saw the queen of France, then the dauphiness, at Versailles; and surely never lighted on this orb, which she hardly seemed to touch, a more delightful vision. I saw her just above the horizon, decorating and cheering the elevated sphere she just began to move in,—glittering like the morning-star, full of life, and splendour, and joy. Oh! what a revolution! and what a heart must I have to contemplate without emotion that elevation and that fall! Little did I dream when she added titles of veneration to those of enthusiastic, distant, respectful love, that she should ever be obliged to carry the sharp antidote against disgrace concealed in that bosom; little did I dream that I should have lived to see such disasters fallen upon her in a nation of gallant men, in a nation of men of honour, and of cavaliers. I thought ten thousand swords must have leaped from their scabbards to avenge even a look that threatened her with insult. But the age of chivalry is gone. That of sophisters, economists, and calculators, has succeeded; and the glory of Europe is extinguished for ever. Never, never more shall we behold that generous loyalty to rank and sex, that proud submission, that dignified obedience, that subordination of the heart, which kept alive, even in servitude itself, the spirit of an exalted freedom. The unbought grace of life, the cheap defence of nations, the nurse of manly sentiment and heroic enterprise, is gone! It is gone, that sensibility of principle, that charity of honor, which felt a stain like a wound, which inspired courage whilst it mitigated ferocity, which ennobled whatever it touched, and under which vice itself lost half its evil, by losing all its grossness.

This mixed system of opinion and sentiment had its origin in the ancient chivalry; and the principle, though varied in its appearance by the varying state of human affairs, subsisted and influenced through a long succession of generations, even to the time we live in. If it should ever be totally extinguished, the loss I fear will be great. It is this which has given its character to modern Europe. It is this which has distinguished it under all its forms of government, and distinguished it to its advantage, from the states of Asia, and possibly from those states which flourished in the most brilliant periods of the antique world. It was this, which, without confounding ranks, had produced a noble equality, and handed it down through all the gradations of social life. It was this opinion which mitigated kings into companions, and raised private men to be fellows with kings. Without force or opposition, it subdued the fierceness of pride and power; it obliged sovereigns to submit to the soft collar of social esteem, compelled stern authority to submit to elegance, and gave a dominating vanquisher of laws to be subdued by manners.

But now all is to be changed. All the pleasing illusions, which made power gentle and obedience liberal, which harmonized the different shades of life, and which, by a bland assimilation, incorporated into politics the sentiments which beautify and soften private society, are to be dissolved by this new conquering empire of light and reason. All the decent drapery of life is to be rudely torn off. All the superadded ideas, furnished from the wardrobe of a moral imagination, which the heart owns, and the understanding ratifies,

as necessary to cover the defects of our naked, shivering nature, and
to raise it to dignity in our own estimation, are to be exploded as a
ridiculous, absurd, and antiquated fashion.

On this scheme of things, a king is but a man, a queen is but a
woman; a woman is but an animal, and an animal not of the highest
order. All homage paid to the sex in general as such, and without
distinct views, is to be regarded as romance and folly. Regicide, and
parricide, and sacrilege, are but fictions of superstition, corrupting
jurisprudence by destroying its simplicity. The murder of a king, or
a queen, or a bishop, or a father, are only common homicide; and if
the people are by any chance, or in any way, gainers by it, a sort of
homicide much the most pardonable, and into which we ought not
to make too severe a scrutiny.

On the scheme of this barbarous philosophy, which is the offspring
of cold hearts and muddy understandings, and which is as void of
solid wisdom as it is destitute of all taste and elegance, laws are to
be supported only by their own terrors, and by the concern which
each individual may find in them from his own private speculations,
or can spare to them from his own private interests. In the groves
of *their* academy, at the end of every vista, you see nothing but the
gallows. Nothing is left which engages the affections on the part
of the commonwealth. On the principles of this mechanic philosophy, our institutions can never be embodied, if I may use the expression, in persons; so as to create in us love, veneration, admiration, or attachment. But that sort of reason which banishes the
affections is incapable of filling their place. These public affections,
combined with manners, are required sometimes as supplements,
sometimes as correctives, always as aids to law. The precept given
by a wise man, as well as a great critic, for the construction of poems,
is equally true as to states:—*Non satis est pulchra esse poemata,
dulcia sunto.* There ought to be a system of manners in every nation, which a well-formed mind would be disposed to relish. To
make us love our country, our country ought to be lovely.

But power, of some kind or other, will survive the shock in which
manners and opinions perish; and it will find other and worse means
for its support. The usurpation which, in order to subvert ancient

institutions, has destroyed ancient principles, will hold power by arts similar to those by which it has acquired it. When the old feudal and chivalrous spirit of *fealty,* which, by freeing kings from fear, freed both kings and subjects from the precautions of tyranny, shall be extinct in the minds of men, plots and assassinations will be anticipated by preventive murder and preventive confiscation, and that long roll of grim and bloody maxims, which form the political code of all power, not standing on its own honour, and the honour of those who are to obey it. Kings will be tyrants from policy, when subjects are rebels from principle.

When ancient opinions and rules of life are taken away, the loss cannot possibly be estimated. From that moment we have no compass to govern us; nor can we know distinctly to what port we steer. Europe, undoubtedly, taken in a mass, was in a flourishing condition the day on which your revolution was completed. How much of that prosperous state was owing to the spirit of our old manners and opinions is not easy to say; but as such causes cannot be indifferent in their operation, we must presume, that, on the whole, their operation was beneficial.

We are but too apt to consider things in the state in which we find them, without sufficiently adverting to the causes by which they have been produced, and possibly may be upheld. Nothing is more certain, than that our manners, our civilization, and all the good things which are connected with manners and with civilization, have, in this European world of ours, depended for ages upon two principles; and were indeed the result of both combined; I mean the spirit of a gentleman, and the spirit of religion. The nobility and the clergy, the one by profession, the other by patronage, kept learning in existence, even in the midst of arms and confusions, and whilst governments were rather in their causes than formed. Learning paid back what it received to nobility and to priesthood, and paid it with usury, by enlarging their ideas, and by furnishing their minds. Happy if they had all continued to know their indissoluble union, and their proper place! Happy if learning, not debauched by ambition, had been satisfied to continue the instructor, and not aspired to be the master! Along with its natural protector and guardians, learning will be cast into the mire, and trodden down under the hoofs of a swinish multitude.[17]

If, as I suspect, modern letters owe more than they are always willing to owe to ancient manners, so do other interests which we value full as much as they are worth. Even commerce, and trade, and manufacture, the gods of our economical politicians, are themselves perhaps but creatures; are themselves but effects, which, as first causes, we choose to worship. They certainly grew under the same shade in which learning flourished. They too may decay with their natural protecting principles. With you, for the present at least, they all threaten to disappear together. Where trade and manufactures are wanting to a people, and the spirit of nobility and religion remains, sentiment supplies, and not always ill supplies, their place; but if commerce and the arts should be lost in an experiment to try how well a state may stand without these old fundamental principles, what sort of a thing must be a nation of gross, stupid, ferocious, and, at the same time, poor and sordid, barbarians, destitute of religion, honour, or manly pride, possessing nothing at present, and hoping for nothing hereafter?

I wish you may not be going fast, and by the shortest cut, to that horrible and disgustful situation. Already there appears a poverty of conception, a coarseness and a vulgarity, in all the proceedings of the Assembly and of all their instructors. Their liberty is not liberal. Their science is presumptuous ignorance. Their humanity is savage and brutal.

It is not clear, whether in England we learned those grand and decorous principles and manners, of which considerable traces yet remain, from you, or whether you took them from us. But to you, I think, we trace them best. You seem to me to be—*gentis incunabula nostræ.* France has always more or less influenced manners in England; and when your fountain is choked up and polluted, the stream will not run long, or not run clear, with us, or perhaps with any nation. This gives all Europe, in my opinion, but too close and connected a concern in what is done in France. Excuse me, therefore, if I have dwelt too long on the atrocious spectacle of

[17 See the fate of Bailly and Condorcet, supposed to be here particularly alluded to. Compare the circumstances of the trial and execution of the former with this prediction.]

the 6th of October, 1789, or have given too much scope to the reflections which have arisen in my mind on occasion of the most important of all revolutions, which may be dated from that day, I
mean a revolution in sentiments, manners, and moral opinions. As
things now stand, with everything respectable destroyed without us,
and an attempt to destroy within us every principle of respect, one is
almost forced to apologize for harbouring the common feelings of
men.

Why do I feel so differently from the Reverend Dr. Price, and
those of his lay flock who will choose to adopt the sentiments of his
discourse?—For this plain reason—because it is *natural* I should;
because we are so made, as to be affected at such spectacles with
melancholy sentiments upon the unstable condition of mortal prosperity, and the tremendous uncertainty of human greatness; because in those natural feelings we learn great lessons; because in
events like these our passions instruct our reason; because when
kings are hurled from their thrones by the Supreme Director of
this great drama, and become the objects of insult to the base, and
of pity to the good, we behold such disasters in the moral, as we
should behold a miracle in the physical, order of things. We are
alarmed into reflection; our minds (as it has long since been observed) are purified by terror and pity; our weak, unthinking pride
is humbled under the dispensations of a mysterious wisdom. Some
tears might be drawn from me, if such a spectacle were exhibited on
the stage. I should be truly ashamed of finding in myself that
superficial, theatric sense of painted distress, whilst I could exult
over it in real life. With such a perverted mind, I could never
venture to show my face at a tragedy. People would think the tears
that Garrick formerly, or that Siddons not long since, have extorted
from me, were the tears of hypocrisy; I should know them to be the
tears of folly.

Indeed the theatre is a better school of moral sentiments than
churches, where the feelings of humanity are thus outraged. Poets
who have to deal with an audience not yet graduated in the school
of the rights of men, and who must apply themselves to the moral
constitution of the heart, would not dare to produce such a triumph
as a matter of exultation. There, where men follow their natural

impulses, they would not bear the odious maxims of a Machiavelian policy, whether applied to the attainments of monarchical or democratic tyranny. They would reject them on the modern, as they once did on the ancient stage, where they could not bear even the hypothetical proposition of such wickedness in the mouth of a personated tyrant, though suitable to the character he sustained. No theatric audience in Athens would bear what has been borne, in the midst of the real tragedy of this triumphal day; a principal actor weighing, as it were in scales hung in a shop of horrors,—so much actual crime against so much contingent advantage,—and after putting in and out weights, declaring that the balance was on the side of the advantages. They would not bear to see the crimes of new democracy posted as in a ledger against the crimes of old despotism, and the book-keepers of politics finding democracy still in debt, but by no means unable or unwilling to pay the balance. In the theatre, the first intuitive glance, without any elaborate process of reasoning, will show, that this method of political computation would justify every extent of crime. They would see, that on these principles, even where the very worst acts were not perpetrated, it was owing rather to the fortune of the conspirators, than to their parsimony in the expenditure of treachery and blood. They would soon see, that criminal means once tolerated are soon preferred. They present a shorter cut to the object than through the highway of the moral virtues. Justifying perfidy and murder for public benefit, public benefit would soon become the pretext, and perfidy and murder the end; until rapacity, malice, revenge, and fear more dreadful than revenge, could satiate their insatiable appetites. Such must be the consequences of losing, in the splendour of these triumphs of the rights of men, all natural sense of wrong and right.

But the Reverend Pastor exults in this "leading in triumph," because truly Louis the Sixteenth was "an arbitrary monarch;" that is, in other words, neither more nor less than because he was Louis the Sixteenth, and because he had the misfortune to be born king of France, with the prerogatives of which, a long line of ancestors, and a long acquiescence of the people, without any act of his, had put him in possession. A misfortune it has indeed turned out to him, that he was born king of France. But misfortune is not crime, nor is indiscretion always the greatest guilt. I shall never think that a prince, the acts of whose whole reign was a series of concessions to his subjects, who was willing to relax his authority, to remit his prerogatives, to call his people to a share of freedom, not known, perhaps not desired by their ancestors; such a prince, though he should be subjected to the common frailties attached to men and to princes, though he should have once thought it necessary to provide force against the desperate designs manifestly carrying on against his person, and the remnants of his authority; though all this should be taken into consideration, I shall be led with great difficulty to think he deserves the cruel and insulting triumph of Paris and of Dr. Price. I tremble for the cause of liberty, from such an example to kings. I tremble for the cause of humanity, in the unpunished outrages of the most wicked of mankind. But there are some people of that low and degenerate fashion of mind, that they look up with a sort of complacent awe and admiration to kings, who know to keep firm in their seat, to hold a strict hand over their subjects, to assert their prerogative, and, by the awakened vigilance of a severe despotism, to guard against the very first approaches of freedom. Against such as these they never elevate their voice. Deserters from principle, listed with fortune, they never see any good in suffering virtue, nor any crime in prosperous usurpation.

If it could have been made clear to me, that the king and queen of France (those I mean who were such before the triumph) were inexorable and cruel tyrants, that they had formed a deliberate scheme for massacring the National Assembly, (I think I have seen something like the latter insinuated in certain publications) I should think their captivity just. If this be true, much more ought to have been done, but done, in my opinion, in another manner. The punishment of real tyrants is a noble and awful act of justice; and it has with truth been said to be consolatory to the human mind. But if I were to punish a wicked king, I should regard the dignity in avenging the crime. Justice is grave and decorous, and in its punishments rather seems to submit to a necessity, than to make a choice. Had Nero, or Agrippina, or Louis the Eleventh, or Charles the Ninth, been the subject; if Charles the Twelfth of Sweden, after the murder of Patkul, or his predecessor Christina, after the murder of Monaldeschi, had fallen into your hands, Sir, or into mine, I am sure our conduct would have been different.

If the French king, or king of the French, (or by whatever name he is known in the new vocabulary of your constitution) has in his own person, and that of his queen, really deserved these unavowed, but unavenged, murderous attempts, and those frequent indignities more cruel than murder, such a person would ill deserve even that subordinate executory trust, which I understand is to be placed in him; nor is he fit to be called chief in a nation which he has outraged and oppressed. A worse choice for such an office in a new commonwealth, than that of a deposed tyrant, could not possibly be made. But to degrade and insult a man as the worst of criminals, and afterwards to trust him in your highest concerns, as a faithful, honest, and zealous servant, is not consistent with reasoning, nor prudent in policy, nor safe in practice. Those who could make such an appointment must be guilty of a more flagrant breach of trust than any they have yet committed against the people. As this is the only crime in which your leading politicians could have acted inconsistently, I conclude that there is no sort of ground for these horrid insinuations. I think no better of all the other calumnies.

In England, we give no credit to them. We are generous enemies: we are faithful allies. We spurn from us with disgust and indignation the slanders of those who bring us their anecdotes with the attestation of the flower-de-luce on their shoulder. We have Lord George Gordon fast in Newgate; and neither his being a public proselyte to Judaism, nor his having, in his zeal against Catholic priests and all sorts of ecclesiastics, raised a mob (excuse the term, it is still in use here) which pulled down all our prisons, have preserved to him a liberty, of which he did not render himself worthy by a virtuous use of it. We have rebuilt Newgate, and tenanted the mansion. We have prisons almost as strong as the Bastile, for those who dare to libel the queens of France. In this spiritual retreat, let the noble libeller remain. Let him there meditate on his Thalmud, until he learns a conduct more becoming his birth and parts, and not so disgraceful to the ancient religion to which he has become a proselyte; or until some persons from your side of the water, to please your new Hebrew brethren, shall ransom him. He may then be enabled to purchase, with the old hoards of the synagogue, and a very small poundage on the long compound interest of the thirty pieces of silver, (Dr. Price has shown us what miracles compound interest will perform in 1790 years,) the lands which are lately discovered to have been usurped by the Gallican church. Send us your Popish archbishop of Paris, and we will send you our Protestant Rabbin. We shall treat the person you send us in exchange like a gentleman and an honest man, as he is; but pray let him bring with him the fund of his hospitality, bounty, and charity; and, depend upon it, we shall never confiscate a shilling of that honourable and pious fund, nor think of enriching the treasury with the spoils of the poor-box.

To tell you the truth, my dear Sir, I think the honour of our nation to be somewhat concerned in the disclaimer of the proceedings of this society of the Old Jewry and the London Tavern. I have no man's proxy. I speak only for myself, when I disclaim, as I do with all possible earnestness, all communion with the actors in that triumph, or with the admirers of it. When I assert anything else, as concerning the people of England, I speak from observation, not from authority; but I speak from the experience I have had in a pretty extensive and mixed communication with the inhabitants of this kingdom, of all descriptions and ranks, and after a course of attentive observations, began early in life, and continued for nearly forty years. I have often been astonished, considering that we are divided from you but by a slender dyke of about twenty-four miles, and that the mutual intercourse between the two countries has lately been very great, to find how little you seem to know of us. I suspect that this is owing to your forming a judgment of this nation from certain publications, which do, very erroneously, if they do at all, represent the opinions and dispositions generally prevalent in England. The vanity, restlessness, petulance, and spirit of intrigue, of several petty cabals, who attempt to hide their total want of consequence in bustle and noise, and puffing, and mutual quotation of each other, makes you imagine that our contemptuous neglect of their abilities is a mark of general acquiescence in their opinions. No such thing, I assure you. Because half a dozen grasshoppers under a fern make the field ring with their importunate chink, whilst thousands of great cattle, reposed beneath the shadow of the British oak, chew the cud and are silent, pray do not imagine that those who make the noise are the only inhabitants of the field; that, of course, they are many in number; or that, after all, they are other than the little, shrivelled, meagre, hopping, though loud and troublesome, insects of the hour.

I almost venture to affirm, that not one in a hundred amongst us participates in the "triumph" of the Revolution Society. If the king and queen of France, and their children, were to fall into our hands by the chance of war, in the most acrimonious of all hostilities, (I deprecate such an event, I deprecate such hostility,) they would be treated with another sort of triumphal entry into London. We formerly have had a king of France in that situation; you have read how he was treated by the victor in the field; and in what manner he was afterwards received in England. Four hundred years have gone over us; but I believe we are not materially changed since that period. Thanks to our sullen resistance to innovation, thanks to the cold sluggishness of our national character, we still bear the stamp of our forefathers. We have not (as I conceive) lost the generosity and dignity of thinking of the fourteenth century; nor as yet have we subtilized ourselves into savages. We are not the converts of Rousseau; we are not the disciples of Voltaire; Helvetius has made no progress amongst us. Atheists are not our preachers; madmen are not our lawgivers. We know that *we* have made no discoveries, and we think that no discoveries are to be made, in morality; nor many in the great principles of government, nor in the ideas of liberty, which were understood long before we were born, altogether as well as they will be after the grave has heaped its mould upon our presumption, and the silent tomb shall have imposed its law on our pert loquacity. In England we have not yet been completely embowelled of our natural entrails; we still feel within us, and we cherish and cultivate, those inbred sentiments which are the faithful guardians, the active monitors of our duty, the true supporters of all liberal and manly morals. We have not been drawn and trussed, in order that we may be filled, like stuffed birds in a museum, with chaff and rags and paltry blurred shreds of paper about the rights of man. We preserve the whole of our feelings still native and entire, unsophisticated by pedantry and infidelity. We have real hearts of flesh and blood beating in our bosoms. We fear God; we look up with awe to kings; with affection to parliaments; with duty to magistrates; with reverence to priests; and with respect to nobility.[18] Why? Because when such ideas are brought before our minds, it is *natural* to be so affected; because all other feelings are false and spurious, and tend to corrupt our minds, to vitiate our primary morals, to render us unfit for rational liberty; and by teaching us a servile, licentious, and abandoned insolence, to be our low sport for a few holidays, to make us perfectly fit for, and justly deserving of, slavery, through the whole course of our lives.

You see, Sir, that in this enlightened age I am bold enough to confess, that we are generally men of untaught feelings; that instead of casting away all our old prejudices, we cherish them to a very considerable degree, and, to take more shame to ourselves, we cherish them because they are prejudices; and the longer they have lasted, and the more generally they have prevailed, the more we cherish them. We are afraid to put men to live and trade each on his own private stock of reason; because we suspect that this stock in each man is small, and that the individuals would do better to avail themselves of the general bank and capital of nations and of ages. Many of our men of speculation, instead of exploding general prejudices, employ their sagacity to discover the latent wisdom which prevails in them. If they find what they seek, and they seldom fail, they think it more wise to continue the prejudice, with the reason involved, than to cast away the coat of prejudice, and to leave nothing but the naked reason; because prejudice, with its reason, has a motive to give action to that reason, and an affection which will give it permanence. Prejudice is of ready application in the emergency; it previously engages the mind in a steady course of

---

[18] The English are, I conceive, misrepresented in a letter published in one of the papers, by a gentleman thought to be a dissenting minister.—When writing to Dr. Price of the spirit which prevails at Paris, he says, "The spirit of the people in this place has abolished all the proud *distinctions* which the *king* and *nobles* had usurped in their minds; whether they talk of *the king, the noble, or the priest,* their whole language is that of the most *enlightened and liberal amongst the English.*" If this gentleman means to confine the terms *enlightened and liberal* to one set of men in England, it may be true. It is not generally so.

wisdom and virtue, and does not leave the man hesitating in the moment of decision, sceptical, puzzled, and unresolved. Prejudice renders a man's virtue his habit; and not a series of unconnected acts. Through just prejudice, his duty becomes a part of his nature.

Your literary men, and your politicians, and so do the whole clan of the enlightened among us, essentially differ in these points. They have no respect for the wisdom of others; but they pay it off by a very full measure of confidence in their own. With them it is a sufficient motive to destroy an old scheme of things, because it is an old one. As to the new, they are in no sort of fear with regard to the duration of a building run up in haste; because duration is no object to those who think little or nothing has been done before their time, and who place all their hopes in discovery. They conceive, very systematically, that all things which give perpetuity are mischievous, and therefore they are at inexpiable war with all establishments. They think that government may vary like modes of dress, and with as little ill effect: that there needs no principle of attachment, except a sense of present conveniency, to any constitution of the state. They always speak as if they were of opinion that there is a singular species of compact between them and their magistrates, which binds the magistrate, but which has nothing reciprocal in it, but that the majesty of the people has a right to dissolve it without any reason, but its will. Their attachment to their country itself is only so far as it agrees with some of their fleeting projects; it begins and ends with that scheme of polity which falls in with their momentary opinion.

These doctrines, or rather sentiments, seem prevalent with your new statesmen. But they are wholly different from those on which we have always acted in this country.

I hear it is sometimes given out in France, that what is doing among you is after the example of England. I beg leave to affirm, that scarcely anything done with you has originated from the practice or the prevalent opinions of this people, either in the act or in the spirit of the proceeding. Let me add, that we are as unwilling to learn these lessons from France, as we are sure that we never taught them to that nation. The cabals here, who take a sort of share in your transactions, as yet consist of but a handful of people. If unfortunately by their intrigues, their sermons, their publications, and by a confidence derived from an expected union with the counsels and forces of the French nation, they should draw considerable numbers into their faction, and in consequence should seriously attempt anything here in imitation of what has been done with you, the event, I dare venture to prophesy, will be, that, with some trouble to their country, they will soon accomplish their own destruction. This people refused to change their law in remote ages from respect to the infallibility of popes; and they will not now alter it from a pious implicit faith in the dogmatism of philosophers; though the former was armed with the anathema and crusade, and though the latter should act with the libel and the lamp-iron.

Formerly your affairs were your own concern only. We felt for them as men; but we kept aloof from them, because we were not citizens of France. But when we see the model held up to ourselves, we must feel as Englishmen, and feeling, we must provide as Englishmen. Your affairs, in spite of us, are made a part of our interest; so far at least as to keep at a distance your panacea, or your plague. If it be a panacea, we do not want it. We know the consequences of unnecessary physic. If it be a plague, it is such a plague that the precautions of the most severe quarantine ought to be established against it.

I hear on all hands that a cabal, calling itself philosophic, receives the glory of many of the late proceedings; and that their opinions and systems are the true actuating spirit of the whole of them. I have heard of no party in England, literary or political, at any time, known by such a description. It is not with you composed of those men, is it? whom the vulgar, in their blunt, homely style, commonly call atheists and infidels? If it be, I admit that we too have had writers of that description, who made some noise in their day. At present they repose in lasting oblivion. Who, born within the last forty years, has read one word of Collins, and Toland, and Tindal, and Chubb, and Morgan, and that whole race who called themselves Freethinkers? Who now reads Bolingbroke? Who ever read him through? Ask the booksellers of London what is become of all these lights of the world. In as few years their few successors will go to the family vault of "all the Capulets." But whatever they were, or are, with us, they were and are wholly unconnected individuals. With us they kept the common nature of their kind, and were not gregarious. They never acted in corps, or were known as a faction in the state, nor presumed to influence in that name or character, or for the purposes of such a faction, on any of our public concerns. Whether they ought so to exist, and so be permitted to act, is another question. As such cabals have not existed in England, so neither has the spirit of them had any influence in establishing the original frame of our constitution, or in any one of the several reparations and improvements it has undergone. The whole has been done under the auspices, and is confirmed by the sanctions, of religion and piety. The whole has emanated from the simplicity of our national character, and from a sort of native plainness and directness of understanding, which for a long time characterized those men who have successively obtained authority amongst us. This disposition still remains; at least in the great body of the people.

We know, and what is better, we feel inwardly, that religion is the basis of civil society, and the source of all good and of all comfort.[19] In England we are so convinced of this, that there is no rust of superstition, with which the accumulated absurdity of the human mind might have crusted it over in the course of ages, that ninety-nine in a hundred of the people of England would not prefer to impiety. We shall never be such fools as to call in an enemy to the substance of any system to remove its corruptions, to supply its defects, or to perfect its construction. If our religious tenets should ever want a further elucidation, we shall not call on atheism to explain them. We shall not light up our temple from that unhallowed fire. It will be illuminated with other lights. It will be perfumed with other incense, than the infectious stuff which is imported by the smugglers of adulterated metaphysics. If our ecclesiastical establishment should want a revision, it is not avarice or rapacity, public or private, that we shall employ for the audit, or receipt, or application of its con-

[19] Sit igitur hoc ab initio persuasum civibus, dominos esse omnium rerum ac moderatores, deos; eaque, quæ gerantur, eorum geri vi, ditione, ac numine; eosdemque optime de genere hominum mereri; et qualis quisque sit, quid agat, quid in se admittat, qua mente, qua pietate colat religiones intueri; piorum et impiorum habere rationem. His enim rebus imbutæ mentes haud sane abhorrebunt ab utili et à vera sententia. Cic. de Legibus, l. 2.

secrated revenue. Violently condemning neither the Greek nor the Armenian, nor, since heats are subsided, the Roman system of religion, we prefer the Protestant; not because we think it has less of the Christian religion in it, but because, in our judgment, it has more. We are Protestants, not from indifference, but from zeal.

We know, and it is our pride to know, that man is by his constitution a religious animal; that atheism is against, not only our reason, but our instincts; and that it cannot prevail long. But if, in the moment of riot, and in a drunken delirium from the hot spirit drawn out of the alembic of hell, which in France is now so furiously boiling, we should uncover our nakedness, by throwing off that Christian religion which has hitherto been our boast and comfort, and one great source of civilization amongst us, and amongst many other nations, we are apprehensive (being well aware that the mind will not endure a void) that some uncouth, pernicious, and degrading superstition might take place of it.

For that reason, before we take from our establishment the natural, human means of estimation, and give it up to contempt, as you have done, and in doing it have incurred the penalties you well deserve to suffer, we desire that some other may be presented to us in the place of it. We shall then form our judgment.

On these ideas, instead of quarrelling with establishments, as some do, who have made a philosophy and a religion of their hostility to such institutions, we cleave closely to them. We are resolved to keep an established church, an established monarchy, an established aristocracy, and an established democracy, each in the degree it exists, and in no greater. I shall show you presently how much of each of these we possess.

It has been the misfortune (not, as these gentlemen think it, the glory) of this age, that everything is to be discussed, as if the constitution of our country were to be always a subject rather of altercation, than enjoyment. For this reason, as well as for the satisfaction of those among you (if any such you have among you) who may wish to profit of examples, I venture to trouble you with a few thoughts upon each of these establishments. I do not think they were unwise in ancient Rome, who, when they wished to new-model their laws, set commissioners to examine the best constituted republics within their reach.

First, I beg leave to speak of our church establishment, which is the first of our prejudices, not a prejudice destitute of reason, but involving in it profound and extensive wisdom. I speak of it first. It is first, and last, and midst in our minds. For, taking ground on that religious system, of which we are now in possession, we continue to act on the early received and uniformly continued sense of mankind. That sense not only, like a wise architect, hath built up the august fabric of states, but like a provident proprietor, to preserve the structure from profanation and ruin, as a sacred temple purged from all the impurities of fraud, and violence, and injustice, and tyranny, hath solemnly and for ever consecrated the commonwealth, and all that officiate in it. This consecration is made, that all who administer in the government of men, in which they stand in the person of God himself, should have high and worthy notions of their function and destination; that their hope should be full of immortality; that they should not look to the paltry pelf of the moment, nor to the temporary and transient praise of the vulgar, but to a solid, permanent existence, in the permanent part of their nature, and to a permanent fame and glory, in the example they leave as a rich inheritance to the world.

Such sublime principles ought to be infused into persons of exalted situations; and religious establishments provided, that may continually revive and enforce them. Every sort of moral, every sort of civil, every sort of politic institution, aiding the rational and natural ties that connect the human understanding and affections to the divine, are not more than necessary, in order to build up that wonderful structure, Man; whose prerogative it is, to be in a great degree a creature of his own making; and who, when made as he ought to be made, is destined to hold no trivial place in the creation. But whenever man is put over men, as the better nature ought ever to preside, in that case more particularly, he should as nearly as possible be approximated to his perfection.

The consecration of the state, by a state religious establishment, is necessary also to operate with a wholesale awe upon free citizens; because, in order to secure their freedom, they must enjoy some determinate portion of power. To them therefore a religion connected with the state, and with their duty towards it, becomes even more necessary than in such societies, where the people, by the terms of their subjection, are confined to private sentiments, and the management of their own family concerns. All persons possessing any portion of power ought to be strongly and awfully impressed with an idea that they act in trust: and that they are to account for their conduct in that trust to the one great Master, Author, and Founder of society.

This principle ought even to be more strongly impressed upon the minds of those who compose the collective sovereignty, than upon those of single princes. Without instruments, these princes can do nothing. Whoever uses instruments, in finding helps, finds also impediments. Their power is therefore by no means complete; nor are they safe in extreme abuse. Such persons, however elevated by flattery, arrogance, and self-opinion, must be sensible, that, whether covered or not by positive law, in some way or other they are accountable even here for the abuse of their trust. If they are not cut off by a rebellion of their people, they may be strangled by the very janissaries kept for their security against all other rebellion. Thus we have seen the king of France sold by his soldiers for an increase of pay. But where popular authority is absolute and unrestrained, the people have an infinitely greater, because a far better founded, confidence in their own power. They are themselves, in a great measure, their own instruments. They are nearer to their objects. Besides, they are less under responsibility to one of the greatest controlling powers on earth, the sense of fame and estimation. The share of infamy, that is likely to fall to the lot of each individual in public acts, is small indeed; the operation of opinion being in the inverse ratio to the number of those who abuse power. Their own approbation of their own acts has to them the appearance of a public judgment in their favour. A perfect democracy is therefore the most shameless thing in the world. As it is the most shameless, it is also the most fearless. No man apprehends in his person that he can be made subject to punishment. Certainly the people at large never ought: for as all punishments are for example towards the conservation of the people at large, the people at large can never become the subject of punishment by any human hand.[20] It is therefore of infinite importance that they should not be suffered to imagine that their will, any more than that of kings, is the standard of right and wrong. They ought to be persuaded that they are full as little entitled, and far less qualified with safety to themselves, to use any arbitrary power whatsoever; that therefore they are not, under a false show of liberty, but in truth, to exercise an unnatural, inverted domination, tyrannically to exact, from those who officiate in the state, not an entire devotion to their interest, which is their right, but an abject submission to their occasional will; extinguishing thereby, in all those who serve them, all moral principle, all sense of dignity, all use of judgment, and all consistency of character; whilst by the very same process they give themselves up a proper, a suitable, but a most contemptible prey to the servile ambition of popular sycophants, or courtly flatterers.

When the people have emptied themselves of all the lust of selfish will, which without religion it is utterly impossible they ever should, when they are conscious that they exercise, and exercise perhaps in a higher link of the order of delegation, the power, which to be legitimate must be according to that eternal, immutable law, in which will and reason are the same, they will be more careful how they place power in base and incapable hands. In their nomination to office, they will not appoint to the exercise of authority, as to a pitiful job, but as to a holy function; not according to their sordid, selfish interest, nor to their wanton caprice, nor to their arbitrary will; but they will confer that power (which any man may well tremble to give or to receive) on those only, in whom they may discern that predominant proportion of active virtue and wisdom, taken together and fitted to the charge, such, as in the great and inevitable mixed mass of human imperfections and infirmities, is to be found.

When they are habitually convinced that no evil can be acceptable, either in the act or the permission, to him whose essence is good, they will be better able to extirpate out of the minds of all magistrates, civil, ecclesiastical, or military, anything that bears the least resemblance to a proud and lawless domination.

[20] Quicquid multis peccatur inultem.

But one of the first and most leading principles on which the commonwealth and the laws are consecrated, is lest the temporary possessors and life-renters in it, unmindful of what they have received from their ancestors, or of what is due to their posterity, should act as if they were the entire masters; that they should not think it among their rights to cut off the entail, or commit waste on the inheritance, by destroying at their pleasure the whole original fabric of their society; hazarding to leave to those who come after them a ruin instead of an habitation—and teaching these successors as little to respect their contrivances, as they had themselves respected the institutions of their forefathers. By this unprincipled facility of changing the state as often, and as much, and in as many ways, as there are floating fancies or fashions, the whole chain and continuity of the commonwealth would be broken. No one generation could link with the other. Men would become little better than the flies of a summer.

And first of all, the science of jurisprudence, the pride of the human intellect, which, with all its defects, redundancies, and errors, is the collected reason of ages, combining the principles of original justice with the infinite variety of human concerns, as a heap of old exploded errors, would be no longer studied. Personal self-sufficiency and arrogance (the certain attendants upon all those who have never experienced a wisdom greater than their own) would usurp the tribunal. Of course no certain laws, establishing invariable grounds of hope and fear, would keep the actions of men in a certain course, or direct them to a certain end. Nothing stable in the modes of holding property, or exercising function, could form a solid ground on which any parent could speculate in the education of his offspring, or in a choice for their future establishment in the world. No principles would be early worked into the habits. As soon as the most able instructor had completed his laborious course of institution, instead of sending forth his pupil, accomplished in a virtuous discipline, fitted to procure him attention and respect, in his place in society, he would find everything altered; and that he had turned out a poor creature to the contempt and derision of the world, ignorant of the true grounds of estimation. Who would insure a tender and delicate sense of honour to beat almost with the first pulses of the heart, when no man could know what would be the test of honour in a nation, continually varying the standard of its coin? No part of life would retain its acquisitions. Barbarism with regard to science and literature, unskilfulness with regard to arts and manufactures, would infallibly succeed to the want of a steady education and settled principle; and thus the commonwealth itself would, in a few generations, crumble away, be disconnected into the dust and powder of individuality, and at length dispersed to all the winds of heaven.

To avoid therefore the evils of inconstancy and versatility, ten thousand times worse than those of obstinacy and the blindest prejudice, we have *consecrated* the state, that no man should approach to look into its defects or corruptions but with due caution; that he should never dream of beginning its reformation by its subversion; that he should approach to the faults of the state as to the wounds of a father, with pious awe and trembling solicitude. By this wise prejudice we are taught to look with horror on those children of their country, who are prompt rashly to hack that aged parent in pieces, and put him into the kettle of magicians, in hopes that by their poisonous weeds, and wild incantations, they may regenerate the paternal constitution, and renovate their father's life.

Society is indeed a contract. Subordinate contracts for objects of mere occasional interest may be dissolved at pleasure—but the state ought not to be considered as nothing better than a partnership agreement in a trade of pepper and coffee, calico or tobacco, or some other such low concern, to be taken up for a little temporary interest, and to be dissolved by the fancy of the parties. It is to be looked on with other reverence; because it is not a partnership in things subservient only to the gross animal existence of a temporary and perishable nature. It is a partnership in all science; a partnership in all art; a partnership in every virtue, and in all perfection. As the ends of such a partnership cannot be obtained in many generations, it becomes a partnership not only between those who are living, but between those who are living, those who are dead, and those who are to be born. Each contract of each particular state is but a clause in the great primæval contract of eternal society, linking the lower with the higher natures, connecting the visible and in-

visible world, according to a fixed compact sanctioned by the inviolable oath which holds all physical and all moral natures, each in
their appointed place. This law is not subject to the will of those,
who by an obligation above them, and infinitely superior, are bound
to submit their will to that law. The municipal corporations of that
universal kingdom are not morally at liberty at their pleasure, and
on their speculations of a contingent improvement, wholly to separate and tear asunder the bands of their subordinate community, and
to dissolve it into an unsocial, uncivil, unconnected chaos of elemen-
tary principles. It is the first and supreme necessity only, a necessity
that is not chosen, but chooses, a necessity paramount to deliberation,
that admits no discussion, and demands no evidence, which alone
can justify a resort to anarchy. This necessity is no exception to
the rule; because this necessity itself is a part too of that moral and
physical disposition of things, to which man must be obedient by
consent or force; but if that which is only submission to necessity
should be made the object of choice, the law is broken, nature is dis-
obeyed, and the rebellious are outlawed, cast forth, and exiled, from
this world of reason, and order, and peace, and virtue, and fruitful
penitence, into the antagonist world of madness, discord, vice, confusion, and unavailing sorrow.

These, my dear Sir, are, were, and, I think, long will be, the sentiments of not the least learned and reflecting part of this kingdom.
They, who are included in this description, form their opinions on
such grounds as such persons ought to form them. The less inquiring receive them from an authority, which those whom Providence dooms to live on trust need not be ashamed to rely on. These
two sorts of men move in the same direction, though in a different
place. They both move with the order of the universe. They all
know or feel this great ancient truth: "Quod illi principi et præpo-
tenti Deo qui omnem hunc mundum regit, nihil eorum quæ quidem
fiant in terris acceptius quam concilia et cœtus hominum jure sociati
quæ civitates appellantur." They take this tenet of the head and
heart, not from the great name which it immediately bears, nor
from the greater from whence it is derived; but from that which
alone can give true weight and sanction to any learned opinion, the
common nature and common relation of men. Persuaded that all

things ought to be done with reference, and referring all to the point of reference to which all should be directed, they think themselves bound, not only as individuals in the sanctuary of the heart, or as congregated in that personal capacity, to renew the memory of their high origin and cast; but also in their corporate character to perform their national homage to the institutor, and author, and protector of civil society; without which civil society man could not by any possibility arrive at the perfection of which his nature is capable, nor even make a remote and faint approach to it. They conceive that He who gave our nature to be perfected by our virtue, willed also the necessary means of its perfection.—He willed therefore the state—He willed its connexion with the source and original archetype of all perfection. They who are convinced of this his will, which is the law of laws, and the sovereign of sovereigns, cannot think it reprehensible that this our corporate fealty and homage, that this our recognition of a seigniory paramount, I had almost said this oblation of the state itself, as a worthy offering on the high altar of universal praise, should be performed as all public, solemn acts are performed, in buildings, in music, in decoration, in speech, in the dignity of persons, according to the customs of mankind, taught by their nature; this is, with modest splendour and unassuming state, with mild majesty and sober pomp. For those purposes they think some part of the wealth of the country is as usefully employed as it can be in fomenting the luxury of individuals. It is the public ornament. It is the public consolation. It nourishes the public hope. The poorest man finds his own importance and dignity in it, whilst the wealth and pride of individuals at every moment makes the man of humble rank and fortune sensible of his inferiority, and degrades and vilifies his condition. It is for the man in humble life, and to raise his nature, and to put him in mind of a state in which the privileges of opulence will cease, when he will be equal by nature, and may be more than equal by virtue, that this portion of the general wealth of his country is employed and sanctified.

I assure you I do not aim at singularity. I give you opinions which have been accepted amongst us, from very early times to this moment, with a continued and general approbation, and which indeed are so worked into my mind, that I am unable to distinguish what I have learned from others from the results of my own meditation.

It is on some such principles that the majority of the people of England, far from thinking a religious national establishment unlawful, hardly think it lawful to be without one. In France you are wholly mistaken if you do not believe us above all other things attached to it, and beyond all other nations; and when this people has acted unwisely and unjustifiably in its favour, (as in some instances they have done most certainly) in their very errors you will at least discover their zeal.

This principle runs through the whole system of their polity. They do not consider their church establishment as convenient, but as essential to their state; not as a thing heterogeneous and separable; something added for accommodation; what they may either keep or lay aside, according to their temporary ideas of convenience. They consider it as the foundation of their whole constitution, with which, and with every part of which, it holds an indissoluble union. Church and state are ideas inseparable in their minds, and scarcely is the one ever mentioned without mentioning the other.

Our education is so formed as to confirm and fix this impression. Our education is in a manner wholly in the hands of ecclesiastics, and in all stages from infancy to manhood. Even when our youth, leaving schools and universities, enter that most important period of life which begins to link experience and study together, and when with that view they visit other countries, instead of old domestics whom we have seen as governors to principal men from other parts, three-fourths of those who go abroad with our young nobility and gentlemen are ecclesiastics; not as austere masters, nor as mere followers; but as friends and companions of a graver character, and not seldom persons as well born as themselves. With them, as relations, they most constantly keep up a close connexion through life. By this connexion we conceive that we attach our gentlemen to the church; and we liberalize the church by an intercourse with the leading characters of the country.

So tenacious are we of the old ecclesiastical modes and fashions of institution, that very little alteration has been made in them since the fourteenth or fifteenth century: adhering in this particular, as in all things else, to our old settled maxim, never entirely nor at once to depart from antiquity. We found these old institutions, on the whole, favourable to morality and discipline; and we thought they were susceptible of amendment, without altering the ground. We thought that they were capable of receiving and meliorating, and above all of preserving, the accessions of science and literature, as the order of Providence should successively produce them. And after all, with this Gothic and monkish education (for such it is in the ground-work) we may put in our claim to as ample and as early a share in all the improvements in science, in arts, and in literature, which have illuminated and adorned the modern world, as any other nation in Europe: we think one main cause of this improvement was our not despising the patrimony of knowledge which was left us by our forefathers.

It is from our attachment to a church establishment, that the English nation did not think it wise to intrust that great, fundamental interest of the whole to what they trust no part of their civil or military public service, that is, to the unsteady and precarious contribution of individuals. They go further. They certainly never have suffered, and never will suffer, the fixed estate of the church to be converted into a pension, to depend on the treasury, and to be delayed, withheld, or perhaps to be extinguished, by fiscal difficulties: which difficulties may sometimes be pretended for political purposes, and are in fact often brought on by the extravagance, negligence, and rapacity of politicians. The people of England think that they have constitutional motives, as well as religious, against any project of turning their independent clergy into ecclesiastical pensioners of state. They tremble for their liberty, from the influence of a clergy dependent on the crown; they tremble for the public tranquillity from the disorders of a factious clergy, if it were made to depend upon any other than the crown. They therefore made their church, like their king and their nobility, independent.

From the united considerations of religion and constitutional policy, from their opinion of a duty to make sure provision for the consolation of the feeble and the instruction of the ignorant, they have incorporated and identified the estate of the church with the mass of *private property*, of which the state is not the proprietor, either for use or dominion, but the guardian only and the regulator. They have ordained that the provision of this establishment might be as stable as the earth on which it stands, and should not fluctuate with the Euripus of funds and actions.

The men of England, the men, I mean, of light and leading in England, whose wisdom (if they have any) is open and direct, would be ashamed, as of a silly, deceitful trick, to profess any religion in name, which by their proceedings, they appear to contemn. If by their conduct (the only language that rarely lies) they seemed to regard the great ruling principle of the moral and the natural world, as a mere invention to keep the vulgar in obedience, they apprehend that by such a conduct they would defeat the politic purpose they have in view. They would find it difficult to make others believe in a system to which they manifestly give no credit themselves. The Christian statesmen of this land would indeed first provide for the *multitude;* because it is the *multitude;* and is therefore, as such, the first object in the ecclesiastical institution, and in all institutions. They have been taught, that the circumstance of the gospel's being preached to the poor, was one of the great tests of its true mission. They think, therefore, that those do not believe it, who do not take care it should be preached to the poor. But as they know that charity is not confined to any one description, but ought to apply itself to all men who have wants, they are not deprived of a due and anxious sensation of pity to the distresses of the miserable great. They are not repelled through a fastidious delicacy, at the stench of their arrogance and presumption, from a medicinal attention to their mental blotches and running sores. They are sensible that religious instruction is of more consequence to them than to any others; from the greatness of the temptation to which they are exposed; from the important consequences that attend their faults; from the contagion of their ill example; from the necessity of bowing down the stubborn neck of their pride and ambition to the yoke of moderation and virtue; from a consideration of the fat stupidity and gross ignorance concerning what imports men most to know, which prevails at courts, and at the head of armies, and in senates, as much as at the loom and in the field.

The English people are satisfied, that to the great the consolations of religion are as necessary as its instructions. They too are among the unhappy. They feel personal pain, and domestic sorrow. In these they have no privilege, but are subject to pay their full contingent to the contributions levied on mortality. They want this sovereign balm under their gnawing cares and anxieties, which, being less conversant about the limited wants of animal life, range without limit, and are diversified by infinite combinations, in the wild and unbounded regions of imagination. Some charitable dole is wanting to these, our often very unhappy brethren, to fill the gloomy void that reigns in minds which have nothing on earth to hope or fear; something to relieve in the killing languor and over-laboured lassitude of those who have nothing to do; something to excite an appetite to existence in the palled satiety which attends on all pleasures which may be bought, where nature is not left to her own process, where even desire is anticipated, and therefore fruition defeated by meditated schemes and contrivances of delight; and no interval, no obstacle, is interposed between the wish and the accomplishment.

The people of England know how little influence the teachers of religion are likely to have with the wealthy and powerful of long standing, and how much less with the newly fortunate, if they appear in a manner no way assorted to those with whom they must associate, and over whom they must even exercise, in some cases, something like an authority. What must they think of that body of teachers, if they see it in no part above the establishment of their domestic servants? If the poverty were voluntary, there might be some difference. Strong instances of self-denial operate powerfully on our minds; and a man who has no wants has obtained great freedom, and firmness, and even dignity. But as the mass of any description of men are but men, and their poverty cannot be voluntary, that disrespect, which attends upon all lay poverty, will not depart from the ecclesiastical. Our provident constitution has therefore taken care that those who are to instruct presumptuous ignorance, those who are to be censors over insolent vice, should neither incur their contempt, nor live upon their alms; nor will it tempt the rich to a neglect of the true medicine of their minds. For these reasons, whilst we provide first for the poor, and with a parental solicitude, we have not relegated religion (like something we were ashamed to show) to obscure municipalities, or rustic villages. No! we will have her to exalt her mitred front in courts and parliaments. We will have her mixed throughout the whole mass of life, and blended with all the classes of society. The people of England will show to the haughty potentates of the world, and to their talking sophisters, that a free, a generous, an informed nation honours the high magistrates of its church; that it will not suffer the insolence of wealth and titles, or any other species of proud pretension, to look down with scorn upon what they look up to with reverence; nor presume to trample on that acquired personal nobility, which they intend always to be, and which often is, the fruit, not the reward, (for what can be the reward?) of learning, piety, and virtue. They can see, without pain or grudging, an archbishop precede a duke. They can see a bishop of Durham, or a bishop of Winchester, in possession of ten thousand pounds a year; and cannot conceive why it is in worse hands than estates to the like amount in the hands of this earl, or that squire; although it may be true, that so many dogs and horses are not kept by the former, and fed with the victuals which ought to nourish the children of the people. It is true, the whole church revenue is not always employed, and to every shilling, in charity; nor perhaps ought it; but something is generally so employed. It is better to cherish virtue and humanity, by leaving much to free will, even with some loss to the object, than to attempt to make men mere machines and instruments of a political benevolence. The world on the whole will gain by a liberty, without which virtue cannot exist.

When once the commonwealth has established the estates of the church as property, it can, consistently, hear nothing of the more or the less. Too much and too little are treason against property. What evil can arise from the quantity in any hand, whilst the supreme authority has the full, sovereign superintendence over this, as over all property, to prevent every species of abuse; and, whenever it notably deviates, to give to it a direction agreeable to the purposes of its institution.

In England most of us conceive that it is envy and malignity towards those who are often the beginners of their own fortune, and not a love of the self-denial and mortification of the ancient church, that makes some look askance at the distinctions, and honours, and revenues, which, taken from no person, are set apart for virtue. The ears of the people of England are distinguishing. They hear these men speak broad. Their tongue betrays them. Their language is in the *patois* of fraud; in the cant and gibberish of hypocrisy. The people of England must think so, when these praters affect to carry back the clergy to that primitive, evangelic poverty, which, in the spirit, ought always to exist in them, (and in us too, however we may like it,) but in the thing must be varied, when the relation of that body to the state is altered; when manners, when modes of life, when indeed the whole order of human affairs, has undergone a total revolution. We shall believe those reformers then to be honest enthusiasts, not, as now we think them, cheats and deceivers, when we see them throwing their own goods into common, and submitting their own persons to the austere discipline of the early church.

With these ideas rooted in their minds, the Commons of Great Britain, in the national emergencies, will never seek their resource from the confiscation of the estates of the church and poor. Sacrilege and proscription are not among the ways and means of our committee of supply. The Jews in Change Alley have not yet dared to hint their hopes of a mortgage on the revenues belonging to the see of Canterbury. I am not afraid that I shall be disavowed, when I assure you, that there is not *one* public man in this kingdom, whom you would wish to quote, no not one, of any party or description, who does not reprobate the dishonest, perfidious, and cruel confiscation which the National Assembly has been compelled to make of that property, which it was their first duty to protect.

It is with the exultation of a little national pride I tell you, that those amongst us who have wished to pledge the societies of Paris in the cup of their abominations have been disappointed. The robbery of your church has proved a security to the possession of ours. It has roused the people. They see with horror and alarm that enormous and shameless act of proscription. It has opened, and will more and more open, their eyes upon the selfish enlargement of mind, and the narrow liberality of sentiment, of insidious men, which, commencing in close hypocrisy and fraud, have ended in open violence and rapine. At home we behold similar beginnings. We are on our guard against similar conclusions.

I hope we shall never be so totally lost to all sense of the duties imposed upon us by the law of social union, as upon any pretext of public service, to confiscate the goods of a single unoffending citizen. Who but a tyrant (a name expressive of everything which can vitiate and degrade human nature) could think of seizing on the property of men, unaccused, unheard, untried, by whole descriptions, by hundreds and thousands together? Who, that had not lost every trace of humanity, could think of casting down men of exalted rank and sacred function, some of them of an age to call at once for reverence and compassion, of casting them down from the highest situation in the commonwealth, wherein they were maintained by their own landed property, to a state of indigence, depression, and contempt?

The confiscators truly have made some allowance to their victims from the scraps and fragments of their own tables, from which they have been so harshly driven, and which have been so bountifully spread for a feast to the harpies of usury. But to drive men from independence to live on alms, is itself great cruelty. That which might be a tolerable condition to men in one state of life, and not habituated to other things, may, when all these circumstances are altered, be a dreadful revolution; and one to which a virtuous mind would feel pain in condemning any guilt, except that which would demand the life of the offender. But to many minds this punishment of *degradation* and *infamy* is worse than death. Undoubtedly it is an infinite aggravation of this cruel suffering, that the persons who were taught a double prejudice in favour of religion, by education, and by the place they held in the administration of its functions, are to receive the remnants of their property as alms from the profane and impious hands of those who had plundered them of all the rest; to receive (if they are at all to receive) not from the charitable contributions of the faithful, but from the insolent tenderness of known and avowed atheism, the maintenance of religion, measured out to them on the standard of the contempt in which it is held; and for the purpose of rendering those who receive the allowance vile, and of no estimation, in the eyes of mankind.

But this act of seizure of property, it seems, is a judgment in law and not a confiscation. They have, it seems, found out in the acad emies of the *Palais Royal,* and the *Jacobins,* that certain men had no right to the possessions which they held under law, usage, the decisions of courts, and the accumulated prescription of a thousand years. They say that ecclesiastics are fictitious persons, creatures of the state, whom at pleasure they may destroy, and of course limit and modify in every particular; that the goods they possess are not prop erly theirs, but belong to the state which created the fiction; and we are therefore not to trouble ourselves with what they may suffer in their natural feelings and natural persons, on account of what is done towards them in this their constructive character. Of what import is it under what names you injure men, and deprive them of the just emoluments of a profession, in which they were not only permitted but encouraged by the state to engage; and upon the supposed certainty of which emoluments they had formed the plan of their lives, contracted debts, and led multitudes to an entire de- pendence upon them?

You do not imagine, Sir, that I am going to compliment this miserable distinction of persons with any long discussion. The arguments of tyranny are as contemptible as its force is dreadful. Had not your confiscators, by their early crimes, obtained a power which secures indemnity to all the crimes of which they have since been guilty, or that they can commit, it is not the syllogism of the logician, but the lash of the executioner, that would have refuted a sophistry which becomes an accomplice of theft and murder. The sophistic tyrants of Paris are loud in their declamations against the departed regal tyrants, who in former ages have vexed the world. They are thus bold, because they are safe from the dungeons and iron cages of their old masters. Shall we be more tender of the tyrants of our own time, when we see them acting worse tragedies under our eyes? shall we not use the same liberty that they do, when we can use it with the same safety? when to speak honest truth only requires a contempt of the opinions of those whose actions we abhor?

This outrage on all the rights of property was at first covered with what, on the system of their conduct, was the most astonishing of all pretexts—a regard to national faith. The enemies to property at first pretended a most tender, delicate, and scrupulous anxiety for keeping the king's engagements with the public creditor. These professors of the rights of men are so busy in teaching others, that they have not leisure to learn anything themselves; otherwise they would have known, that it is to the property of the citizen, and not to the demands of the creditor of the state, that the first and original faith of civil society is pledged. The claim of the citizen is prior in time, paramount in title, superior in equity. The fortunes of individuals, whether possessed by acquisition, or by descent, or in virtue of a participation in the goods of some community, were no part of the creditor's security, expressed or implied. They never so much as entered into his head when he made his bargain. He well knew that the public, whether represented by a monarch or by a senate, can pledge nothing but the public estate; and it can have no public estate, except in what it derives from a just and proportioned imposition upon the citizens at large. This was engaged, and nothing else could be engaged, to the public creditor. No man can mortgage his injustice as a pawn for his fidelity.

It is impossible to avoid some observation on the contradictions caused by the extreme rigour and the extreme laxity of this new public faith, which influenced in this transaction, and which influenced not according to the nature of the obligation, but to the description of the persons to whom it was engaged. No acts of the old government of the kings of France are held valid in the National Assembly, except his pecuniary engagements; acts of all others of the most ambiguous legality. The rest of all the acts of that royal government are considered in so odious a light, that to have a claim under its authority is looked on as a sort of crime. A pension, given as a reward for service to the state, is surely as good a ground of property as any security for money advanced to the state. It is better; for money is paid, and well paid, to obtain that service. We have, however, seen multitudes of people under this description in France, who never had been deprived of their allowances by the most arbitrary ministers, in the most arbitrary times, by this assembly of the rights of men, robbed without mercy. They were told, in answer to their claim to the bread earned with their blood, that their services had not been rendered to the country that now exists.

This laxity of public faith is not confined to those unfortunate persons. The Assembly, with perfect consistency it must be owned, is engaged in a respectable deliberation how far it is bound by the treaties made with other nations under the former government, and their committee is to report which of them they ought to ratify, and which not. By this means they have put the external fidelity of this virgin state on a par with its internal.

It is not easy to conceive upon what rational principle the royal government should not, of the two, rather have possessed the power of rewarding service, and making treaties, in virtue of its prerogative, than that of pledging to creditors the revenue of the state, actual and possible. The treasure of the nation, of all things, has been the least allowed to the prerogative of the king of France, or to the prerogative of any king in Europe. To mortgage the public revenue implies the sovereign dominion, in the fullest sense, over the public purse. It goes far beyond the trust even of a temporary and occasional taxation. The acts, however, of that dangerous power (the distinctive mark of a boundless despotism) have been alone held sacred. Whence arose this preference given by a democratic assembly to a body of property deriving its title from the most critical and obnoxious of all the exertions of monarchical authority? Reason can furnish nothing to reconcile inconsistency; nor can partial favour be accounted for upon equitable principles. But the contradiction and partiality which admit no justification, are not the less without an adequate cause; and that cause I do not think it difficult to discover.

By the vast debt of France a great monied interest has insensibly grown up, and with it a great power. By the ancient usages which prevailed in that kingdom, the general circulation of property, and in particular the mutual convertibility of land into money, and of money into land, had always been a matter of difficulty. Family settlements, rather more general and more strict than they are in England, the *jus retractus,* the great mass of landed property held by the crown, and, by a maxim of the French law, held inalienably, the vast estates of the ecclesiastical corporations,—all these had kept the landed and monied interests more separated in France, less miscible, and the owners of the two distinct species of property not so well disposed to each other as they are in this country.

The monied property was long looked on with rather an evil eye by the people. They saw it connected with their distresses, and aggravating them. It was no less envied by the old landed interests, partly for the same reasons that rendered it obnoxious to the people, but much more so as it eclipsed, by the splendour of an ostentatious luxury, the unendowed pedigrees and naked titles of several among the nobility. Even when the nobility, which represented the more permanent landed interest, united themselves by marriage (which sometimes was the case) with the other description, the wealth which saved the family from ruin, was supposed to contaminate and degrade it. Thus the enmities and heart-burnings of these parties were increased even by the usual means by which discord is made to cease and quarrels are turned into friendship. In the mean time, the pride of the wealthy men, not noble or newly noble, increased with its cause. They felt with resentment an inferiority, the grounds of which they did not acknowledge. There was no measure to which they were not willing to lend themselves, in order to be revenged of the outrages of this rival pride, and to exalt their wealth to what they considered as its natural rank and estimation. They struck at the nobility through the crown and the church. They attacked them particularly on the side on which they thought them the most vulnerable, that is, the possessions of the church, which, through the patronage of the crown, generally devolved upon the nobility. The bishoprics, and the great commendatory abbeys, were, with few exceptions, held by that order.

In this state of real, though not always perceived, warfare between the noble ancient landed interest and the new monied interest, the greatest because the most applicable strength was in the hands of the latter. The monied interest is in its nature more ready for any adventure; and its possessors more disposed to new enterprises of any kind. Being of a recent acquisition, it falls in more naturally with any novelties. It is therefore the kind of wealth which will be resorted to by all who wish for change.

Along with the monied interest, a new description of men had grown up, with whom that interest soon formed a close and marked union; I mean the political men of letters. Men of letters, fond of distinguishing themselves, are rarely averse to innovation. Since the decline of the life and greatness of Louis the Fourteenth, they were not so much cultivated either by him, or by the regent, or the successors to the crown; nor were they engaged to the court by favours and emoluments so systematically as during the splendid period of that ostentatious and not impolitic reign. What they lost in the old court protection, they endeavoured to make up by joining in a sort of incorporation of their own; to which the two academies of France, and afterwards the vast undertaking of the Encyclopædia, carried on by a society of these gentlemen, did not a little contribute.

The literary cabal had some years ago formed something like a regular plan for the destruction of the Christian religion. This object they pursued with a degree of zeal which hitherto had been discovered only in the propagators of some system of piety. They were possessed with a spirit of proselytism in the most fanatical degree; and from thence, by an easy progress, with the spirit of persecution according to their means.[21] What was not to be done towards their great end by any direct or immediate act, might be wrought by a longer process through the medium of opinion. To command that opinion, the first step is to establish a dominion over those who direct it. They contrived to possess themselves, with great method and perseverance, of all the avenues to literary fame. Many of them indeed stood high in the ranks of literature and science. The world had done them justice; and in favour of general talents forgave the evil tendency of their peculiar principles. This was true liberality; which they returned by endeavouring to confine the reputation of sense, learning, and taste to themselves or their followers. I will venture to say that this narrow, exclusive spirit has not been less prejudicial to literature and to taste, than to morals and true philosophy. These atheistical fathers have a bigotry of their own; and they have learnt to talk against monks with the spirit of a monk. But in some things they are men of the world. The resources of intrigue are called in to supply the defects of argument and wit. To this

---

[21] This (down to the end of the first sentence in the next paragraph) and some other parts here and there, were inserted on his reading the manuscript, by my lost Son.

system of literary monopoly was joined an unremitting industry to blacken and discredit in every way, and by every means, all those who did not hold to their faction. To those who have observed the spirit of their conduct, it has long been clear that nothing was wanted but the power of carrying the intolerance of the tongue and of the pen into a persecution which would strike at property, liberty, and life.

The desultory and faint persecution carried on against them, more from compliance with form and decency, than with serious resentment, neither weakened their strength, nor relaxed their efforts. The issue of the whole was, that, what with opposition, and what with success, a violent and malignant zeal, of a kind hitherto unknown in the world, had taken an entire possession of their minds, and rendered their whole conversation, which otherwise would have been pleasing and instructive, perfectly disgusting. A spirit of cabal, intrigue, and proselytism, pervaded all their thoughts, words, and actions. And, as controversial zeal soon turns its thoughts on force, they began to insinuate themselves into a correspondence with foreign princes; in hopes, through their authority, which at first they flattered, they might bring about the changes they had in view. To them it was indifferent whether these changes were to be accomplished by the thunderbolt of despotism, or by the earthquake of popular commotion. The correspondence between this cabal and the late king of Prussia will throw no small light upon the spirit of all their proceedings.[22] For the same purpose for which they intrigued with princes, they cultivated, in a distinguished manner, the monied interest of France; and partly through the means furnished by those whose peculiar offices gave them the most extensive and certain means of communication, they carefully occupied all the avenues to opinion.

Writers, especially when they act in a body, and with one direction, have great influence on the public mind; the alliance, therefore, of these writers with the monied interest[23] had no small effect in removing the popular odium and envy which attended that species of wealth. These writers, like the propagators of all novelties, pre-

[22] I do not choose to shock the feeling of the moral reader with any quotation of their vulgar, base, and profane language.
[23] Their connexion with Turgot and almost all the people of the finance.

tended to a great zeal for the poor, and the lower orders, whilst in their satires they rendered hateful, by every exaggeration, the faults of courts, of nobility, and of priesthood. They became a sort of demagogues. They served as a link to unite, in favour of one object, obnoxious wealth to restless and desperate poverty.

As these two kinds of men appear principal leaders in all the late transactions, their junction and politics will serve to account, not upon any principles of law or of policy, but as a *cause,* for the general fury with which all the landed property of ecclesiastical corporations has been attacked; and the great care which, contrary to their pretended principles, has been taken, of a monied interest originating from the authority of the crown. All the envy against wealth and power was artificially directed against other descriptions of riches. On what other principle than that which I have stated can we account for an appearance so extraordinary and unnatural as that of the ecclesiastical possessions, which had stood so many successions of ages and shocks of civil violences, and were girded at once by justice, and by prejudice, being applied to the payment of debts, comparatively recent, invidious, and contracted by a decried and subverted government?

Was the public estate a sufficient stake for the public debts? Assume that it was not, and that a loss *must* be incurred somewhere— When the only estate lawfully possessed, and which the contracting parties had in contemplation at the time in which their bargain was made, happens to fail, who according to the principles of natural and legal equity, ought to be the sufferer? Certainly it ought to be either the party who trusted, or the party who persuaded him to trust; or both; and not third parties who had no concern with the transaction. Upon any insolvency they ought to suffer who are weak enough to lend upon bad security, or they who fraudulently held out a security that was not valid. Laws are acquainted with no other rules of decision. But by the new institute of the rights of men, the only persons, who in equity ought to suffer, are the only persons who are to be saved harmless: those are to answer the debt who neither were lenders nor borrowers, mortgagers nor mortgagees.

What had the clergy to do with these transactions? What had

they to do with any public engagement further than the extent of their own debt? To that, to be sure, their estates were bound to the last acre. Nothing can lead more to the true spirit of the Assembly, which fits for public confiscation, with its new equity, and its new morality, than an attention to their proceeding with regard to this debt of the clergy. The body of confiscators, true to that monied interest for which they were false to every other, have found the clergy competent to incur a legal debt. Of course they declared them legally entitled to the property which their power of incurring the debt and mortgaging the estate implied; recognizing the rights of those persecuted citizens, in the very act in which they were thus grossly violated.

If, as I said, any persons are to make good deficiencies to the public creditor, besides the public at large, they must be those who managed the agreement. Why therefore are not the estates of all the comptrollers-general confiscated?[24] Why not those of the long succession of ministers, financiers, and bankers who have been enriched whilst the nation was impoverished by their dealings and their counsels? Why is not the estate of M. Laborde declared forfeited rather than of the archbishop of Paris, who has had nothing to do in the creation or in the jobbing of the public funds? Or, if you must confiscate old landed estates in favour of the money-jobbers, why is the penalty confined to one description? I do not know whether the expenses of the Duke de Choiseul have left anything of the infinite sums which he had derived from the bounty of his master, during the transactions of a reign which contributed largely by every species of prodigality in war and peace, to the present debt of France. If any such remains, why is not this confiscated? I remember to have been in Paris during the time of the old government. I was there just after the Duke d'Aiguillon had been snatched (as it was generally thought) from the block by the hand of a protecting despotism. He was a minister, and had some concern in the affairs of that prodigal period. Why do I not see his estate delivered up to the municipalities in which it is situated? The noble family of Noailles have long been servants (meritorious servants I admit) to the crown of France, and have had of course

[24] All have been confiscated in their turn.

some share in its bounties. Why do I hear nothing of the application of their estates to the public debt? Why is the estate of the Duke de Rochefoucault more sacred than that of the Cardinal de Rochefoucault? The former is, I doubt not, a worthy person; and (if it were not a sort of profaneness to talk of the use, as affecting the title to the property) he makes a good use of his revenues; but it is no disrespect to him to say, what authentic information well warrants me in saying, that the use made of a property equally valid, by his brother[25] the cardinal archbishop of Rouen, was far more laudable and far more public-spirited. Can one hear of the proscription of such persons, and the confiscation of their effects, without indignation and horror? He is not a man who does not feel such emotions on such occasions. He does not deserve the name of a free-man who will not express them.

Few barbarous conquerors have ever made so terrible a revolution in property. None of the heads of the Roman factions, when they established *"crudelem illam hastam"* in all their auctions of rapine, have ever set up to sale the goods of the conquered citizen to such an enormous amount. It must be allowed in favour of those tyrants of antiquity, that what was done by them could hardly be said to be done in cold blood. Their passions were inflamed, their tempers soured, their understandings confused, with the spirit of revenge, with the innumerable reciprocated and recent inflictions and retaliations of blood and rapine. They were driven beyond all bounds of moderation by the apprehension of the return of power with the return of property, to the families of those they had injured beyond all hope of forgiveness.

These Roman confiscators, who were yet only in the elements of tyranny, and were not instructed in the rights of men to exercise all sorts of cruelties on each other without provocation, thought it necessary to spread a sort of colour over their injustice. They considered the vanquished party as composed of traitors who had borne arms, or otherwise had acted with hostility, against the commonwealth. They regarded them as persons who had forfeited their property by their crimes. With you, in your improved state of the

[25] Not his brother, nor any near relation; but this mistake does not affect the argument.

human mind, there was no such formality. You seized upon five millions sterling of annual rent, and turned forty or fifty thousand human creatures out of their houses, because "such was your pleasure." The tyrant Harry the Eighth of England, as he was not better enlightened than the Roman Mariuses and Syllas, and had not studied in your new schools, did not know what an effectual instrument of despotism was to be found in that grand magazine of offensive weapons, the rights of men. When he resolved to rob the abbeys, as the club of the Jacobins have robbed all the ecclesiastics, he began by setting on foot a commission to examine into the crimes and abuses which prevailed in those communities. As it might be expected, his commission reported truths, exaggerations, and falsehoods. But truly or falsely, it reported abuses and offences. However, as abuses might be corrected, as every crime of persons does not infer a forfeiture with regard to communities, and as property, in that dark age, was not discovered to be a creature of prejudice, all those abuses (and there were enow of them) were hardly thought sufficient ground for such a confiscation as it was for his purpose to make. He therefore procured the formal surrender of these estates. All these operose proceedings were adopted by one of the most decided tyrants in the rolls of history, as necessary preliminaries, before he could venture, by bribing the members of his two servile houses with a share of the spoil, and holding out to them an eternal immunity from taxation, to demand a confirmation of his iniquitous proceedings by an act of Parliament. Had fate reserved him to our times, four technical terms would have done his business, and saved him all this trouble; he needed nothing more than one short form of incantation—"*Philosophy, Light, Liberality, the Rights of Men.*"

I can say nothing in praise of those acts of tyranny, which no voice has hitherto ever commended under any of their false colours; yet in these false colours an homage was paid by despotism to justice. The power which was above all fear and all remorse was not set above all shame. Whilst shame keeps its watch, virtue is not wholly extinguished in the heart; nor will moderation be utterly exiled from the minds of tyrants.

I believe every honest man sympathizes in his reflections with our political poet on that occasion, and will pray to avert the omen whenever these acts of rapacious despotism present themselves to his view or his imagination:

—"May no such storm
Fall on our times, where ruin must reform.
Tell me (my Muse) what monstrous dire offence,
What crimes could any Christian king incense
To such a rage? Was 't luxury, or lust?
Was *he* so temperate, so chaste, so just?
Were these their crimes? they were his own much more,
But wealth is crime enough to him that's poor."[26]

This same wealth, which is at all times treason and *lese nation* to indigent and rapacious despotism, under all modes of polity, was

---

[26] The rest of the passage is this—

"Who having spent the treasures of his crown,
Condemns their luxury to feed his own.
And yet this act, to varnish o'er the shame
Of sacrilege, must bear devotion's name.
No crime so bold, but would be understood
A real, or at least a seeming good;
Who fears not to do ill, yet fears the name,
And, free from conscience, is a slave to fame.
Thus he the church at once protects, and spoils;
But princes' swords are sharper than their styles.
And thus to th' ages past he makes amends,
Their charity destroys, their faith defends.
Then did religion in a lazy cell,
In empty aery contemplation dwell;
And, like the block, unmoved lay; but ours,
As much too active, like the stork devours.
Is there no temperate region can be known,
Betwixt their frigid and our torrid zone?
Could we not wake from that lethargic dream,
But to be restless in a worse extreme?
And for that lethargy was there no cure,
But to be cast into a calenture;
Can knowledge have no bound, but must advance
So far, to make us wish for ignorance?
And rather in the dark to grope our way,
Than, led by a false guide, to err by day?
Who sees these dismal heaps, but would demand,
What barbarous invader sacked the land?
But when he hears, no Goth, no Turk did bring
This desolation, but a Christian king;
When nothing, but the name of zeal, appears
'Twixt our best actions and the worst of theirs,
What does he think our sacrilege would spare,
When such th' effects of our devotion are?"

COOPER'S HILL, by SIR JOHN DENHAM.

your temptation to violate property, law, and religion, united in one object. But was the state of France so wretched and undone, that no other recourse but rapine remained to preserve its existence? On this point I wish to receive some information. When the states met, was the condition of the finances of France such, that, after economizing on principles of justice and mercy through all departments, no fair repartition of burthens upon all the orders could possibly restore them? If such an equal imposition would have been sufficient, you well know it might easily have been made. M. Necker, in the budget which he laid before the orders assembled at Versailles, made a detailed exposition of the state of the French nation.[27]

If we give credit to him, it was not necessary to have recourse to any new impositions whatsoever, to put the receipts of France on a balance with its expenses. He stated the permanent charges of all descriptions, including the interest of a new loan of four hundred millions, at 531,444,000 livres; the fixed revenue at 475,294,000, making the deficiency 56,150,000, or short of £2,200,000 sterling. But to balance it, he brought forward savings and improvements of revenue (considered as entirely certain) to rather more than the amount of that deficiency; and he concludes with these emphatical words, (p. 39,) "Quel pays, Messieurs, que celui, où, *sans impôts* et avec de simples objets *inappercus,* on peut faire disparoître un deficit qui a fait tant de bruit en Europe." As to the reimbursement, the sinking of debt, and the other great objects of public credit and political arrangement indicated in Mons. Necker's speech, no doubt could be entertained, but that a very moderate and proportioned assessment on the citizens without distinction would have provided for all of them to the fullest extent of their demand.

If this representation of Mons. Necker was false, then the Assembly are in the highest degree culpable for having forced the king to accept as his minister, and since the king's deposition, for having employed, as *their* minister, a man who had been capable of abusing so notoriously the confidence of his master and their own; in a matter too of the highest moment, and directly appertaining to his

[27] Rapport de Mons. le Directeur-Général des Finances, fait par ordre du Roi à Versailles. Mai 5, 1789.

particular office. But if the representation was exact, (as having always, along with you, conceived a high degree of respect for M. Necker, I make no doubt it was,) then what can be said in favour of those, who, instead of moderate, reasonable, and general contribution, have in cold blood, and impelled by no necessity, had recourse to a partial and cruel confiscation?

Was that contribution refused on a pretext of privilege, either on the part of the clergy, or on that of the nobility? No, certainly. As to the clergy, they even ran before the wishes of the third order. Previous to the meeting of the states, they had in all their instructions expressly directed their deputies to renounce every immunity, which put them upon a footing distinct from the condition of their fellow-subjects. In this renunciation the clergy were even more explicit than the nobility.

But let us suppose that the deficiency had remained at the fifty-six millions, (or £2,200,000 sterling), as at first stated by M. Necker. Let us allow that all the resources he opposed to that deficiency were impudent and groundless fictions; and that the Assembly (or their lords of articles[28] at the Jacobins) were from thence justified in laying the whole burthen of that deficiency on the clergy,—yet allowing all this, a necessity of £2,200,000 sterling will not support a confiscation to the amount of five millions. The imposition of £2,200,000 on the clergy, as partial, would have been oppressive and unjust, but it would not have been altogether ruinous to those on whom it was imposed; and therefore it would not have answered the real purpose of the managers.

Perhaps persons unacquainted with the state of France, on hearing the clergy and the noblesse were privileged in point of taxation, may be led to imagine, that, previous to the Revolution, these bodies had contributed nothing to the state. This is a great mistake. They certainly did not contribute equally with each other, nor either of them equally with the commons. They both, however, contributed largely. Neither nobility nor clergy enjoyed any exemption from the excise on consumable commodities, from duties of custom, or from any of the other numerous *indirect* impositions, which in

---

[28] In the constitution of Scotland, during the Stuart reigns, a committee sat for preparing bills; and none could pass, but those previously approved by them. This committee was called lords of articles.

France, as well as here, make so very large a proportion of all payments to the public. The noblesse paid the capitation. They paid also a land-tax, called the twentieth penny, to the height sometimes of three, sometimes of four, shillings in the pound; both of them *direct* impositions of no light nature, and no trivial produce. The clergy of the provinces annexed by conquest to France, (which in extent make about an eighth part of the whole, but in wealth a much larger proportion,) paid likewise to the capitation and the twentieth penny, at the rate paid by the nobility. The clergy in the old provinces did not pay the capitation; but they had redeemed themselves at the expense of about 24 millions, or a little more than a million sterling. They were exempted from the twentieths: but then they made free gifts; they contracted debts for the state; and they were subject to some other charges, the whole computed at about a thirteenth part of their clear income. They ought to have paid annually about forty thousand pounds more, to put them on a par with the contribution of the nobility.

When the terrors of this tremendous proscription hung over the clergy, they made an offer of a contribution, through the archbishop of Aix, which, for its extravagance, ought not to have been accepted. But it was evidently and obviously more advantageous to the public creditor than anything which could rationally be promised by the confiscation. Why was it not accepted? The reason is plain—There was no desire that the church should be brought to serve the state. The service of the state was made a pretext to destroy the church. In their way to the destruction of the church they would not scruple to destroy their country: and they have destroyed it. One great end in the project would have been defeated if the plan of extortion had been adopted in lieu of the scheme of confiscation. The new landed interest connected with the new republic, and connected with it for its very being, could not have been created. This was among the reasons why that extravagant ransom was not accepted.

The madness of the project of confiscation, on the plan that was first pretended, soon became apparent. To bring this unwieldy mass of landed property, enlarged by the confiscation of all the vast landed domain of the crown, at once into market, was obviously to defeat the profits proposed by the confiscation, by depreciating the value of those lands, and indeed of all the landed estates throughout France. Such a sudden diversion of all its circulating money from trade to land, must be an additional mischief. What step was taken? Did the Assembly, on becoming sensible of the inevitable ill effects of their projected sale, revert to the offers of the clergy? No distress could oblige them to travel in a course which was disgraced by any appearance of justice. Giving over all hopes from a general immediate sale, another project seems to have succeeded. They proposed to take stock in exchange for the church lands. In that project great difficulties arose in equalizing the objects to be exchanged. Other obstacles also presented themselves, which threw them back again upon some project of sale. The municipalities had taken an alarm. They would not hear of transferring the whole plunder of the kingdom to the stock-holders in Paris. Many of those municipalities had been (upon system) reduced to the most deplorable indigence. Money was nowhere to be seen. They were therefore led to the point that was so ardently desired. They panted for a currency of any kind which might revive their perishing industry. The municipalities were then to be admitted to a share in the spoil, which evidently rendered the first scheme (if ever it had been seriously entertained) altogether impracticable. Public exigencies pressed upon all sides. The minister of finance reiterated his call for supply with a most urgent, anxious, and boding voice. Thus pressed on all sides, instead of the first plan of converting their bankers into bishops and abbots, instead of paying the old debt, they contracted a new debt, at 3 per cent., creating a new paper currency, founded on an eventual sale of the church lands. They issued this paper currency to satisfy in the first instance chiefly the demands made upon them by the *bank of discount*, the great machine, or paper-mill, of their fictitious wealth.

The spoil of the church was now become the only resource of all their operations in finance, the vital principle of all their politics, the sole security for the existence of their power. It was necessary by all, even the most violent means, to put every individual on the same bottom, and to bind the nation in one guilty interest to uphold this act, and the authority of those by whom it was done. In order to force the most reluctant into a participation of their pillage, they rendered their paper circulation compulsory in all payments. Those who consider the general tendency of their schemes to this one object as a centre, and a centre from which afterwards all their measures radiate, will not think that I dwell too long upon this part of the proceedings of the National Assembly.

To cut off all appearance of connexion between the crown and public justice, and to bring the whole under implicit obedience to the dictators in Paris, the old independent judicature of the parliaments, with all its merits, and all its faults, was wholly abolished. Whilst the parliaments existed, it was evident that the people might some time or other come to resort to them, and rally under the standard of their ancient laws. It became however a matter of consideration that the magistrates and officers, in the courts now abolished, *had purchased their places* at a very high rate, for which, as well as for the duty they performed, they received but a very low return of interest. Simple confiscation is a boon only for the clergy; —to the lawyers some appearances of equity are to be observed; and they are to receive compensation to an immense amount. Their compensation becomes part of the national debt, for the liquidation of which there is the one exhaustless fund. The lawyers are to obtain their compensation in the new church paper, which is to march with the new principles of judicature and legislature. The dismissed magistrates are to take their share of martyrdom with the ecclesiastics, or to receive their own property from such a fund, and in such a manner, as all those, who have been seasoned with the ancient principles of jurisprudence, and had been the sworn guardians of property, must look upon with horror. Even the clergy are to receive their miserable allowance out of the depreciated paper, which is stamped with the indelible character of sacrilege, and with the symbols of their own ruin, or they must starve. So violent an outrage upon credit, property, and liberty, as this compulsory paper currency, has seldom been exhibited by the alliance of bankruptcy and tyranny, at any time, or in any nation.

In the course of all these operations, at length comes out the grand *arcanum;*—that in reality, and in a fair sense, the lands of the church (so far as anything certain can be gathered from their proceedings) are not to be sold at all. By the late resolutions of the National Assembly, they are indeed to be delivered to the highest bidder. But it is to be observed, that *a certain portion only of the purchase money is to be laid down*. A period of twelve years is to be given for the payment of the rest. The philosophic purchasers are therefore, on payment of a sort of fine, to be put instantly into possession of the estate. It becomes in some respects a sort of gift to them; to be held on the feudal tenure of zeal to the new establishment. This project is evidently to let in a body of purchasers without money. The consequence will be, that these purchasers, or rather grantees, will pay, not only from the rents as they accrue, which might as well be received by the state, but from the spoil of the materials of buildings, from waste in woods, and from whatever money, by hands habituated to the gripings of usury, they can wring from the miserable peasant. He is to be delivered over to the mercenary and arbitrary discretion of men, who will be stimulated to every species of extortion by the growing demands on the growing profits of an estate held under the precarious settlement of a new political system.

When all the frauds, impostures, violences, rapines, burnings, murders, confiscations, compulsory paper currencies, and every description of tyranny and cruelty employed to bring about and to uphold this Revolution, have their natural effect, that is, to shock the moral sentiments of all virtuous and sober minds, the abettors of this philosophic system immediately strain their throats in a declamation against the old monarchical government of France. When they have rendered that deposed power sufficiently black, they then proceed in argument, as if all those who disapprove of their new abuses must of course be partisans of the old; that those who reprobate their crude and violent schemes of liberty ought to be treated as advocates for servitude. I admit that their necessities do compel them to this base and contemptible fraud. Nothing can reconcile men to their proceedings and projects, but the supposition that there is no third option between them and some tyranny as odious as can be furnished by the records of history, or by the invention of poets. This prattling of theirs hardly deserves the name of sophistry. It is nothing but plain impudence. Have these gentlemen never heard, in the whole circle of the worlds of theory and practice, of anything between the despotism of the monarch and the despotism of the multitude? Have they never heard of a monarchy directed by laws, controlled and balanced by the great hereditary wealth and hereditary dignity of a nation; and both again controlled by a judicious check from the reason and feeling of the people at large, acting by a suitable and permanent organ? Is it then impossible that a man may be found, who, without criminal ill intention, or pitiable absurdity, shall prefer such a mixed and tempered government to either of the extremes; and who may repute that nation to be destitute of all wisdom and of all virtue, which, having in its choice to obtain such a government with ease, *or rather to confirm it when actually possessed,* thought proper to commit a thousand crimes, and to subject their country to a thousand evils, in order to avoid it? Is it then a truth so universally acknowledged, that a pure democracy is the only tolerable form into which human society can be thrown, that a man is not permitted to hesitate about its merits, without the suspicion of being a friend to tyranny, that is, of being a foe to mankind?

I do not know under what description to class the present ruling authority in France. It affects to be a pure democracy, though I think it in a direct train of becoming shortly a mischievous and ignoble oligarchy. But for the present I admit it to be a contrivance of the nature and effect of what it pretends to. I reprobate no form of government merely upon abstract principles. There may be situations in which the purely democratic form will become necessary. There may be some (very few, and very particularly circumstanced) where it would be clearly desirable. This I do not take to be the case of France, or of any other great country. Until now, we have seen no examples of considerable democracies. The ancients were better acquainted with them. Not being wholly unread in the authors, who had seen the most of those constitutions, and who best understood them, I cannot help concurring with their opinion, that an absolute democracy, no more than absolute monarchy, is to be reckoned among the legitimate forms of government. They think it rather the corruption and degeneracy, than the sound constitution of a republic. If I recollect rightly, Aristotle observes, that a democracy has many striking points of resemblance with a tyranny.[29] Of this I am certain, that in a democracy, the majority of the citizens is capable of exercising the most cruel oppressions upon the minority, whenever strong divisions prevail in that kind of polity, as they often must; and that oppression of the minority will extend to far greater numbers, and will be carried on with much greater fury, than can almost ever be apprehended from the dominion of a single sceptre. In such a popular persecution, individual sufferers are in a much more deplorable condition than in any other. Under a cruel prince they have the balmy compassion of mankind to assuage the smart of their wounds; they have the plaudits of the people to animate their generous constancy under their sufferings: but those who are subjected to wrong under multitudes, are deprived of all external consolation. They seem deserted by mankind, overpowered by a conspiracy of their whole species.

But admitting democracy not to have that inevitable tendency to party tyranny, which I suppose it to have, and admitting it to possess as much good in it when unmixed, as I am sure it possesses when compounded with other forms; does monarchy, on its part, contain nothing at all to recommend it? I do not often quote Bolingbroke, nor have his works in general left any permanent impression on my mind. He is a presumptuous and a superficial writer. But he has one observation, which, in my opinion, is not without depth and solidity. He says, that he prefers a monarchy to other governments; because you can better ingraft any description of republic on a monarchy than anything of monarchy upon the republican forms. I think him perfectly in the right. The fact is so historically; and it agrees well with the speculation.

[29] When I wrote this I quoted from memory, after many years had elapsed from my reading the passage. A learned friend has found it, and it is as follows:

Τὸ ἦθος τὸ αὐτό, καὶ ἄμφω δεσποτικὰ τῶν βελτιόνων, καὶ τὰ ψηφίσματα, ὥσπερ ἐκεῖ τὰ ἐπιταγματα· καὶ ὁ δημαγωγος καὶ ὁ κόλαξ, οἱ αὐτοὶ καὶ ἀνάλογοι· καὶ μάλιστα ἑκάτεροι παρ᾽ ἑκατέροις ἰσχύουσιν, οἱ μὲν κόλακες παρὰ τυράννοις, οἱ δὲ δημαγωγοὶ παρὰ τοῖς δήμοις τοῖς τοιούτοις.—

"The ethical character is the same; both exercise despotism over the better class of citizens; and decrees are in the one, what ordinances and arrêts are in the other: the demagogue too, and the court favourite, are not unfrequently the same identical men, and always bear a close analogy; and these have the principal power, each in their respective forms of government, favourites with the absolute monarch, and demagogues with a people such as I have described." Arist. Politic. lib. iv. cap. 4.

I know how easy a topic it is to dwell on the faults of departed greatness. By a revolution in the state, the fawning sycophant of yesterday is converted into the austere critic of the present hour. But steady, independent minds, when they have an object of so serious a concern to mankind as government under their contemplation, will disdain to assume the part of satirists and declaimers. They will judge of human institutions as they do of human characters. They will sort out the good from the evil, which is mixed in mortal institutions, as it is in mortal men.

Your government in France, though usually, and I think justly, reputed the best of the unqualified or ill-qualified monarchies, was still full of abuses. These abuses accumulated in a length of time, as they must accumulate in every monarchy not under the constant inspection of a popular representative. I am no stranger to the faults and defects of the subverted government of France; and I think I am not inclined by nature or policy to make a panegyric upon anything which is a just and natural object of censure. But the question is not now of the vices of that monarchy, but of its existence. Is it then true, that the French government was such as to be incapable or undeserving of reform; so that it was of absolute necessity that the whole fabric should be at once pulled down, and the area cleared for the erection of a theoretic, experimental edifice in its place? All France was of a different opinion in the beginning of the year 1789. The instructions to the representatives to the states-general, from every district in that kingdom, were filled with projects for the reformation of that government, without the remotest suggestion of a design to destroy it. Had such a design been even insinuated, I believe there would have been but one voice, and that voice for rejecting it with scorn and horror. Men have been sometimes led by degrees, sometimes hurried, into things of which, if they could have seen the whole together, they never would have permitted the most remote approach. When those instructions were given, there was no question but that abuses existed, and that they demanded a reform; nor is there now. In the interval between the instructions and the Revolution, things changed their shape; and, in consequence of that change, the true question at present is, Whether those who would have reformed, or those who have destroyed, are in the right?

To hear some men speak of the late monarchy of France, you would imagine that they were talking of Persia bleeding under the ferocious sword of Tahmas Kouli Khân; or at least describing the barbarous anarchic despotism of Turkey, where the finest countries in the most genial climates in the world are wasted by peace more than any countries have been worried by war; where arts are unknown, where manufactures languish, where science is extinguished, where agriculture decays, where the human race itself melts away and perishes under the eye of the observer. Was this the case of France? I have no way of determining the question but by reference to facts. Facts do not support this resemblance. Along with much evil, there is some good in monarchy itself; and some corrective to its evil from religion, from laws, from manners, from opinions, the French monarchy must have received; which rendered it (though by no means a free, and therefore by no means a good, constitution) a despotism rather in appearance than in reality.

Among the standards upon which the effects of government on any country are to be estimated, I must consider the state of its population as not the least certain. No country in which population flourishes, and is in progressive improvement, can be under a *very* mischievous government. About sixty years ago, the Intendants of the generalities of France made, with other matters, a report of the population of their several districts. I have not the books, which are very voluminous, by me, nor do I know where to procure them, (I am obliged to speak by memory, and therefore the less positively,) but I think the population of France was by them, even at that period, estimated at twenty-two millions of souls. At the end of the last century it had been generally calculated at eighteen. On either of these estimations, France was not ill peopled. M. Necker, who is an authority for his own time at least equal to the Intendants for theirs, reckons, and upon apparently sure principles, the people of France, in the year 1780, at twenty-four millions six hundred and seventy thousand. But was this the probable ultimate term under the old establishment? Dr. Price is of opinion, that the growth of population in France was by no means at its *acmé* in that year. I certainly defer to Dr. Price's authority a good deal more in these speculations, than I do in his general politics. This gentleman, taking ground on M. Necker's data, is very confident that since the period of that minister's calculation, the French population has increased rapidly; so rapidly, that in the year 1789 he will not consent to rate the people of that kingdom at a lower number than thirty millions. After abating much (and much I think ought to be abated) from the sanguine calculation of Dr. Price, I have no doubt that the population of France did increase considerably during this later period: but supposing that it increased to nothing more than will be sufficient to complete the twenty-four millions six hundred and seventy thousand to twenty-five millions, still a population of twenty-five millions, and that in an increasing progress, on a space of about twenty-seven thousand square leagues, is immense. It is, for instance, a good deal more than the proportionable population of this island, or even than that of England, the best peopled part of the united kingdom.

It is not universally true, that France is a fertile country. Considerable tracts of it are barren, and labour under other natural disadvantages. In the portions of that territory where things are more favourable, as far as I am able to discover, the numbers of the people correspond to the indulgence of nature.[30] The Generality of Lisle (this I admit is the strongest example) upon an extent of four hundred and four leagues and a half, about ten years ago, contained seven hundred and thirty-four thousand six hundred souls, which is one thousand seven hundred and seventy-two inhabitants to each square league. The middle term for the rest of France is about nine hundred inhabitants to the same admeasurement.

I do not attribute this population to the deposed government; because I do not like to compliment the contrivances of men with what is due in a great degree to the bounty of Providence. But that decried government could not have obstructed, most probably it favoured, the operation of those causes, (whatever they were,) whether of nature in the soil, or habits of industry among the people, which has produced so large a number of the species throughout that whole kingdom, and exhibited in some particular places such prodigies of population. I never will suppose that fabric of a state to be

[30] De l'Administration des Finances de la France, par Mons. Necker, vol. i. p. 288.

the worst of all political institutions, which, by experience, is found to contain a principle favourable (however latent it may be) to the increase of mankind.

The wealth of a country is another, and no contemptible standard, by which we may judge whether, on the whole, a government be protecting or destructive. France far exceeds England in the multitude of her people; but I apprehend that her comparative wealth is much inferior to ours; that it is not so equal in the distribution, nor so ready in the circulation. I believe the difference in the form of the two governments to be amongst the causes of this advantage on the side of England. I speak of England, not of the whole British dominions; which, if compared with those of France, will, in some degree, weaken the comparative rate of wealth upon our side. But that wealth, which will not endure a comparison with the riches of England, may constitute a very respectable degree of opulence. M. Necker's book published in 1785,[31] contains an accurate and interesting collection of facts relative to public economy and to political arithmetic; and his speculations on the subject are in general wise and liberal. In that work he gives an idea of the state of France, very remote from the portrait of a country whose government was a perfect grievance, an absolute evil, admitting no cure but through the violent and uncertain remedy of a total revolution. He affirms, that from the year 1726 to the year 1784, there was coined at the mint of France, in the species of gold and silver, to the amount of about one hundred millions of pounds sterling.[32]

It is impossible that M. Necker should be mistaken in the amount of the bullion which has been coined in the mint. It is a matter of official record. The reasonings of this able financier, concerning the quantity of gold and silver which remained for circulation, when he wrote in 1785, that is, about four years before the deposition and imprisonment of the French king, are not of equal certainty; but they are laid on grounds so apparently solid, that it is not easy to refuse a considerable degree of assent to his calculation. He calculates the *numeraire,* or what we call *specie,* then actually existing in France, at about eighty-eight millions of the same English money. A great accumulation of wealth for one country, large as that country is!

---

[31] De l'Administration des Finances de la France, par Mons. Necker.
[32] Vol. iii. chap. 8 and chap. 9.

M. Necker was so far from considering this influx of wealth as likely to cease, when he wrote in 1785, that he presumes upon a future annual increase of two per cent. upon the money brought into France during the periods from which he computed.

Some adequate cause must have originally introduced all the money coined at its mint into that kingdom; and some cause as operative must have kept at home, or returned into its bosom, such a vast flood of treasure as M. Necker calculates to remain for domestic circulation. Suppose any reasonable deductions from M. Necker's computation, the remainder must still amount to an immense sum. Causes thus powerful to acquire, and to retain, cannot be found in discouraged industry, insecure property, and a positively destructive government. Indeed, when I consider the face of the kingdom of France; the multitude and opulence of her cities; the useful magnificence of her spacious high roads and bridges; the opportunity of her artificial canals and navigations opening the conveniences of maritime communication through a solid continent of so immense an extent; when I turn my eyes to the stupendous works of her ports and harbours, and to her whole naval apparatus, whether for war or trade; when I bring before my view the number of her fortifications, constructed with so bold and masterly a skill, and made and maintained at so prodigious a charge, presenting an armed front and impenetrable barrier to her enemies upon every side; when I recollect how very small a part of that extensive region is without cultivation, and to what complete perfection the culture of many of the best productions of the earth have been brought in France; when I reflect on the excellence of her manufactures and fabrics, second to none but ours, and in some particulars not second; when I contemplate the grand foundations of charity, public and private; when I survey the state of all the arts that beautify and polish life; when I reckon the men she has bred for extending her fame in war, her able statesmen, the multitude of her profound lawyers and theologians, her philosophers, her critics, her historians and antiquaries, her poets and her orators, sacred and profane; I behold in all this something which awes and commands the imagination, which checks the mind on the brink of precipitate and indiscriminate censure, and which demands that we should very seriously examine, what and how great are the latent vices that could authorize us at once to level so spacious a fabric with the ground. I do not recognize in this view of things, the despotism of Turkey. Nor do I discern the character of a government, that has been, on the whole, so oppressive, or so corrupt, or so negligent, as to be utterly unfit *for all reformation*. I must think such a government well deserved to have its excellencies heightened, its faults corrected, and its capacities improved into a British constitution.

Whoever has examined into the proceedings of that deposed government for several years back, cannot fail to have observed, amidst the inconstancy and fluctuation natural to courts, an earnest endeavour towards the prosperity and improvement of the country; he must admit, that it had long been employed, in some instances wholly to remove, in many considerably to correct, the abusive practices and usages that had prevailed in the state; and that even the unlimited power of the sovereign over the persons of his subjects, inconsistent, as undoubtedly it was, with law and liberty, had yet been every day growing more mitigated in the exercise. So far from refusing itself to reformation, that government was open, with a censurable degree of facility, to all sorts of projects and projectors on the subject. Rather too much countenance was given to the spirit of innovation, which soon was turned against those who fostered it, and ended in their ruin. It is but cold, and no very flattering, justice to that fallen monarchy, to say, that, for many years, it trespassed more by levity and want of judgment in several of its schemes, than from any defect in diligence or in public spirit. To compare the government of France for the last fifteen or sixteen years with wise and well-constituted establishments during that, or during any period, is not to act with fairness. But if in point of prodigality in the expenditure of money, or in point of rigour in the exercise of power, it be compared with any of the former reigns, I believe candid judges will give little credit to the good intentions of those who dwell perpetually on the donations to favourites, or on the expenses of the court, or on the horrors of the Bastile, in the reign of Louis the Sixteenth.[33]

[33] The world is obliged to M. de Calonne for the pains he has taken to refute the scandalous exaggerations relative to some of the royal expenses, and to detect the fallacious account given of pensions, for the wicked purpose of provoking the populace to all sorts of crimes.

Whether the system, if it deserves such a name, now built on the ruins of that ancient monarchy, will be able to give a better account of the population and wealth of the country, which it has taken under its care, is a matter very doubtful. Instead of improving by the change, I apprehend that a long series of years must be told, before it can recover in any degree the effects of this philosophic revolution, and before the nation can be replaced on its former footing. If Dr. Price should think fit, a few years hence, to favour us with an estimate of the population of France, he will hardly be able to make up his tale of thirty millions of souls, as computed in 1789, or the Assembly's computation of twenty-six millions of that year; or even M. Necker's twenty-five millions in 1780. I hear that there are considerable emigrations from France; and that many, quitting that voluptuous climate, and that seductive *Circean* liberty, have taken refuge in the frozen regions, and under the British despotism, of Canada.

In the present disappearance of coin, no person could think it the same country, in which the present minister of the finances has been able to discover fourscore millions sterling in specie. From its general aspect one would conclude that it had been for some time past under the special direction of the learned academicians of Laputa and Balnibarbi.[34] Already the population of Paris has so declined, that M. Necker stated to the National Assembly the provision to be made for its subsistence at a fifth less than what had formerly been found requisite.[35] It is said (and I have never heard it contradicted) that a hundred thousand people are out of employment in that city, though it is become the seat of the imprisoned court and National Assembly. Nothing, I am credibly informed, can exceed the shocking and disgusting spectacle of mendicancy displayed in that capital. Indeed the votes of the National Assembly leave no doubt of the fact. They have lately appointed a standing committee of mendicancy. They are contriving at once a vigorous police on this subject, and, for the first time, the imposition of a tax to maintain the poor, for whose present relief great sums appear on the face of the public accounts of the

[34] See Gulliver's Travels for the idea of countries governed by philosophers.
[35] M. de Calonne states the falling off of the population of Paris as far more considerable; and it may be so, since the period of M. Necker's calculation.

year.[36] In the meantime the leaders of the legislative clubs and coffeehouses are intoxicated with admiration at their own wisdom and ability. They speak with the most sovereign contempt of the rest of the world. They tell the people, to comfort them in the rags with which they have clothed them, that they are a nation of philosophers; and sometimes, by all the arts of quackish parade, by show, tumult, and bustle, sometimes by the alarms of plots and invasions, they attempt to drown the cries of indigence, and to divert the eyes of the observer from the ruin and wretchedness of the state. A brave people will certainly prefer liberty accompanied with a virtuous poverty to a depraved and wealthy servitude. But before the price of comfort and opulence is paid, one ought to be pretty sure it is real liberty which is purchased, and that she is to be purchased at no other price. I shall always, however, consider that liberty as very equivocal in her appearance, which has not wisdom and justice for her companions; and does not lead prosperity and plenty in her train.

The advocates for this Revolution, not satisfied with exaggerating the vices of their ancient government, strike at the fame of their country itself, by painting almost all that could have attracted the attention of strangers, I mean their nobility and their clergy, as objects of horror. If this were only a libel, there had not been much in it. But it has practical consequences. Had your nobility and gentry, who formed the great body of your landed men, and the

[36] Travaux de charité pour subvenir au manque de	*Livres.*	£	s.	d.
travail à Paris et dans les provinces	3,866,920 —	161,121	13	4
Destruction de vagabondage et de la mendicité .	1,671,417 —	69,642	7	6
Primes pour l'importation de grains	5,671,907 —	236,329	9	2
Dépenses relatives aux subsistances, déduction fait des récouvrements qui ont eu lieu . . .	39,871,790 —	1,661,324	11	8

Total   *Liv.* 51,082,034—£2,128,418   1   8

When I sent this book to the press, I entertained some doubt concerning the nature and extent of the last article in the above accounts, which is only under a general head, without any detail. Since then I have seen M. de Calonne's work. I must think it a great loss to me that I had not that advantage earlier. M. de Calonne thinks this article to be on account of general subsistence; but as he is not able to comprehend how so great a loss as upwards of £1,661,000 sterling could be sustained on the difference between the price and the sale of grain, he seems to attribute this enormous head of charge to secret expenses of the Revolution. I cannot say anything positively on that subject. The reader is capable of judging, by the aggregate of these immense charges, on the state and condition of France; and the system of public economy adopted in that nation. These articles of account produced no inquiry or discussion in the National Assembly.

whole of your military officers, resembled those of Germany, at the period when the Hanse-towns were necessitated to confederate against the nobles in defence of their property—had they been like the *Orsini* and *Vitelli* in Italy, who used to sally from their fortified dens to rob the trader and traveller—had they been such as the *Mamelukes* in Egypt, or the *Nayres* on the coast of Malabar, I do admit, that too critical an inquiry might not be advisable into the means of freeing the world from such a nuisance. The statues of Equity and Mercy might be veiled for a moment. The tenderest minds, confounded with the dreadful exigence in which morality submits to the suspension of its own rules in favour of its own principles, might turn aside whilst fraud and violence were accomplishing the destruction of a pretended nobility which disgraced, whilst it persecuted, human nature. The persons most abhorrent from blood, and treason, and arbitrary confiscation, might remain silent spectators of this civil war between the vices.

But did the privileged nobility who met under the king's precept at Versailles, in 1789, or their constituents, deserve to be looked on as the *Nayres* or *Mamelukes* of this age, or as the *Orsini* and *Vitelli* of ancient times? If I had then asked the question I should have passed for a madman. What have they since done that they were to be driven into exile, that their persons should be hunted about, mangled, and tortured, their families dispersed, their houses laid in ashes, and that their order should be abolished, and the memory of it, if possible, extinguished, by ordaining them to change the very names by which they were usually known? Read their instructions to their representatives. They breathe the spirit of liberty as warmly, and they recommend reformation as strongly, as any other order. Their privileges relative to contribution were voluntarily surrendered; as the king, from the beginning, surrendered all pretence to a right of taxation. Upon a free constitution there was but one opinion in France. The absolute monarchy was at an end. It breathed its last, without a groan, without struggle, without convulsion. All the struggle, all the dissension, arose afterwards upon the preference of a despotic democracy to a government of reciprocal control. The triumph of the victorious party was over the principles of a British constitution.

I have observed the affectation, which for many years past, has prevailed in Paris even to a degree perfectly childish, of idolizing the memory of your Henry the Fourth. If anything could put one out of humour with that ornament to the kingly character, it would be this overdone style of insidious panegyric. The persons who have worked this engine the most busily, are those who have ended their panegyrics in dethroning his successor and descendant; a man, as good-natured, at the least, as Henry the Fourth; altogether as fond of his people; and who has done infinitely more to correct the ancient vices of the state than that great monarch did, or we are sure he ever meant to do. Well it is for his panegyrists that they have not him to deal with. For Henry of Navarre was a resolute, active, and politic prince. He possessed indeed great humanity and mildness; but a humanity and mildness that never stood in the way of his interests. He never sought to be loved without putting himself first in a condition to be feared. He used soft language with determined conduct. He asserted and maintained his authority in the gross, and distributed his acts of concession only in the detail. He spent the income of his prerogative nobly; but he took care not to break in upon the capital; never abandoning for a moment any of the claims which he made under the fundamental laws, nor sparing to shed the blood of those who opposed him, often in the field, sometimes upon the scaffold. Because he knew how to make his virtues respected by the ungrateful, he has merited the praises of those, whom, if they had lived in his time, he would have shut up in the Bastile, and brought to punishment along with the regicides whom he hanged after he had famished Paris into a surrender.

If these panegyrists are in earnest in their admiration of Henry the Fourth, they must remember, that they cannot think more highly of him than he did of the noblesse of France; whose virtue, honour, courage, patriotism, and loyalty were his constant theme.

But the nobility of France are degenerated since the days of Henry the Fourth. This is possible. But it is more than I can believe to be true in any great degree. I do not pretend to know France as correctly as some others; but I have endeavoured through my whole life to make myself acquainted with human nature; otherwise I should be unfit to take even my humble part in the service of mankind. In that study I could not pass by a vast portion of our nature, as it appeared modified in a country but twenty-four miles from the shore of this island. On my best observation, compared with my best inquiries, I found your nobility for the greater part composed of men of high spirit, and of a delicate sense of honour, both with regard to themselves individually, and with regard to their whole corps, over whom they kept, beyond what is common in other countries, a censorial eye. They were tolerably well bred; very officious, humane, and hospitable; in their conversation frank and open; with a good military tone; and reasonably tinctured with literature, particularly of the authors in their own language. Many had pretensions far above this description. I speak of those who were generally met with.

As to their behaviour to the inferior classes, they appeared to me to comport themselves towards them with good-nature, and with something more nearly approaching to familiarity, than is generally practised with us in the intercourse between the higher and lower ranks of life. To strike any person, even in the most abject condition, was a thing in a manner unknown, and would be highly disgraceful. Instances of other ill-treatment of the humble part of the community were rare: and as to attacks made upon the property or the personal liberty of the commons, I never heard of any whatsoever from *them;* nor, whilst the laws were in vigour under the ancient government, would such tyranny in subjects have been permitted. As men of landed estates, I had no fault to find with their conduct, though much to reprehend, and much to wish changed, in many of the old tenures. Where the letting of their land was by rent, I could not discover that their agreements with their farmers were oppressive; nor when they were in partnership with the farmer, as often was the case, have I heard that they had taken the lion's share. The proportions seemed not inequitable. There might be exceptions; but certainly they were exceptions only. I have no reason to believe that in these respects the landed noblesse of France were worse than the landed gentry of this country; certainly in no respect more vexatious than the landholders, not noble, of their own nation. In cities the nobility had no manner of power; in the country very little. You know, Sir, that much of the civil government, and the police in the most essential parts was not in the hands of that nobility which presents itself first to our consideration. The revenue, the system and collection of which were the most grievous parts of the French government, was not administered by the men of the sword; nor were they answerable for the vices of its principle, or the vexations, where any such existed, in its management.

Denying, as I am well warranted to do, that the nobility had any considerable share in the oppression of the people, in cases in which real oppression existed, I am ready to admit that they were not without considerable faults and errors. A foolish imitation of the worst part of the manners of England, which impaired their natural character, without substituting in its place what perhaps, they meant to copy, has certainly rendered them worse than formerly they were. Habitual dissoluteness of manners continued beyond the pardonable period of life, was more common amongst them than it is with us; and it reigned with the less hope of remedy, though possibly with something of less mischief by being covered with more exterior decorum. They countenanced too much that licentious philosophy, which has helped to bring on their ruin. There was another error amongst them more fatal. Those of the commons, who approached to or exceeded many of the nobility in point of wealth, were not fully admitted to the rank and estimation which wealth, in reason and good policy, ought to bestow in every country; though I think not equally with that of other nobility. The two kinds of aristocracy were too punctiliously kept asunder, less so, however, than in Germany and some other nations.

This separation, as I have already taken the liberty of suggesting to you, I conceive to be one principal cause of the destruction of the old nobility. The military, particularly, was too exclusively reserved for men of family. But, after all, this was an error of opinion, which a conflicting opinion would have rectified. A permanent assembly, in which the commons had their share of power, would soon abolish whatever was too invidious and insulting in these distinctions; and even the faults in the morals of the nobility would have been probably corrected, by the greater varieties of occupation and pursuit to which a constitution by orders would have given rise.

All this violent cry against the nobility I take to be a mere work of art. To be honoured and even privileged by the laws, opinions, and inveterate usages of our country, growing out of the prejudice of ages, has nothing to provoke horror and indignation in any man. Even to be too tenacious of those privileges is not absolutely a crime. The strong struggle in every individual to preserve possession of what he has found to belong to him, and to distinguish him is one of the securities against injustice and despotism implanted in our nature. It operates as an instinct to secure property, and to preserve communities in a settled state. What is there to shock in this? Nobility is a graceful ornament to the civil order. It is the Corinthian capital of polished society. *Omnes boni nobilitati semper favemus,* was the saying of a wise and good man. It is indeed one sign of a liberal and benevolent mind to incline to it with some sort of partial propensity. He feels no ennobling principle in his own heart, who wishes to level all the artificial institutions which have been adopted for giving a body to opinion, and permanence to fugitive esteem. It is a sour, malignant, envious disposition, without taste for the reality, or for any image or representation of virtue, that sees with joy the unmerited fall of what had long flourished in splendour and in honour. I do not like to see anything destroyed; any void produced in society; any ruin on the face of the land. It was therefore with no disappointment or dissatisfaction that my inquiries and observations did not present to me any incorrigible vices in the noblesse of France, or any abuse which could not be removed by a reform very short of abolition. Your noblesse did not deserve punishment: but to degrade is to punish.

It was with the same satisfaction I found that the result of my inquiry concerning your clergy was not dissimilar. It is no soothing news to my ears, that great bodies of men are incurably corrupt. It is not with much credulity I listen to any, when they speak evil of those whom they are going to plunder. I rather suspect that vices are feigned or exaggerated, when profit is looked for in their punishment. An enemy is a bad witness; a robber is a worse. Vices and abuses there were undoubtedly in that order, and must be. It was an old establishment, and not frequently revised. But I saw no crimes in the individuals that merited confiscation of their substance, nor those cruel insults and degradations, and that unnatural persecution, which have been substituted in the place of meliorating regulation.

If there had been any just cause for this new religious persecution, the atheistic libellers, who act as trumpeters to animate the populace to plunder, do not love any body so much as not to dwell with complacence on the vices of the existing clergy. This they have not done. They find themselves obliged to rake into the histories of former ages (which they have ransacked with a malignant and profligate industry) for every instance of oppression and persecution which has been made by that body or in its favour, in order to justify, upon very iniquitous, because very illogical, principles of retaliation, their own persecutions, and their own cruelties. After destroying all other genealogies and family distinctions, they invent a sort of pedigree of crimes. It is not very just to chastise men for the offences of their natural ancestors: but to take the fiction of ancestry in a corporate succession, as a ground for punishing men who have no relation to guilty acts, except in names and general descriptions, is a sort of refinement in injustice belonging to the philosophy of this enlightened age. The Assembly punishes men, many, if not most, of whom abhor the violent conduct of ecclesiastics in former times as much as their present persecutors can do, and who would be as loud and as strong in the expression of that sense, if they were not well aware of the purposes for which all this declamation is employed.

Corporate bodies are immortal for the good of the members, but not for their punishment. Nations themselves are such corporations. As well might we in England think of waging inexpiable war upon all Frenchmen for the evils which they have brought upon us in the several periods of our mutual hostilities. You might, on your part, think yourselves justified in falling upon all Englishmen on account of the unparalleled calamities brought on the people of France by the unjust invasions of our Henries and our Edwards. Indeed we should be mutually justified in this exterminatory war upon each other, full as much as you are in the unprovoked persecution of your present countrymen, on account of the conduct of men of the same name in other times.

We do not draw the moral lessons we might from history. On the contrary, without care it may be used to vitiate our minds and to destroy our happiness. In history a great volume is unrolled for our instruction, drawing the materials of future wisdom from the past errors and infirmities of mankind. It may, in the perversion, serve for a magazine, furnishing offensive and defensive weapons for parties in church and state, and supplying the means of keeping alive, or reviving, dissensions and animosities, and adding fuel to civil fury. History consists, for the greater part, of the miseries brought upon the world by pride, ambition, avarice, revenge, lust, sedition, hypocrisy, ungoverned zeal, and all the train of disorderly appetites, which shake the public with the same

> —"troublous storms that toss
> The private state, and render life unsweet."

These vices are the *causes* of those storms. Religion, morals, laws, prerogatives, privileges, liberties, rights of men, are the *pretexts*. The pretexts are always found in some specious appearance of a real good. You would not secure men from tyranny and sedition, by rooting out of the mind the principles to which these fraudulent pretexts apply? If you did, you would root out everything that is valuable in the human breast. As these are the pretexts, so the ordinary actors and instruments in great public evils are kings, priests, magistrates, senates, parliaments, national assemblies, judges, and captains. You would not cure the evil by resolving, that there should be no more monarchs, nor ministers of state, nor of the gospel; no interpreters of law; no general officers; no public councils. You might change the names. The things in some shape must remain. A certain *quantum* of power must always exist in the community, in some hands, and under some appellation. Wise men will apply their remedies to vices, not to names; to the causes of evil which are permanent, not to the occasional organs by which they act, and the transitory modes in which they appear. Otherwise you will be wise historically, a fool in practice. Seldom have two ages the same fashion in their pretexts and the same modes of mischief. Wickedness is a little more inventive. Whilst you are discussing fashion, the fashion is gone by. The very same vice assumes a new body. The spirit transmigrates; and, far from losing its principle of life by the change of its appearance, it is renovated in its new organs with a fresh vigour of a juvenile activity. It walks abroad, it continues its ravages, whilst you are gibbeting the carcase, or demolishing the tomb. You are terrifying yourselves with ghosts and apparitions, whilst your house is the haunt of robbers. It is thus with all those, who, attending only to the shell and husk of history, think they are waging war with intolerance, pride, and cruelty, whilst, under colour of abhorring the ill principles of antiquated parties, they are authorizing and feeding the same odious vices in different factions, and perhaps in worse.

Your citizens of Paris formerly had lent themselves as the ready instruments to slaughter the followers of Calvin, at the infamous massacre of St. Bartholomew. What should we say to those who could think of retaliating on the Parisians of this day the abominations and horrors of that time? They are indeed brought to abhor *that* massacre. Ferocious as they are, it is not difficult to make them dislike it; because the politicians and fashionable teachers have no interest in giving their passions exactly the same direction. Still, however, they find it their interest to keep the same savage dispositions alive. It was but the other day that they caused this very massacre to be acted on the stage for the diversion of the descendants of those who committed it. In this tragic farce they produced the cardinal of Lorraine in his robes of function, ordering general slaughter. Was this spectacle intended to make the Parisians abhor persecution, and loathe the effusion of blood?—No; it was to teach them to persecute their own pastors; it was to excite them, by raising a disgust and horror of their clergy, to an alacrity in hunting down to destruction an order, which, if it ought to exist at all, ought to exist not only in safety, but in reverence. It was to stimulate their cannibal appetites (which one would think had been gorged sufficiently) by variety and seasoning; and to quicken them to an alertness in new murders and massacres, if it should suit the purpose of the Guises of the day. An assembly, in which sat a multitude of priests and prelates, was obliged to suffer this indignity at its door. The author was not sent to the galleys, nor the players to the house of correction. Not long after this exhibition, those players came forward to the Assembly to claim the rites of that very religion which they had dared to expose, and to show their prostituted faces in the senate, whilst the archbishop of Paris, whose function was known to his people only by his prayers and benedictions, and his wealth only by his alms, is forced to abandon his house, and to fly from his flock, (as from ravenous wolves,) because, truly, in the sixteenth century, the cardinal of Lorraine was a rebel and a murderer.[37]

Such is the effect of the perversion of history, by those, who, for the same nefarious purposes, have perverted every other part of learning. But those who will stand upon that elevation of reason, which places centuries under our eye, and brings things to the true point of comparison, which obscures little names, and effaces the colours of little parties, and to which nothing can ascend but the spirit and moral quality of human actions, will say to the teachers of the Palais Royal,—The cardinal of Lorraine was the murderer of the sixteenth century, you have the glory of being the murderers in the eighteenth; and this is the only difference between you. But history in the nineteenth century, better understood, and better employed, will, I trust, teach a civilized posterity to abhor the misdeeds of both these barbarous ages. It will teach future priests and magistrates not to retaliate upon the speculative and inactive atheists of future times, the enormities committed by the present practical zealots and furious fanatics of that wretched error, which, in its quiescent state, is more than punished, whenever it is embraced. It will teach posterity not to make war upon either religion or philosophy, for the abuse which the hypocrites of both have made of the two most valuable blessings conferred upon us by the bounty of the universal Patron, who in all things eminently favours and protects the race of man.

If your clergy, or any clergy, should show themselves vicious beyond the fair bounds allowed to human infirmity, and to those professional faults which can hardly be separated from professional virtues, though their vices never can countenance the exercise of oppression, I do admit, that they would naturally have the effect of abating very much of our indignation against the tyrants who exceed measure and justice in their punishment. I can allow in clergymen, through all their divisions, some tenaciousness of their own

[37] This is on a supposition of the truth of this story, but he was not in France at the time. One name serves as well as another.

opinion, some overflowings of zeal for its propagation, some predilection to their own state and office, some attachment to the interests of their own corps, some preference to those who listen with docility to their doctrines, beyond those who scorn and deride them. I allow all this, because I am a man who have to deal with men, and who would not, through a violence of toleration, run into the greatest of all intolerance. I must bear with infirmities until they fester into crimes.

Undoubtedly, the natural progress of the passions, from frailty to vice, ought to be prevented by a watchful eye and a firm hand. But it is true that the body of your clergy had past those limits of a just allowance. From the general style of your late publications of all sorts, one would be led to believe that your clergy in France were a sort of monsters; an horrible composition of superstition, ignorance, sloth, fraud, avarice, and tyranny. But is this true? Is it true, that the lapse of time, the cessation of conflicting interests, the woeful experience of the evils resulting from party rage, have had no sort of influence gradually to meliorate their minds? Is it true, that they were daily renewing invasions on the civil power, troubling the domestic quiet of their country, and rendering the operations of its government feeble and precarious? Is it true, that the clergy of our times have pressed down the laity with an iron hand, and were in all places, lighting up the fires of a savage persecution? Did they by every fraud endeavour to increase their estates? Did they use to exceed the due demands on estates that were their own? Or, rigidly screwing up right into wrong, did they convert a legal claim into a vexatious extortion? When not possessed of power, were they filled with the vices of those who envy it? Were they inflamed with a violent, litigious spirit of controversy? Goaded on with the ambition of intellectual sovereignty, were they ready to fly in the face of all magistracy, to fire churches, to massacre the priests of other descriptions, to pull down altars, and to make their way over the ruins of subverted governments to an empire or doctrine sometimes flattering, sometimes forcing the consciences of men from the jurisdiction of public institutions into a submission of their personal authority, beginning with a claim of liberty, and ending with an abuse of power?

These, or some of these, were the vices objected, and not wholly without foundation, to several of the churchmen of former times, who belonged to the two great parties, which then divided and distracted Europe.

If there was in France, as in other countries there visibly is, a great abatement, rather than any increase of these vices, instead of loading the present clergy with the crimes of other men, and the odious character of other times, in common equity they ought to be praised, encouraged, and supported, in their departure from a spirit which disgraced their predecessors, and for having assumed a temper of mind and manners more suitable to their sacred function.

When my occasions took me into France, towards the close of the late reign, the clergy, under all their forms, engaged a considerable part of my curiosity. So far from finding (except from one set of men, not then very numerous, though very active) the complaints and discontents against that body, which some publications had given me reason to expect, I perceived little or no public or private uneasiness on their account. On further examination, I found the clergy, in general, persons of moderate minds and decorous manners; I include the seculars, and the regulars of both sexes. I had not the good fortune to know a great many of the parochial clergy: but in general I received a perfectly good account of their morals, and of their attention to their duties. With some of the higher clergy I had a personal acquaintance; and of the rest in that class, a very good means of information. They were, almost all of them, persons of noble birth. They resembled others of their own rank; and where there was any difference, it was in their favour. They were more fully educated than the military noblesse; so as by no means to disgrace their profession by ignorance, or by want of fitness for the exercise of their authority. They seemed to me, beyond the clerical character, liberal and open; with the hearts of gentlemen, and men of honour; neither insolent nor servile in their manners and conduct. They seemed to me rather a superior class; a set of men, amongst whom you would not be surprised to find a *Fenelon*. I saw among the clergy in Paris (many of the description are not to be met with anywhere) men of great learning and candour; and I had reason to believe, that this description was not confined to Paris.

What I found in other places, I know was accidental; and therefore to be presumed a fair example. I spent a few days in a provincial town, where, in the absence of the bishop, I passed my evenings with three clergymen, his vicars-general, persons who would have done honour to any church. They were all well informed; two of them of deep, general, and extensive erudition, ancient and modern, oriental and western; particularly in their own profession. They had a more extensive knowledge of our English divines than I expected and they entered into the genius of those writers with a critical accuracy. One of these gentlemen is since dead, the Abbé *Morangis*. I pay this tribute, without reluctance, to the memory of that noble, reverend, learned, and excellent person; and I should do the same with equal cheerfulness, to the merits of the others, who I believe are still living, if I did not fear to hurt those whom I am unable to serve.

Some of these ecclesiastics of rank are, by all titles, persons deserving of general respect. They are deserving of gratitude from me, and from many English. If this letter should ever come into their hands, I hope they will believe there are those of our nation who feel for their unmerited fall, and for the cruel confiscation of their fortunes, with no common sensibility. What I say of them is a testimony, as far as one feeble voice can go, which I owe to truth. Whenever the question of this unnatural persecution is concerned, I will pay it. No one shall prevent me from being just and grateful. The time is fitted for the duty; and it is particularly becoming to show our justice and gratitude, when those, who have deserved well of us and of mankind, are labouring under popular obloquy, and the persecutions of oppressive power.

You had before your Revolution about an hundred and twenty bishops. A few of them were men of eminent sanctity, and charity without limit. When we talk of the heroic, of course we talk of rare virtue. I believe the instances of eminent depravity may be as rare amongst them as those of transcendent goodness. Examples of avarice and of licentiousness may be picked out, I do not question it, by those who delight in the investigation which leads to such discoveries. A man as old as I am will not be astonished that several, in every description, do not lead that perfect life of self-denial, with regard to wealth or to pleasure, which is wished for by all, by some expected, but by none exacted with more rigour, than by those who are the most attentive to their own interests, or the most indulgent to their own passions. When I was in France, I am certain that the number of vicious prelates was not great. Certain individuals among them, not distinguishable for the regularity of their lives, made some amends for their want of the severe virtues, in their possession of the liberal; and were endowed with qualities which made them useful in the church and state. I am told, that, with few exceptions, Louis the Sixteenth had been more attentive to character, in his promotions to that rank, than his immediate predecessor; and I believe (as some spirit of reform has prevailed through the whole reign) that it may be true. But the present ruling power has shown a disposition only to plunder the church. It has punished *all* prelates; which is to favour the vicious, at least in point of reputation. It has made a degrading pensionary establishment, to which no man of liberal ideas or liberal condition will destine his children. It must settle into the lowest classes of the people. As with you the inferior clergy are not numerous enough for their duties; as these duties are, beyond measure, minute and toilsome, as you have left no middle classes of clergy at their ease, in future nothing of science or erudition can exist in the Gallican church. To complete the project, without the least attention to the rights of patrons, the Assembly has provided in future an elective clergy; an arrangement which will drive out of the clerical profession all men of sobriety; all who can pretend to independence in their function or their conduct; and which will throw the whole direction of the public mind into the hands of a set of licentious, bold, crafty, factious, flattering wretches, of such condition and such habits of life as will make their contemptible pensions (in comparison of which the stipend of an exciseman is lucrative and honourable) an object of low and illiberal intrigue. Those officers, whom they still call bishops, are to be elected to a provision comparatively mean, through the same arts, (that is, electioneering arts,) by men of all religious tenets that are known or can be invented. The new lawgivers have not ascertained anything whatsoever concerning their qualifications, relative either to doctrine or to morals; no more than they have done with regard to the subordinate clergy: nor does it appear but that both the higher and the lower may, at their discretion, practise or preach any mode of religion or irreligion that they please. I do not yet see what the jurisdiction of bishops over their subordinates is to be, or whether they are to have any jurisdiction at all.

In short, Sir, it seems to me, that this new ecclesiastical establishment is intended only to be temporary, and preparatory to the utter abolition, under any of its forms, of the Christian religion, whenever the minds of men are prepared for this last stroke against it, by the accomplishment of the plan for bringing its ministers into universal contempt. They who will not believe, that the philosophical fanatics, who guide in these matters, have long entertained such a design, are utterly ignorant of their character and proceedings. These enthusiasts do not scruple to avow their opinion, that a state can subsist without any religion better than with one and that they are able to supply the place of any good which may be in it, by a project of their own—namely, by a sort of education they have imagined, founded in a knowledge of the physical wants of men; progressively carried to an enlightened self-interest, which, when well understood, they tell us, will identify with an interest more enlarged and public. The scheme of this education has been long known. Of late they distinguish it (as they have got an entirely new nomenclature of technical terms) by the name of a *Civic Education*.

I hope their partisans in England (to whom I rather attribute very inconsiderate conduct, than the ultimate object in this detestable design) will succeed neither in the pillage of the ecclesiastics, nor in the introduction of a principle of popular election to our bishoprics and parochial cures. This, in the present condition of the world, would be the last corruption of the church; the utter ruin of the clerical character; the most dangerous shock that the state ever received through a misunderstood arrangement of religion. I know well enough that the bishoprics and cures, under kingly and seignioral patronage, as now they are in England, and as they have been lately in France, are sometimes acquired by unworthy methods; but the other mode of ecclesiastical canvass subjects them infinitely more surely and more generally to all the evil arts of low ambition, which, operating on and through greater numbers, will produce mischief in proportion.

Those of you, who have robbed the clergy, think that they shall easily reconcile their conduct to all Protestant nations; because the clergy, whom they have thus plundered, degraded, and given over to mockery and scorn, are of the Roman Catholic, that is, of *their own* pretended persuasion. I have no doubt that some miserable bigots will be found here, as well as elsewhere, who hate sects and parties different from their own, more than they love the substance of religion; and who are more angry with those who differ from them in their particular plans and systems, than displeased with those who attack the foundation of our common hope. These men will write and speak on the subject in the manner that is to be expected from their temper and character. Burnet says, that when he was in France, in the year 1683, "the method which carried over the men of the finest parts to Popery was this—they brought themselves to doubt of the whole Christian religion. When that was once done, it seemed a more indifferent thing of what side or form they continued outwardly." If this was then the ecclesiastical policy of France, it is what they have since but too much reason to repent of. They preferred atheism to a form of religion not agreeable to their ideas. They succeeded in destroying that form; and atheism has succeeded in destroying them. I can readily give credit to Burnet's story; because I have observed too much of a similar spirit (for a little of it is "much too much") amongst ourselves. The humour, however, is not general.

The teachers who reformed our religion in England bore no sort of resemblance to your present reforming doctors in Paris. Perhaps they were (like those whom they opposed) rather more than could be wished under the influence of a party spirit; but they were more sincere believers; men of the most fervent and exalted piety; ready to die (as some of them did die) like true heroes in defence of their particular ideas of Christianity; as they would with equal fortitude, and more cheerfully, for that stock of general truth, for the branches of which they contended with their blood. These men would have disavowed with horror those wretches who claimed a fellowship with them upon no other titles than those of their having pillaged the persons with whom they maintained controversies, and their having despised the common religion, for the purity of which they exerted themselves with a zeal, which unequivocally bespoke their highest reverence for the substance of that system which they wished to reform. Many of their descendants have retained the same zeal, but (as less engaged in conflict) with more moderation. They do not forget that justice and mercy are substantial parts of religion. Impious men do not recommend themselves to their communion by iniquity and cruelty towards any description of their fellow-creatures.

We hear these new teachers continually boasting of their spirit of toleration. That those persons should tolerate all opinions, who think none to be of estimation, is a matter of small merit. Equal neglect is not impartial kindness. The species of benevolence, which arises from contempt, is no true charity. There are in England abundance of men who tolerate in the true spirit of toleration. They think the dogmas of religion, though in different degrees, are all of moment: and that amongst them there is, as amongst all things of value, a just ground of preference. They favour, therefore, and they tolerate. They tolerate, not because they despise opinions, but because they respect justice. They would reverently and affectionately protect all religions, because they love and venerate the great principle upon which they all agree, and the great object to which they are all directed. They begin more and more plainly to discern, that we have all a common cause, as against a common enemy. They will not be so misled by the spirit of faction, as not to distinguish what is done in favour of their subdivision, from those acts of hostility, which, through some particular description, are aimed at the whole corps, in which they themselves, under another denomination, are included. It is impossible for me to say what may be the character of every description of men amongst us. But I speak for the greater part; and for them, I must tell you, that sacrilege is no part of their doctrine of good works; that, so far from calling you into their fellowship on such title, if your professors are admitted to their communion, they must carefully conceal their doctrine of the lawfulness of the prescription of innocent men; and that they must make restitution of all stolen goods whatsoever. Till then they are none of ours.

You may suppose that we do not approve your confiscation of the revenues of bishops, and deans, and chapters, and parochial clergy possessing independent estates arising from land, because we have the same sort of establishment in England. That objection, you will say, cannot hold as to the confiscation of the goods of monks and nuns, and the abolition of their order. It is true that this particular part of your general confiscation does not affect England, as a precedent in point: but the reason implies, and it goes a great way. The long parliament confiscated the lands of deans and chapters in England on the same ideas upon which your assembly set to sale the lands of the monastic orders. But it is in the principle of injustice that the danger lies, and not in the description of persons on whom it is first exercised. I see, in a country very near us, a course of policy pursued, which sets justice, the common concern of mankind, at defiance. With the National Assembly of France, possession is nothing, law and usage are nothing. I see the National Assembly openly reprobate the doctrine of prescription, which one of the greatest of their own lawyers[38] tells us, with great truth, is a part of the law of nature. He tells us, that the positive ascertainment of its limits, and its security from invasion, were among the causes for which civil society itself has been instituted. If prescription be once shaken, no species of property is secure, when it once becomes an object large enough to tempt the cupidity of indigent power. I see a practice perfectly correspondent to their contempt of this great fundamental part of natural law. I see the confiscators begin with bishops and chapters, and monasteries; but I do not see them end there. I see the princes of the blood, who by the oldest usages of that kingdom, held large landed estates, (hardly with the compliment of a debate,) deprived of their possessions, and, in lieu of their stable, independent property, reduced to the hope of some precarious, charitable pension, at the pleasure of an assembly, which of course will pay little regard to the rights of pensioners at pleasure, when it despises those of legal proprietors. Flushed with the insolence of their first inglorious victories, and pressed by the distresses caused by their lust of unhallowed lucre, disappointed but not discouraged, they have at length ventured completely to subvert all

[38] Domat.

property of all descriptions throughout the extent of a great kingdom. They have compelled all men, in all transactions of commerce, in the disposal of lands, in civil dealing, and through the whole communion of life, to accept as perfect payment and good and lawful tender, the symbols of their speculations on a projected sale of their plunder. What vestiges of liberty or property have they left? The tenant-right of a cabbage-garden, a year's interest in a hovel, the good-will of an ale-house or a baker's shop, the very shadow of a constructive property, are more ceremoniously treated in our parliament, than with you the oldest and most valuable landed possessions, in the hands of the most respectable personages, or than the whole body of the monied and commercial interest of your country. We entertain a high opinion of the legislative authority; but we have never dreamt that parliaments had any right whatever to violate property, to overrule prescription, or to force a currency of their own fiction in the place of that which is real, and recognised by the law of nations. But you, who began with refusing to submit to the most moderate restraints, have ended by establishing an unheard-of despotism. I find the ground upon which your confiscators go is this; that indeed their proceedings could not be supported in a court of justice; but that the rules of prescription cannot bind a legislative assembly.[39] So that this legislative assembly of a free nation sits, not for the security, but for the destruction, of property, and not of property only, but of every rule and maxim which can give it stability, and of those instruments which can alone give it circulation.

When the Anabaptists of Munster, in the sixteenth century, had filled Germany with confusion, by their system of levelling, and their wild opinions concerning property, to what country in Europe did not the progress of their fury furnish just cause of alarm? Of all things, wisdom is the most terrified with epidemical fanaticism, because of all enemies it is that against which she is the least able to furnish any kind of resource. We cannot be ignorant of the spirit of atheistical fanaticism, that is inspired by a multitude of writings, dispersed with incredible assiduity and expense, and by sermons delivered in all the streets and places of public resort in Paris. These writings and sermons have filled the populace with a black and sav-

---

[39] Speech of Mr. Camus, published by order of the National Assembly.

age atrocity of mind, which supersedes in them the common feelings of nature, as well as all sentiments of morality and religion; insomuch that these wretches are induced to bear with a sullen patience the intolerable distresses brought upon them by the violent convulsions and permutations that have been made in property.[40] The spirit of proselytism attends this spirit of fanaticism. They have societies to cabal and correspond at home and abroad for the propagation of their tenets. The republic of Berne, one of the happiest, the most prosperous, and the best governed countries upon earth, is one of the great objects, at the destruction of which they aim. I am told they have in some measure succeeded in sowing there the seeds of discontent. They are busy throughout Germany. Spain and Italy have not been untried. England is not left out of the comprehensive scheme of their malignant charity: and in England we find those who stretch out their arms to them, who recommend their example from more than one pulpit, and who choose in more than one periodical meeting, publicly to correspond with them, to applaud them, and to hold them up as objects for imitation; who receive from them tokens of confraternity, and standards consecrated amidst their rights and mysteries;[41] who suggest to them leagues of perpetual amity, at the very time when the power, to which our constitution has exclusively delegated the federative capacity of this kingdom, may find it expedient to make war upon them.

It is not the confiscation of our church property from this example

[40] Whether the following description is strictly true, I know not; but it is what the publishers would have pass for true in order to animate others. In a letter from Toul, given in one of their papers, is the following passage concerning the people of that district: "Dans la Révolution actuelle, ils ont résisté à toutes les *séductions du bigotisme, aux persécutions, et aux tracasseries* des ennemis de la Révolution. *Oubliant leurs plus grânds intérêts* pour rendre hommage aux vues d'ordre général qui ont déterminé l'Assemblée Nationale, ils voient, *sans se plaindre,* supprimer cette foule d'établissemens ecclésiastiques par lesquels *ils subsistoient;* et même, en perdant leur siège épiscopal, la seul de toutes ses ressources qui pouvoit, ou plutôt *qui devoit, en toute équité,* leur être conservée; condamnés *à la plus effrayante misère,* sans avoir *été ni pu être entendus, ils ne murmurent point,* ils restent fidèles aux principes du plus pur patriotisme; ils sont encore prêts à *verser leur sang* pour le maintien de la Constitution, qui va réduire leur ville *à la plus déplorable nullité.*" These people are not supposed to have endured those sufferings and injustices in a struggle for liberty, for the same account states truly that they had been always free; their patience in beggary and ruin, and their suffering, without remonstrance, the most flagrant and confessed injustice, if strictly true, can be nothing but the effect of this dire fanaticism. A great multitude all over France is in the same condition and the same temper.

[41] See the proceedings of the confederation at *Nantz.*

in France that I dread, though I think this would be no trifling evil. The great source of my solicitude is, lest it should ever be considered in England as the policy of a state to seek a resource in confiscations of any kind; or that any one description of citizens should be brought to regard any of the others as their proper prey.[42] Nations are wading deeper and deeper into an ocean of boundless debt. Public debts, which at first were a security to governments, by interesting many in the public tranquillity, are likely in their excess to become the means of their subversion. If governments provide for these debts by heavy impositions, they perish by becoming odious to the people. If they do not provide for them they will be undone by the efforts of the most dangerous of all parties; I mean an extensive, discontented monied interest, injured and not destroyed. The men who compose this interest look for their security, in the first instance, to the fidelity of government; in the second, to its power. If they find the old governments effete, worn out, and with their springs relaxed, so as not to be of sufficient vigour for their purposes, they may seek new ones that shall be possessed of more energy; and this energy will be derived, not from an acquisition of resources, but from a contempt of justice. Revolutions are favourable to confiscation; and it is impossible to know under what obnoxious names the next confiscations will be authorized. I am sure that the principles predominant in France extend to very many persons, and descriptions of persons, in all countries who think their innoxious indolence their security. This kind of innocence in proprietors may be argued into inutility; and inutility into an unfitness for their

---

[42] "Si plures sunt ii quibus improbe datum est, quam illi quibus injuste ademptum est, idcirco plus etiam valent? Non enim numero hæc judicantur sed pondere. Quam autem habet æquitatem, ut agrum multis annis, aut etiam sæculis ante possessum, qui nullum habuit habeat; qui autem habuit amittat? Ac, propter hoc injuriæ genus, Lacedæmonii Lysandrum Ephorum expulerunt: Agin regem (quod nunquam antea apud eos acciderat) necaverunt: exque eo tempore tantæ discordiae secutæ sunt, ut et tyranni existerint, et optimates exterminarentur, et preclarissime constituta respublica dilaberetur. Nec vero solum ipsa cecidit, sed etiam reliquam Græciam evertit contagionibus malorum, quæ a Lacedæmoniis profectæ manarunt latius."—After speaking of the conduct of the model of true patriots, Aratus of Sicyon, which was in a very different spirit, he says, "Sic par est agere cum civibus; non ut bis jam vidimus, hastam in foro ponere et bona civium voci subjicere præconis. At ille Græcus (id quod fuit sapientis et præstantis viri) omnibus consulendum esse putavit: eaque est summa ratio et sapientia boni civis, commoda civium non divellere, sed omnes eadem æquitate continere."—Cic. Off. l. 2.

estates. Many parts of Europe are in open disorder. In many others there is a hollow murmuring under ground; a confused movement is felt, that threatens a general earthquake in the political world. Already confederacies and correspondencies of the most extraordinary nature are forming, in several countries.[43] In such a state of things we ought to hold ourselves upon our guard. In all mutations (if mutations must be) the circumstance which will serve most to blunt the edge of their mischief, and to promote what good may be in them, is that they should find us with our minds tenacious of justice, and tender of property.

But it will be argued, that this confiscation in France ought not to alarm other nations. They say it is not made from wanton rapacity; that it is a great measure of national policy, adopted to remove an extensive, inveterate, superstitious mischief. It is with the greatest difficulty that I am able to separate policy from justice. Justice itself is the great standing policy of civil society; and any eminent departure from it, under any circumstances, lies under the suspicion of being no policy at all.

When men are encouraged to go into a certain mode of life by the existing laws, and protected in that mode as in a lawful occupation—when they have accommodated all their ideas and all their habits to it—when the law had long made their adherence to its rules a ground of reputation, and their departure from them a ground of disgrace and even of penalty—I am sure it is unjust in legislature, by an arbitrary act, to offer a sudden violence to their minds and their feelings; forcibly to degrade them from their state and condition, and to stigmatize with shame and infamy that character, and those customs, which before had been made the measure of their happiness and honour. If to this be added an expulsion from their habitations, and a confiscation of all their goods, I am not sagacious enough to discover how this despotic sport, made of the feelings, consciences, prejudices, and properties of men, can be discriminated from the rankest tyranny.

If the injustice of the course pursued in France be clear, the policy of the measure, that is, the public benefit to be expected from it,

[43] See two books entitled, Enige Originalschriften des Illuminatenordens.—System und Folgen des Illuminatenordens. Munchen, 1787.

ought to be at least as evident, and at least as important. To a
man who acts under the influence of no passion, who has nothing
in view in his projects but the public good, a great difference will
immediately strike him between what policy would dictate on the
original introduction of such institutions, and on a question of their
total abolition, where they have cast their roots wide and deep, and
where, by long habit, things more valuable than themselves are so
adapted to them, and in a manner interwoven with them, that the
one cannot be destroyed without notably impairing the other. He
might be embarrassed if the case were really such as sophisters represent it in their paltry style of debating. But in this, as in most
questions of state, there is a middle. There is something else than
the mere alternative of absolute destruction, or unreformed existence. *Spartam nactus es; hanc exorna.* This is, in my opinion, a
rule of profound sense, and ought never to depart from the mind of
an honest reformer. I cannot conceive how any man can have
brought himself to that pitch of presumption, to consider his country as nothing but *carte blanche,* upon which he may scribble whatever he pleases. A man full of warm, speculative benevolence may
wish his society otherwise constituted than he finds it; but a good
patriot, and a true politician, always considers how he shall make
the most of the existing materials of his country. A disposition to
preserve, and an ability to improve, taken together, would be my
standard of a statesman. Everything else is vulgar in the conception, perilous in the execution.

There are moments in the fortune of states, when particular men
are called to make improvements, by great mental exertion. In those
moments, even when they seem to enjoy the confidence of their
prince and country, and to be invested with full authority, they have
not always apt instruments. A politician, to do great things, looks
for a *power,* what our workmen call a *purchase;* and if he finds that
power, in politics as in mechanics, he cannot be at a loss to apply it.
In the monastic institutions, in my opinion, was found a great *power*
for the mechanism of politic benevolence. There were revenues with
a public direction; there were men wholly set apart and dedicated
to public purposes, without any other than public ties and public
principles; men without the possibility of converting the estate of

the community into a private fortune; men denied to self-interests, whose avarice is for some community; men to whom personal poverty is honour, and implicit obedience stands in the place of freedom. In vain shall a man look to the possibility of making such things when he wants them. The winds blow as they list. These institutions are the products of enthusiasm; they are the instruments of wisdom. Wisdom cannot create materials; they are the gifts of nature or of chance; her pride is in the use. The perennial existence of bodies corporate and their fortunes are things particularly suited to a man who has long views; who meditates designs that require time in fashioning, and which propose duration when they are accomplished. He is not deserving to rank high, or even to be mentioned in the order of great statesmen, who, having obtained the command and direction of such a power as existed in the wealth, the discipline, and the habits of such corporations, as those which you have rashly destroyed, cannot find any way of converting it to the great and lasting benefit of his country. On the view of this subject, a thousand uses suggest themselves to a contriving mind. To destroy any power, growing wild from the rank productive force of the human mind, is almost tantamount, in the moral world, to the destruction of the apparently active properties of bodies in the material. It would be like the attempt to destroy (if it were in our competence to destroy) the expansive force of fixed air in nitre, or the power of steam, or of electricity, or of magnetism. These energies always existed in nature, and they were always discernible. They seemed, some of them unserviceable, some noxious, some no better than a sport to children; until contemplative ability, combining with practic skill, tamed their wild nature, subdued them to use, and rendered them at once the most powerful and the most tractable agents, in subservience to the great views and designs of men. Did fifty thousand persons, whose mental and whose bodily labour you might direct, and so many hundred thousand a year of a revenue, which was neither lazy nor superstitious, appear too big for your abilities to wield? Had you no way of using them but by converting monks into pensioners? Had you no way of turning the revenue to account, but through the improvident resource of a spendthrift sale? If you were thus destitute of mental funds, the proceeding is in its natural course. Your politicians do not understand their trade; and therefore they sell their tools.

But the institutions savour of superstition in their very principle; and they nourish it by a permanent and standing influence. This I do not mean to dispute; but this ought not to hinder you from deriving from superstition itself any resources which may thence be furnished for the public advantage. You derive benefits from many dispositions and many passions of the human mind, which are of as doubtful a colour, in the moral eye, as superstition itself. It was your business to correct and mitigate everything which was noxious in this passion, as in all the passions. But is superstition the greatest of all possible vices? In its possible excess I think it becomes a very great evil. It is, however, a moral subject; and of course admits of all degrees and all modifications. Superstition is the religion of feeble minds; and they must be tolerated in an intermixture of it, in some trifling or some enthusiastic shape or other, else you will deprive weak minds of a resource found necessary to the strongest. The body of all true religion consists, to be sure, in obedience to the will of the Sovereign of the world; in a confidence in his declarations; and in imitation of his perfections. The rest is our own. It may be prejudicial to the great end; it may be auxiliary. Wise men, who as such are not *admirers,* (not admirers at least of the *Munera Terræ,*) are not violently attached to these things, nor do they violently hate them. Wisdom is not the most severe corrector of folly. They are the rival follies, which mutually wage so unrelenting a war; and which make so cruel a use of their advantages, as they can happen to engage the immoderate vulgar, on the one side, or the other, in their quarrels. Prudence would be neuter; but if, in the contention between fond attachment and fierce antipathy concerning things in their nature not made to produce such heats, a prudent man were obliged to make a choice of what errors and excesses of enthusiasm he would condemn or bear, perhaps he would think the superstition which builds, to be more tolerable than that which demolishes—that which adorns a country, than that which deforms it—that which endows, than that which plunders—that which disposes to mistaken beneficence, than that which stimulates to real justice—that which leads a man to refuse to himself lawful pleasures, than that which snatches from others the scanty subsistence of their self-denial. Such, I think, is very nearly the state of the question between the ancient founders of monkish superstition, and the superstition of the pretended philosophers of the hour.

For the present I postpone all consideration of the supposed public profit of the sale, which however I conceive to be perfectly delusive. I shall here only consider it as a transfer of property. On the policy of that transfer I shall trouble you with a few thoughts.

In every prosperous community something more is produced than goes to the immediate support of the producer. This surplus forms the income of the landed capitalist. It will be spent by a proprietor who does not labour. But this idleness is itself the spring of labour; this repose the spur to industry. The only concern of the state is, that the capital taken in rent from the land, should be returned again to the industry from whence it came; and that its expenditure should be with the least possible detriment to the morals of those who expend it, and to those of the people to whom it is returned.

In all the views of receipt, expenditure, and personal employment, a sober legislator would carefully compare the possessor whom he was recommended to expel, with the stranger who was proposed to fill his place. Before the inconveniencies are incurred which *must* attend all violent revolutions in property through extensive confiscation, we ought to have some rational assurance that the purchasers of the confiscated property will be in a considerable degree more laborious, more virtuous, more sober, less disposed to extort an unreasonable proportion of the gains of the labourer, or to consume on themselves a larger share than is fit for the measure of an individual; or that they should be qualified to dispense the surplus in a more steady and equal mode, so as to answer the purposes of a politic expenditure, than the old possessors, call those possessors bishops, or canons, or commendatory abbots, or monks, or what you please. The monks are lazy. Be it so. Suppose them no otherwise employed than by singing in the choir. They are as usefully employed as those who neither sing nor say. As usefully even as those who sing upon the stage. They are as usefully employed as if they worked from dawn to dark in the innumerable servile, degrading, unseemly, unmanly, and often most unwholesome and pestiferous occupations, to which by the social economy so many wretches are inevitably doomed. If it were not generally pernicious to disturb the natural course of things, and to impede in any degree, the great wheel of circulation which is turned by the strangely-directed labour of these unhappy people, I should be infinitely more inclined forcibly to rescue them from their miserable industry, than violently to disturb the tranquil repose of monastic quietude. Humanity, and perhaps policy, might better justify me in the one than in the other. It is a subject on which I have often reflected, and never reflected without feeling from it. I am sure that no consideration, except the necessity of submitting to the yoke of luxury, and the despotism of fancy, who in their own imperious way will distribute the surplus product of the soil, can justify the toleration of such trades and employments in a well-regulated state. But for this purpose of distribution, it seems to me, that the idle expenses of monks are quite as well directed as the idle expenses of us lay-loiterers.

When the advantages of the possession and of the project are on a par, there is no motive for a change. But in the present case, perhaps, they are not upon a par, and the difference is in favour of the possession. It does not appear to me, that the expenses of those whom you are going to expel, do in fact take a course so directly and so generally leading to vitiate and degrade and render miserable those through whom they pass, as the expenses of those favourites whom you are intruding into their houses. Why should the expenditure of a great landed property, which is a dispersion of the surplus product of the soil, appear intolerable to you or to me, when it takes its course through the accumulation of vast libraries, which are the history of the force and weakness of the human mind; through great collections of ancient records, medals, and coins, which attest and explain laws and customs; through paintings and statues, that, by imitating nature, seem to extend the limits of creation; through grand monuments of the dead, which continue the regards and connexions of life beyond the grave; through collections of the specimens of nature which become a representative assembly of all the classes and families of the world, that by disposition facilitate, and, by exciting curiosity, open the avenues to science? If by great permanent establishments, all these objects of expense are better secured from the inconstant sport of personal caprice and personal extravagance, are they worse than if the same tastes prevailed in scattered individuals? Does not the sweat of the mason and carpenter, who toil in order to partake of the sweat of the peasant, flow as pleasantly and as salubriously, in the construction and repair of the majestic edifices of religion, as in the painted booths and sordid sties of vice and luxury; as honourably and as profitably in repairing those sacred works, which grow hoary with innumerable years, as on the momentary receptacles of transient voluptuousness; in opera-houses, and brothels, and gaming-houses, and club-houses, and obelisks in the Champ de Mars? Is the surplus product of the olive and the vine worse employed in the frugal sustenance of persons, whom the fictions of a pious imagination raise to dignity by construing in the service of God, than in pampering the innumerable multitude of those who are degraded by being made useless domestics, subservient to the pride of man? Are the decorations of temples an expenditure less worthy a wise man, than ribbons, and laces, and national cockades, and petit maisons, and petit soupers, and all the innumerable fopperies and follies, in which opulence sports away the burthen of its superfluity?

We tolerate even these; not from love of them, but for fear of worse. We tolerate them, because property and liberty, to a degree, require that toleration. But why proscribe the other, and surely, in every point of view, the more laudable use of estates? Why, through the violation of all property, through an outrage upon every principle of liberty, forcibly carry them from the better to the worse?

This comparison between the new individuals and the old corps is made upon a supposition that no reform could be made in the latter. But in a question of reformation, I always consider corporate bodies, whether sole or consisting of many, to be much more susceptible of a public direction by the power of the state, in the use of their property, and in the regulation of modes and habits of life in their members, than private citizens ever can be, or perhaps ought to be: and this seems to me a very material consideration for those who undertake anything which merits the name of a politic enterprise.—So far as to the estates of monasteries.

With regard to the estates possessed by bishops and canons, and commendatory abbots, I cannot find out for what reason some landed estates may not be held otherwise than by inheritance. Can any philosophic spoiler undertake to demonstrate the positive or the comparative evil of having a certain, and that too a large, portion of landed property, passing in succession through persons whose title to it is, always in theory, and often in fact, an eminent degree of piety, morals, and learning; a property, which, by its destination, in their turn, and on the score of merit, gives to the noblest families renovation and support, to the lowest the means of dignity and elevation; a property, the tenure of which is the performance of some duty, (whatever value you may choose to set upon that duty,) and the character of whose proprietors demands, at least, an exterior decorum, and gravity of manners; who are to exercise a generous but temperate hospitality; part of whose income they are to consider as a trust for charity; and who, even when they fail in their trust, when they slide from their character, and degenerate into a mere common secular nobleman or gentleman, are in no respect worse than those who may succeed them in their forfeited possessions? Is it better that estates should be held by those who have no duty, than by those who have one?—by those whose character and destination point to virtues, than by those who have no rule and direction in the expenditure of their estates but their own will and appetite? Nor are these estates held altogether in the character or with the evils supposed inherent in mortmain. They pass from hand to hand with a more rapid circulation than any other. No excess is good; and therefore too great a proportion of landed property may be held officially for life: but it does not seem to me of material injury to any commonwealth, that there should exist some estates that have a chance of being acquired by other means than the previous acquisition of money.

This letter has grown to a great length, though it is indeed short with regard to the infinite extent of the subject. Various avocations have from time to time called my mind from the subject. I was not sorry to give myself leisure to observe whether, in the proceedings of the National Assembly, I might not find reasons to change or to qualify some of my first sentiments. Everything has confirmed me more strongly in my first opinions. It was my original purpose to take a view of the principles of the National Assembly with regard to the great and fundamental establishments; and to compare the whole of what you have substituted in the place of what you have destroyed, with the several members of our British constitution. But this plan is of a greater extent than at first I computed, and I find that you have little desire to take the advantage of any examples. At present I must content myself with some remarks upon your establishments; reserving for another time what I proposed to say concerning the spirit of our British monarchy, aristocracy, and democracy, as practically they exist.

I have taken a view of what has been done by the governing power in France. I have certainly spoke of it with freedom. Those whose principle it is to despise the ancient, permanent sense of mankind, and to set up a scheme of society on new principles, must naturally expect that such of us, who think better of the judgment of the human race than of theirs, should consider both them and their devices, as men and schemes upon their trial. They must take it for granted that we attend much to their reason, but not at all to their authority. They have not one of the great influencing prejudices of mankind in their favor. They avow their hostility to opinion. Of course they must expect no support from that influence, which, with every other authority, they have deposed from the seat of its jurisdiction.

I can never consider this Assembly as anything else than a voluntary association of men, who have availed themselves of circumstances to seize upon the power of the state. They have not the sanction and authority of the character under which they first met. They have assumed another of a very different nature; and have completely altered and inverted all the relations in which they originally stood. They do not hold the authority they exercise under any constitutional law of the state. They have departed from the instructions, of the people by whom they were sent; which instructions, as the Assembly did not act in virtue of any ancient usage or settled law, were the sole source of their authority. The most considerable of their acts have not been done by great majorities; and in this sort of near divisions, which carry only the constructive authority of the whole, strangers will consider reasons as well as resolutions.

If they had set up this new experimental government, as a necessary substitute for an expelled tyranny, mankind would anticipate the time of prescription, which, through long usage, mellows into legality governments that were violent in their commencement. All those who have affections which lead them to the conservation of civil order would recognize, even in its cradle, the child as legitimate, which has been produced from those principles of cogent expediency to which all just governments owe their birth, and on which they justify their continuance. But they will be late and reluctant in giving any sort of countenance to the operations of a power, which has derived its birth from no law and no necessity; but which on the contrary has had its origin in those vices and sinister practices by which the social union is often disturbed and sometimes destroyed. This Assembly has hardly a year's prescription. We have their own word for it that they have made a revolution. To make a revolution is a measure which, *prima fronte,* requires an apology. To make a revolution is to subvert the ancient state of our country; and no common reasons are called for to justify so violent a proceeding. The sense of mankind authorizes us to examine into the mode of acquiring new power, and to criticise on the use that is made of it, with less awe and reverence than that which is usually conceded to a settled and recognized authority.

In obtaining and securing their power, the Assembly proceeds upon principles the most opposite to those which appear to direct them in the use of it. An observation on this difference will let us into the true spirit of their conduct. Everything which they have done, or continue to do, in order to obtain and keep their power, is by the most common arts. They proceed exactly as their ancestors of ambition have done before them.—Trace them through all their artifices, frauds, and violences, you can find nothing at all that is new. They follow precedents and examples with the punctilious exactness of a pleader. They never depart an iota from the authentic formulas of tyranny and usurpation. But in all the regulations relative to the public good, the spirit has been the very reverse of this. There they commit the whole to the mercy of untried speculations;

they abandon the dearest interests of the public to those loose theories, to which none of them would choose to trust the slightest of his private concerns. They make this difference, because in their desire of obtaining and securing power they are thoroughly in earnest; there they travel in the beaten road. The public interests, because about them they have no real solicitude, they abandon wholly to chance: I say to chance, because their schemes have nothing in experience to prove their tendency beneficial.

We must always see with a pity not unmixed with respect, the errors of those who are timid and doubtful of themselves with regard to points wherein the happiness of mankind is concerned. But in these gentlemen there is nothing of the tender, parental solicitude, which fears to cut up the infant for the sake of an experiment. In the vastness of their promises, and the confidence of their predictions, they far outdo all the boasting of empirics. The arrogance of their pretensions, in a manner provokes and challenges us to an inquiry into their foundation.

I am convinced that there are men of considerable parts among the popular leaders in the National Assembly. Some of them display eloquence in their speeches and their writings. This cannot be without powerful and cultivated talents. But eloquence may exist without a proportionable degree of wisdom. When I speak of ability, I am obliged to distinguish. What they have done towards the support of their system bespeaks no ordinary men. In the system itself, taken as the scheme of a republic constructed for procuring the prosperity and security of the citizen, and for promoting the strength and grandeur of the state, I confess myself unable to find out anything which displays, in a single instance the work of a comprehensive and disposing mind, or even the provisions of a vulgar prudence. Their purpose everywhere seems to have been to evade and slip aside from *difficulty*. This it has been the glory of the great masters in all the arts to confront, and to overcome; and when they had overcome the first difficulty, to turn it into an instrument for new conquests over new difficulties; thus to enable them to extend the empire of their science; and even to push forward, beyond the reach of their original thoughts, the land-marks of the human understanding itself. Difficulty is a severe instructor, set over us by the supreme ordinance of a parental Guardian and Legislator, who knows us better than we know ourselves, as he loves us better too. *Pater ipse colendi haud facilem esse viam voluit.* He that wrestles with us strengthens our nerves, and sharpens our skill. Our antagonist is our helper. This amicable conflict with difficulty obliges us to an intimate acquaintance with our object, and compels us to consider it in all its relations. It will not suffer us to be superficial. It is the want of nerves of understanding for such a task, it is the degenerate fondness for tricking short-cuts, and little fallacious facilities, that has in so many parts of the world created governments with arbitrary powers. They have created the late arbitrary monarchy of France. They have created the arbitrary republic of Paris. With them defects in wisdom are to be supplied by the plentitude of force. They get nothing by it. Commencing their labours on a principle of sloth, they have the common fortune of slothful men. The difficulties, which they rather had eluded than escaped, meet them again in their course; they multiply and thicken on them; they are involved, through a labyrinth of confused detail, in an industry without limit, and without direction; and, in conclusion, the whole of their work becomes feeble, vicious, and insecure.

It is this inability to wrestle with difficulty which has obliged the arbitrary Assembly of France to commence their schemes of reform with abolition and total destruction.[44] But is it in destroying and pulling down that skill is displayed? Your mob can do this as well at least as your assemblies. The shallowest understanding, the rudest hand, is more than equal to that task. Rage and phrensy will pull down more in half an hour, than prudence, deliberation, and foresight can build up in a hundred years. The errors and defects of old establishments are visible and palpable. It calls for little

[44] A leading member of the Assembly, M. Rabaud de St. Etienne, has expressed the principle of all their proceedings as clearly as possible.—Nothing can be more simple:— *"Tous les établissemens en France couronnent le malheur du peuple: pour le rendre heureux il faut le rénouveler; changer ses idées; changer ses loix; changer ses mœurs; . . . changer les hommes; changer les choses; changer les mots . . . tout détruire; oui, tout détruire; puisque tout est à recréer."* This gentleman was chosen president in an assembly not sitting at the *Quinze-vingt,* or the *Petits Maisons;* and composed of persons giving themselves out to be rational beings; but neither his ideas, language, or conduct, differ in the smallest degree from the discourses, opinions, and actions of those within and without the Assembly, who direct the operations of the machine now at work in France.

ability to point them out; and where absolute power is given, it requires but a word wholly to abolish the vice and the establishment together. The same lazy but restless disposition, which loves sloth and hates quiet, directs the politicians, when they come to work for supplying the place of what they have destroyed. To make everything the reverse of what they have seen is quite as easy as to destroy. No difficulties occur in what has never been tried. Criticism is almost baffled in discovering the defects of what has not existed; and eager enthusiasm and cheating hope have all the wide field of imagination, in which they may expatiate with little or no opposition.

At once to preserve and to reform is quite another thing. When the useful parts of an old establishment are kept, and what is superadded is to be fitted to what is retained, a vigorous mind, steady, persevering attention, various powers of comparison and combination, and the resources of an understanding fruitful in expedients, are to be exercised; they are to be exercised in a continued conflict with the combined force of opposite vices, with the obstinacy that rejects all improvement, and the levity that is fatigued and disgusted with everything of which it is in possession. But you may object—"A process of this kind is slow. It is not fit for an assembly, which glories in performing in a few months the work of ages. Such a mode of reforming, possibly, might take up many years." Without question it might; and it ought. It is one of the excellencies of a method in which time is amongst the assistants, that its operation is slow, and in some cases almost imperceptible. If circumspection and caution are a part of wisdom, when we work only upon inanimate matter, surely they become a part of duty too, when the subject of our demolition and construction is not brick and timber, but sentient beings, by the sudden alteration of whose state, condition, and habits, multitudes may be rendered miserable. But it seems as if it were the prevalent opinion in Paris, that an unfeeling heart, and an undoubting confidence, are the sole qualifications for a perfect legislator. Far different are my ideas of that high office. The true lawgiver ought to have a heart full of sensibility. He ought to love and respect his kind, and to fear himself. It may be allowed to his temperament to catch his ultimate object with an intuitive glance; but his movements towards it ought to be deliberate. Political arrangement, as it is a work for social ends, is to be only wrought by social means. There mind must conspire with mind. Time is required to produce that union of minds which alone can produce all the good we aim at. Our patience will achieve more than our force. If I might venture to appeal to what is so much out of fashion in Paris, I mean to experience, I should tell you, that in my course I have known, and, according to my measure, have co-operated with great men; and I have never yet seen any plan which has not been mended by the observations of those who were much inferior in understanding to the person who took the lead in the business. By a slow but well-sustained progress, the effect of each step is watched; the good or ill success of the first gives light to us in the second; and so, from light to light, we are conducted with safety through the whole series. We see that the parts or the system do not clash. The evils latent in the most promising contrivances are provided for as they arise. One advantage is as little as possible sacrificed to another. We compensate, we reconcile, we balance. We are enabled to unite into a consistent whole the various anomalies and contending principles that are found in the minds and affairs of men. From hence arises, not an excellence in simplicity, but one far superior, an excellence in composition. Where the great interests of mankind are concerned through a long succession of generations, that succession ought to be admitted into some share in the councils, which are so deeply to affect them. If justice requires this, the work itself requires the aid of more minds than one age can furnish. It is from this view of things that the best legislators have been often satisfied with the establishment of some sure, solid, and ruling principle in government; a power like that which some of the philosophers have called a plastic nature; and having fixed the principle, they have left it afterwards to its own operation.

To proceed in this manner, that is, to proceed with a presiding principle, and a prolific energy, is with me the criterion of profound wisdom. What your politicians think the marks of a bold, hardy genius, are only proofs of a deplorable want of ability. By their violent haste and their defiance of the process of nature, they are delivered over blindly to every projector and adventurer, to every alchymist and empiric. They despair of turning to account anything that is common. Diet is nothing in their system of remedy. The worst of it is, that this their despair of curing common distempers by regular methods, arises not only from defect of comprehension, but, I fear, from some malignity of disposition. Your legislators seem to have taken their opinions of all professions, ranks, and offices, from the declamations and buffooneries of satirists; who would themselves be astonished if they were held to the letter of their own descriptions. By listening only to these, your leaders regard all things only on the side of their vices and faults, and view those vices and faults under every colour of exaggeration. It is undoubtedly true, though it may seem paradoxical; but in general, those who are habitually employed in finding and displaying faults, are unqualified for the work of reformation: because their minds are not only unfurnished with patterns of the fair and good, but by habit they come to take no delight in the contemplation of those things. By hating vices too much, they come to love men too little. It is therefore not wonderful, that they should be indisposed and unable to serve them. From hence arises the complexional disposition of some of your guides to pull everything in pieces. At this malicious game they display the whole of their *quadrimanous* activity. As to the rest, the paradoxes of eloquent writers, brought forth purely as a sport of fancy, to try their talents, to rouse attention and excite surprise, are taken up by these gentlemen, not in the spirit of the original authors, as means of cultivating their taste and improving their style. These paradoxes become with them serious grounds of action, upon which they proceed in regulating the most important concerns of the state. Cicero ludicrously describes Cato as endeavouring to act, in the commonwealth, upon the school paradoxes, which exercised the wits of the junior students in the Stoic philosophy. If this was true of Cato, these gentlemen copy after him in the manner of some persons who lived about his time— *pede nudo Catonem.* Mr. Hume told me that he had from Rousseau himself the secret of his principles of composition. That acute though eccentric observer had perceived, that to strike and interest the public, the marvellous must be produced; that the marvellous of the heathen mythology had long since lost its effect; that giants, magicians, fairies, and heroes of romance which succeeded, had exhausted the portion of credulity which belonged to their age; that now nothing was left to the writer but that species of the marvellous which might still be produced, and with as great an effect as ever, though in another way; that is, the marvellous in life, in manners, in characters, and in extraordinary situations, giving rise to new and unlooked-for strokes in politics and morals. I believe, that were Rousseau alive, and in one of his lucid intervals, he would be shocked at the practical phrensy of his scholars, who in their paradoxes are servile imitators, and even in their incredulity discover an implicit faith.

Men who undertake considerable things, even in a regular way, ought to give us ground to presume ability. But the physician of the state, who, not satisfied with the cure of distempers, undertakes to regenerate constitutions, ought to show uncommon powers. Some very unusual appearances of wisdom ought to display themselves on the face of the designs of those, who appeal to no practice, and who copy after no model. Has any such been manifested? I shall take a view (it shall for the subject be a very short one) of what the Assembly has done, with regard, first, to the constitution of the legislature; in the next place, to that of the executive power; then to that of the judicature; afterwards to the model of the army; and conclude with the system of finance; to see whether we can discover in any part of their schemes the portentous ability, which may justify these bold undertakers in the superiority which they assume over mankind.

It is in the model of the sovereign and presiding part of this new republic, that we should expect their grand display. Here they were to prove their title to their proud demands. For the plan itself at large, and for the reasons on which it is grounded, I refer to the journals of the Assembly of the 29th of September, 1789, and to the subsequent proceedings which have made any alterations in the plan. So far as in a matter somewhat confused I can see light, the system remains substantially as it has been originally framed. My few remarks will be such as regard its spirit, its tendency, and its fitness for framing a popular commonwealth, which they profess theirs to be, suited to the ends for which any commonwealth, and particularly such a commonwealth, is made. At the same time, I mean to consider its consistency with itself and its own principles.

Old establishments are tried by their effects. If the people are happy, united, wealthy, and powerful, we presume the rest. We conclude that to be good from whence good is derived. In old establishments various correctives have been found for their aberrations from theory. Indeed they are the results of various necessities and expediences. They are not often constructed after any theory; theories are rather drawn from them. In them we often see the end best obtained, where the means seem not perfectly reconcilable to what we may fancy was the original scheme. The means taught by experience may be better suited to political ends than those contrived in the original project. They again react upon the primitive constitution, and sometimes improve the design itself, from which they seem to have departed. I think all this might be curiously exemplified in the British Constitution. At worst, the errors and deviations of every kind in reckoning are found and computed, and the ship proceeds in her course. This is the case of old establishments; but in a new and merely theoretic system, it is expected that every contrivance shall appear, on the face of it, to answer its ends; especially where the projectors are no way embarrassed with an endeavour to accommodate the new building to an old one, neither in the walls or on the foundations.

The French builders, clearing away as mere rubbish whatever they found, and, like their ornamental gardeners, forming everything into an exact level, propose to rest the whole local and general legislature on three bases of three different kinds; one geometrical, one arithmetical, and the third financial; the first of which they call the *basis of territory;* the second, the *basis of population;* and the third, the *basis of contribution.* For the accomplishment of the first of these purposes, they divide the area of their country into eighty-three pieces, regularly square, of eighteen leagues by eighteen. These large divisions are called *Departments.* These they portion, proceeding by square measurement, into seventeen hundred and twenty districts, called *Communes.* These again they subdivide, still proceeding by square measurement, into smaller districts called *Cantons*, making in all 6400.

At first view this geometrical basis of theirs, presents not much to admire or to blame. It calls for no great legislative talents. Nothing more than an accurate land surveyor, with his chain, sight, and theodolite, is requisite for such a plan as this. In the old divisions of the country, various accidents at various times, and the ebb and flow of various properties and jurisdictions, settled their bounds. These bounds were not made upon any fixed system undoubtedly. They were subject to some inconveniences: but they were inconveniences for which use had found remedies, and habit had supplied accommodation and patience. In this new pavement of square within square, and this organization, and semi-organization, made on the system of Empedocles and Buffon, and not upon any politic principle, it is impossible that innumerable local inconveniences, to which men are not habituated, must not arise. But these I pass over, because it requires an accurate knowledge of the country, which I do not possess, to specify them.

When these state surveyors came to take a view of their work of measurement they soon found, that in politics the most fallacious of all things was geometrical demonstration. They had then recourse to another basis (or rather buttress) to support the building, which tottered on that false foundation. It was evident, that the goodness of the soil, the number of the people, their wealth, and the largeness of their contribution, made such infinite variations between square and square, as to render mensuration a ridiculous standard of power in the commonwealth, and equality in geometry the most unequal of all measures in the distribution of men. However, they could not give it up. But dividing their political and civil representation into three parts, they allotted one of those parts to the square measurement, without a single fact or calculation to ascertain whether this territorial proportion of representation was fairly assigned, and ought upon any principle really to be a third. Having however given to geometry this portion (of a third for her dower) out of compliment, I suppose, to that sublime science, they left the other two to be scuffled for between the other parts, population and contribution.

When they came to provide for population, they were not able to proceed quite so smoothly as they had done in the field of their geometry. Here their arithmetic came to bear upon their juridical metaphysics. Had they stuck to their metaphysic principles, the arithmetical process would be simple indeed. Men, with them, are strictly equal, and are entitled to equal rights in their own government. Each head, on this system, would have its vote, and every man would vote directly for the person who was to represent him in the legislature. "But soft—by regular degrees, not yet." This metaphysic principle, to which law, custom, usage, policy, reason, were to yield, is to yield itself to their pleasure. There must be many degrees, and some stages, before the representative can come in contact with his constituent. Indeed, as we shall soon see, these two persons are to have no sort of communion with each other. First, the voters in the *Canton,* who compose what they call *primary assemblies,* are to have a *qualification.* What! a qualification on the indefeasible rights of men? Yes; but it shall be a very small qualification. Our injustice shall be very little oppressive; only the local valuation of three days' labour paid to the public. Why, this is not much, I readily admit, for anything but the utter subversion of your equalising principle. As a qualification it might as well be let alone; for it answers no one purpose for which qualifications are established; and, on your ideas, it excludes from a vote the man of all others whose natural equality stands the most in need of protection and defence: I mean the man who has nothing else but his natural equality to guard him. You order him to buy the right, which you before told him nature had given to him gratuitously at his birth, and of which no authority on earth could lawfully deprive him. With regard to the person who cannot come up to your market, a tyrannous aristocracy, as against him, is established at the very outset, by you who pretend to be its sworn foe.

The gradation proceeds. These primary assemblies of the *Canton* elect deputies to the *Commune;* one for every two hundred qualified inhabitants. Here is the first medium put between the primary elector and the representative legislator; and here a new turnpike is fixed for taxing the rights of men with a second qualification: for none can be elected into the *Commune* who does not pay the amount of ten days' labour. Nor have we yet done. There is still to be another gradation.[45] These *Communes,* chosen by the *Canton,* choose to the *Department;* and the deputies of the *Department* choose their deputies to the *National Assembly.* Here is a third barrier of a senseless qualification. Every deputy to the National Assembly must pay, in direct contribution, to the value of a *mark of silver.* Of all these qualifying barriers we must think alike; that they are impotent to secure independence; strong only to destroy the rights of men.

In all this process, which in its fundamental elements affects to consider only *population* upon a principle of natural right, there is a manifest attention to *property;* which, however just and reasonable on other schemes, is on theirs perfectly unsupportable.

When they come to their third basis, that of *Contribution,* we find that they have more completely lost sight of their rights of men. This last basis rests *entirely* on property. A principle totally different from the equality of men, and utterly irreconcilable to it, is thereby admitted; but no sooner is this principle admitted, than (as usual) it is subverted; and it is not subverted (as we shall presently see) to approximate the inequality of riches to the level of nature. The additional share in the third portion of representation (a portion reserved exclusively for the higher contribution) is made to regard the *district* only, and not the individuals in it who pay. It is easy to perceive, by the course of their reasonings, how much they were embarrassed by their contradictory ideas of the rights of men and the privileges of riches. The committee of constitution do as good as admit that they are wholly irreconcilable. "The relation with regard to the contributions, is without doubt *null* (say they) when the question is on the balance of the political rights as between individual and individual; without which *personal equality would be destroyed,* and *an aristocracy of the rich* would be established. But this inconvenience entirely disappears when the proportional

---

[45] The Assembly, in executing the plan of their committee, made some alterations. They have struck out one stage in these gradations; this removes a part of the objection; but the main objection, namely, that in their scheme the first constituent voter has no connexion with the representative legislator, remains in all its force. There are other alterations, some possibly for the better, some certainly for the worse; but to the author the merit or demerit of these smaller alterations appears to be of no moment, where the scheme itself is fundamentally vicious and absurd.

relation of the contribution is only considered in the *great masses,* and is solely between province and province; it serves in that case only to form a just reciprocal proportion between the cities, without affecting the personal rights of the citizens."

Here the principle of *contribution,* as taken between man and man, is reprobated as *null,* and destructive to equality and as pernicious too; because it leads to the establishment of an *aristocracy of the rich.* However, it must not be abandoned. And the way of getting rid of the difficulty is to establish the inequality as between department and department, leaving all the individuals in each department upon an exact par. Observe, that this parity between individuals had been before destroyed, when the qualifications within the departments were settled; nor does it seem a matter of great importance whether the equality of men be injured by masses or individually. An individual is not of the same importance in a mass represented by a few, as in a mass represented by many. It would be too much to tell a man jealous of his equality, that the elector has the same franchise who votes for three members as he who votes for ten.

Now take it in the other point of view, and let us suppose their principle of representation according to contribution, that is, according to riches, to be well imagined, and to be a necessary basis for their republic. In this their third basis they assume, that riches ought to be respected, and that justice and policy require that they should entitle men, in some mode or other, to a larger share in the administration of public affairs; it is now to be seen how the Assembly provides for the pre-eminence, or even for the security, of the rich, by conferring, in virtue of their opulence, that larger measure of power to their district which is denied to them personally. I readily admit (indeed I should lay it down as a fundamental principle) that in a republican government, which has a democratic basis, the rich do require an additional security above what is necessary to them in monarchies. They are subject to envy, and through envy to oppression. On the present scheme it is impossible to divine what advantage they derive from the aristocratic preference upon which the unequal representation of the masses is founded. The rich cannot feel it, either as a support to dignity, or as security

to fortune: for the aristocratic mass is generated from purely democratic principles; and the preference given to it in the general representation has no sort of reference to, or connexion with, the persons,
upon account of whose property this superiority of the mass is established. If the contrivers of this scheme meant any sort of favour
to the rich, in consequence of their contribution, they ought to have
conferred the privilege either on the individual rich, or on some
class formed of rich persons (as historians represent Servius Tullius
to have done in the early constitution of Rome); because the contest between the rich and the poor is not a struggle between corporation and corporation, but a contest between men and men; a
competition not between districts, but between descriptions. It
would answer its purpose better if the scheme were inverted; that
the votes of the masses were rendered equal; and that the votes
within each mass were proportioned to property.

Let us suppose one man in a district (it is an easy supposition) to
contribute as much as an hundred of his neighbours. Against these
he has but one vote. If there were but one representative for the
mass, his poor neighbours would outvote him by an hundred to
one for that single representative. Bad enough. But amends are to
be made him. How? The district, in virtue of his wealth, is to
choose, say ten members instead of one: that is to say, by paying a
very large contribution he has the happiness of being outvoted, an
hundred to one, by the poor, for ten representatives, instead of being
outvoted exactly in the same proportion for a single member. In
truth, instead of benefiting by this superior quantity of representation, the rich man is subjected to an additional hardship. The increase of representation within his province sets up nine persons
more, and as many more than nine as there may be democratic
candidates, to cabal and intrigue, and to flatter the people at his
expense and to his oppression. An interest is by this means held out
to multitudes of the inferior sort, in obtaining a salary of eighteen
livres a day, (to them a vast object,) besides the pleasure of a residence in Paris, and their share in the government of the kingdom.
The more the objects of ambition are multiplied and become democratic, just in that proportion the rich are endangered.

Thus it must fare between the poor and the rich in the province deemed aristocratic, which in its internal relation is the very reverse of that character. In its external relation, that is, its relation to the other provinces, I cannot see how the unequal representation, which is given to masses on account of wealth, becomes the means of preserving the equipoise and the tranquillity of the commonwealth. For if it be one of the objects to secure the weak from being crushed by the strong, (as in all society undoubtedly it is,) how are the smaller and poorer of these masses to be saved from the tyranny of the more wealthy? Is it by adding to the wealthy further and more systematical means of oppressing them? When we come to a balance of representation between corporate bodies, provincial interests, emulations, and jealousies are full as likely to arise among them as among individuals; and their divisions are likely to produce a much hotter spirit of dissension, and something leading much more nearly to a war.

I see that these aristocratic masses are made upon what is called the principle of direct contribution. Nothing can be a more unequal standard than this. The indirect contribution, that which arises from duties on consumption, is in truth a better standard, and follows and discovers wealth more naturally than this of direct contribution. It is difficult indeed to fix a standard of local preference on account of the one, or of the other, or of both, because some provinces may pay the more of either or of both, on account of causes not intrinsic, but originating from those very districts over whom they have obtained a preference in consequence of their ostensible contribution. If the masses were independent, sovereign bodies, who were to provide for a federative treasury by distinct contingents, and that the revenue had not (as it has) many impositions running through the whole, which affect men individually, and not corporately, and which, by their nature, confound all territorial limits, something might be said for the basis of contribution as founded on masses. But of all things, this representation, to be measured by contribution, is the most difficult to settle upon principles of equity in a country, which considers its districts as members of a whole. For a great city, such as Bourdeaux, or Paris, appears to pay a vast body of duties, almost out of all assignable proportion to other places, and its mass is considered accordingly. But are these cities the true contributors in that proportion? No. The consumers of the commodities imported into Bourdeaux, who are scattered through all France, pay the import duties of Bourdeaux. The produce of the vintage in Guienne and Languedoc, give to that city the means of its contribution growing out of an export commerce. The landholders who spend their estates in Paris, and are thereby the creators of that city, contribute for Paris from the provinces out of which their revenues arise. Very nearly the same arguments will apply to the representative share given on account of *direct* contributions: because the direct contribution must be assessed on wealth real or presumed; and that local wealth will itself arise from causes not local, and which therefore in equity ought not to produce a local preference.

It is very remarkable, that in this fundamental regulation, which settles the representation of the mass upon the direct contribution, they have not yet settled how that direct contribution shall be laid, and how apportioned. Perhaps there is some latent policy towards the continuance of the present Assembly in this strange procedure. However, until they do this, they can have no certain constitution. It must depend at last upon the system of taxation, and must vary with every variation in that system. As they have contrived matters, their taxation does not so much depend on their constitution, as their constitution on their taxation. This must introduce great confusion among the masses; as the variable qualification for votes within the district must, if ever real contested elections take place, cause infinite internal controversies.

To compare together the three bases, not on their political reason, but on the ideas on which the Assembly works, and to try its consistency with itself, we cannot avoid observing, that the principle which the committee call the basis of *population,* does not begin to operate from the same point with the two other principles called the bases of *territory* and of *contribution,* which are both of an aristocratic nature. The consequence is, that, where all three begin to operate together, there is the most absurd inequality produced by the operation of the former on the two latter principles. Every canton contains four square leagues, and is estimated to contain, on the average, 4000 inhabitants, or 680 voters in the *primary assemblies,* which vary in numbers with the population of the canton, and send *one deputy* to the *commune* for every 200 voters. *Nine cantons* make a *commune*.

Now let us take *a canton* containing *a sea-port town of trade,* or *a great manufacturing town.* Let us suppose the population of this canton to be 12,700 inhabitants, or 2193 voters, forming *three primary assemblies,* and sending *ten deputies* to the *commune.*

Oppose to this *one* canton *two* others of the remaining eight in the same commune. These we may suppose to have their fair population of 4000 inhabitants and 680 voters each, or 8000 inhabitants and 1360 voters, both together. These will form only *two primary assemblies,* and send only *six* deputies to the *commune.*

When the assembly of the *commune* comes to vote on the *basis of territory,* which principle is first admitted to operate in that assembly, the *single canton,* which has *half* the territory of the *other two,* will have *ten* voices to *six* in the election of *three deputies* to the assembly of the department, chosen on the express ground of a representation of territory. This inequality, striking as it is, will be yet highly aggravated, if we suppose, as we fairly may, the *several* other cantons of the *commune* to fall proportionably short of the average population, as much as the *principal canton* exceeds it.

Now as to *the basis of contribution,* which also is a principle admitted first to operate in the assembly of the *commune.* Let us again take *one* canton, such as is stated above. If the whole of the direct contributions paid by a great trading or manufacturing town be divided equally among the inhabitants, each individual will be found to pay much more than an individual living in the country according to the same average. The whole paid by the inhabitants of the former will be more than the whole paid by the inhabitants of the latter—we may fairly assume one-third more. Then the 12,700 inhabitants, or 2193 voters of the canton, will pay as much as 19,050 inhabitants, or 3289 voters of the *other cantons,* which are nearly the estimated proportion of inhabitants and voters of *five* other cantons. Now the 2193 voters will, as I before said, send only *ten* deputies to the assembly; the 3289 voters will send *sixteen.* Thus, for an *equal* share in the contribution of the whole *commune,* there will be a difference of *sixteen* voices to *ten* in voting for deputies to be chosen on the principle of representing the general contribution of the whole *commune*.

By the same mode of computation we shall find 15,875 inhabitants, or 2741 voters of the *other* cantons, who pay *one-sixth* LESS to the contribution of the whole *commune,* will have *three* VOICES MORE than the 12,700 inhabitants, or 2193 voters of the *one* canton.

Such is the fantastical and unjust inequality between mass and mass, in this curious repartition of the rights of representation arising out of *territory* and *contribution*. The qualifications which these confer are in truth negative qualifications, that give a right in an inverse proportion to the possession of them.

In this whole contrivance of the three bases, consider it in any light you please, I do not see a variety of objects reconciled in one consistent whole, but several contradictory principles reluctantly and irreconcilably brought and held together by your philosophers, like wild beasts shut up in a cage, to claw and bite each other to their mutual destruction.

I am afraid I have gone too far into their way of considering the formation of a constitution. They have much, but bad, metaphysics; much, but bad, geometry; much, but false, proportionate arithmetic; but if it were all as exact as metaphysics, geometry, and arithmetic ought to be, and if their schemes were perfectly consistent in all their parts, it would make only a more fair and sightly vision. It is remarkable, that, in a great arrangement of mankind, not one reference whatsoever is to be found to anything moral or anything politic; nothing that relates to the concerns, the actions, the passions, the interests of men. *Hominem non sapiunt.*

You see I only consider this constitution as electoral, and leading by steps to the National Assembly. I do not enter into the internal government of the departments, and their genealogy through the communes and cantons. These local governments are, in the original plan, to be as nearly as possible composed in the same manner and on the same principles with the elective assemblies. They are each of them bodies perfectly compact and rounded in themselves.

You cannot but perceive in this scheme, that it has a direct and immediate tendency to sever France into a variety of republics, and to render them totally independent of each other without any direct constitutional means of coherence, connexion, or subordination, except what may be derived from their acquiescence in the determinations of the general congress of the ambassadors from each independent republic. Such in reality is the National Assembly, and such governments I admit do exist in the world, though in forms infinitely more suitable to the local and habitual circumstances of their people. But such associations, rather than bodies politic, have generally been the effect of necessity, not choice; and I believe the present French power is the very first body of citizens, who, having obtained full authority to do with their country what they pleased, have chosen to dissever it in this barbarous manner.

It is impossible not to observe, that, in the spirit of this geometrical distribution, and arithmetical arrangement, these pretended citizens treat France exactly like a country of conquest. Acting as conquerors, they have imitated the policy of the harshest of that harsh race. The policy of such barbarous victors, who contemn a subdued people, and insult their feelings, has ever been, as much as in them lay, to destroy all vestiges of the ancient country, in religion, in polity, in laws, and in manners; to confound all territorial limits; to produce a general poverty; to put up their properties to auction; to crush their princes, nobles, and pontiffs; to lay low everything which had lifted its head above the level, or which could serve to combine or rally, in their distresses, the disbanded people, under the standard of old opinion. They have made France free in the manner in which those sincere friends to the rights of mankind, the Romans, freed Greece, Macedon, and other nations. They destroyed the bonds of their union, under colour of providing for the independence of each of their cities.

When the members who compose these new bodies of cantons, communes, and departments, arrangements purposely produced through the medium of confusion, begin to act, they will find themselves in a great measure strangers to one another. The electors and elected throughout, especially in the rural *cantons,* will be frequently without any civil habitudes or connexions, or any of that natural discipline which is the soul of a true republic. Magistrates and collectors of revenue are now no longer acquainted with their districts, bishops with their dioceses, or curates with their parishes. These

new colonies of the rights of men bear a strong resemblance to that
sort of military colonies which Tacitus has observed upon in the
declining policy of Rome. In better and wiser days (whatever course
they took with foreign nations) they were careful to make the elements of methodical subordination and settlement to be coeval; and
even to lay the foundations of civil discipline in the military.[46] But,
when all the good arts had fallen into ruin, they proceeded, as your
Assembly does, upon the equality of men, and with as little judgment, and as little care for those things which make a republic tolerable or durable. But in this, as well as almost every instance,
your new commonwealth is born, and bred, and fed, in those corruptions which mark degenerated and worn-out republics. Your
child comes into the world with the symptoms of death; the *facies
Hippocratica* forms the character of its physiognomy, and the prognostic of its fate.

The legislators who framed the ancient republics knew that their
business was too arduous to be accomplished with no better apparatus than the metaphysics of an undergraduate, and the mathematics and arithmetic of an exciseman. They had to do with men,
and they were obliged to study human nature. They had to do
with citizens, and they were obliged to study the effects of those
habits which are communicated by the circumstances of civil life.
They were sensible that the operation of this second nature on the
first produced a new combination; and thence arose many diversities amongst men, according to their birth, their education, their
professions, the periods of their lives, their residence in towns or
in the country, their several ways of acquiring and of fixing property, and according to the quality of the property itself, all which
rendered them as it were so many different species of animals.
From hence they thought themselves obliged to dispose their citizens into such classes, and to place them in such situations in the
state, as their peculiar habits might qualify them to fill, and to
allot to them such appropriated privileges as might secure to them

[46] Non, ut olim, universæ legiones deducebantur cum tribunis, et centurionibus, et
sui cujusque ordinis militibus, ut consensu et caritate rempublicam afficerent; sed
ignoti inter se, diversis manipulis, sine rectore, sine affectibus mutuis, quasi ex alio
genere mortalium, repente in unum collecti, numerus magis quam colonia. Tac.
Annal. l. 14, sect. 27. All this will be still more applicable to the unconnected,
rotatory, biennial national assemblies, in this absurd and senseless constitution.

what their specific occasions required, and which might furnish
to each description such force as might protect it in the conflict
caused by the diversity of interests, that must exist, and must contend, in all complex society: for the legislator would have been
ashamed, that the coarse husbandman should well know how to
assort and to use his sheep, horses, and oxen, and should have enough
of common sense, not to abstract and equalize them all into animals, without providing for each kind an appropriate food, care, and
employment; whilst he, the economist, disposer, and shepherd of
his own kindred, subliming himself into an airy metaphysician, was
resolved to know nothing of his flocks but as men in general. It is
for this reason that Montesquieu observed very justly, that in their
classification of the citizens, the great legislators of antiquity made
the greatest display of their powers, and even soared above themselves. It is here that your modern legislators have gone deep into
the negative series, and sunk even below their own nothing. As the
first sort of legislators attended to the different kinds of citizens,
and combined them into one commonwealth, the others, the metaphysical and alchemistical legislators, have taken the direct contrary
course. They have attempted to confound all sorts of citizens, as
well as they could, into one homogeneous mass; and then they divided this their amalgama into a number of incoherent republics.
They reduce men to loose counters, merely for the sake of simple
telling, and not to figures whose power is to arise from their place
in the table. The elements of their own metaphysics might have
taught them better lessons. The troll of their categorical table might
have informed them that there was something else in the intellectual world besides *substance* and *quantity*. They might learn from
the catechism of metaphysics that there were eight heads more,[47] in
every complex deliberation, which they have never thought of;
though these, of all the ten, are the subjects on which the skill of
man can operate anything at all.

So far from this able disposition of some of the old republican
legislators, which follows with a solicitous accuracy the moral
conditions and propensities of men, they have levelled and crushed
together all the orders which they found, even under the coarse

[47] Qualitas, Relatio, Actio, Passio, Ubi, Quando, Situs, Habitus.

unartificial arrangement of the monarchy, in which mode of government the classing of the citizens is not of so much importance as in a republic. It is true, however, that every such classification, if properly ordered, is good in all forms of government; and composes a strong barrier against the excesses of despotism, as well as it is the necessary means of giving effect and permanence to a republic. For want of something of this kind, if the present project of a republic should fail, all securities to a moderated freedom fail along with it; all the indirect restraints which mitigate despotism are removed; insomuch that if monarchy should ever again obtain an entire ascendancy in France, under this or under any other dynasty, it will probably be, if not voluntarily tempered, at setting out, by the wise and virtuous counsels of the prince, the most completely arbitrary power that has ever appeared on earth. This is to play a most desperate game.

The confusion which attends on all such proceedings, they even declare to be one of their objects, and they hope to secure their constitution by a terror of a return of those evils which attended their making it. "By this," say they, "its destruction will become difficult to authority, which cannot break it up without the entire disorganization of the whole state." They presume, that if this authority should ever come to the same degree of power that they have acquired, it would make a more moderate and chastised use of it, and would piously tremble entirely to disorganize the state in the savage manner that they have done. They expect, from the virtues of returning despotism, the security which is to be enjoyed by the offspring of their popular vices.

I wish, Sir, that you and my readers would give an attentive perusal to the work of M. de Calonne, on this subject. It is indeed not only an eloquent, but an able and instructive, performance. I confine myself to what he says relative to the constitution of the new state, and to the condition of the revenue. As to the disputes of this minister with his rivals, I do not wish to pronounce upon them. As little do I mean to hazard any opinion concerning his ways and means, financial or political, for taking his country out of its present disgraceful and deplorable situation of servitude, anarchy, bankruptcy, and beggary. I cannot speculate quite so sanguinely as he does: but he is a Frenchman, and has a closer duty relative to those objects, and better means of judging of them, than I can have. I wish that the formal avowal which he refers to, made by one of the principal leaders in the Assembly, concerning the tendency of their scheme to bring France not only from a monarchy to a republic, but from a republic to a mere confederacy, may be very particularly attended to. It adds new force to my observations: and indeed M. de Calonne's work supplies my deficiencies by many new and striking arguments on most of the subjects of this letter.[48]

It is this resolution, to break their country into separate republics, which has driven them into the greatest number of their difficulties and contradictions. If it were not for this, all the questions of exact equality, and these balances, never to be settled, of individual rights, population, and contribution, would be wholly useless. The representation, though derived from parts, would be a duty which equally regarded the whole. Each deputy to the Assembly would be the representative of France, and of all its descriptions, of the many and of the few, of the rich and of the poor, of the great districts and of the small. All these districts would themselves be subordinate to some standing authority, existing independently of them, an authority in which their representation, and everything that belongs to it, originated, and to which it was pointed. This standing, unalterable, fundamental government would make, and it is the only thing which could make, that territory truly and properly a whole. With us, when we elect popular representatives, we send them to a council, in which each man individually is a subject, and submitted to a government complete in all its ordinary functions. With you the elective Assembly is the sovereign, and the sole sovereign; all the members are therefore integral parts of this sole sovereignty. But with us it is totally different. With us the representative, separated from the other parts, can have no action and no existence. The government is the point of reference of the several members and districts of our representation. This is the centre of our unity. This government of reference is a trustee for the *whole,* and not for the parts. So is the other branch of our public council, I mean the House of Lords. With us the king and the lords are

[48] See l'Etat de la France, p. 363.

several and joint securities for the equality of each district, each
province, each city. When did you hear in Great Britain of any
province suffering from the inequality of its representation; what
district from having no representation at all? Not only our monarchy and our peerage secure the equality on which our unity depends, but it is the spirit of the House of Commons itself. The
very inequality of representation, which is so foolishly complained
of, is perhaps the very thing which prevents us from thinking or
acting as members for districts. Cornwall elects as many members
as all Scotland. But is Cornwall better taken care of than Scotland?
Few trouble their heads about any of your bases, out of some giddy
clubs. Most of those who wish for any change, upon any plausible
grounds, desire it on different ideas.

Your new constitution is the very reverse of ours in its principle; and I am astonished how any persons could dream of holding
out anything done in it, as an example for Great Britain. With
you there is little, or rather no, connexion between the last representative and the first constituent. The member who goes to the
National Assembly is not chosen by the people, nor accountable to
them. There are three elections before he is chosen: two sets of
magistracy intervene between him and the primary assembly, so as
to render him, as I have said, an ambassador of a state, and not
the representative of the people within a state. By this the whole
spirit of the election is changed; nor can any corrective, which your
constitution-mongers have devised, render him anything else than
what he is. The very attempt to do it would inevitably introduce
a confusion, if possible, more horrid than the present. There is no
way to make a connexion between the original constituent and the
representative, but by the circuitous means which may lead the
candidate to apply in the first instance to the primary electors, in
order that by their authoritative instructions (and something more
perhaps) these primary electors may force the two succeeding bodies
of electors to make a choice agreeable to their wishes. But this
would plainly subvert the whole scheme. It would be to plunge
them back into that tumult and confusion of popular election,
which, by their interposed gradation of elections, they mean to
avoid, and at length to risk the whole fortune of the state with those

who have the least knowledge of it, and the least interest in it. This is a perpetual dilemma, into which they are thrown by the vicious, weak, and contradictory principles they have chosen. Unless the people break up and level this gradation, it is plain that they do not at all substantially elect to the Assembly; indeed they elect as little in appearance as reality.

What is it we all seek for in an election? To answer its real purposes, you must first possess the means of knowing the fitness of your man; and then you must retain some hold upon him by personal obligation or dependence. For what end are these primary electors complimented, or rather mocked, with a choice? They can never know anything of the qualities of him that is to serve them, nor has he any obligation whatsoever to them. Of all the powers unfit to be delegated by those who have any real means of judging, that most peculiarly unfit is what relates to a *personal* choice. In case of abuse, that body of primary electors never can call the representative to an account for his conduct. He is too far removed from them in the chain of representation. If he acts improperly at the end of his two years' lease, it does not concern him for two years more. By the new French constitution the best and the wisest representatives go equally with the worst into this *Limbus Patrum*. Their bottoms are supposed foul, and they must go into dock to be refitted. Every man who has served in an assembly is ineligible for two years after. Just as these magistrates begin to learn their trade, like chimney-sweepers, they are disqualified for exercising it. Superficial, new, petulant acquisition, and interrupted, dronish, broken, ill recollection, is to be the destined character of all your future governors. Your constitution has too much of jealousy to have much of sense in it. You consider the breach of trust in the representative so principally, that you do not at all regard the question of his fitness to execute it.

This purgatory interval is not unfavorable to a faithless representative, who may be as good a canvasser as he was a bad governor. In this time he may cabal himself into a superiority over the wisest and most virtuous. As, in the end, all the members of this elective constitution are equally fugitive, and exist only for the election, they may be no longer the same persons who had chosen him, to whom he is to be responsible when he solicits for a renewal of his trust. To call all the secondary electors of the *Commune* to account, is ridiculous, impracticable, and unjust; they may themselves have been deceived in their choice, as the third set of electors, those of the *Department,* may be in theirs. In your elections responsibility cannot exist.

Finding no sort of principle of coherence with each other in the nature and constitution of the several new republics of France, I considered what cement the legislators had provided for them from any extraneous materials. Their confederations, their *spectacles,* their civic feasts, and their enthusiasm, I take no notice of; they are nothing but mere tricks; but tracing their policy through their actions, I think I can distinguish the arrangements by which they propose to hold these republics together. The first, is the *confiscation,* with the compulsory paper currency annexed to it; the second, is the supreme power of the city of Paris; the third, is the general army of the state. Of this last I shall reserve what I have to say, until I come to consider the army as a head by itself.

As to the operation of the first (the confiscation and paper currency) merely as a cement, I cannot deny that these, the one depending on the other, may for some time compose some sort of cement, if their madness and folly in the management, and in the tempering of the parts together, does not produce a repulsion in the very outset. But allowing to the scheme some coherence and some duration, it appears to me, that if, after a while, the confiscation should not be found sufficient to support the paper coinage, (as I am morally certain it will not,) then, instead of cementing, it will add infinitely to the dissociation, distraction, and confusion of these confederate republics, both with relation to each other, and to the several parts within themselves. But if the confiscation should so far succeed as to sink the paper currency, the cement is gone with the circulation. In the mean time its binding force will be very uncertain, and it will straiten or relax with every variation in the credit of the paper.

One thing only is certain in this scheme, which is an effect seemingly collateral, but direct, I have no doubt, in the minds of those who conduct this business, that is, its effect in producing an *Oligarchy* in every one of the republics. A paper circulation, not founded on any real money deposited or engaged for, amounting already to four-and-forty millions of English money, and this currency by force substituted in the place of the coin of the kingdom, becoming thereby the substance of its revenue, as well as the medium of all its commercial and civil intercourse, must put the whole of what power, authority, and influence is left, in any form whatsoever it may assume, into the hands of the managers and conductors of this circulation.

In England we feel the influence of the bank; though it is only the centre of a voluntary dealing. He knows little indeed of the influence of money upon mankind, who does not see the force of the management of a monied concern, which is so much more extensive, and in its nature so much more depending on the managers, than any of ours. But this is not merely a money concern. There is another member in the system inseparably connected with this money management. It consists in the means of drawing out at discretion portions of the confiscated lands for sale; and carrying on a process of continual transmutation of paper into land, and land into paper. When we follow this process in its effects, we may conceive something of the intensity of the force with which this system must operate. By this means the spirit of money-jobbing and speculation goes into the mass of land itself, and incorporates with it. By this kind of operation, that species of property becomes (as it were) volatilized; it assumes an unnatural and monstrous activity, and thereby throws into the hands of the several managers, principal and subordinate, Parisian and provincial, all the representative of money, and perhaps a full tenth part of all the land in France, which has now acquired the worst and most pernicious part of the evil of a paper circulation, the greatest possible uncertainty in its value. They have reversed the Latonian kindness to the landed property of Delos. They have sent theirs to be blown about, like the light fragments of a wreck, *oras et littora circum*.

The new dealers, being all habitually adventurers, and without any fixed habits or local predilections, will purchase to job out again, as the market of paper, or of money, or of land, shall present an advantage. For though a holy bishop thinks that agriculture will derive great advantages from the *"enlightened"* usurers who are to purchase the church confiscations, I, who am not a good, but an old farmer, with great humility beg leave to tell his late lordship, that usury is not a tutor of agriculture; and if the word "enlightened" be understood according to the new dictionary, as it always is in your new schools, I cannot conceive how a man's not believing in God can teach him to cultivate the earth with the least of any additional skill or encouragement. "Diis immortalibus sero," said an old Roman, when he held one handle of the plough, whilst Death held the other. Though you were to join in the commission all the directors of the two academies to the directors of the *Caisse d'Escompte,* one old, experienced peasant is worth them all. I have got more information upon a curious and interesting branch of husbandry, in one short conversation with an old Carthusian monk, than I have derived from all the Bank directors that I have ever conversed with. However, there is no cause for apprehension from the meddling of money-dealers with rural economy. These gentlemen are too wise in their generation. At first, perhaps, their tender and susceptible imaginations may be captivated with the innocent and unprofitable delights of a pastoral life; but in a little time they will find that agriculture is a trade much more laborious, and much less lucrative, than that which they had left. After making its panegyric, they will turn their backs on it like their great precursor and prototype. They may, like him, begin by singing *"Beatus ille"*—but what will be the end?

> *Hæc ubi locutus fænerator Alphius,*
> *Jam jam futurus rusticus*
> *Omnem relegit idibus pecuniam;*
> *Quærit calendis ponere.*

They will cultivate the *Caisse d'Eglise,* under the sacred auspices of this prelate, with much more profit than its vineyards and its corn-fields. They will employ their talents according to their habits and their interests. They will not follow the plough whilst they can direct treasuries, and govern provinces.

Your legislators, in everything new, are the very first who have founded a commonwealth upon gaming, and infused this spirit into it as its vital breath. The great object in these politics is to metamorphose France from a great kingdom into one great play-table;

to turn its inhabitants into a nation of gamesters; to make speculation as extensive as life; to mix it with all its concerns; and to divert
the whole of the hopes and fears of the people from their usual
channels into the impulses, passions, and superstitions of those who
live on chances. They loudly proclaim their opinion, that this their
present system of a republic cannot possibly exist without this kind
of gaming fund; and that the very thread of its life is spun out of
the staple of these speculations. The old gaming in funds was mischievous enough undoubtedly; but it was so only to individuals.
Even when it had its greatest extent, in the Mississippi and South
Sea, it affected but few, comparatively; where it extends further, as
in lotteries, the spirit has but a single object. But where the law,
which in most circumstances forbids, and in none countenances,
gaming, is itself debauched, so as to reverse its nature and policy,
and expressly to force the subject to this destructive table, by bringing the spirit and symbols of gaming into the minutest matters, and
engaging everybody in it, and in everything, a more dreadful epi-
demic distemper of that kind is spread than yet has appeared in the
world. With you a man can neither earn nor buy his dinner without a speculation. What he receives in the morning will not have
the same value at night. What he is compelled to take as pay for
an old debt will not be received as the same when he comes to pay
a debt contracted by himself; nor will it be the same when by
prompt payment he would avoid contracting any debt at all. Industry must wither away. Economy must be driven from your country. Careful provision will have no existence. Who will labour
without knowing the amount of his pay? Who will study to increase what none can estimate? Who will accumulate, when he
does not know the value of what he saves? If you abstract it from
its uses in gaming, to accumulate your paper wealth, would be
not the providence of a man, but the distempered instinct of a
jackdaw.

The truly melancholy part of the policy of systematically making
a nation of gamesters is this, that though all are forced to play, few
can understand the game; and fewer still are in a condition to avail
themselves of the knowledge. The many must be the dupes of the
few who conduct the machine of these speculations. What effect it

must have on the country people is visible. The townsman can calculate from day to day; not so the inhabitant of the country. When the peasant first brings his corn to market, the magistrate in the towns obliges him to take the assignat at par; when he goes to the shop with his money, he finds it seven per cent. the worse for crossing the way. This market he will not readily resort to again. The towns-people will be inflamed; they will force the country people to bring their corn. Resistance will begin, and the murders of Paris and St. Denis may be renewed through all France.

What signifies the empty compliment paid to the country, by giving it, perhaps, more than its share in the theory of your representation? Where have you placed the real power over monied and landed circulation? Where have you placed the means of raising and falling the value of every man's freehold? Those, whose operations can take from, or add ten per cent. to, the possessions of every man in France, must be the masters of every man in France. The whole of the power obtained by this revolution will settle in the towns among the burghers, and the monied directors who lead them. The landed gentleman, the yeoman, and the peasant, have, none of them, habits, or inclinations, or experience, which can lead them to any share in this the sole source of power and influence now left in France. The very nature of a country life, the very nature of landed property, in all the occupations, and all the pleasures they afford, render combination and arrangement (the sole way of procuring and exerting influence) in a manner impossible amongst country people. Combine them by all the art you can, and all the industry, they are always dissolving into individuality. Anything in the nature of incorporation is almost impracticable amongst them. Hope, fear, alarm, jealousy, the ephemerous tale that does its business and dies in a day, all these things, which are the reins and spurs by which leaders check or urge the minds of followers, are not easily employed, or hardly at all, amongst scattered people. They assemble, they arm, they act, with the utmost difficulty, and at the greatest charge. Their efforts, if ever they can be commenced, cannot be sustained. They cannot proceed systematically. If the country gentlemen attempt an influence through the mere income of their property, what is it to that of those who have ten times their income to sell, and who can ruin their property by bringing their plunder to meet it at market? If the landed man wishes to mortgage, he falls the value of his land, and raises the value of assignats. He augments the power of his enemy by the very means he must take to contend with him. The country gentleman therefore, the officer by sea and land, the man of liberal views and habits, attached to no profession, will be as completely excluded from the government of his country as if he were legislatively proscribed. It is obvious, that in the towns, all things which conspire against the country gentleman combine in favour of the money manager and director. In towns combination is natural. The habits of burghers, their occupations, their diversion, their business, their idleness, continually bring them into mutual contact. Their virtues and their vices are sociable; they are always in garrison; and they come embodied and half disciplined into the hands of those who mean to form them for civil or military action.

All these considerations leave no doubt on my mind, that if this monster of a constitution can continue, France will be wholly governed by the agitators in corporations, by societies in the towns formed of directors of assignats, and trustees for the sale of church lands, attornies, agents, money-jobbers, speculators, and adventurers, composing an ignoble oligarchy, founded on the destruction of the crown, the church, the nobility, and the people. Here end all the deceitful dreams and visions of the equality and rights of men. In "the Serbonian bog" of this base oligarchy they are all absorbed, sunk, and lost for ever.

Though human eyes cannot trace them, one would be tempted to think some great offences in France must cry to heaven, which has thought fit to punish it with a subjection to a vile and inglorious domination, in which no comfort or compensation is to be found in any even of those false splendours, which, playing about other tyrannies, prevent mankind from feeling themselves dishonoured even whilst they are oppressed. I must confess I am touched with a sorrow, mixed with some indignation, at the conduct of a few men, once of great rank, and still of great character, who, deluded with specious names, have engaged in a business too deep for the line of their understanding to fathom; who have lent their fair reputation, and the authority of their high-sounding names, to the designs of men with whom they could not be acquainted; and have thereby made their very virtues operate to the ruin of their country.

So far as to the first cementing principle.

The second material of cement for their new republic is the superiority of the city of Paris: and this I admit is strongly connected with the other cementing principle of paper circulation and confiscation. It is in this part of the project we must look for the cause of the destruction of all the old bounds of provinces and jurisdictions, ecclesiastical and secular, and the dissolution of all ancient combinations of things, as well as the formation of so many small unconnected republics. The power of the city of Paris is evidently one great spring of all their politics. It is through the power of Paris, now become the centre and focus of jobbing, that the leaders of this faction direct, or rather command, the whole legislative and the whole executive government. Everything therefore must be done which can confirm the authority of that city over the other republics. Paris is compact; she has an enormous strength, wholly disproportioned to the force of any of the square republics; and this strength is collected and condensed within a narrow compass. Paris has a natural and easy connexion of its parts, which will not be affected by any scheme of a geometrical constitution, nor does it much signify whether its proportion of representation be more or less, since it has the whole draft of fishes in its drag-net. The other divisions of the kingdom being hackled and torn to pieces, and separated from all their habitual means, and even principles of union, cannot, for some time at least, confederate against her. Nothing was to be left in all the subordinate members, but weakness, disconnexion, and confusion. To confirm this part of the plan, the Assembly has lately come to a resolution, that no two of their republics shall have the same commander-in-chief.

To a person who takes a view of the whole, the strength of Paris, thus formed, will appear a system of general weakness. It is boasted that the geometrical policy has been adopted, that all local ideas should be sunk, and that the people should no longer be Gascons, Picards, Bretons, Normans; but Frenchmen, with one country, one heart, and one Assembly. But instead of being all Frenchmen, the greater likelihood is, that the inhabitants of that region will shortly have no country. No man ever was attached by a sense of pride, partiality, or real affection, to a description of square measurement. He never will glory in belonging to the Chequer No. 71, or to any other badge-ticket. We begin our public affections in our families. No cold relation is a zealous citizen. We pass on to our neighbourhoods, and our habitual provincial connexions. These are inns and resting-places. Such divisions of our country as have been formed by habit, and not by a sudden jerk of authority, were so many little images of the great country in which the heart found something which it could fill. The love to the whole is not extinguished by this subordinate partiality. Perhaps it is a sort of elemental training to those higher and more large regards, by which alone men come to be affected, as with their own concern, in the prosperity of a kingdom so extensive as that of France. In that general territory itself, as in the old name of provinces, the citizens are interested from old prejudices and unreasoned habits, and not on account of the geometric properties of its figure. The power and pre-eminence of Paris does certainly press down and hold these republics together as long as it lasts. But, for the reasons I have already given you, I think it cannot last very long.

Passing from the civil creating and the civil cementing principles of this constitution, to the National Assembly, which is to appear and act as sovereign, we see a body in its constitution with every possible power, and no possible external control. We see a body without fundamental laws, without established maxims, without respected rules of proceeding, which nothing can keep firm to any system whatsoever. Their idea of their powers is always taken at the utmost stretch of legislative competency, and their examples for common cases from the exceptions of the most urgent necessity. The future is to be in most respects like the present Assembly; but, by the mode of the new elections and the tendency of the new circulations, it will be purged of the small degree of internal control existing in a minority chosen originally from various interests, and preserving something of their spirit. If possible, the next Assembly must be worse than the present. The present, by destroying and altering everything, will leave to their successors apparently nothing popular to do. They will be roused by emulation and example to enterprises the boldest and the most absurd. To suppose such an Assembly sitting in perfect quietude is ridiculous.

Your all-sufficient legislators, in their hurry to do everything at once, have forgot one thing that seems essential, and which I believe never has been before, in the theory or the practice, omitted by any projector of a republic. They have forgot to constitute a *senate,* or something of that nature and character. Never, before this time, was heard of a body politic composed of one legislative and active assembly, and its executive officers, without such a council; without something to which foreign states might connect themselves; something to which, in the ordinary detail of government, the people could look up; something which might give a bias, and steadiness, and preserve something like consistency in the proceedings of state. Such a body kings generally have as a council. A monarchy may exist without it; but it seems to be in the very essence of a republican government. It holds a sort of middle place between the supreme power exercised by the people, or immediately delegated from them, and the mere executive. Of this there are no traces in your constitution; and, in providing nothing of this kind, your Solons and Numas have, as much as in anything else, discovered a sovereign incapacity.

Let us now turn our eyes to what they have done towards the formation of an executive power. For this they have chosen a degraded king. This their first executive officer is to be a machine, without any sort of deliberative discretion in any one act of his function. At best he is but a channel to convey to the National Assembly such matter as it may import that body to know. If he had been made the exclusive channel, the power would not have been without its importance; though infinitely perilous to those who would choose to exercise it. But public intelligence and statement of facts may pass to the Assembly with equal authenticity, through any other conveyance. As to the means, therefore, of giving a direction to measures by the statement of an authorized reporter, this office of intelligence is as nothing.

To consider the French scheme of an executive officer, in its two natural divisions of civil and political.—In the first it must be observed, that, according to the new constitution, the higher parts of judicature, in either of its lines, are not in the king. The king of France is not the fountain of justice. The judges, neither the original nor the appellate, are of his nomination. He neither proposes the candidates, nor has a negative on the choice. He is not even the public prosecutor. He serves only as a notary to authenticate the choice made of the judges in the several districts. By his officers he is to execute their sentence. When we look into the true nature of his authority, he appears to be nothing more than a chief of bum-bailiffs, sergeants at mace, catch-poles, jailers, and hangmen. It is impossible to place anything called royalty in a more degrading point of view. A thousand times better had it been for the dignity of this unhappy prince, that he had nothing at all to do with the administration of justice, deprived as he is of all that is venerable, and all that is consolatory, in that function, without power of originating any process; without a power of suspension, mitigation, or pardon. Everything in justice that is vile and odious is thrown upon him. It was not for nothing that the Assembly has been at such pains to remove the stigma from certain offices, when they are resolved to place the persons who had lately been their king in a situation but one degree above the executioner, and in an office nearly of the same quality. It is not in nature, that, situated as the king of the French now is, he can respect himself, or can be respected by others.

View this new executive officer on the side of his political capacity, as he acts under the orders of the National Assembly. To execute laws is a royal office; to execute orders is not to be a king. However, a political executive magistracy, though merely such, is a great trust. It is a trust indeed that has much depending upon its faithful and diligent performance, both in the person presiding in it and in all its subordinates. Means of performing this duty ought to be given by regulation; and dispositions toward it ought to be infused by the circumstances attendant on the trust. It ought to be environed with dignity, authority, and consideration, and it ought to lead to glory. The office of execution is an office of exertion. It is not from impotence we are to expect the tasks of power. What sort of a person is a king to command executory service, who has no means whatsoever to reward it? Not in a permanent office; not in a grant of land; no, not in a pension of fifty pounds a year; not in the vainest and most trivial title. In France the king is no more the fountain of honour than he is the fountain of justice. All rewards, all distinctions, are in other hands. Those who serve the king can be actuated by no natural motive but fear; by a fear of everything except their master. His functions of internal coercion are as odious as those which he exercises in the department of justice. If relief is to be given to any municipality, the Assembly gives it. If troops are to be sent to reduce them to obedience to the Assembly, the king is to execute the order; and upon every occasion he is to be spattered over with the blood of his people. He has no negative; yet his name and authority is used to enforce every harsh decree. Nay, he must concur in the butchery of those who shall attempt to free him from his imprisonment, or show the slightest attachment to his person or to his ancient authority.

Executive magistracy ought to be constituted in such a manner, that those who compose it should be disposed to love and to venerate those whom they are bound to obey. A purposed neglect, or, what is worse, a literal but perverse and malignant obedience, must be the ruin of the wisest counsels. In vain will the law attempt to anticipate or to follow such studied neglects and fraudulent attentions. To make them act zealously is not in the competence of law. Kings, even such as are truly kings, may and ought to bear the freedom of subjects that are obnoxious to them. They may too, without derogating from themselves, bear even the authority of such persons, if it promotes their service. Louis the Thirteenth mortally hated the Cardinal de Richelieu; but his support of that minister against his rivals was the source of all the glory of his reign, and the solid foundation of his throne itself. Louis the Fourteenth, when come to the throne, did not love the Cardinal Mazarin; but for his interests he preserved him in power. When old, he detested Louvois; but for years, whilst he faithfully served his greatness, he endured his person. When George the Second took Mr. Pitt, who certainly was not agreeable to him, into his councils, he did nothing which could humble a wise sovereign. But these ministers, who were chosen by affairs, not by affections, acted in the name of, and in trust for, kings; and not as their avowed, constitutional, and ostensible masters. I think it impossible that any king, when he has recovered his first terrors, can cordially infuse vivacity and vigour into measures which he knows to be dictated by those, who, he must be persuaded, are in the highest degree ill affected to his person. Will any ministers, who serve such a king (or whatever he may be called) with but a decent appearance of respect, cordially obey the orders of those whom but the other day in his name they had committed to the Bastile? will they obey the orders of those whom, whilst they were exercising despotic justice upon them, they conceived they were treating with lenity; and from whom, in a prison, they thought they had provided an asylum? If you expect such obedience, amongst your other innovations and regenerations, you ought to make a revolution in nature, and provide a new constitution for the human mind. Otherwise, your supreme government cannot harmonize with its executory system. There are cases in which we cannot take up with names and abstractions. You may call half a dozen leading individuals, whom we have reason to fear and hate, the nation. It makes no other difference, than to make us fear and hate them the more. If it had been thought justifiable and expedient to make such a revolution by such means, and through such persons, as you have made yours, it would have been more wise to have completed the business of the fifth and sixth of October. The new executive officer would then owe his situation to those who are his creators as well as his masters; and he might be bound in interest, in the society of crime, and (if in crimes there could be virtues) in gratitude, to serve those who had promoted him to a place of great lucre and great sensual indulgence; and of something more: for more he must have received from those who certainly would not have limited an aggrandized creature, as they have done a submitting antagonist.

A king circumstanced as the present, if he is totally stupefied by his misfortunes, so as to think it not the necessity, but the premium and privilege of life, to eat and sleep, without any regard to glory, can never be fit for the office. If he feels as men commonly feel, he must be sensible, that an office so circumstanced is one in which he can obtain no fame or reputation. He has no generous interest that can excite him to action. At best, his conduct will be passive and defensive. To inferior people such an office might be matter of honour. But to be raised to it, and to descend to it, are different things,

and suggest different sentiments. Does he *really* name the ministers?
They will have a sympathy with him. Are they forced upon him?
The whole business between them and the nominal king will be
mutual counteraction. In all other countries, the office of ministers
of state is of the highest dignity. In France it is full of peril, and
incapable of glory. Rivals, however, they will have in their nothing-
ness, whilst shallow ambition exists in the world, or the desire of a
miserable salary is an incentive to short-sighted avarice. Those competitors of the ministers are enabled by your constitution to attack
them in their vital parts, whilst they have not the means of repelling
their charges in any other than the degrading character of culprits.
The ministers of state in France are the only persons in that country
who are incapable of a share in the national councils. What ministers! What councils! What a nation!—But they are responsible.
It is a poor service that is to be had from responsibility. The elevation of mind to be derived from fear will never make a nation glorious. Responsibility prevents crimes. It makes all attempts against
the laws dangerous. But for a principle of active and zealous service,
none but idiots could think of it. Is the conduct of a war to be trusted
to a man who may abhor its principle; who, in every step he may
take to render it successful, confirms the power of those by whom he
is oppressed? Will foreign states seriously treat with him who has no
prerogative of peace or war; no, not so much as in a single vote by
himself or his ministers, or by any one whom he can possibly influence? A state of contempt is not a state for a prince: better get rid of
him at once.

I know it will be said that these humours in the court and executive government will continue only through this generation; and that
the king has been brought to declare the dauphin shall be educated
in a conformity to his situation. If he is made to conform to his
situation, he will have no education at all. His training must be
worse even than that of an arbitrary monarch. If he reads—whether
he reads or not, some good or evil genius will tell him his ancestors
were kings. Thenceforward his object must be to assert himself and
to avenge his parents. This you will say is not his duty. That may
be; but it is nature; and whilst you pique nature against you, you do
unwisely to trust to duty. In this futile scheme of polity, the state

nurses in its bosom, for the present, a source of weakness, perplexity, counteraction, inefficiency, and decay; and it prepares the means of its final ruin. In short, I see nothing in the executive force (I cannot call it authority) that has even an appearance of vigour, or that has the smallest degree of just correspondence or symmetry, or amicable relation with the supreme power, either as it now exists, or as it is planned for the future government.

You have settled, by an economy as perverted as the policy, two[49] establishments of government; one real, one fictitious. Both maintained at a vast expense; but the fictitious at, I think, the greatest. Such a machine as the latter is not worth the grease of its wheels. The expense is exorbitant; and neither the show nor the use deserve the tenth part of the charge. Oh! but I don't do justice to the talents of the legislators: I don't allow, as I ought to do, for necessity. Their scheme of executive force was not their choice. This pageant must be kept. The people would not consent to part with it. Right; I understand you. You do, in spite of your grand theories, to which you would have heaven and earth to bend, you do know how to conform yourselves to the nature and circumstances of things. But when you were obliged to conform thus far to circumstances, you ought to have carried your submission farther, and to have made, what you were obliged to take, a proper instrument, and useful to its end. That was in your power. For instance, among many others, it was in your power to leave to your king the right of peace and war. What! to leave to the executive magistrate the most dangerous of all prerogatives? I know none more dangerous; nor any one more necessary to be so trusted. I do not say that this prerogative ought to be trusted to your king, unless he enjoyed other auxiliary trusts along with it, which he does not now hold. But, if he did possess them, hazardous as they are undoubtedly, advantages would arise from such a constitution, more than compensating the risk. There is no other way of keeping the several potentates of Europe from intriguing distinctly and personally with the members of your Assembly, from intermeddling in all your concerns, and fomenting, in the heart of your country, the most pernicious of all factions; factions in the interest and under the direction of foreign powers. From that worst of evils,

[49] In reality three, to reckon the provincial republican establishments.

thank God, we are still free. Your skill, if you had any, would be well employed to find out indirect correctives and controls upon this perilous trust. If you did not like those which in England we have chosen, your leaders might have exerted their abilities in contriving better. If it were necessary to exemplify the consequences of such an executive government as yours, in the management of great affairs, I should refer you to the late reports of M. de Montmorin to the National Assembly, and all the other proceedings relative to the differences between Great Britain and Spain. It would be treating your understanding with disrespect to point them out to you.

I hear that the persons who are called ministers have signified an intention of resigning their places. I am rather astonished that they have not resigned long since. For the universe I would not have stood in the situation in which they have been for this last twelvemonth. They wished well, I take it for granted, to the Revolution. Let this fact be as it may, they could not, placed as they were upon an eminence, though an eminence of humiliation, but be the first to see collectively, and to feel each in his own department, the evils which have been produced by that revolution. In every step which they took, or forbore to take, they must have felt the degraded situation of their country, and their utter incapacity of serving it. They are in a species of subordinate servitude, in which no men before them were ever seen. Without confidence from their sovereign, on whom they were forced, or from the Assembly who forced them upon him, all the noble functions of their office are executed by committees of the Assembly, without any regard whatsoever to their personal or their official authority. They are to execute, without power; they are to be responsible, without discretion; they are to deliberate, without choice. In their puzzled situation, under two sovereigns, over neither of whom they have any influence, they must act in such a manner as (in effect, whatever they may intend) sometimes to betray the one, sometimes the other, and always to betray themselves. Such has been their situation; such must be the situation of those who succeed them. I have much respect, and many good wishes, for M. Necker. I am obliged to him for attentions. I thought when his enemies had driven him from Versailles, that his exile was a subject of most serious congratulation—*sed multæ urbes et publica vota vicerunt.* He is now sitting on the ruins of the finances, and of the monarchy of France.

A great deal more might be observed on the strange constitution of the executory part of the new government; but fatigue must give bounds to the discussion of subjects, which in themselves have hardly any limits.

As little genius and talent am I able to perceive in the plan of judicature formed by the National Assembly. According to their invariable course, the framers of your constitution have begun with the utter abolition of the parliaments. These venerable bodies, like the rest of the old government, stood in need of reform, even though there should be no change made in the monarchy. They required several more alterations to adapt them to the system of a free constitution. But they had particulars in their constitution, and those not a few, which deserved approbation from the wise. They possessed one fundamental excellence; they were independent. The most doubtful circumstance attendant on their office, that of its being vendible, contributed however to this independency of character. They held for life. Indeed they may be said to have held by inheritance. Appointed by the monarch, they were considered as nearly out of his power. The most determined exertions of that authority against them only showed their radical independence. They composed permanent bodies politic, constituted to resist arbitrary innovation; and from that corporate constitution, and from most of their forms, they were well calculated to afford both certainty and stability to the laws. They had been a safe asylum to secure these laws, in all the revolutions of humour and opinion. They had saved that sacred deposit of the country during the reigns of arbitrary princes, and the struggles of arbitrary factions. They kept alive the memory and record of the constitution. They were the great security to private property; which might be said (when personal liberty had no existence) to be, in fact, as well guarded in France as in any other country. Whatever is supreme in a state, ought to have, as much as possible, its judicial authority so constituted as not only not to depend upon it, but in some sort to balance it. It ought to give a security to its justice against its power. It ought to make its judicature, as it were, something exterior to the state.

These parliaments had furnished, not the best certainly, but some considerable corrective to the excesses and vices of the monarchy. Such an independent judicature was ten times more necessary when a democracy became the absolute power of the country. In that constitution, elective, temporary, local judges, such as you have contrived, exercising their dependent functions in a narrow society, must be the worst of all tribunals. In them it will be vain to look for any appearance of justice towards strangers, towards the obnoxious rich, towards the minority of routed parties, towards all those who in the election have supported unsuccessful candidates. It will be impossible to keep the new tribunals clear of the worst spirit of faction. All contrivances by ballot we know experimentally to be vain and childish to prevent a discovery of inclinations. Where they may the best answer the purposes of concealment, they answer to produce suspicion, and this is a still more mischievous cause of partiality.

If the parliaments had been preserved, instead of being dissolved at so ruinous a change to the nation, they might have served in this new commonwealth, perhaps not precisely the same, (I do not mean an exact parallel,) but nearly the same, purposes as the court and senate of Areopagus did in Athens; that is, as one of the balances and correctives to the evils of a light and unjust democracy. Every one knows that this tribunal was the great stay of that state; every one knows with what care it was upheld, and with what a religious awe it was consecrated. The parliaments were not wholly free from faction, I admit; but this evil was exterior and accidental, and not so much the vice of their constitution itself, as it must be in your new contrivance of sexennial elective judicatories. Several English commend the abolition of the old tribunals, as supposing that they determined everything by bribery and corruption. But they have stood the test of monarchic and republican scrutiny. The court was well disposed to prove corruption on those bodies when they were dissolved in 1771.—Those who have again dissolved them would have done the same if they could—but both inquisitions having failed, I conclude, that gross pecuniary corruption must have been rather rare amongst them.

It would have been prudent, along with the parliaments, to preserve their ancient power of registering, and of remonstrating at least, upon all the decrees of the National Assembly, as they did upon those which passed in the time of the monarchy. It would be a means of squaring the occasional decrees of a democracy to some principles of general jurisprudence. The vice of the ancient democracies, and one cause of their ruin, was, that they ruled, as you do, by occasional decrees, *psephismata*. This practice soon broke in upon the tenour and consistency of the laws; it abated the respect of the people towards them; and totally destroyed them in the end.

Your vesting the power of remonstrance, which, in the time of the monarchy, existed in the parliament of Paris, in your principal executive officer, whom, in spite of common sense, you persevere in calling king, is the height of absurdity. You ought never to suffer remonstrance from him who is to execute. This is to understand neither council nor execution; neither authority nor obedience. The person whom you call king, ought not to have this power, or he ought to have more.

Your present arrangement is strictly judicial. Instead of imitating your monarchy, and seating your judges on a bench of independence, your object is to reduce them to the most blind obedience. As you have changed all things, you have invented new principles of order. You first appoint judges, who, I suppose, are to determine according to law, and then you let them know, that at some time or other, you intend to give them some law by which they are to determine. Any studies which they have made (if any they have made) are to be useless to them. But to supply these studies, they are to be sworn to obey all the rules, orders, and instructions which from time to time they are to receive from the National Assembly. These if they submit to, they leave no ground of law to the subject. They become complete and most dangerous instruments in the hands of the governing power, which, in the midst of a cause, or on the prospect of it, may wholly change the rule of decision. If these orders of the National Assembly come to be contrary to the will of the people, who locally choose those judges, such confusion must happen as is terrible to think of. For the judges owe their places to the local authority; and the commands they are sworn to obey come from those who have no share in their appointment. In the mean time they have the example of the court of *Chatelet* to encourage and guide them in the exercise of their functions. That court is to try criminals sent to it by the National Assembly, or brought before it by other courses of delation. They sit under a guard to save their own lives. They know not by what law they judge, nor under what authority they act, nor by what tenure they hold. It is thought that they are sometimes obliged to condemn at peril of their lives. This is not perhaps certain, nor can it be ascertained; but when they acquit, we know they have seen the persons whom they discharge, with perfect impunity to the actors, hanged at the door of their court.

The Assembly indeed promises that they will form a body of law, which shall be short, simple, clear, and so forth. That is, by their short laws, they will leave much to the discretion of the judge; whilst they have exploded the authority of all the learning which could make judicial discretion (a thing perilous at best) deserving the appellation of a *sound* discretion.

It is curious to observe, that the administrative bodies are carefully exempted from the jurisdiction of these new tribunals. That is, those persons are exempted from the power of the laws, who ought to be the most entirely submitted to them. Those who execute public pecuniary trusts, ought of all men to be the most strictly held to their duty. One would have thought that it must have been among your earliest cares, if you did not mean that those administrative bodies should be real, sovereign, independent states, to form an awful tribunal, like your late parliaments, or like our king's bench, where all corporate officers might obtain protection in the legal exercise of their functions, and would find coercion if they trespassed against their legal duty. But the cause of the exemption is plain. These administrative bodies are the great instruments of the present leaders in their progress through democracy to oligarchy. They must therefore be put above the law. It will be said, that the legal tribunals which you have made are unfit to coerce them. They are undoubtedly. They are unfit for any rational purpose. It will be said too, that the administrative bodies will be accountable to the General Assembly. This I fear is talking without much consideration of the nature of that Assembly, or of these corporations. However, to be subject to the pleasure of that Assembly, is not to be subject to law either for protection or for constraint.

This establishment of judges as yet wants something to its completion. It is to be crowned by a new tribunal. This is to be a grand state judicature; and it is to judge of crimes committed against the nation, that is, against the power of the Assembly. It seems as if they had something in their view of the nature of the high court of justice erected in England during the time of the great usurpation. As they have not yet finished this part of the scheme, it is impossible to form a right judgment upon it. However, if great care is not taken to form it in a spirit very different from that which has guided them in their proceedings relative to state offences, this tribunal, subservient to their inquisition, *the committee of research,* will extinguish the last sparks of liberty in France, and settle the most dreadful and arbitrary tyranny ever known in any nation. If they wish to give to this tribunal any appearance of liberty and justice, they must not evoke from or send to it the causes relative to their own members, at their pleasure. They must also remove the seat of that tribunal out of the republic of Paris.[50]

Has more wisdom been displayed in the constitution of your army than what is discoverable in your plan of judicature? The able arrangement of this part is the more difficult, and requires the greatest skill and attention, not only as the great concern in itself, but as it is the third cementing principle in the new body of republics, which you call the French nation. Truly it is not easy to divine what that army may become at last. You have voted a very large one, and on good appointments, at least fully equal to your apparent means of payment. But what is the principle of its discipline? or whom is it to obey? You have got the wolf by the ears, and I wish you joy of the happy position in which you have chosen to place yourselves, and in which you are well circumstanced for a free deliberation, relatively to that army, or to anything else.

The minister and secretary of state for the war department is M. de la Tour du Pin. This gentleman, like his colleagues in administration, is a most zealous assertor of the Revolution, and a sanguine

---

[50] For further elucidations upon the subject of all these judicatures, and of the committee of research, see M. de Calonne's work.

admirer of the new constitution, which originated in that event.
His statement of facts, relative to the military of France, is important, not only from his official and personal authority, but because it
displays very clearly the actual condition of the army in France, and
because it throws light on the principles upon which the Assembly
proceeds, in the administration of this critical object. It may enable
us to form some judgment, how far it may be expedient in this country to imitate the martial policy of France.

M. de la Tour du Pin, on the fourth of last June, comes to give an
account of the state of his department, as it exists under the auspices
of the National Assembly. No man knows it so well; no man can
express it better. Addressing himself to the National Assembly, he
says, "His Majesty has *this day* sent me to apprize you of the multiplied disorders of which *every day* he receives the most distressing
intelligence. The army (le corps militaire) threatens to fall into the
most turbulent anarchy. Entire regiments have dared to violate at
once the respect due to the laws, to the king, to the order established
by your decrees, and to the oaths which they have taken with the
most awful solemnity. Compelled by my duty to give you information of these excesses, my heart bleeds when I consider who they are
that have committed them. Those, against whom it is not in my
power to withhold the most grievous complaints, are a part of that
very soldiery which to this day have been so full of honour and loyalty, and with whom, for fifty years, I have lived the comrade and
the friend.

"What incomprehensible spirit of delirium and delusion has all at
once led them astray? Whilst you are indefatigable in establishing
uniformity in the empire, and moulding the whole into one coherent
and consistent body; whilst the French are taught by you at once the
respect which the laws owe to the rights of man, and that which the
citizens owe to the laws, the administration of the army presents
nothing but disturbance and confusion. I see in more than one corps
the bonds of discipline relaxed or broken; the most unheard-of pretensions avowed directly and without any disguise; the ordinances
without force; the chiefs without authority; the military chest and
the colours carried off; the authority of the king himself [*risum
teneatis?*] proudly defied; the officers despised, degraded, threatened,

driven away, and some of them prisoners in the midst of their corps, dragging on a precarious life in the bosom of disgust and humiliation. To fill up the measure of all these horrors, the commandants of places have had their throats cut, under the eyes, and almost in the arms, of their own soldiers.

"These evils are great; but they are not the worst consequences which may be produced by such military insurrections. Sooner or later they may menace the nation itself. *The nature of things requires* that the army should never act but as *an instrument*. The moment that, erecting itself into a deliberative body, it shall act according to its own resolutions, the *government, be it what it may, will immediately degenerate into a military democracy;* a species of political monster, which has always ended by devouring those who have produced it.

"After all this, who must not be alarmed at the irregular consultations, and turbulent committees, formed in some regiments by the common soldiers and non-commissioned officers, without the knowledge, or even in contempt of the authority, of their superiors; although the presence and concurrence of those superiors could give no authority to such monstrous democratic assemblies [comices]."

It is not necessary to add much to this finished picture: finished as far as its canvas admits; but as I apprehend, not taking in the whole of the nature and complexity of the disorders of this military democracy, which, the minister at war truly and wisely observes, wherever it exists, must be the true constitution of the state, by whatever formal appellation it may pass. For, though he informs the Assembly that the more considerable part of the army have not cast off their obedience, but are still attached to their duty, yet those travellers, who have seen the corps whose conduct is the best, rather observe in them the absence of mutiny, than the existence of discipline.

I cannot help pausing here for a moment, to reflect upon the expressions of surprise which this minister has let fall, relative to the excesses he relates. To him the departure of the troops from their ancient principles of loyalty and honour seems quite inconceivable. Surely those to whom he addresses himself know the causes of it but too well. They know the doctrines which they have preached, the decrees which they have passed, the practices which they have countenanced. The soldiers remember the 6th of October. They recollect the French guards. They have not forgotten the taking of the king's castles in Paris and Marseilles. That the governors in both places were murdered with impunity, is a fact that has not passed out of their minds. They do not abandon the principles laid down so ostentatiously and laboriously of the quality of men. They cannot shut their eyes to the degradation of the whole noblesse of France, and the suppression of the very idea of a gentleman. The total abolition of titles and distinctions is not lost upon them. But M. de la Tour du Pin is astonished at their disloyalty, when the doctors of the Assembly have taught them at the same time the respect due to laws. It is easy to judge which of the two sorts of lessons men with arms in their hands are likely to learn. As to the authority of the king, we may collect from the minister himself (if any argument on that head were not quite superfluous) that it is not of more consideration with these troops, than it is with everybody else. "The king," says he, "has over and over again repeated his orders to put a stop to these excesses: but, in so terrible a crisis, *your* [the Assembly's] concurrence is become indispensably necessary to prevent the evils which menace the state. *You* unite to the force of the legislative power, *that of opinion* still more important." To be sure the army can have no opinion of the power or authority of the king. Perhaps the soldier has by this time learned, that the Assembly itself does not enjoy a much greater degree of liberty than that royal figure.

It is now to be seen what has been proposed in this exigency, one of the greatest that can happen in a state. The minister requests the Assembly to array itself in all its terrors, and to call forth all its majesty. He desires that the grave and severe principles announced by them may give vigour to the king's proclamation. After this we should have looked for courts civil and martial; breaking of some corps, decimating of others, and all the terrible means which necessity has employed in such cases to arrest the progress of the most terrible of all evils; particularly, one might expect, that a serious inquiry would be made into the murder of commandants in the view of their soldiers. Not one word of all this, or of anything like it. After they had been told that the soldiery trampled upon the decrees of the Assembly promulgated by the king, the Assembly pass new decrees; and they authorize the king to make new proclamations. After the secretary at war had stated that the regiments had paid no regard to oaths *prêtés avec la plus imposante solemnité*—they propose—what? More oaths. They renew decrees and proclamations as they experience their insufficiency, and they multiply oaths in proportion as they weaken, in the minds of men, the sanctions of religion. I hope that handy abridgments of the excellent sermons of Voltaire, d'Alembert, Diderot, and Helvetius, on the Immortality of the Soul, on a particular superintending Providence, and on a Future State of Rewards and Punishments, are sent down to the soldiers along with their civic oaths. Of this I have no doubt; as I understand that a certain description of reading makes no inconsiderable part of their military exercises, and that they are full as well supplied with the ammunition of pamphlets as of cartridges.

To prevent the mischiefs arising from conspiracies, irregular consultations, seditious committees, and monstrous democratic assemblies ["comitia, comices"] of the soldiers, and all the disorders arising from idleness, luxury, dissipation, and insubordination, I believe the most astonishing means have been used that ever occurred to men, even in all the inventions of this prolific age. It is no less than this:— The king has promulgated in circular letters to all the regiments his direct authority and encouragement, that the several corps should join themselves with the clubs and confederations in the several municipalities, and mix with them in their feasts and civic entertainments! This jolly discipline, it seems, is to soften the ferocity of their minds; to reconcile them to their bottle companions of other descriptions; and to merge particular conspiracies in more general associations.[51] That this remedy would be pleasing to the soldiers, as they are described by M. de la Tour du Pin, I can readily believe; and that, however mutinous otherwise, they will dutifully submit themselves to *these* royal proclamations. But I should question whether all this civic swearing, clubbing, and feasting, would dispose them, more than at present they are disposed, to an obedience to their

[51] Comme sa majesté y a reconnu, non une système d'associations particulières, mais une réunion de volontés de tous les François pour la liberté et la prospérité communes, ainsi pour la maintien de l'ordre publique; il a pensé qu'il convenoit que chaque régiment prit part à ces fêtes civiques pour multiplier les rapports et referrer les liens d'union entre les citoyens et les troupes.—Lest I should not be credited, I insert the words, authorizing the troops to feast with the popular confederacies.

officers; or teach them better to submit to the austere rules of military discipline. It will make them admirable citizens after the French mode, but not quite so good soldiers after any mode. A doubt might well arise, whether the conversations at these good tables would fit them a great deal the better for the character of *mere instruments,* which this veteran officer and statesman justly observes the nature of things always requires an army to be.

Concerning the likelihood of this improvement in discipline, by the free conversation of the soldiers with municipal festive societies, which is thus officially encouraged by royal authority and sanction, we may judge by the state of the municipalities themselves, furnished to us by the war minister in this very speech. He conceives good hopes of the success of his endeavours towards restoring order *for the present* from the good disposition of certain regiments; but he finds something cloudy with regard to the future. As to preventing the return of confusion, "for this, the administration (says he) cannot be answerable to you, as long as they see the municipalities arrogate to themselves an authority over the troops, which your institutions have reserved wholly to the monarch. You have fixed the limits of the military authority and the municipal authority. You have bounded the action, which you have permitted to the latter over the former, to the right of requisition; but never did the letter or the spirit of your decrees authorize the commons in these municipalities to break the officers, to try them, to give orders to the soldiers, to drive them from the posts committed to their guard, to stop them in their marches ordered by the king, or, in a word, to enslave the troops to the caprice of each of the cities, or even market town, through which they are to pass."

Such is the character and disposition of the municipal society which is to reclaim the soldiery, to bring them back to the true principles of military subordination, and to render them machines in the hands of the supreme power of the country! Such are the distempers of the French troops! Such is their cure! As the army is, so is the navy. The municipalities supersede the orders of the Assembly, and the seamen in their turn supersede the orders of the municipalities. From my heart I pity the condition of a respectable servant of the public, like this war minister, obliged in his old age to pledge the Assembly in their civic cups, and to enter with a hoary head into all the fantastic vagaries of these juvenile politicians. Such schemes are not like propositions coming from a man of fifty years' wear and tear amongst mankind. They seem rather such as ought to be expected from those grand compounders in politics, who shorten the road to their degrees in the state; and have a certain inward fanatical assurance and illumination upon all subjects; upon the credit of which one of their doctors has thought fit, with great applause, and greater success, to caution the Assembly not to attend to old men, or to any persons who valued themselves upon their experience. I suppose all the ministers of state must qualify, and take this test; wholly abjuring the errors and heresies of experience and observation. Every man has his own relish. But I think if I could not attain to the wisdom, I would at least preserve something of the stiff and peremptory dignity of age. These gentlemen deal in regeneration: but at any price I should hardly yield my rigid fibres to be regenerated by them; nor begin, in my grand climacteric, to squall in their new accents, or to stammer, in my second cradle, the elemental sounds of their barbarous metaphysics.[52] *Si isti mihi largiantur ut repueriscam, et in eorum cunis vagiam, valde recusem!*

The imbecility of any part of the puerile and pedantic system, which they call a constitution, cannot be laid open without discovering the utter insufficiency and mischief of every other part with which it comes in contact, or that bears any the remotest relation to it. You cannot propose a remedy for the incompetence of the crown, without displaying the debility of the Assembly. You cannot deliberate on the confusion of the army of the state, without disclosing the worse disorders of the armed municipalities. The military lays open the civil, and the civil betrays the military, anarchy. I wish everybody carefully to peruse the eloquent speech (such it is) of Mons. de la Tour du Pin. He attributes the salvation of the municipalities to the good behaviour of some of the troops. These troops are to preserve the well-disposed part of those municipalities, which is confessed to be the weakest, from the pillage of the worst disposed, which is the strongest. But the municipalities affect a sovereignty, and will command those troops which are necessary for their pro-

[52] This war minister has since quitted the school, and resigned his office.

tection. Indeed they must command them or court them. The municipalities, by the necessity of their situation, and by the republican powers they have obtained, must, with relation to the military, be the masters, or the servants, or the confederates, or each successively; or they must make a jumble of all together, according to circumstances. What government is there to coerce the army but the municipality, or the municipality but the army? To preserve concord where authority is extinguished, at the hazard of all consequences, the Assembly attempts to cure the distempers by the distempers themselves; and they hope to preserve themselves from a purely military democracy, by giving it a debauched interest in the municipal.

If the soldiers once come to mix for any time in the municipal clubs, cabals, and confederacies, an elective attraction will draw them to the lowest and most desperate part. With them will be their habits, affections, and sympathies. The military conspiracies, which are to be remedied by civic confederacies; the rebellious municipalities, which are to be rendered obedient by furnishing them with the means of seducing the very armies of the state that are to keep them in order; all these chimeras of a monstrous and portentous policy must aggravate the confusion from which they have arisen. There must be blood. The want of common judgment manifested in the construction of all their descriptions of forces, and in all their kinds of civil and judicial authorities, will make it flow. Disorders may be quieted in one time and in one part. They will break out in others; because the evil is radical and intrinsic. All these schemes of mixing mutinous soldiers with seditious citizens must weaken still more and more the military connexion of soldiers with their officers, as well as add military and mutinous audacity to turbulent artificers and peasants. To secure a real army, the officer should be first and last in the eye of the soldier; first and last in his attention, observance, and esteem. Officers it seems there are to be, whose chief qualification must be temper and patience. They are to manage their troops by electioneering arts. They must bear themselves as candidates, not as commanders. But as by such means power may be occasionally in their hands, the authority by which they are to be nominated becomes of high importance.

What you may do finally does not appear; nor is it of much moment, whilst the strange and contradictory relation between your army and all the parts of your republic, as well as the puzzled relation of those parts to each other and to the whole, remain as they are. You seem to have given the provisional nomination of the officers, in the first instance, to the king, with a reserve of approbation by the National Assembly. Men who have an interest to pursue are extremely sagacious in discovering the true seat of power. They must soon perceive that those, who can negative indefinitely, in reality appoint. The officers must therefore look to their intrigues in that Assembly, as the sole, certain road to promotion. Still, however, by your new constitution they must begin their solicitation at court. This double negotiation for military rank seems to me a contrivance as well adapted, as if it were studied for no other end, to promote faction in the Assembly itself, relative to this vast military patronage; and then to poison the corps of officers with factions of a nature still more dangerous to the safety of government, upon any bottom on which it can be placed, and destructive in the end to the efficiency of the army itself. Those officers, who lose the promotions intended for them by the crown, must become of a faction opposite to that of the Assembly, which has rejected their claims, and must nourish discontents in the heart of the army against the ruling powers. Those officers, on the other hand, who, by carrying their point through an interest in the Assembly, feel themselves to be at best only second in the good-will of the crown, though first in that of the Assembly, must slight an authority which would not advance and could not retard their promotion. If to avoid these evils you will have no other rule for command or promotion than seniority, you will have an army of formality; at the same time it will become more independent, and more of a military republic. Not they, but the king is the machine. A king is not to be deposed by halves. If he is not everything in the command of an army, he is nothing. What is the effect of a power placed nominally at the head of the army, who to that army is no object of gratitude, or of fear? Such a cipher is not fit for the administration of an object, of all things the most delicate, the supreme command of military men. They must be constrained (and their inclinations lead them to what their necessities require) by a real, vigorous, effective, decided, personal authority. The authority of the Assembly itself suffers by passing through such a debilitating channel as they have chosen. The army will not long look to an assembly acting through the organ of false show, and palpable imposition. They will not seriously yield obedience to a prisoner. They will either despise a pageant, or they will pity a captive king. This relation of your army to the crown will, if I am not greatly mistaken, become a serious dilemma in your politics.

It is besides to be considered, whether an assembly like yours, even supposing that it was in possession of another sort of organ through which its orders were to pass, is fit for promoting the obedience and discipline of an army. It is known, that armies have hitherto yielded a very precarious and uncertain obedience to any senate, or popular authority; and they will least of all yield it to an assembly which is only to have a continuance of two years. The officers must totally lose the characteristic disposition of military men, if they see with perfect submission and due admiration, the dominion of pleaders; especially when they find that they have a new court to pay to an endless succession of those pleaders; whose military policy, and the genius of whose command, (if they should have any,) must be as uncertain as their duration is transient. In the weakness of one kind of authority, and in the fluctuation of all, the officers of an army will remain for some time mutinous and full of faction, until some popular general, who understands the art of conciliating the soldiery, and who possesses the true spirit of command, shall draw the eyes of all men upon himself. Armies will obey him on his personal account. There is no other way of securing military obedience in this state of things. But the moment in which that event shall happen, the person who really commands the army is your master; the master (that is little) of your king, the master of your Assembly, the master of your whole republic.

How came the Assembly by their present power over the army? Chiefly, to be sure, by debauching the soldiers from their officers. They have begun by a most terrible operation. They have touched the central point, about which the particles that compose armies are at repose. They have destroyed the principle of obedience in the great, essential, critical link between the officer and the soldier, just where the chain of military subordination commences and on which the whole of that system depends. The soldier is told he is a citizen, and has the rights of man and citizen. The right of a man, he is told, is to be his own governor, and to be ruled only by those to whom he delegates that self-government. It is very natural he should think that he ought most of all to have his choice where he is to yield the great est degree of obedience. He will therefore, in all probability, systematically do, what he does at present occasionally; that is, he will exercise at least a negative in the choice of his officers. At present the officers are known at best to be only permissive, and on their good behaviour. In fact, there have been many instances in which they have been cashiered by their corps. Here is a second negative on the choice of the king; a negative as effectual at least as the other of the Assembly. The soldiers know already that it has been a question, not ill received in the National Assembly, whether they ought not to have the direct choice of their officers, or some proportion of them? When such matters are in deliberation it is no extravagant supposition that they will incline to the opinion most favourable to their pretensions. They will not bear to be deemed the army of an imprisoned king, whilst another army in the same country, with whom too they are to feast and confederate, is to be considered as the free army of a free constitution. They will cast their eyes on the other and more permanent army; I mean the municipal. That corps, they well know, does actually elect its own officers. They may not be able to discern the grounds of distinction on which they are not to elect a Marquis de la Fayette (or what is his new name?) of their own. If this election of a commander-in-chief be a part of the rights of men, why not of theirs? They see elective justices of peace, elective judges, elective curates, elective bishops, elective municipalities, and elective commanders of the Parisian army.—Why should they alone be excluded? Are the brave troops of France the only men in that nation who are not the fit judges of military merit, and of the qualifications necessary for a commander-in-chief? Are they paid by the state, and do they therefore lose the rights of men? They are a part of that nation themselves, and contribute to that pay. And is not the king, is not the National Assembly, and are not all who elect the National Assembly likewise paid? Instead of seeing all these forfeit their rights by their receiving a salary, they perceive that in all these cases a salary is given for the exercise of those rights. All your resolutions, all your proceedings, all your debates, all the works of your doctors in religion and politics, have industriously been put into their hands; and you expect that they will apply to their own case just as much of your doctrines and examples as suits your pleasure.

Everything depends upon the army in such a government as yours; for you have industriously destroyed all the opinions, and prejudices, and, as far as in you lay, all the instincts which support government. Therefore the moment any difference arises between your National Assembly and any part of the nation, you must have recourse to force. Nothing else is left to you; or rather you have left nothing else to yourselves. You see, by the report of your war minister, that the distribution of the army is in a great measure made with a view of internal coercion.[53] You must rule by an army; and you have infused into that army by which you rule, as well as into the whole body of the nation, principles which after a time must disable you in the use you resolve to make of it. The king is to call out troops to act against his people, when the world has been told, and the assertion is still ringing in our ears, that troops ought not to fire on citizens. The colonies assert to themselves an independent constitution and a free trade. They must be constrained by troops. In what chapter of your code of the rights of men are they able to read, that it is a part of the rights of men to have their commerce monopolized and restrained for the benefit of others? As the colonists rise on you, the negroes rise on them. Troops again—Massacre, torture, hanging! These are your rights of men! These are the fruits of metaphysic declarations wantonly made, and shamefully retracted! It was but the other day, that the farmers of land in one of your provinces refused to pay some sort of rents to the lord of the soil. In consequence of this, you decree, that the country people shall pay all rents and dues, except those which as grievances you have abolished; and if they refuse, then you order the king to march troops against them. You lay down metaphysic propositions which infer universal consequences, and then you attempt to limit logic by

[53] Courier François, 30th July, 1790. Assemblée Nationale, Numero 210.

despotism. The leaders of the present system tell them of their rights, as men, to take fortresses, to murder guards, to seize on kings without the least appearance of authority even from the Assembly, whilst, as the sovereign legislative body, that Assembly was sitting in the name of the nation—and yet these leaders presume to order out the troops which have acted in these very disorders, to coerce those who shall judge on the principles, and follow the examples, which have been guaranteed by their own approbation.

The leaders teach the people to abhor and reject all feodality as the barbarism of tyranny, and they tell them afterwards how much of that barbarous tyranny they are to bear with patience. As they are prodigal of light with regard to grievances, so the people find them sparing in the extreme with regard to redress. They know that not only certain quit-rents and personal duties, which you have permitted them to redeem, (but have furnished no money for the redemption,) are as nothing to those burthens for which you have made no provision at all. They know, that almost the whole system of landed property in its origin is feudal; that it is the distribution of the possessions of the original proprietors, made by a barbarous conqueror to his barbarous instruments; and that the most grievous effects of the conquest are the land rents of every kind, as without question they are.

The peasants, in all probability, are the descendants of these ancient proprietors, Romans or Gauls. But if they fail, in any degree, in the titles which they make on the principles of antiquaries and lawyers, they retreat into the citadel of the rights of men. There they find that men are equal; and the earth, the kind and equal mother of all, ought not to be monopolized to foster the pride and luxury of any men, who by nature are no better than themselves, and who, if they do not labour for their bread, are worse. They find, that by the laws of nature the occupant and subduer of the soil is the true proprietor; that there is no prescription against nature; and that the agreements (where any there are) which have been made with the landlords, during the time of slavery, are only the effect of duresse and force; and that when the people re-entered into the rights of men, those agreements were made as void, as everything else which had been settled under the prevalence of the old feudal and aristocratic tyranny. They will tell you that they see no difference between an idler with a hat and a national cockade, and an idler in a cowl, or in a rochet. If you ground the title to rents on succession and prescription, they tell you from the speech of M. *Camus,* published by the National Assembly for their information, that things ill begun cannot avail themselves of prescription; that the title of these lords was vicious in its origin; and that force is at least as bad as fraud. As to the title by succession, they will tell you, that the succession of those who have cultivated the soil is the true pedigree of property, and not rotten parchments and silly substitutions; that the lords have enjoyed their usurpation too long; and that if they allow to these lay monks any charitable pension, they ought to be thankful to the bounty of the true proprietor, who is so generous towards a false claimant to his goods.

When the peasants give you back that coin of sophistic reason, on which you have set your image and superscription, you cry it down as base money, and tell them you will pay for the future with French guards, and dragoons, and hussars. You hold up, to chastise them, the second-hand authority of a king, who is only the instrument of destroying, without any power of protecting either the people or his own person. Through him it seems you will make yourselves obeyed. They answer, You have taught us that there are no gentlemen; and which of your principles teach us to bow to kings whom we have not elected? We know without your teaching, that lands were given for the support of feudal dignities, feudal titles, and feudal offices. When you took down the cause as a grievance, why should the more grievous effect remain? As there are now no hereditary honours, and no distinguished families, why are we taxed to maintain what you tell us ought not to exist? You have sent down our old aristocratic landlords in no other character, and with no other title, but that of exactors under your authority. Have you endeavoured to make these your rent-gatherers respectable to us? No. You have sent them to us with their arms reversed, their shields broken, their impresses defaced; and so displumed, degraded, and metamorphosed, such unfeathered two-legged things, that we no longer know them. They are strangers to us. They do not even go by the names of our ancient lords. Physically they may be the same men; though we are not quite sure of that, on your new philosophic doctrines of personal identity. In all other respects they are totally changed. We do not see why we have not as good a right to refuse them their rents as you have to abrogate all their honours, titles, and distinctions. This we have never commissioned you to do; and it is one instance, among many indeed, of your assumption of undelegated power. We see the burghers of Paris, through their clubs, their mobs, and their national guards, directing you at their pleasure, and giving that as law to you, which, under your authority is transmitted as law to us. Through you these burghers dispose of the lives and fortunes of us all. Why should not you attend as much to the desires of the laborious husbandman with regard to our rent, by which we are affected in the most serious manner, as you do to the demands of these insolent burghers, relative to distinctions and titles of honour, by which neither they nor we are affected at all? But we find you pay more regard to their fancies than to our necessities. Is it among the rights of man to pay tribute to his equals? Before this measure of yours, we might have thought we were not perfectly equal. We might have entertained some old, habitual, unmeaning prepossession in favour of those landlords; but we cannot conceive with what other view than that of destroying all respect to them, you could have made the law that degrades them. You have forbidden us to treat them with any of the old formalities of respect, and now you send troops to sabre and to bayonet us into a submission to fear and force, which you did not suffer us to yield to the mild authority of opinion.

The ground of some of these arguments is horrid and ridiculous to all rational ears; but to the politicians of metaphysics who have opened schools for sophistry, and made establishments for anarchy, it is solid and conclusive. It is obvious, that on a mere consideration of the right, the leaders in the Assembly would not in the least have scrupled to abrogate the rents along with the titles and family ensigns. It would be only to follow up the principle of their reasonings, and to complete the analogy of their conduct. But they had newly possessed themselves of a great body of landed property by confiscation. They had this commodity at market; and the market would have been wholly destroyed, if they were to permit the hus-

bandmen to riot in the speculations with which they so freely intoxicated themselves. The only security which property enjoys in any
one of its descriptions, is from the interests of their rapacity with
regard to some other. They have left nothing but their own arbitrary pleasure, to determine what property is to be protected and
what subverted.

Neither have they left any principle by which any of their municipalities can be bound to obedience; or even conscientiously obliged
not to separate from the whole to become independent, or to connect
itself with some other state. The people of Lyons, it seems, have refused lately to pay taxes. Why should they not? What lawful authority is there left to exact them? The king imposed some of them.
The old states, methodized by orders, settled the more ancient. They
may say to the Assembly, Who are you, that are not our kings, nor
the states we have elected, nor sit on the principles on which we have
elected you? And who are we, that when we see the gabelles, which
you have ordered to be paid, wholly shaken off, when we see the
act of disobedience afterwards ratified by yourselves, who are we,
that we are not to judge what taxes we ought or ought not to pay,
and who are not to avail ourselves of the same powers, the validity of
which you have approved in others? To this the answer is, We
will send troops. The last reason of kings is always the first with
your Assembly. This military aid may serve for a time, whilst the
impression of the increase of pay remains, and the vanity of being
umpires in all disputes is flattered. But this weapon will snap short,
unfaithful to the hand that employs it. The Assembly keep a school,
where, systematically, and with unremitting perseverance, they teach
principles, and form regulations, destructive to all spirit of subordination, civil and military—and then they expect that they shall hold
in obedience an anarchic people by an anarchic army.

The municipal army which, according to the new policy, is to
balance this national army, if considered in itself only, is of a constitution much more simple, and in every respect less exceptionable.
It is a mere democratic body, unconnected with the crown or the
kingdom; armed, and trained, and officered at the pleasure of the
districts to which the corps severally belong; and the personal service

of the individuals, who compose, or the fine in lieu of personal service, are directed by the same authority.[54] Nothing is more uniform. If, however, considered in any relation to the crown, to the National Assembly, to the public tribunals, or to the other army, or considered in a view to any coherence or connexion between its parts, it seems a monster, and can hardly fail to terminate its perplexed movements in some great national calamity. It is a worse preservative of a general constitution, than the systasis of Crete, or the confederation of Poland, or any other ill-devised corrective which has yet been imagined, in the necessities produced by an ill-constructed system of government.

Having concluded my few remarks on the constitution of the supreme power, the executive, the judicature, the military, and on the reciprocal relation of all these establishments, I shall say something of the ability showed by your legislators with regard to the revenue.

In their proceedings relative to this object, if possible, still fewer traces appear of political judgment or financial resource. When the states met, it seemed to be the great object to improve the system of revenue, to enlarge its collection, to cleanse it of oppression and vexation, and to establish it on the most solid footing. Great were the expectations entertained on that head throughout Europe. It was by this grand arrangement that France was to stand or fall; and this became, in my opinion, very properly, the test by which the skill and patriotism of those who ruled in that Assembly would be tried. The revenue of the state is the state. In effect all depends upon it, whether for support or for reformation. The dignity of every occupation wholly depends upon the quantity and the kind of virtue that may be exerted in it. As all great qualities of the mind which operate in public, and are not merely suffering and passive, require force for their display, I had almost said for their unequivocal existence, the revenue, which is the spring of all power, becomes in its

---

[54] I see by M. Necker's account, that the national guards of Paris have received, over and above the money levied within their own city, about £145,000 sterling out of the public treasure. Whether this be an actual payment for the nine months of their existence, or an estimate of their yearly charge, I do not clearly perceive. It is of no great importance, as certainly they may take whatever they please.

administration the sphere of every active virtue. Public virtue, being of a nature magnificent and splendid, instituted for great things, and conversant about great concerns, requires abundant scope and room and cannot spread and grow under confinement, and in circumstances straitened, narrow, and sordid. Through the revenue alone the body politic can act in its true genius and character, and therefore it will display just as much of its collective virtue, and as much of that virtue which may characterize those who move it, and are, as it were, its life and guiding principle, as it is possessed of a just revenue. For from hence not only magnanimity, and liberality, and beneficence, and fortitude, and providence, and the tutelary protection of all good arts, derive their food, and the growth of their organs, but continence, and self-denial, and labour, and vigilance, and frugality, and whatever else there is in which the mind shows itself above the appetite, are nowhere more in their proper element than in the provision and distribution of the public wealth. It is therefore not without reason that the science of speculative and practical finance, which must take to its aid so many auxiliary branches of knowledge, stands high in the estimation not only of the ordinary sort, but of the wisest and best men; and as this science has grown with the progress of its object, the prosperity and improvement of nations has generally increased with the increase of their revenues; and they will both continue to grow and flourish, as long as the balance between what is left to strengthen the efforts of individuals, and what is collected for the common efforts of the state, bear to each other a due reciprocal proportion, and are kept in a close correspondence and communication. And perhaps it may be owing to the greatness of revenues, and to the urgency of state necessities, that old abuses in the constitution of finances are discovered, and their true nature and rational theory comes to be more perfectly understood; insomuch, that a smaller revenue might have been more distressing in one period than a far greater is found to be in another; the proportionate wealth even remaining the same. In this state of things, the French Assembly found something in their revenues to preserve, to secure, and wisely to administer, as well as to abrogate and alter. Though their proud assumption might justify the severest tests, yet in trying their abilities on their financial proceedings, I would only consider what is the plain, obvious duty of a common finance minister, and try them upon that, and not upon models of ideal perfection.

The objects of a financier are, then, to secure an ample revenue; to impose it with judgment and equality; to employ it economically; and, when necessity obliges him to make use of credit, to secure its foundations in that instance, and for ever, by the clearness and candour of his proceedings, the exactness of his calculations, and the solidity of his funds. On these heads we may take a short and distinct view of the merits and abilities of those in the National Assembly, who have taken to themselves the management of this arduous concern. Far from any increase of revenue in their hands, I find, by a report of M. Vernier, from the committee of finances, of the second of August last, that the amount of the national revenue, as compared with its produce before the Revolution, was diminished by the sum of two hundred millions, or *eight millions sterling* of the annual income, considerably more than one-third of the whole.

If this be the result of great ability, never surely was ability displayed in a more distinguished manner, or with so powerful an effect. No common folly, no vulgar incapacity, no ordinary official negligence, even no official crime, no corruption, no peculation, hardly any direct hostility which we have seen in the modern world, could in so short a time have made so complete an overthrow of the finances, and with them, of the strength of a great kingdom.—*Cedò qui vestram rempublicam tantam amisistis tam cito?*

The sophisters and declaimers, as soon as the Assembly met, began with decrying the ancient constitution of the revenue in many of its most essential branches, such as the public monopoly of salt. They charged it, as truly as unwisely, with being ill-contrived, oppressive, and partial. This representation they were not satisfied to make use of in speeches preliminary to some plan of reform; they declared it in a solemn resolution or public sentence, as it were judicially, passed upon it; and this they dispersed throughout the nation. At the time they passed the decree, with the same gravity they ordered the same absurd, oppressive, and partial tax to be paid, until they could find a revenue to replace it. The consequence was inevitable. The provinces which had been always exempted from this salt monopoly, some of whom were charged with other contributions, perhaps equivalent, were totally disinclined to bear any part of the burthen, which by an equal distribution was to redeem the others. As to the Assembly, occupied as it was with the declaration and violation of the rights of men, and with their arrangements for general confusion, it had neither leisure nor capacity to contrive, nor authority to enforce, any plan of any kind relative to the replacing the tax or equalizing it, or compensating the provinces, or for conducting their minds to any scheme of accommodation with other districts which were to be relieved.

The people of the salt provinces, impatient under taxes, damned by the authority which had directed their payment, very soon found their patience exhausted. They thought themselves as skilful in demolishing as the Assembly could be. They relieved themselves by throwing off the whole burthen. Animated by this example, each district, or part of a district, judging of its own grievance by its own feeling, and of its remedy by its own opinion, did as it pleased with other taxes.

We are next to see how they have conducted themselves in contriving equal impositions, proportioned to the means of the citizens, and the least likely to lean heavy on the active capital employed in the generation of that private wealth, from whence the public fortune must be derived. By suffering the several districts, and several of the individuals in each district, to judge of what part of the old revenue they might withhold, instead of better principles of equality, a new inequality was introduced of the most oppressive kind. Payments were regulated by dispositions. The parts of the kingdom which were the most submissive, the most orderly, or the most affectionate to the commonwealth, bore the whole burthen of the state. Nothing turns out to be so oppressive and unjust as a feeble government. To fill up all the deficiencies in the old impositions, and the new deficiencies of every kind which were to be expected, what remained to a state without authority? The National Assembly called for a voluntary benevolence; for a fourth part of the income of all the citizens, to be estimated on the honour of those who were to pay. They obtained something more than could be rationally calculated, but what was far indeed from answerable to their real necessities, and much less to their fond expectations. Rational people could have hoped for little from this their tax in the disguise of a benevolence; a tax weak, ineffective, and unequal; a tax by which luxury, avarice, and selfishness were screened, and the load thrown upon productive capital, upon integrity, generosity, and public spirit—a tax of regulation upon virtue. At length the mask is thrown off, and they are now trying means (with little success) of exacting their benevolence by force.

This benevolence, the ricketty offspring of weakness, was to be supported by another resource, the twin brother of the same prolific imbecility. The patriotic donations were to make good the failure of the patriotic contribution. John Doe was to become security for Richard Roe. By this scheme they took things of much price from the giver, comparatively of small value to the receiver; they ruined several trades; they pillaged the crown of its ornaments, the churches of their plate, and the people of their personal decorations. The invention of these juvenile pretenders to liberty was in reality nothing more than a servile imitation of one of the poorest resources of doting despotism. They took an old huge full-bottomed periwig out of the wardrobe of the antiquated frippery of Louis the Fourteenth, to cover the premature baldness of the National Assembly. They produced this old-fashioned formal folly, though it had been so abundantly exposed in the Memoirs of the Duke de St. Simon, if to reasonable men it had wanted any arguments to display its mischief and insufficiency. A device of the same kind was tried in my memory by Louis the Fifteenth, but it answered at no time. However, the necessities of ruinous wars were some excuse for desperate projects. The deliberations of calamity are rarely wise. But here was a season for disposition and providence. It was in a time of profound peace, then enjoyed for five years, and promising a much longer continuance, that they had recourse to this desperate trifling. They were sure to lose more reputation by sporting, in their serious situation, with these toys and playthings of finance, which have filled half their journals, than could possibly be compensated by the poor temporary supply which they afforded. It seemed as if those who adopted such projects were wholly ignorant of their circumstances, or wholly unequal to their necessities. Whatever virtue may be in these devices, it is obvious that neither the patriotic gifts, nor the patriotic contribution, can ever be resorted to again. The resources of public folly are soon exhausted. The whole indeed of their scheme of revenue is to make, by any artifice, an appearance of a full reservoir for the hour, whilst at the same time they cut off the springs and living fountains of perennial supply. The account not long since furnished by M. Necker was meant, without question, to be favourable. He gives a flattering view of the means of getting through the year; but he expresses, as it is natural he should, some apprehension for that which was to succeed. On this last prognostic, instead of entering into the grounds of this apprehension, in order, by a proper foresight, to prevent the prognosticated evil, M. Necker receives a sort of friendly reprimand from the president of the Assembly.

As to their other schemes of taxation, it is impossible to say anything of them with certainty; because they have not yet had their operation: but nobody is so sanguine as to imagine they will fill up any perceptible part of the wide gaping breach which their incapacity has made in their revenues. At present the state of their treasury sinks every day more and more in cash, and swells more and more in fictitious representation. When so little within or without is now found but paper, the representative not of opulence but of want, the creature not of credit but of power, they imagine that our flourishing state in England is owing to that bank-paper, and not the bank-paper to the flourishing condition of our commerce, to the solidity of our credit, and to the total exclusion of all idea of power from any part of the transaction. They forget that, in England, not one shilling of paper-money of any description is received but of choice; that the whole has had its origin in cash actually deposited; and that it is convertible at pleasure, in an instant, and without the smallest loss, into cash again. Our paper is of value in commerce, because in law it is of none. It is powerful on 'Change, because in Westminster Hall it is impotent. In payment of a debt of twenty shillings, a creditor may refuse all the paper of the bank of England. Nor is there amongst us a single public security, of any quality or nature whatsoever, that is enforced by authority. In fact it might be easily shown, that our paper wealth, instead of lessening the real coin, has a tendency to increase it; instead of being a substitute for money, it only facilitates its entry, its exit, and its circulation; that it is the symbol of prosperity, and not the badge of distress. Never was a scarcity of cash, and an exuberance of paper, a subject of complaint in this nation.

Well! but a lessening of prodigal expenses, and the economy which has been introduced by the virtuous and sapient Assembly, make amends for the losses sustained in the receipt of revenue. In this at least they have fulfilled the duty of a financier.—Have those, who say so, looked at the expenses of the National Assembly itself? of the municipalities? of the city of Paris? of the increased pay of the two armies? of the new police? of the new judicatures? Have they even carefully compared the present pension list with the former? These politicians have been cruel, not economical. Comparing the expense of the former prodigal government and its relation to the then revenues with the expenses of this new system as opposed to the state of its new treasury, I believe the present will be found beyond all comparison more chargeable.[55]

It remains only to consider the proofs of financial ability, furnished by the present French managers when they are to raise supplies on credit. Here I am a little at a stand; for credit, properly speaking, they have none. The credit of the ancient government was not indeed the best; but they could always, on some terms, command money, not only at home, but from most of the countries of Europe where a surplus capital was accumulated; and the credit of that government was improving daily. The establishment of a system of liberty would of course be supposed to give it new strength: and so it would actually have done, if a system of liberty had been established.

[55] The reader will observe, that I have but lightly touched (my plan demanded nothing more) on the condition of the French finances, as connected with the demands upon them. If I had intended to do otherwise, the materials in my hands for such a task are not altogether perfect. On this subject I refer the reader to M. de Calonne's work; and the tremendous display that he has made of the havoc and devastation in the public estate, and in all the affairs of France, caused by the presumptuous good intentions of ignorance and incapacity. Such effects those causes will always produce. Looking over that account with a pretty strict eye, and, with perhaps too much rigour, deducting everything which may be placed to the account of a financier out of place, who might be supposed by his enemies desirous of making the most of his cause, I believe it will be found, that a more salutary lesson of caution against the daring spirit of innovators, than what has been supplied at the expense of France, never was at any time furnished to mankind.

What offers has their government of pretended liberty had from Holland, from Hamburgh, from Switzerland, from Genoa, from England, for a dealing in their paper? Why should these nations of commerce and economy enter into any pecuniary dealings with a people, who attempt to reverse the very nature of things; amongst whom they see the debtor prescribing at the point of the bayonet, the medium of his solvency to the creditor; discharging one of his engagements with another; turning his very penury into his resource; and paying his interest with his rags?

Their fanatical confidence in the omnipotence of church plunder has induced these philosophers to overlook all care of the public estate, just as the dream of the philosopher's stone induces dupes, under the more plausible delusion of the hermetic art, to neglect all rational means of improving their fortunes. With these philosophic financiers, this universal medicine made of church mummy is to cure all the evils of the state. These gentlemen perhaps do not believe a great deal in the miracles of piety; but it cannot be questioned, that they have an undoubting faith in the prodigies of sacrilege. Is there a debt which presses them?—Issue *assignats*. Are compensations to be made, or a maintenance decreed to those whom they have robbed of their freehold in their office, or expelled from their profession?— *Assignats*. Is a fleet to be fitted out?—*Assignats*. If sixteen millions sterling of these *assignats,* forced on the people, leave the wants of the state as urgent as ever—issue, says one, thirty millions sterling of *assignats*—says another, issue fourscore millions more of *assignats*. The only difference among their financial factions is on the greater or the lesser quantity of *assignats* to be imposed on the public sufferance. They are all professors of *assignats*. Even those, whose natural good sense and knowledge of commerce, not obliterated by philosophy, furnish decisive arguments against this delusion, conclude their arguments, by proposing the emission of *assignats*. I suppose they must talk of *assignats,* as no other language would be understood. All experience of their inefficiency does not in the least discourage them. Are the old *assignats* depreciated at market?— What is the remedy? Issue new *assignats.—Mais si maladia, oponia-tria, non vult se garire, quid illi facere? assignare—postea assignare; ensuita assignare.* The word is a trifle altered. The Latin of your present doctors may be better than that of your old comedy; their wisdom and the variety of their resources are the same. They have not more notes in their song than the cuckoo; though, far from the softness of that harbinger of summer and plenty, their voice is as harsh and as ominous as that of the raven.

Who but the most desperate adventurers in philosophy and finance could at all have thought of destroying the settled revenue of the state, the sole security for the public credit, in the hope of rebuilding it with the materials of confiscated property? If, however, an excessive zeal for the state should have led a pious and venerable prelate (by anticipation a father of the church[56]) to pillage his own order, and, for the good of the church and people, to take upon himself the place of grand financier of confiscation, and comptroller-general of sacrilege, he and his coadjutors were in my opinion, bound to show, by their subsequent conduct, that they knew something of the office they assumed. When they had resolved to appropriate to the *Fisc,* a certain portion of the landed property of their conquered country, it was their business to render their bank a real fund of credit, as far as such a bank was capable of becoming so.

To establish a current circulating credit upon any *Land-bank,* under any circumstances whatsoever, has hitherto proved difficult at the very least. The attempt has commonly ended in bankruptcy. But when the Assembly were led, through a contempt of moral, to a defiance of economical, principles, it might at least have been expected, that nothing would be omitted on their part to lessen this difficulty, to prevent any aggravation of this bankruptcy. It might be expected, that to render your *Land-bank* tolerable, every means would be adopted that could display openness and candour in the statement of the security; everything which could aid the recovery of the demand. To take things in their most favourable point of view, your condition was that of a man of a large landed estate, which he wished to dispose of for the discharge of a debt, and the supply of certain services. Not being able instantly to sell, you wished to mortgage. What would a man of fair intentions, and a commonly clear understanding, do in such circumstances? Ought

[56] La Bruyère of Bossuet.

he not first to ascertain the gross value of the estate; the charges of its management and disposition; the encumbrances perpetual and temporary of all kinds that affect it; then, striking a net surplus, to calculate the just value of the security? When that surplus (the only security to the creditor) had been clearly ascertained, and properly vested in the hands of trustees; then he would indicate the parcels to be sold, and the time and conditions of sale; after this, he would admit the public creditor, if he chose it, to subscribe his stock into this new fund; or he might receive proposals for an *assignat* from those who would advance money to purchase this species of security.

This would be to proceed like men of business, methodically and rationally; and on the only principles of public and private credit that have an existence. The dealer would then know exactly what he purchased; and the only doubt which could hang upon his mind would be, the dread of the resumption of the spoil, which one day might be made (perhaps with an addition of punishment) from the sacrilegious gripe of those execrable wretches who could become purchasers at the auction of their innocent fellow-citizens.

An open and exact statement of the clear value of the property, and of the time, the circumstances, and the place of sale, were all necessary, to efface as much as possible the stigma that has hitherto been branded on every kind of Land-bank. It became necessary on another principle, that is, on account of a pledge of faith previously given on that subject, that their future fidelity in a slippery concern might be established by their adherence to their first engagement. When they had finally determined on a state resource from church booty, they came, on the 14th of April, 1790, to a solemn resolution on the subject; and pledged themselves to their country, "that in the statement of the public charges for each year, there should be brought to account a sum sufficient for defraying the expenses of the R. C. A. religion, the support of the ministers at the altars, the relief of the poor, the pensions to the ecclesiastics, secular as well as regular, of the one and of the other sex, *in order that the estates and goods which are at the disposal of the nation may be disengaged of all charges, and employed by the representatives, or the legislative body, to the great and most pressing exigencies of the state.*" They further engaged, on the same day, that the sum necessary for the year 1791 should be forthwith determined.

In this resolution they admit it their duty to show distinctly the expense of the above objects, which, by other resolutions, they had before engaged should be first in the order of provision. They admit that they ought to show the estate clear and disengaged of all charges, and that they should show it immediately. Have they done this immediately, or at any time? Have they ever furnished a rent-roll of the immovable estates, or given in an inventory of the movable effects, which they confiscate to their assignats? In what manner they can fulfill their engagements of holding out to public service, "an estate disengaged of all charges," without authenticating the value of the estate, or the quantum of the charges, I leave it to their English admirers to explain. Instantly upon this assurance, and previously to any one step towards making it good, they issue, on the credit of so handsome a declaration, sixteen millions sterling of their paper. This was manly. Who, after this masterly stroke, can doubt of their abilities in finance?—But then, before any other emission of these financial *indulgences*, they took care at least to make good their original promise!—If such estimate, either of the value of the estate or the amount of the encumbrances, has been made, it has escaped me. I never heard of it.

At length they have spoken out, and they have made a full discovery of their abominable fraud, in holding out the church lands as a security for any debts, or any service whatsoever. They rob only to enable them to cheat; but in a very short time they defeat the ends both of the robbery and the fraud, by making out accounts for other purposes, which blow up their whole apparatus of force and of deception. I am obliged to M. de Calonne for his reference to the document which proves this extraordinary fact; it had by some means escaped me. Indeed it was not necessary to make out my assertion as to the breach of faith on the declaration of the 14th of April, 1790. By a report of their committee it now appears, that the charge of keeping up the reduced ecclesiastical establishments, and other expenses attendant on religion, and maintaining the religious of both sexes, retained or pensioned, and the other concomitant expenses of the same nature, which they have brought upon

themselves by this convulsion in property, exceeds the income of the
estates acquired by it in the enormous sum of two millions sterling
annually; besides a debt of seven millions and upwards. These are
the calculating powers of imposture! This is the finance of philosophy! This is the result of all the delusions held out to engage a
miserable people in rebellion, murder, and sacrilege, and to make
them prompt and zealous instruments in the ruin of their country!
Never did a state, in any case, enrich itself by the confiscations of
the citizens. This new experiment has succeeded like all the rest.
Every honest mind, every true lover of liberty and humanity, must
rejoice to find that injustice is not always good policy, nor rapine the
high road to riches. I subjoin with pleasure, in a note, the able and
spirited observations of M. de Calonne on this subject.[57]

In order to persuade the world of the bottomless resource of
ecclesiastical confiscation, the Assembly have proceeded to other confiscations of estates in offices, which could not be done with any
common colour without being compensated out of this grand confiscation of landed property. They have thrown upon this fund,
which was to show a surplus disengaged of all charges, a new
charge; namely, the compensation to the whole body of the disbanded judicature; and of all suppressed offices and estates; a
charge which I cannot ascertain, but which unquestionably amounts
to many French millions. Another of the new charges in an annuity

[57] "Ce n'est point à l'assemblée entière que je m'adresse ici; je ne parle qu'à ceux
qui l'égarent, en lui cachant sous des gazes séduisantes le but où ils l'entraînent.
C'est à eux que je dis: votre objet, vous n'en disconviendrez pas, c'est d'ôter tout
espoir au clergé, et de consommer sa ruine; c'est-là, en ne vous soupçonnant d'aucune
combinaison de cupidité, d'aucun regard sur le jeu des effets publics, c'est-là ce qu'on
doit croire que vous avez en vue dans la terrible opération que vous proposez; c'est
ce qui doit en être le fruit. Mais le peuple que vous y intéressez, quel avantage peut-il
y trouver? En vous servant sans cesse de lui, que faites vous pour lui? Rien,
absolument rien; et, au contraire, vous faites ce qui ne conduit qu'à l'accabler de
nouvelles charges. Vous avez rejeté, à son préjudice, une offre de 400 millions, dont
l'acceptation pouvoit devenir un moyen de soulagement en sa faveur; et à cette
ressource, aussi profitable que legitime, vous avez substitué une injustice ruineuse,
qui, de votre propre aveu, charge le trésor public, et par conséquent le peuple, d'un
surcroît de dépense annuelle de 50 millions au moins, et d'un remboursement de
150 millions.

"Malheureux peuple! voilà ce que vous vaut en dernier résultat l'expropriation de
l'Eglise, et la dureté des décrets taxateurs du traitement des ministres d'une religion
bienfaisante; et désormais ils seront à votre charge: leurs charités soulageoient les
pauvres; et vous allez être imposés pour subvenir à leur entretien!"—*De l'Etat de la
France*, p. 81. See also p. 92, and the following pages.

of four hundred and eighty thousand pounds sterling, to be paid (if they choose to keep faith) by daily payments, for the interest of the first assignats. Have they ever given themselves the trouble to state fairly the expense of the management of the church lands in the hands of the municipalities, to whose care, skill, and diligence, and that of their legion of unknown under-agents, they have chosen to commit the charge of the forfeited estates, and the consequence of which had been so ably pointed out by the bishop of Nancy?

But it is unnecessary to dwell on these obvious heads of encumbrance. Have they made out any clear state of the grand encumbrance of all, I mean the whole of the general and municipal establishments of all sorts, and compared it with the regular income by revenue? Every deficiency in these becomes a charge on the confiscated estate, before the creditor can plant his cabbages on an acre of church property. There is no other prop than this confiscation to keep the whole state from tumbling to the ground. In this situation they have purposely covered all, that they ought industriously to have cleared, with a thick fog; and then, blindfold themselves, like bulls that shut their eyes when they push, they drive, by the point of the bayonets, their slaves, blindfolded indeed no worse than their lords, to take their fictions for currencies, and to swallow down paper pills by thirty-four millions sterling at a dose. Then they proudly lay in their claim to a future credit, on failure of all their past engagements, and at a time when (if in such a matter anything can be clear) it is clear that the surplus estates will never answer even the first of their mortgages, I mean that of the four hundred millions (or sixteen millions sterling) of *assignats*. In all this procedure I can discern neither the solid sense of plain dealing, nor the subtle dexterity of ingenious fraud. The objections within the Assembly to pulling up the flood-gates for this inundation of fraud are unanswered; but they are thoroughly refuted by an hundred thousand financiers in the street. These are the numbers by which the metaphysic arithmeticians compute. These are the grand calculations on which a philosophical public credit is founded in France. They cannot raise supplies; but they can raise mobs. Let them rejoice in the applauses of the club at Dundee, for their wisdom and patriotism in having thus applied the plunder of the citizens to the

service of the state. I hear of no address upon this subject from
the directors of the bank of England; though their approbation
would be of a *little* more weight in the scale of credit than that of
the club at Dundee. But, to do justice to the club, I believe the
gentlemen who compose it to be wiser than they appear; that they
will be less liberal of their money than of their addresses; and that
they would not give a dog's-ear of their most rumpled and ragged
Scotch paper for twenty of your fairest assignats.

Early in this year the Assembly issued paper to the amount of
sixteen millions sterling: what must have been the state into which
the Assembly has brought your affairs, that the relief afforded by
so vast a supply has been hardly perceptible? This paper also felt
an almost immediate depreciation of five per cent., which in a little
time came to about seven. The effect of these assignats on the receipt of the revenue is remarkable. M. Necker found that the collectors of the revenue, who received in coin, paid the treasury in
assignats. The collectors made seven per cent. by thus receiving in
money, and accounting in depreciated paper. It was not very difficult to foresee, that this must be inevitable. It was, however, not the
less embarrassing. M. Necker was obliged (I believe, for a considerable part, in the market of London) to buy gold and silver for the
mint, which amounted to about twelve thousand pounds above the
value of the commodity gained. That minister was of opinion,
that, whatever their secret nutritive virtue might be, the state could
not live upon *assignats* alone; that some real silver was necessary,
particularly for the satisfaction of those who, having iron in their
hands, were not likely to distinguish themselves for patience, when
they should perceive that, whilst an increase of pay was held out to
them in real money, it was again to be fraudulently drawn back by
depreciated paper. The minister, in this very natural distress, applied to the Assembly, that they should order the collectors to pay
in specie what in specie they had received. It could not escape him,
that if the treasury paid three per cent. for the use of a currency,
which should be returned seven per cent. worse than the minister
issued it, such a dealing could not very greatly tend to enrich the
public. The Assembly took no notice of his recommendation. They
were in this dilemma—If they continued to receive the assignats,

cash must become an alien to their treasury: if the treasury should refuse those paper *amulets,* or should discountenance them in any degree, they must destroy the credit of their sole resource. They seem then to have made their option; and to have given some sort of credit to their paper by taking it themselves; at the same time in their speeches they made a sort of swaggering declaration, something, I rather think, above legislative competence; that is, that there is no difference in value between metallic money and their assignats. This was a good, stout, proof article of faith, pronounced under an anathema, by the venerable fathers of this philosophic synod. *Credat* who will—certainly not *Judæus Apella.*

A noble indignation rises in the minds of your popular leaders, on hearing the magic lantern in their show of finance compared to the fraudulent exhibitions of Mr. Law. They cannot bear to hear the sands of his Mississippi compared with the rock of the church, on which they build their system. Pray let them suppress this glorious spirit, until they show to the world what piece of solid ground there is for their assignats, which they have not pre-occupied by other charges. They do injustice to that great, mother fraud, to compare it with their degenerate imitation. It is not true that Law built solely on a speculation concerning the Mississippi. He added the East India trade; he added the African trade; he added the farms of all the farmed revenue of France. All these together unquestionably could not support the structure which the public enthusiasm, not he, chose to build upon these bases. But these were, however, in comparison, generous delusions. They supposed, and they aimed at, an increase of the commerce of France. They opened to it the whole range of the two hemispheres. They did not think of feeding France from its own substance. A grand imagination found in this flight of commerce something to captivate. It was wherewithal to dazzle the eye of an eagle. It was not made to entice the smell of a mole, nuzzling and burying himself in his mother earth, as yours is. Men were not then quite shrunk from their natural dimensions by a degrading and sordid philosophy, and fitted for low and vulgar deceptions. Above all, remember, that, in imposing on the imagination, the then managers of the system made a compliment to the freedom of men. In their fraud there was no mixture of force. This was reserved to our time, to quench the little glimmerings of reason which might break in upon the solid darkness of this enlightened age.

On recollection, I have said nothing of a scheme of finance which may be urged in favor of the abilities of these gentlemen, and which has been introduced with great pomp, though not yet finally adopted, in the National Assembly. It comes with something solid in aid of the credit of the paper circulation; and much has been said of its utility and its elegance. I mean the project for coining into money the bells of the suppressed churches. This is their alchemy. There are some follies which baffle argument; which go beyond ridicule; and which excite no feeling in us but disgust; and therefore I say no more upon it.

It is as little worth remarking any further upon all their drawing and re-drawing, on their circulation for putting off the evil day, on the play between the treasury and the *Caisse d'Escompte,* and on all these old, exploded contrivances of mercantile fraud, now exalted into policy of state. The revenue will not be trifled with. The prattling about the rights of men will not be accepted in payment for a biscuit or a pound of gunpowder. Here then the metaphysicians descend from their airy speculations, and faithfully follow examples. What examples? The examples of bankrupts. But defeated, baffled, disgraced, when their breath, their strength, their inventions, their fancies desert them, their confidence still maintains its ground. In the manifest failure of their abilities, they take credit for their benevolence. When the revenue disappears in their hands, they have the presumption, in some of their late proceedings, to value *themselves* on the relief given to the people. They did not relieve the people. If they entertained such intentions, why did they order the obnoxious taxes to be paid? The people relieved themselves in spite of the Assembly.

But waiving all discussion on the parties who may claim the merit of this fallacious relief, has there been, in effect, any relief to the people in any form? Mr. Bailly, one of the grand agents of paper circulation, lets you into the nature of this relief. His speech to the National Assembly contained a high and laboured panegyric on the inhabitants of Paris, for the constancy and unbroken resolution with which they have borne their distress and misery. A fine picture of public felicity! What! great courage and unconquerable firmness of mind to endure benefits, and sustain redress? One would think from the speech of this learned lord mayor, that the Parisians, for this twelvemonth past, had been suffering the straits of some dreadful blockade; that Henry the Fourth had been stopping up the avenues to their supply, and Sully thundering with his ordnance at the gates of Paris; when in reality they are besieged by no other enemies than their own madness and folly, their own credulity and perverseness. But Mr. Bailly will sooner thaw the eternal ice of his Atlantic regions, than restore the central heat to Paris, whilst it remains "smitten with the cold, dry, petrific mace" of a false and unfeeling philosophy. Some time after this speech, that is, on the thirteenth of last August, the same magistrate, giving an account of his government at the bar of the same Assembly, expresses himself as follows: "In the month of July, 1789," [the period of everlasting commemoration,] "the finances of the city of Paris were *yet* in good order; the expenditure was counterbalanced by the receipt, and she had at that time a million" [forty thousand pounds sterling] "in bank. The expenses which she has been constrained to incur, *subsequent to the Revolution,* amount to 2,500,000 livres. From these expenses, and the great falling off in the product of *the free gifts,* not only a momentary, but a *total,* want of money has taken place." This is the Paris, upon whose nourishment, in the course of the last year, such immense sums, drawn from the vitals of all France, have been expended. As long as Paris stands in the place of ancient Rome, so long she will be maintained by the subject provinces. It is an evil inevitably attendant on the dominion of sovereign democratic republics. As it happened in Rome, it may survive that republican domination which gave rise to it. In that case despotism itself must submit to the vices of popularity. Rome, under her emperors, united the evils of both systems; and this unnatural combination was one great cause of her ruin.

To tell the people that they are relieved by the dilapidation of their public estate, is a cruel and insolent imposition. Statesmen, before they valued themselves on the relief given to the people by the destruction of their revenue, ought first to have carefully attended to the solution of this problem:—Whether it be more advantageous to the people to pay considerably, and to gain in proportion; or to gain little or nothing, and to be disburthened of all contribution? My mind is made up to decide in favour of the first proposition. Experience is with me, and, I believe, the best opinions also. To keep a balance between the power of acquisition on the part of the subject, and the demands he is to answer on the part of the state, is the fundamental part of the skill of a true politician. The means of acquisition are prior in time and in arrangement. Good order is the foundation of all good things. To be enabled to acquire, the people, without being servile, must be tractable and obedient. The magistrate must have his reverence, the laws their authority. The body of the people must not find the principles of natural subordination by art rooted out of their minds. They must respect that property of which they cannot partake. They must labour to obtain what by labour can be obtained; and when they find, as they commonly do, the success disproportioned to the endeavour, they must be taught their consolation in the final proportions of eternal justice. Of this consolation whoever deprives them, deadens their industry, and strikes at the root of all acquisition as of all conservation. He that does this is the cruel oppressor, the merciless enemy of the poor and wretched; at the same time that by his wicked speculations he exposes the fruits of successful industry, and the accumulations of fortune, to the plunder of the negligent, the disappointed, and the unprosperous.

Too many of the financiers by profession are apt to see nothing in revenue but banks, and circulations, and annuities on lives, and tontines, and perpetual rents, and all the small wares of the shop. In a settled order of the state, these things are not to be slighted, nor is the skill in them to be held of trivial estimation. They are good, but then only good, when they assume the effects of that settled order, and are built upon it. But when men think that these beggarly contrivances may supply a resource for the evils which result from breaking up the foundations of public order, and from causing or suffering the principles of property to be subverted, they will, in the ruin of their country, leave a melancholy and lasting monument of the effect of preposterous politics, and presumptuous, short-sighted, narrow-minded wisdom.

The effects of the incapacity shown by the popular leaders in all the great members of the commonwealth are to be covered with the "all-atoning name" of liberty. In some people I see great liberty indeed; in many, if not in the most, an oppressive, degrading servitude. But what is liberty without wisdom, and without virtue? It is the greatest of all possible evils; for it is folly, vice, and madness, without tuition or restraint. Those who know what virtuous liberty is, cannot bear to see it disgraced by incapable heads, on account of their having high-sounding words in their mouths. Grand, swelling sentiments of liberty I am sure I do not despise. They warm the heart; they enlarge and liberalize our minds; they animate our courage in a time of conflict. Old as I am, I read the fine raptures of Lucan and Corneille with pleasure. Neither do I wholly condemn the little arts and devices of popularity. They facilitate the carrying of many points of moment; they keep the people together; they refresh the mind in its exertions; and they diffuse occasional gaiety over the severe brow of moral freedom. Every politician ought to sacrifice to the graces; and to join compliance with reason. But in such an undertaking as that in France, all these subsidiary sentiments and artifices are of little avail. To make a government requires no great prudence. Settle the seat of power; teach obedience and the work is done. To give freedom is still more easy. It is not necessary to guide; it only requires to let go the rein. But to form a *free government;* that is, to temper together these opposite elements of liberty and restraint in one consistent work, requires much thought, deep reflection, a sagacious, powerful, and combining mind. This I do not find in those who take the lead in the National Assembly. Perhaps they are not so miserably deficient as they appear. I rather believe it. It would put them below the common level of human understanding. But when the leaders choose to make themselves bidders at an auction of popularity, their talents, in the construction of the state, will be of no service. They will become flatterers instead of legislators; the instruments, not the guides, of the people. If any of them should happen to propose a scheme of liberty, soberly limited, and defined with proper qualifications, he will be immediately outbid by his competitors, who will produce something more splendidly popular. Suspicions will be raised of his fidelity to his cause. Moderation will be stigmatized as the virtue of cowards; and compromise as the prudence of traitors; until, in hopes of preserving the credit which may enable him to temper, and moderate, on some occasions, the popular leader is obliged to become active in propagating doctrines, and establishing powers, that will afterwards defeat any sober purpose at which he ultimately might have aimed.

But am I so unreasonable as to see nothing at all that deserves commendation in the indefatigable labours of this Assembly? I do not deny that, among an infinite number of acts of violence and folly, some good may have been done. They who destroy everything certainly will remove some grievance. They who make everything new, have a chance that they may establish something beneficial. To give them credit for what they have done in virtue of the authority they have usurped, or which can excuse them in the crimes by which that authority has been acquired, it must appear, that the same things could not have been accomplished without producing such a revolution. Most assuredly they might; because almost every one of the regulations made by them, which is not very equivocal, was either in the cession of the king, voluntarily made at the meeting of the states, or in the concurrent instructions to the orders. Some usages have been abolished on just grounds; but they were such, that if they had stood as they were to all eternity, they would little detract from the happiness and prosperity of any state. The improvements of the National Assembly are superficial, their errors fundamental.

Whatever they are, I wish my countrymen rather to recommend to our neighbours the example of the British constitution, than to take models from them for the improvement of our own. In the former they have got an invaluable treasure. They are not, I think, without some causes of apprehension and complaint; but these they do not owe to their constitution, but to their own conduct. I think our happy situation owing to our constitution; but owing to the whole of it, and not to any part singly; owing in a great measure to what we have left standing in our several reviews and reformations, as well as to what we have altered or superadded. Our people will find employment enough for a truly patriotic, free, and independent spirit, in guarding what they possess from violation. I would not exclude alteration neither; but even when I changed, it should be to preserve. I should be led to my remedy by a great grievance. In what I did, I should follow the example of our ancestors. I would make the reparation as nearly as possible in the style of the building. A politic caution, a guarded circumspection, a moral rather than a complexional timidity, were among the ruling principles of our forefathers in their most decided conduct. Not being illuminated with the light of which the gentlemen of France tell us they have got so abundant a share, they acted under a strong impression of the ignorance and fallibility of mankind. He that had made them thus fallible, rewarded them for having in their conduct attended to their nature. Let us imitate their caution, if we wish to deserve their fortune, or to retain their bequests. Let us add, if we please, but let us preserve what they have left; and standing on the firm ground of the British constitution, let us be satisfied to admire, rather than attempt to follow in their desperate flights, the aëronauts of France.

I have told you candidly my sentiments. I think they are not likely to alter yours. I do know that they ought. You are young; you cannot guide, but must follow the fortune of your country. But hereafter they may be of some use to you, in some future form which your commonwealth may take. In the present it can hardly remain; but before its final settlement it may be obliged to pass, as one of our poets says, "through great varieties of untried being," and in all its transmigrations to be purified by fire and blood.

I have little to recommend my opinions but long observation and much impartiality. They come from one who has been no tool of power, no flatterer of greatness; and who in his last acts does not wish to belie the tenour of his life. They come from one, almost the whole of whose public exertion has been a struggle for the liberty of others; from one in whose breast no anger durable or vehement has ever been kindled, but by what he considered as tyranny; and who snatches from his share in the endeavours which are used by good men to discredit opulent oppression, the hours he has employed on your affairs; and who in so doing persuades himself he has not departed from his usual office: they come from one who desires honours, distinctions, and emoluments, but little; and who expects them not at all; who has no contempt for fame, and no fear of obloquy; who shuns contention, though he will hazard an opinion: from one who wishes to preserve consistency, but who would preserve consistency by varying his means to secure the unity of his end; and, when the equipoise of the vessel in which he sails may be endangered by overloading it upon one side, is desirous of carrying the small weight of his reasons to that which may preserve its equipoise.

A LETTER

FROM

THE RIGHT HON. EDMUND BURKE

TO A NOBLE LORD

ON THE ATTACKS MADE UPON HIM AND HIS PENSION, IN THE
HOUSE OF LORDS, BY THE DUKE OF BEDFORD AND THE
EARL OF LAUDERDALE, EARLY IN THE PRESENT
SESSION OF PARLIAMENT

1796

INTRODUCTORY NOTE

When Burke retired from Parliament at the close of his labors in the trial of Warren Hastings, it was proposed to raise him to the peerage as Lord Beaconsfield; but before the matter came to a point, Burke's son Richard, in whom all his hopes and affections were centered, died and left his father desolate. A hereditary honor was no longer in question, and it was arranged, since Burke was now, as always, in financial difficulties, that he should get £1,200 a year from the Civil List so long as his wife lived, and that the King should propose to Parliament a more liberal recognition of his services. But Pitt, probably in order to avoid unseemly opposition from Burke's enemies, arranged a grant of £2,500 a year directly from the Crown, so that Burke, though glad to get the money, was disappointed in its not being a more broadly national reward.

Pitt's caution seems to have been justified, for in the next year, when party feeling was running high, the Duke of Bedford and Lord Lauderdale seized upon the granting of the pension as a weapon with which to attack the administration. Burke at once saw, in the fact that the assault came from the head of the house of Bedford, an opportunity for the most telling repartee, and this opportunity he availed himself of with tremendous effect. As politics, it gives us Burke's own view of his record as an administrator; as literature, the piece is probably unsurpassed in the language for lofty and scornful invective.

A LETTER

FROM

THE RIGHT HON. EDMUND BURKE

TO A NOBLE LORD

[1796]

My Lord,

ICOULD hardly flatter myself with the hope, that so very early in the season I should have to acknowledge obligations to the Duke of BEDFORD, and to the Earl of LAUDERDALE. These noble persons have lost no time in conferring upon me that sort of honour, which it is alone within their competence, and which it is certainly most congenial to their nature, and to their manners, to bestow.

To be ill spoken of, in whatever language they speak, by the zealots of the new sect in philosophy and politics, of which these noble persons think so charitably, and of which others think so justly, to me, is no matter of uneasiness or surprise. To have incurred the displeasure of the Duke of Orleans or the Duke of Bedford, to fall under the censure of citizen Brissot or of his friend the Earl of Lauderdale, I ought to consider as proofs, not the least satisfactory, that I have produced some part to the effect I proposed by my endeavours. I have laboured hard to earn, what the noble lords are generous enough to pay. Personal offence I have given them none. The part they take against me is from zeal to the cause. It is well! It is perfectly well! I have to do homage to their justice. I have to thank the Bedfords and the Lauderdales for having so faithfully and so fully acquitted towards me whatever arrear of debt was left undischarged by the Priestleys and the Paines.

Some, perhaps, may think them executors in their own wrong: I at least have nothing to complain of. They have gone beyond the demands of justice. They have been (a little perhaps beyond their intention) favourable to me. They have been the means of bringing

out, by their invectives, the handsome things which Lord Grenville
has had the goodness and condescension to say in my behalf. Retired as I am from the world, and from all its affairs and all its
pleasures, I confess it does kindle, in my nearly extinguished feelings, a very vivid satisfaction to be so attacked and so commended.
It is soothing to my wounded mind, to be commended by an able,
vigorous, and well-informed statesman, and at the very moment
when he stands forth with a manliness and resolution, worthy of
himself and of his cause, for the preservation of the person and government of our sovereign, and therein for the security of the laws,
the liberties, the morals, and the lives of his people. To be in any
fair way connected with such things, is indeed a distinction. No
philosophy can make me above it; no melancholy can depress me
so low, as to make me wholly insensible to such an honour.

Why will they not let me remain in obscurity and inaction?
Are they apprehensive, that if an atom of me remains, the sect has
something to fear? Must I be annihilated, lest, like old *John Zisca's,*
my skin might be made into a drum, to animate Europe to eternal
battle, against a tyranny that threatens to overwhelm all Europe,
and all the human race?

My Lord, it is a subject of awful meditation. Before this of
France, the annals of all time have not furnished an instance of a
complete revolution. That Revolution seems to have extended even
to the constitution of the mind of man. It has this of wonderful in
it, that it resembles what Lord Verulam says of the operations of
nature. It was perfect, not only in its elements and principles, but
in all its members and its organs from the very beginning. The
moral scheme of France furnishes the only pattern ever known,
which they who admire will *instantly* resemble. It is indeed an
inexhaustible repertory of one kind of examples. In my wretched
condition, though hardly to be classed with the living, I am not
safe from them. They have tigers to fall upon animated strength.
They have hyenas to prey upon carcasses. The national menagerie
is collected by the first physiologists of the time; and it is defective
in no description of savage nature. They pursue even such as me,
into the obscurest retreats, and haul them before their revolutionary tribunals. Neither sex, nor age, nor the sanctuary of the tomb,

is sacred to them. They have so determined a hatred to all privileged orders, that they deny even to the departed the sad immunities of the grave. They are not wholly without an object. Their turpitude purveys to their malice; and they unplumb the dead for bullets to assassinate the living. If all revolutionists were not proof against all caution, I should recommend it to their consideration, that no persons were ever known in history, either sacred or profane, to vex the sepulchre, and, by their sorceries, to call up the prophetic dead, with any other event, than the prediction of their own disastrous fate.—"Leave me, oh leave me to repose!"

In one thing I can excuse the Duke of Bedford for his attack upon me and my mortuary pension. He cannot readily comprehend the transaction he condemns. What I have obtained was the fruit of no bargain; the production of no intrigue; the result of no compromise; the effect of no solicitation. The first suggestion of it never came from me, mediately or immediately, to his Majesty or any of his ministers. It was long known that the instant my engagements would permit it, and before the heaviest of all calamities had for ever condemned me to obscurity and sorrow, I had resolved on a total retreat. I had executed that design. I was entirely out of the way of serving or of hurting any statesman, or any party, when the ministers so generously and so nobly carried into effect the spontaneous bounty of the crown. Both descriptions have acted as became them. When I could no longer serve them, the ministers have considered my situation. When I could no longer hurt them, the revolutionists have trampled on my infirmity. My gratitude, I trust, is equal to the manner in which the benefit was conferred. It came to me indeed, at a time of life, and in a state of mind and body, in which no circumstance of fortune could afford me any real pleasure. But this was no fault in the royal donor, or in his ministers, who were pleased, in acknowledging the merits of an invalid servant of the public, to assuage the sorrows of a desolate old man.

It would ill become me to boast of anything. It would as ill become me, thus called upon, to depreciate the value of a long life, spent with unexampled toil in the service of my country. Since the total body of my services, on account of the industry which was shown in them, and the fairness of my intentions, have obtained the acceptance of my sovereign, it would be absurd in me to range myself on the side of the Duke of Bedford and the corresponding society, or, as far as in me lies, to permit a dispute on the rate at which the authority appointed by *our* constitution to estimate such things has been pleased to set them.

Loose libels ought to be passed by in silence and contempt. By me they have been so always. I knew that as long as I remained in public, I should live down the calumnies of malice, and the judgments of ignorance. If I happened to be now and then in the wrong, (as who is not?) like all other men, I must bear the consequence of my faults and my mistakes. The libels of the present day are just of the same stuff as the libels of the past. But they derive an importance from the rank of the persons they come from, and the gravity of the place where they were uttered. In some way or other I ought to take some notice of them. To assert myself thus traduced is not vanity or arrogance. It is a demand of justice; it is a demonstration of gratitude. If I am unworthy, the ministers are worse than prodigal. On that hypothesis, I perfectly agree with the Duke of Bedford.

For whatever I have been (I am now no more) I put myself on my country. I ought to be allowed a reasonable freedom, because I stand upon my deliverance; and no culprit ought to plead in irons. Even in the utmost latitude of defensive liberty, I wish to preserve all possible decorum. Whatever it may be in the eyes of these noble persons themselves, to me their situation calls for the most profound respect. If I should happen to trespass a little, which I trust I shall not, let it always be supposed, that a confusion of characters may produce mistakes; that, in the masquerades of the grand carnival of our age, whimsical adventures happen; odd things are said and pass off. If I should fail a single point in the high respect I owe to those illustrious persons, I cannot be supposed to mean the Duke of Bedford and the Earl of Lauderdale of the House of Peers, but the Duke of Bedford and the Earl of Lauderdale of Palace-Yard!—The Dukes and Earls of Brentford. There they are on the pavement; there they seem to come nearer to my humble level; and, virtually at least, to have waived their high privilege.

Making this protestation, I refuse all revolutionary tribunals, where men have been put to death for no other reason, than that they had obtained favours from the Crown. I claim, not the letter, but the spirit, of the old English law, that is, to be tried by my peers. I decline his Grace's jurisdiction as a judge. I challenge the Duke of Bedford as a juror to pass upon the value of my services. Whatever his natural parts may be, I cannot recognize, in his few and idle years, the competence to judge of my long and laborious life. If I can help it, he shall not be on the inquest of my *quantum meruit*. Poor rich man! He can hardly know anything of public industry in its exertions, or can estimate its compensations when its work is done. I have no doubt of his Grace's readiness in all the calculations of vulgar arithmetic; but I shrewdly suspect, that he is little studied in the theory of moral proportions; and has never learned the rule of three in the arithmetic of policy and state.

His Grace thinks I have obtained too much. I answer, that my exertions, whatever they have been, were such as no hopes of pecuniary reward could possibly excite; and no pecuniary compensation can possibly reward them. Between money and such services, if done by abler men than I am, there is no common principle of comparison; they are quantities incommensurable. Money is made for the comfort and convenience of animal life. It cannot be a reward for what mere animal life must indeed sustain, but never can inspire. With submission to his Grace, I have not had more than sufficient. As to any noble use, I trust I know how to employ, as well as he, a much greater fortune than he possesses. In a more confined application, I certainly stand in need of every kind of relief and easement much more than he does. When I say I have not received more than I deserve, is this the language I hold to Majesty? No! Far, very far, from it! Before that presence, I claim no merit at all. Everything towards me is favour, and bounty. One style to a gracious benefactor; another to a proud and insulting foe.

His Grace is pleased to aggravate my guilt, by charging my acceptance of his Majesty's grant as a departure from my ideas, and the spirit of my conduct with regard to economy. If it be, my ideas of economy were false and ill-founded. But they are the Duke of Bedford's ideas of economy I have contradicted, and not my own. If he means to allude to certain bills brought in by me on a message from the throne in 1782, I tell him that there is nothing in my conduct that can contradict either the letter or the spirit of those acts. Does he mean the pay-office act? I take it for granted he does not. The act to which he alludes, is, I suppose, the establishment act. I greatly doubt whether his Grace has ever read the one or the other. The first of these systems cost me, with every assistance which my then situation gave me, pains incredible. I found an opinion common through all the offices, and general in the public at large, that it would prove impossible to reform and methodize the office of paymaster-general. I undertook it, however; and I succeeded in my undertaking. Whether the military service, or whether the general economy of our finances, have profited by that act, I leave to those who are acquainted with the army, and with the treasury, to judge.

An opinion full as general prevailed also at the same time, that nothing could be done for the regulation of the civil-list establishment. The very attempt to introduce method into it, and any limitations to its services, was held absurd. I had not seen the man, who so much as suggested one economical principle, or an economical expedient, upon that subject. Nothing but coarse amputation, or coarser taxation, were then talked of, both of them without design, combination, or the least shadow of principle. Blind and headlong zeal, or factious fury, were the whole contribution brought by the most noisy on that occasion, towards the satisfaction of the public, or the relief of the Crown.

Let me tell my youthful censor, that the necessities of that time required something very different from what others then suggested, or what his Grace now conceives. Let me inform him, that it was one of the most critical periods in our annals.

Astronomers have supposed, that if a certain comet, whose path intercepted the ecliptic, had met the earth in some (I forget what) sign, it would have whirled us along with it, in its eccentric course, into God knows what regions of heat and cold. Had the portentous comet of the rights of man, (which "from its horrid hair shakes pestilence and war," and "with fear of change perplexes monarchs,") had that comet crossed upon us in that internal state of England, nothing human could have prevented our being irresistibly hurried, out of the highway of heaven, into all the vices, crimes, horrors, and miseries of the French Revolution.

Happily, France was not then Jacobinised. Her hostility was at a good distance. We had a limb cut off; but we preserved the body. We lost our colonies; but we kept our constitution. There was, indeed, much intestine heat; there was a dreadful fermentation. Wild and savage insurrection quitted the woods, and prowled about our streets in the name of reform. Such was the distemper of the public mind, that there was no madman, in his maddest ideas, and maddest projects, who might not count upon numbers to support his principles and execute his designs.

Many of the changes, by a great misnomer called parliamentary reforms, went, not in the intention of all the professors and sup-porters of them, undoubtedly, but went in their certain, and, in my opinion, not very remote effect, home to the utter destruction of the constitution of this kingdom. Had they taken place, not France, but England, would have had the honour of leading up the death-dance of democratic revolution. Other projects, exactly coincident in time with those, struck at the very existence of the kingdom under any constitution. There are those who remember the blind fury of some, and the lamentable helplessness of others; here, a torpid con-fusion, from a panic fear of the danger; there, the same inaction from a stupid insensibility to it; here, well-wishers to the mischief; there, indifferent lookers-on. At the same time, a sort of national conven-tion, dubious in its nature, and perilous in its example, nosed parlia-ment in the very seat of its authority; sat with a sort of superin-tendence over it; and little less than dictated to it, not only laws, but the very form and essence of legislature itself. In Ireland things ran in a still more eccentric course. Government was unnerved, confounded, and in a manner suspended. Its equipoise was totally gone. I do not mean to speak disrespectfully of Lord North. He was a man of admirable parts; of general knowledge; of a versatile understanding fitted for every sort of business; of infinite wit and pleasantry; of a delightful temper; and with a mind most perfectly disinterested. But it would be only to degrade myself by a weak adulation, and not to honour the memory of a great man, to deny that he wanted something of the vigilance and spirit of command, that the time required. Indeed, a darkness, next to the fog of this awful day, loured over the whole region. For a little time the helm appeared abandoned—

Ipse diem noctemque negat discernere cœlo,
Nec meminisse viæ mediâ Palinurus in undâ.

At that time I was connected with men of high place in the community. They loved liberty as much as the Duke of Bedford can do; and they understood it at least as well. Perhaps their politics, as usual, took a tincture from their character, and they cultivated what they loved. The liberty they pursued was a liberty inseparable from order, from virtue, from morals, and from religion; and was neither hypocritically nor fanatically followed. They did not wish, that liberty, in itself one of the first of blessings, should in its perversion become the greatest curse which could fall upon mankind. To preserve the constitution entire, and practically equal to all the great ends of its formation, not in one single part, but in all its parts, was to them the first object. Popularity and power they regarded alike. These were with them only different means of obtaining that object; and had no preference over each other in their minds, but as one or the other might afford a surer or a less certain prospect of arriving at that end. It is some consolation to me in the cheerless gloom, which darkens the evening of my life, that with them I commenced my political career, and never for a moment, in reality, nor in appearance, for any length of time, was separated from their good wishes and good opinion.

By what accident it matters not, nor upon what desert, but just then, and in the midst of that hunt of obloquy, which ever has pursued me with a full cry through life, I had obtained a very considerable degree of public confidence. I know well enough how equivocal a test this kind of popular opinion forms of the merit that obtained it. I am no stranger to the insecurity of its tenure. I do not boast of it. It is mentioned to show, not how highly I prize the thing, but my right to value the use I made of it. I endeavoured to turn that short-lived advantage to myself into a permanent benefit to my country. Far am I from detracting from the merit of some gentlemen, out of office or in it, on that occasion. No!—It is not my way to refuse a full and heaped measure of justice to the aids that I receive. I have, through life, been willing to give everything to others; and to reserve nothing for myself, but the inward conscience, that I had omitted no pains to discover, to animate, to discipline, to direct the abilities of the country for its service, and to place them in the best light to improve their age, or to adorn it. This conscience I have. I have never suppressed any man; never checked him for a moment in his course, by any jealousy or by any policy. I was always ready, to the height of my means, (and they were always infinitely below my desires,) to forward those abilities which overpowered my own. He is an ill-furnished undertaker, who has no machinery but his own hands to work with. Poor in my own faculties, I ever thought myself rich in theirs. In that period of difficulty and danger, more especially, I consulted, and sincerely co-operated with, men of all parties, who seemed disposed to the same ends, or to any main part of them. Nothing to prevent disorder was omitted: when it appeared, nothing to subdue it was left uncounselled, nor unexecuted, as far as I could prevail. At the time I speak of, and having a momentary lead, so aided and so encouraged, and as a feeble instrument in a mighty hand—I do not say I saved my country; I am sure I did my country important service. There were few, indeed, that did not at that time acknowledge it, and that time was thirteen years ago. It was but one voice, that no man in the kingdom better deserved an honourable provision should be made for him.

So much for my general conduct through the whole of the portentous crisis from 1780 to 1782, and the general sense then entertained of that conduct by my country. But my character, as a reformer, in the particular instances which the Duke of Bedford refers to, is so connected in principle with my opinions on the hideous changes, which have since barbarized France, and, spreading thence, threaten the political and moral order of the whole world, that it seems to demand something of a more detailed discussion.

My economical reforms were not, as his Grace may think, the suppression of a paltry pension or employment, more or less. Economy in my plans was, as it ought to be, secondary, subordinate, instrumental. I acted on state principles. I found a great distemper in the commonwealth; and, according to the nature of the evil and of the object, I treated it. The malady was deep; it was complicated, in the causes and in the symptoms. Throughout it was full of contra-indicants. On one hand government, daily growing more invidious from an apparent increase of the means of strength, was every day growing more contemptible by real weakness. Nor was this dissolution confined to government commonly so called. It extended to parliament; which was losing not a little in its dignity and estimation, by an opinion of its not acting on worthy motives. On the other hand, the desires of the people (partly natural and partly infused into them by art) appeared in so wild and inconsiderate a manner, with regard to the economical object, (for I set aside for a moment the dreadful tampering with the body of the constitution itself,) that, if their petitions had literally been complied with, the state would have been convulsed; and a gate would have been opened, through which all property might be sacked and ravaged. Nothing could have saved the public from the mischiefs of the false reform but its absurdity; which would soon have brought itself, and with it all real reform, into discredit. This would have left a rankling wound in the hearts of the people, who would know they had failed in the accomplishment of their wishes, but who, like the rest of mankind in all ages, would impute the blame to anything rather than to their own proceedings. But there were then persons in the world, who nourished complaint; and would have been thoroughly disappointed if the people were ever satisfied. I was not of that humour. I wished that they *should* be satisfied. It was my aim to give to the people the substance of what I knew they desired, and what I thought was right, whether they desired it or not, before it had been modified for them into senseless petitions. I knew that there is a manifest, marked distinction, which ill men with ill designs, or weak men incapable of any design, will constantly be confounding, that is, a marked distinction between change and reformation. The former alters the substance of the objects themselves; and gets rid of all their essential good, as well as of all the accidental evil, annexed to them. Change is novelty; and whether it is to operate any one of the effects of reformation at all, or whether it may not contradict the very principle upon which reformation is desired, cannot be certainly known beforehand. **Reform is, not a** change in the substance, or in the primary modification, of the object, but, a direct application of a remedy to the grievance complained of. So far as that is removed, all is sure. It stops there; and, if it fails, the substance which underwent the operation, at the very worst, is but where it was.

All this, in effect, I think, but am not sure, I have said elsewhere. It cannot at this time be too often repeated; line upon line; precept upon precept; until it comes into the currency of a proverb, *to innovate is not to reform*. The French revolutionists complained of everything; they refused to reform anything; and they left nothing, no, nothing at all *unchanged*. The consequences are *before* us,— not in remote history; not in future prognostication: they are about us; they are upon us. They shake the public security; they menace private enjoyment. They dwarf the growth of the young; they break the quiet of the old. If we travel, they stop our way. They infest us in town; they pursue us to the country. Our business is interrupted; our repose is troubled; our pleasures are saddened; our very studies are poisoned and perverted, and knowledge is rendered worse than ignorance, by the enormous evils of this dreadful innovation. The revolution harpies of France, sprung from night and hell, or from that chaotic anarchy, which generates equivocally "all monstrous, all prodigious things," cuckoo-like, adulterously lay their eggs, and brood over, and hatch them in the nest of every neighbouring state. These obscene harpies, who deck themselves in I know not what divine attributes, but who in reality are foul and ravenous birds of prey, (both mothers and daughters,) flutter over our heads, and souse down upon our tables, and leave nothing unrent, unrifled, unravaged, or unpolluted with the slime of their filthy offal.[1]

> [1]Tristius haud illis monstrum, nec sævior ulla
> Pestis, et ira Deûm Stygiis sese extulit undis
> Virginei volucrum vultus; fædissima ventris
> Proluvies; uncæque manus; et pallida semper
> Ora fame—

Here the poet breaks the line, because he (and that he is Virgil) had not verse or language to describe that monster even as he had conceived her. Had he lived in our time, he would have been more overpowered with the reality than he was with the imagination. Virgil only knew the horror of the times before him. Had he lived to see the revolutionists and constitutionalists of France, he would have had more horrid and disgusting features of his harpies to describe, and more frequent failures in the attempt to describe them.

If his Grace can contemplate the result of this complete innovation, or, as some friends of his will call it, *reform,* in the whole body of its solidity and compounded mass, at which, as Hamlet says, the face of heaven glows with horror and indignation, and which, in truth, makes every reflecting mind, and every feeling heart, perfectly thought-sick, without a thorough abhorrence of everything they say, and everything they do, I am amazed at the morbid strength or the natural infirmity of his mind.

It was then not my love, but my hatred, to innovation, that produced my plan of reform. Without troubling myself with the exactness of the logical diagram, I considered them as things substantially opposite. It was to prevent that evil, that I proposed the measures, which his Grace is pleased, and I am not sorry he is pleased, to recall to my recollection. I had (what I hope that noble duke will remember in all its operations) a state to preserve, as well as a state to reform. I had a people to gratify, but not to inflame, or to mislead. I do not claim half the credit for what I did, as for what I prevented from being done. In that situation of the public mind, I did not undertake, as was then proposed, to new-model the House of Commons or the House of Lords; or to change the authority under which any officer of the Crown acted, who was suffered at all to exist. Crown, Lords, Commons, judicial system, system of administration, existed as they had existed before; and in the mode and manner in which they had always existed. My measures were, what I then truly stated them to the House to be, in their intent, healing and mediatorial. A complaint was made of too much influence in the House of Commons; I reduced it in both Houses; and I gave my reasons article by article for every reduction, and showed why I thought it safe for the service of the state. I heaved the lead every inch of way I made. A disposition to expense was complained of; to that I opposed, not mere retrenchment, but a system of economy, which would make a random expense, without plan or foresight, in future not easily practicable. I proceeded upon principles of research to put me in possession of my matter; on principles of method to regulate it; and on principles in the human mind and in civil affairs to secure and perpetuate the operation. I conceived nothing arbitrarily; nor proposed anything to be done by the will and pleasure of others, or my own; but by reason, and by reason only. I have ever abhorred, since the first dawn of my understanding to this its obscure twilight, all the operations of opinion, fancy, inclination, and will, in the affairs of government, where only a sovereign reason, paramount to all forms of legislation and administration, should dictate. Government is made for the very purpose of opposing that reason to will and caprice, in the reformers or in the reformed, in the governors or in the governed, in kings, in senates, or in people.

On a careful review, therefore, and analysis, of all the component parts of the civil list, and on weighing them against each other, in order to make, as much as possible, all of them a subject of estimate, (the foundation and cornerstone of all regular provident economy,) is appeared to me evident, that this was impracticable, whilst that part, called the pension list, was totally discretionary in its amount. For this reason, and for this only, I proposed to reduce it, both in its gross quantity, and in its larger individual proportions, to a certainty; lest, if it were left without a *general* limit, it might eat up the civil-list service; if suffered to be granted in portions too great for the fund, it might defeat its own end; and, by unlimited allowances to some, it might disable the Crown in means of providing for others. The pension list was to be kept as a sacred fund; but it could not be kept as a constant, open fund, sufficient for growing demands, if some demands would wholly devour it. The tenour of the act will show that it regarded the civil list *only,* the reduction of which to some sort of estimate was my great object.

No other of the Crown funds did I meddle with, because they had not the same relations. This of the four and a half per cents. does his Grace imagine had escaped me, or had escaped all the men of business, who acted with me in those regulations? I knew that such a fund existed, and that pensions had been always granted on it, before his Grace was born. This fund was full in my eye. It was full in the eyes of those who worked with me. It was left on principle. On principle I did what was then done; and on principle what was left undone was omitted. I did not dare to rob the nation of all funds to reward merit. If I pressed this point too close, I acted contrary to the avowed principles on which I went. Gentlemen are very fond of quoting me; but if any one thinks it worth his while to know the rules that guided me in my plan of reform, he will read my printed speech on that subject; at least what is contained from page 230 to page 241 in the second volume of the collection which a friend has given himself the trouble to make of my publications. Be this as it may, these two bills, (though achieved with the greatest labour, and management of every sort, both within and without the House,) were only a part, and but a small part, of a very large system, comprehending all the objects I stated in opening my proposition, and, indeed, many more, which I just hinted at in my speech to the electors of Bristol, when I was put out of that representation. All these, in some state or other of forwardness, I have long had by me.

But do I justify his Majesty's grace on these grounds? I think them the least of my services! The time gave them an occasional value. What I have done in the way of political economy was far from confined to this body of measures. I did not come into parliament to con my lesson. I had earned my pension before I set my foot in St. Stephen's chapel. I was prepared and disciplined to this political warfare. The first session I sat in parliament, I found it necessary to analyze the whole commercial, financial, constitutional, and foreign interests of Great Britain and its empire. A great deal was then done; and more, far more, would have been done, if more had been permitted by events. Then, in the vigour of my manhood, my constitution sunk under my labour. Had I then died, (and I seemed to myself very near death,) I had then earned for those who belonged to me, more than the Duke of Bedford's ideas of service are of power to estimate. But, in truth, these services I am called to account for are not those on which I value myself the most. If I were to call for a reward, (which I have never done,) it should be for those in which for fourteen years, without intermission, I showed the most industry, and had the least success; I mean in the affairs of India. They are those on which I value myself the most; most for the importance; most for the labour; most for the judgment; most for constancy and perseverance in the pursuit. Others may value them most for the *intention*. In that, surely, they are not mistaken.

Does his Grace think, that they, who advised the Crown to make my retreat easy, considered me only as an economist? That, well understood, however, is a good deal. If I had not deemed it of some value, I should not have made political economy an object of my humble studies, from my very early youth to near the end of my service in parliament, even before (at least to any knowledge of mine) it had employed the thoughts of speculative men in other parts of Europe. At that time it was still in its infancy in England, where, in the last century, it had its origin. Great and learned men thought my studies were not wholly thrown away, and deigned to communicate with me now and then on some particulars of their immortal works. Something of these studies may appear incidentally in some of the earliest things I published. The House has been witness to their effect, and has profited of them more or less for above eight and twenty years.

To their estimate I leave the matter. I was not, like his Grace of Bedford, swaddled, and rocked, and dandled into a legislator; *"Nitor in adversum"* is the motto for a man like me. I possessed not one of the qualities, nor cultivated one of the arts, that recommend men to the favour and protection of the great. I was not made for a minion or a tool. As little did I follow the trade of winning the hearts, by imposing on the understandings, of the people. At every step of my progress in life, (for in every step was I traversed and opposed,) and at every turnpike I met, I was obliged to show my passport, and again and again to prove my sole title to the honour of being useful to my country, by a proof that I was not wholly unacquainted with its laws, and the whole system of its interests both abroad and at home. Otherwise no rank, no toleration, even for me. I had no arts but manly arts. On them I have stood, and, please God, in spite of the Duke of Bedford and the Earl of Lauderdale, to the last gasp will I stand.

Had his Grace condescended to inquire concerning the person, whom he has not thought it below him to reproach, he might have found that, in the whole course of my life, I have never, on any pretence of economy, or on any other pretence, so much as in a single instance, stood between any man and his reward of service, or his encouragement in useful talent and pursuit, from the highest of those services and pursuits to the lowest. On the contrary I have, on an hundred occasions, exerted myself with singular zeal to forward every man's even tolerable pretensions. I have more than once had good-natured reprehensions from my friends for carrying the matter to something bordering on abuse. This line of conduct, whatever its merits might be, was partly owing to natural disposition; but I think full as much to reason and principle. I looked on the consideration of public service, or public ornament, to be real and very justice: and I ever held a scanty and penurious justice to partake of the nature of a wrong. I held it to be, in its consequences, the worst economy in the world. In saving money, I soon can count up all the good I do; but when, by a cold penury, I blast the abilities of a nation, and stunt the growth of its active energies, the ill I may do is beyond all calculation. Whether it be too much or too little, whatever I have done has been general and systematic. I have never entered into those trifling, vexatious, and oppressive details, that have been falsely, and most ridiculously, laid to my charge.

Did I blame the pensions given to Mr. Barré and Mr. Dunning between the proposition and execution of my plan? No! surely no! Those pensions were within my principles. I assert it, those gentlemen deserved their pensions, their titles—all they had; and more had they had, I should have been but pleased the more. They were men of talents; they were men of service. I put the profession of the law out of the question in one of them. It is a service that rewards itself. But their *public service,* though, from their abilities unquestionably of more value than mine, in its quantity and its duration was not to be mentioned with it. But I never could drive a hard bargain in my life, concerning any matter whatever; and least of all do I know how to haggle and huckster with merit. Pension for myself I obtained none; nor did I solicit any. Yet I was loaded with hatred for everything that was withheld, and with obloquy for everything that was given. I was thus left to support the grants of a name ever dear to me, and ever venerable to the world, in favour of those, who were no friends of mine or of his, against the rude attacks of those who were at that time friends to the grantees, and their own zealous partisans. I have never heard the Earl of Lauderdale complain of these pensions. He finds nothing wrong till he comes to me. This is impartiality, in the true, modern, revolutionary style.

Whatever I did at that time, so far as it regarded order and economy, is stable and eternal; as all principles must be. A particular order of things may be altered; order itself cannot lose its value. As to other particulars, they are variable by time and by circumstances. Laws of regulation are not fundamental laws. The public exigencies are the masters of all such laws. They rule the laws, and are not to be ruled by them. They who exercise the legislative power at the time must judge.

It may be new to his Grace, but I beg leave to tell him, that mere parsimony is not economy. It is separable in theory from it; and in fact it may, or it may not, be a *part* of economy, according to circumstances. Expense, and great expense, may be an essential part in true economy. If parsimony were to be considered as one of the kinds of that virtue, there is however another and a higher economy. Economy is a distributive virtue, and consists not in saving, but in selection. Parsimony requires no providence, no sagacity, no powers of combination, no comparison, no judgment. Mere instinct, and that not an instinct of the noblest kind, may produce this false economy in perfection. The other economy has larger views. It demands a discriminating judgment, and a firm, sagacious mind. It shuts one door to impudent importunity, only to open another, and a wider, to unpresuming merit. If none but meritorious service or real talent were to be rewarded, this nation has not wanted, and this nation will not want, the means of rewarding all the service it ever will receive, and encouraging all the merit it ever will produce. No state, since the foundation of society, has been impoverished by that species of profusion. Had the economy of selection and proportion been at all times observed, we should not now have had an overgrown Duke of Bedford, to oppress the industry of humble men, and to limit, by the standard of his own conceptions, the justice, the bounty, or, if he pleases, the charity of the Crown.

His Grace may think as meanly as he will of my deserts in the far greater part of my conduct in life. It is free for him to do so. There will always be some difference of opinion in the value of political services. But there is one merit of mine, which he, of all men living, ought to be the last to call in question. I have supported with very great zeal, and I am told with some degree of success, those opinions, or if his Grace likes another expression better, those old prejudices, which buoy up the ponderous mass of his nobility, wealth, and titles. I have omitted no exertion to prevent him and them from sinking to that level, to which the meretricious French faction, his Grace at least coquets with, omit no exertion to reduce both. I have done all I could to discountenance their inquiries into the fortunes of those, who hold large portions of wealth without any apparent merit of their own. I have strained every nerve to keep the Duke of Bedford in that situation, which alone makes him my superior. Your Lordship has been a witness of the use he makes of that pre-eminence.

But be it, that this is virtue! Be it, that there is virtue in this well-selected rigour; yet all virtues are not equally becoming to all men and at all times. There are crimes, undoubtedly there are crimes, which in all seasons of our existence, ought to put a generous antipathy in action; crimes that provoke an indignant justice, and call forth a warm and animated pursuit. But all things that concern, what I may call, the preventive police of morality, all things merely rigid, harsh, and censorial, the antiquated moralists, at whose feet I was brought up, would not have thought these the fittest matter to form the favourite virtues of young men of rank. What might have been well enough, and have been received with a veneration mixed with awe and terror, from an old, severe, crabbed Cato, would have wanted something of propriety in the young Scipios, the ornament of the Roman nobility, in the flower of their life. But the times, the morals, the masters, the scholars, have all undergone a thorough revolution. It is a vile illiberal school, this new French academy of the *sans culottes*. There is nothing in it that is fit for a gentleman to learn.

Whatever its vogue may be, I still flatter myself, that the parents of the growing generation will be satisfied with what is to be taught to their children in Westminster, in Eton, or in Winchester: I still indulge the hope that no *grown* gentleman or nobleman of our time will think of finishing at Mr. Thelwall's lecture whatever may have been left incomplete at the old universities of his country. I would give to Lord Grenville and Mr. Pitt for a motto, what was said of a Roman censor or prætor (or what was he?) who, in virtue of a Senatus consultum, shut up certain academies,

"Cludere ludum impudentiæ jussit."

Every honest father of a family in the kingdom will rejoice at the breaking up for the holidays, and will pray that there may be a very long vacation in all such schools.

The awful state of the time, and not myself, or my own justification, is my true object in what I now write; or in what I shall ever write or say. It little signifies to the world what becomes of such things as me, or even as the Duke of Bedford. What I say about either of us is nothing more than a vehicle, as you, my Lord, will easily perceive, to convey my sentiments on matters far more worthy of your attention. It is when I stick to my apparent first subject that I ought to apologize, not when I depart from it. I therefore must beg your Lordship's pardon for again resuming it after this very short digression; assuring you that I shall never altogether lose sight of such matter as persons abler than I am may turn to some profit.

The Duke of Bedford conceives, that he is obliged to call the attention of the House of Peers to his Majesty's grant to me, which he considers as excessive, and out of all bounds.

I know not how it has happened, but it really seems, that, whilst his Grace was meditating his well-considered censure upon me, he fell into a sort of sleep. Homer nods; and the Duke of Bedford may dream; and as dreams (even his golden dreams) are apt to be ill-pieced and incongruously put together, his Grace preserved his idea of reproach to *me,* but took the subject-matter from the Crown grants *to his own family.* This is "the stuff of which his dreams are made." In that way of putting things together his Grace is perfectly in the right. The grants to the house of Russell were so enormous, as not only to outrage economy, but even to stagger credibility. The Duke of Bedford is the leviathan among all the creatures of the Crown. He tumbles about his unwieldy bulk; he plays and frolics in the ocean of the royal bounty. Huge as he is, and whilst "he lies floating many a rood," he is still a creature. His ribs, his fins, his whalebone, his blubber, the very spiracles through which he spouts a torrent of brine against his origin, and covers me all over with the spray,—everything of him and about him is from the throne. Is it for *him* to question the dispensation of the royal favour?

I really am at a loss to draw any sort of parallel between the public merits of his Grace, by which he justifies the grants he holds, and these services of mine, on the favourable construction of which I have obtained what his Grace so much disapproves. In private life, I have not at all the honour of acquaintance with the noble Duke. But I ought to presume, and it costs me nothing to do so, that he abundantly deserves the esteem and love of all who live with him. But as to public service, why truly it would not be more ridiculous for me to compare myself in rank, in fortune, in splendid descent, in youth, strength, or figure, with the Duke of Bedford, than to make a parallel between his services and my attempts to be useful to my country. It would not be gross adulation, but uncivil irony, to say, that he has any public merit of his own to keep alive the idea of the services, by which his vast landed pensions were obtained. My merits, whatever they are, are original and personal; his are derivative. It is his ancestor, the original pensioner, that has laid up this inexhaustible fund of merit, which makes his Grace so very delicate and exceptious about the merit of all other grantees of the Crown. Had he permitted me to remain in quiet, I should have said, 'tis his estate; that's enough. It is his by law; what have I to do with it or its history? He would naturally have said on his side, 'tis this man's fortune.—He is as good now as my ancestor was two hundred and fifty years ago. I am a young man with very old pensions; he is an old man with very young pensions,—that's all.

Why will his Grace, by attacking me, force me reluctantly to compare my little merit with that which obtained from the Crown those prodigies of profuse donation, by which he tramples on the mediocrity of humble and laborious individuals? I would willingly leave him to the herald's college, which the philosophy of the sansculottes (prouder by far than all the Garters, and Norroys, and Clarencieux, and Rouge Dragons, that ever pranced in a procession of what his friends call aristocrats and despots) will abolish with contumely and scorn. These historians, recorders, and blazoners of virtues and arms, differ wholly from that other description of historians, who never assign any act of politicians to a good motive. These gentle historians, on the contrary, dip their pens in nothing but the milk of human kindness. They seek no further for merit than the preamble of a patent, or the inscription on a tomb. With them every man created a peer is first a hero ready made. They judge of every man's capacity for office by the offices he has filled; and the more offices the more ability. Every general officer with them is a Marlborough; every statesman a Burleigh; every judge a Murray or a Yorke. They who, alive, were laughed at or pitied by all their acquaintance, make as good a figure as the best of them in the pages of Guillim, Edmondson, and Collins.

To these recorders, so full of good nature to the great and prosperous, I would willingly leave the first Baron Russell, and Earl of Bedford, and the merits of his grants. But the aulnager, the weigher, the meter of grants will not suffer us to acquiesce in the judgment of the prince reigning at the time when they were made. They are never good to those who earn them. Well then; since the new grantees have war made on them by the old, and that the word of the sovereign is not to be taken, let us turn our eyes to history, in which great men have always a pleasure in contemplating the heroic origin of their house.

The first peer of the name, the first purchaser of the grants, was a Mr. Russell, a person of an ancient gentleman's family raised by being a minion of Henry the Eighth. As there generally is some resemblance of character to create these relations, the favourite was in all likelihood much such another as his master. The first of those immoderate grants was not taken from the ancient demesne of the Crown, but from the recent confiscation of the ancient nobility of the land. The lion having sucked the blood of his prey, threw the offal carcass to the jackal in waiting. Having tasted once the food of confiscation, the favourites became fierce and ravenous. This worthy favourite's first grant was from the lay nobility. The second, infinitely improving on the enormity of the first, was from the plunder of the church. In truth his Grace is somewhat excusable for his dislike to a grant like mine, not only in its quantity, but in its kind so different from his own.

Mine was from a mild and benevolent sovereign; his from Henry the Eighth.

Mine had not its fund in the murder of any innocent person of illustrious rank,[2] or in the pillage of any body of unoffending men. His grants were from the aggregate and consolidated funds of judgments iniquitously legal, and from possessions voluntarily surrendered by the lawful proprietors, with the gibbet at their door.

The merit of the grantee whom he derives from was that of being a prompt and greedy instrument of a *levelling* tyrant, who oppressed all descriptions of his people, but who fell with particular fury on everything that was *great and noble*. Mine has been, in endeavouring to screen every man, in every class, from oppression, and particularly in defending the high and eminent, who in the bad times of confiscating princes, confiscating chief governors, or confiscating demagogues, are the most exposed to jealousy, avarice, and envy.

The merit of the original grantee of his Grace's pensions was in giving his hand to the work and partaking the spoil with a prince, who plundered a part of the national church of his time and country. Mine was in defending the whole of the national church of my own time and my own country, and the whole of the national churches of all countries, from the principles and the examples which lead to ecclesiastical pillage, thence to a contempt of *all* prescriptive titles, thence to the pillage of *all* property, and thence to universal desolation.

The merit of the origin of his Grace's fortune was in being a favourite and chief adviser to a prince, who left no liberty to their native country. My endeavour was to obtain liberty for the municipal country in which I was born, and for all descriptions and denominations in it. Mine was to support with unrelaxing vigilance every right, every privilege, every franchise, in this my adopted, my dearer, and more comprehensive country; and not only to preserve those rights in this chief seat of empire, but in every nation, in every land, in every climate, language, and religion, in the vast domain that is still under the protection, and the larger that was once under the protection, of the British Crown.

[2] See the history of the melancholy catastrophe of the Duke of Buckingham. Temp. Hen. 8.

His founder's merits were, by arts in which he served his master and made his fortune, to bring poverty, wretchedness, and depopulation on his country. Mine were, under a benevolent prince, in promoting the commerce, manufactures, and agriculture of his kingdom; in which his Majesty shows an eminent example, who even in his amusements is a patriot, and in hours of leisure an improver of his native soil.

His founder's merit was the merit of a gentleman raised by the arts of a court, and the protection of a Wolsey, to the eminence of a great and potent lord. His merit in that eminence was, by instigating a tyrant to injustice, to provoke a people to rebellion. My merit was, to awaken the sober part of the country, that they might put themselves on their guard against any one potent lord, or any greater number of potent lords, or any combination of great leading men of any sort, if ever they should attempt to proceed in the same courses, but in the reverse order; that is, by instigating a corrupted populace to rebellion, and, through that rebellion, introducing a tyranny yet worse than the tyranny which his Grace's ancestor supported, and of which he profited in the manner we behold in the despotism of Henry the Eighth.

The political merit of the first pensioner of his Grace's house was that of being concerned as a counsellor of state in advising, and in his person executing, the conditions of a dishonourable peace with France; the surrendering the fortress of Boulogne, then our outguard on the continent. By that surrender, Calais, the key of France, and the bridle in the mouth of that power, was, not many years afterwards, finally lost. My merit has been in resisting the power and pride of France, under any form of its rule; but in opposing it with the greatest zeal and earnestness, when that rule appeared in the worst form it could assume; the worst indeed which the prime cause and principle of all evil could possibly give it. It was my endeavour by every means to excite a spirit in the House where I had the honour of a seat, for carrying on, with early vigour and decision, the most clearly just and necessary war, that this or any nation ever carried on; in order to save my country from the iron yoke of its power, and from the more dreadful contagion of its principles; to preserve, while they can be preserved, pure and untainted, the ancient, inbred integrity, piety, good nature, and good humour of the people of England, from the dreadful pestilence, which, beginning in France, threatens to lay waste the whole moral, and in a great degree the whole physical, world, having done both in the focus of its most intense malignity.

The labours of his Grace's founder merited the curses, not loud but deep, of the Commons of England, on whom *he* and his master had effected a *complete parliamentary reform,* by making them, in their slavery and humiliation, the true and adequate representatives of a debased, degraded, and undone people. My merits were, in having had an active, though not always an ostentatious, share, in every one act, without exception, of undisputed constitutional utility in my time, and in having supported, on all occasions, the authority, the efficiency, and the privileges of the Commons of Great Britain. I ended my services by a recorded and fully reasoned assertion on their own journals of their constitutional rights, and a vindication of their constitutional conduct. I laboured in all things to merit their inward approbation, and (along with the assistance of the largest, the greatest, and best of my endeavours) I received their free, unbiassed, public, and solemn thanks.

Thus stands the account of the comparative merits of the Crown grants which compose the Duke of Bedford's fortune as balanced against mine. In the name of common sense, why should the Duke of Bedford think that none but of the House of Russell are entitled to the favour of the Crown? Why should he imagine that no king of England has been capable of judging of merit but King Henry the Eighth? Indeed, he will pardon me; he is a little mistaken; all virtue did not end in the first Earl of Bedford. All discernment did not lose its vision when his Creator closed his eyes. Let him remit his rigour on the disproportion between merit and reward in others, and they will make no inquiry into the origin of his fortune. They will regard with much more satisfaction as he will contemplate with infinitely more advantage, whatever in his pedigree has been dulcified by an exposure to the influence of heaven in a long flow of generations, from the hard, acidulous, metallic tincture of the spring. It is little to be doubted, that several of his forefathers in that long series have degenerated into honour and

virtue. Let the Duke of Bedford (I am sure he will) reject with
scorn and horror the counsels of the lecturers, those wicked panders
to avarice and ambition, who would tempt him, in the troubles of
his country, to seek another enormous fortune from the forfeitures
of another nobility, and the plunder of another church. Let him
(and I trust that yet he will) employ all the energy of his youth,
and all the resources of his wealth, to crush rebellious principles
which have no foundation in morals, and rebellious movements that
have no provocation in tyranny.

Then will be forgot the rebellions, which, by a doubtful priority,
in crime, his ancestor had provoked and extinguished. On such a
conduct in the noble Duke, many of his countrymen might, and
with some excuse might, give way to the enthusiasm of their gratitude, and, in the dashing style of some of the old declaimers, cry
out, that if the fates had found no other way in which they could
give a[3] Duke of Bedford and his opulence as props to a tottering
world, then the butchery of the Duke of Buckingham might be
tolerated; it might be regarded even with complacency, whilst in
the heir of confiscation they saw the sympathizing comforter of the
martyrs, who suffered under the cruel confiscation of this day;
whilst they behold with admiration his zealous protection of the
virtuous and loyal nobility of France, and his manly support of his
brethren, the yet standing nobility and gentry of his native land.
Then his Grace's merit would be pure, and new, and sharp, as fresh
from the mint of honour. As he pleased he might reflect honour on
his predecessors, or throw it forward on those who were to succeed
him. He might be the propagator of the stock of honour, or the root
of it, as he thought proper.

Had it pleased God to continue to me the hopes of succession,
I should have been, according to my mediocrity, and the mediocrity
of the age I live in, a sort of founder of a family. I should have
left a son, who, in all the points in which personal merit can be
viewed, in science, in erudition, in genius, in taste, in honour, in
generosity, in humanity, in every liberal sentiment, and every liberal
accomplishment, would not have shown himself inferior to the Duke
of Bedford or to any of those whom he traces in his line. His Grace

[3] At si non aliam venturo fata Neroni, &c.

very soon would have wanted all plausibility in his attack upon that provision which belonged more to mine than to me. He would soon have supplied every deficiency, and symmetrized every disproportion. It would not have been for that successor to resort to any stagnant wasting reservoir of merit in me, or in any ancestry. He had in himself a salient, living spring of generous and manly action. Every day he lived he would have re-purchased the bounty of the Crown, and ten times more, if ten times more he had received. He was made a public creature; and had no enjoyment whatever, but in the performance of some duty. At this exigent moment, the loss of a finished man is not easily supplied.

But a Disposer whose power we are little able to resist, and whose wisdom it behoves us not at all to dispute, has ordained it in another manner, and (whatever my querulous weakness might suggest) a far better. The storm has gone over me; and I lie like one of those old oaks which the late hurricane has scattered about me. I am stripped of all my honours, I am torn up by the roots, and lie prostrate on the earth! There, and prostrate there, I most unfeignedly recognize the Divine justice, and in some degree submit to it. But whilst I humble myself before God, I do not know that it is forbidden to repel the attacks of unjust and inconsiderate men. The patience of Job is proverbial. After some of the convulsive struggles of our irritable nature, he submitted himself, and repented in dust and ashes. But even so, I do not find him blamed for reprehending, and with a considerable degree of verbal asperity, those ill-natured neighbours of his, who visited his dunghill to read moral, political, and economical lectures on his misery. I am alone, I have none to meet my enemies in the gate. Indeed, my Lord, I greatly deceive myself, if in this hard season I would give a peck of refuse wheat for all that is called fame and honour in the world. This is the appetite but of a few. It is a luxury, it is a privilege, it is an indulgence for those who are at their ease. But we are all of us made to shun disgrace, as we are made to shrink from pain, and poverty, and disease. It is an instinct; and under the direction of reason, instinct is always in the right. I live in an inverted order. They who ought to have succeeded me are gone before me. They who should have been to me a posterity are in the place of ancestors. I owe to the dearest relation (which ever must subsist in memory) that act of piety, which he would have performed to me; I owe it to him to show that he was not descended, as the Duke of Bedford would have it, from an unworthy parent.

The Crown has considered me after long service: the Crown has paid the Duke of Bedford by advance. He has had a long credit for any service which he may perform hereafter. He is secure, and long may he be secure, in his advance, whether he performs any services or not. But let him take care how he endangers the safety of that constitution which secures his own utility or his own insignificance; or how he discourages those, who take up, even puny arms, to defend an order of things, which, like the sun of heaven, shines alike on the useful and the worthless. His grants are ingrafted on the public law of Europe, covered with the awful hoar of innumerable ages. They are guarded by the sacred rules of prescription, found in that full treasury of jurisprudence from which the jejuneness and penury of our municipal law has, by degrees, been enriched and strengthened. This prescription I had my share (a very full share) in bringing to its perfection.[4] The Duke of Bedford will stand as long as prescriptive law endures: as long as the great stable laws of property, common to us with all civilized nations, are kept in their integrity, and without the smallest intermixture of laws, maxims, principles, or precedents of the grand Revolution. They are secure against all changes but one. The whole revolutionary system, institutes, digest, code, novels, text, gloss, comment are, not only not the same, but they are the very reverse, and the reverse fundamentally, of all the laws, on which civil life has hitherto been upheld in all the governments of the world. The learned professors of the rights of man regard prescription, not as a title to bar all claim, set up against all possession—but they look on prescription as itself a bar against the possessor and proprietor. They hold an immemorial possession to be no more than a long-continued, and therefore an aggravated injustice.

Such are *their* ideas; such *their* religion; and such *their* law. But as to *our* country and *our* race, as long as the well-compacted structure of our church and state, the sanctuary, the holy of holies of that

----

[4] Sir George Savile's Act called The *Nullum Tempus* Act.

ancient law, defended by reverence, defended by power, a fortress at once and a temple,[5] shall stand inviolate on the brow of the British Sion—as long as the British monarchy, not more limited than fenced by the orders of the state, shall, like the proud Keep of Windsor, rising in the majesty of proportion, and girt with the double belt of its kindred and coeval towers, as long as this awful structure shall oversee and guard the subjected land—so long the mounds and dykes of the low, fat Bedford level will have nothing to fear from the pickaxes of all the levellers of France. As long as our sovereign lord the king, and his faithful subjects, the Lords and Commons of this realm,—the triple cord, which no man can break; the solemn, sworn, constitutional frank-pledge of this nation; the firm guarantees of each other's being, and each other's rights; the joint and several securities, each in its place and order, for every kind and every quality, of property and of dignity;—as long as these endure, so long the Duke of Bedford is safe: and we are all safe together—the high from the blights of envy and the spoliations of rapacity; the low from the iron hand of oppression and the insolent spurn of contempt. Amen! and so be it: and so it will be,

Dum domus Æneæ Capitoli immobile saxum
Accolet; imperiumque pater Romanus habebit.—

But if the rude inroad of Gallic tumult, with its sophistical rights of man, to falsify the account, and its sword as a make-weight to throw into the scale, shall be introduced into our city by a misguided populace, set on by proud great men, themselves blinded and intoxicated by a frantic ambition, we shall, all of us, perish and be overwhelmed in a common ruin. If a great storm blow on our coast, it will cast the whales on the strand as well as the periwinkles. His Grace will not survive the poor grantee he despises, no, not for a twelvemonth. If the great look for safety in the services they render to this Gallic cause, it is to be foolish, even above the weight of privilege allowed to wealth. If his Grace be one of these whom they endeavour to proselytize, he ought to be aware of the character of the sect, whose doctrines he is invited to embrace. With them insurrection is the most sacred of revolutionary duties to the state.

[5] *Templum in modum arcis.* Tacitus, of the Temple of Jerusalem.

Ingratitude to benefactors is the first of revolutionary virtues. Ingratitude is indeed their four cardinal virtues compacted and amalgamated into one; and he will find it in everything that has happened since the commencement of the philosophic Revolution to this hour. If he pleads the merit of having performed the duty of insurrection against the order he lives, (God forbid he ever should,) the merit of others will be to perform the duty of insurrection against him. If he pleads (again God forbid he should, and I do not suspect he will) his ingratitude to the Crown for its creation of his family, others will plead their right and duty to pay him in kind. They will laugh, indeed they will laugh, at his parchment and his wax. His deeds will be drawn out with the rest of the lumber of his evidence room, and burnt to the tune of *ça ira* in the courts of Bedford (then Equality) house.

Am I to blame, if I attempt to pay his Grace's hostile reproaches to me with a friendly admonition to himself? Can I be blamed, for pointing out to him in what manner he is likely to be affected, if the sect of the cannibal philosophers of France should proselytize any considerable part of this people, and by their joint proselytizing arms, should conquer that government, to which his Grace does not seem to me to give all the support his own security demands? Surely it is proper, that he, and that others like him, should know the true genius of this sect; what their opinions are, what they have done; and to whom; and what (if a prognostic is to be formed from the dispositions and actions of men) it is certain they will do hereafter. He ought to know, that they have sworn assistance, the only engagement they ever will keep, to all in this country, who bear a resemblance to themselves, and who think as such, that *The whole duty of man* consists in destruction. They are a misallied and disparaged branch of the house of Nimrod. They are the Duke of Bedford's natural hunters; and he is their natural game. Because he is not very profoundly reflecting, he sleeps in profound security: they, on the contrary, are always vigilant, active, enterprising, and, though far removed from any knowledge which makes men estimable or useful, in all the instruments and resources of evil, their leaders are not meanly instructed, or insufficiently furnished. In the French Revolution everything is new; and, from want of preparation to meet so unlooked-for an evil, everything is dangerous. Never, before this time, was a set of literary men converted into a gang of robbers and assassins. Never before did a den of bravoes and banditti assume the garb and tone of an academy of philosophers.

Let me tell his Grace, that an union of such characters, monstrous as it seems, is not made for producing despicable enemies. But if they are formidable as foes, as friends they are dreadful indeed. The men of property in France confiding in a force, which seemed to be irresistible, because it had never been tried, neglected to prepare for a conflict with their enemies at their own weapons. They were found in such a situation as the Mexicans were, when they were attacked by the dogs, the cavalry, the iron, and the gunpowder, of a handful of bearded men, whom they did not know to exist in nature. This is a comparison that some, I think, have made; and it is just. In France they had their enemies within their houses. They were even in the bosoms of many of them. But they had not sagacity to discern their savage character. They seemed tame, and even caressing. They had nothing but *douce humanité* in their mouth. They could not bear the punishment of the mildest laws on the greatest criminals. The slightest severity of justice made their flesh creep. The very idea that war existed in the world disturbed their repose. Military glory was no more, with them, than a splendid infamy. Hardly would they hear of self-defence, which they reduced within such bounds, as to leave it no defence at all. All this while they meditated the confiscations and massacres we have seen. Had any one told these unfortunate noblemen and gentlemen, how, and by whom, the grand fabric of the French monarchy under which they flourished would be subverted, they would not have pitied him as a visionary, but would have turned from him as what they call a *mauvais plaisant*. Yet we have seen what has happened. The persons who have suffered from the cannibal philosophy of France, are so like the Duke of Bedford, that nothing but his Grace's probably not speaking quite so good French could enable us to find out any difference. A great many of them had as pompous titles as he, and were of full as illustrious a race: some few of them had fortunes as ample: several of them, without meaning the least disparagement to the Duke of Bedford, were as wise, and as virtuous, and as valiant, and as well educated, and as complete in all the lineaments of men of honour, as he is: and to all this they had added the powerful out-guard of a military profession, which, in its nature, renders men somewhat more cautious than those, who have nothing to attend to but the lazy enjoyment of undisturbed possessions. But security was their ruin. They had dashed to pieces in the storm, and our shores are covered with the wrecks. If they had been aware that such a thing might happen, such a thing never could have happened.

I assure his Grace, that if I state to him the designs of his enemies, in a manner which may appear to him ludicrous and impossible, I tell him nothing that has not exactly happened, point by point, but twenty-four miles from our own shore. I assure him that the Frenchi-fied faction, more encouraged, than others are warned, by what has happened in France, look at him and his landed possessions as an object at once of curiosity and rapacity. He is made for them in every part of their double character. As robbers, to them he is a noble booty; as speculatists, he is a glorious subject for their experi-mental philosophy. He affords matter for an extensive analysis, in all the branches of their science, geometrical, physical, civil, and politi-cal. These philosophers are fanatics; independent of any interest, which if it operated alone would make them much more tractable, they are carried with such a headlong rage towards every desperate trial, that they would sacrifice the whole human race to the slightest of their experiments. I am better able to enter into the character of this description of men than the noble Duke can be. I have lived long and variously in the world. Without any considerable preten-sions to literature in myself, I have aspired to the love of letters. I have lived for a great many years in habitudes with those who pro-fessed them. I can form a tolerable estimate of what is likely to happen from a character, chiefly dependent for fame and fortune on knowledge and talent, as well in its morbid and perverted state, as in that which is sound and natural. Naturally men so formed and finished are the first gifts of Providence to the world. But when they have once thrown off the fear of God, which was in all ages too often the case, and the fear of man, which is now the case, and when in that state they come to understand one another, and to act in corps, a more dreadful calamity cannot arise out of hell to scourge mankind. Nothing can be conceived more hard than the heart of a thoroughbred metaphysician. It comes nearer to the cold malignity of a wicked spirit than to the frailty and passion of a man. It is like that of the principle of evil himself, incorporeal, pure, unmixed, dephlegmated, defecated evil. It is no easy operation to eradicate humanity from the human breast. What Shakspeare calls "the compunctious visitings of nature" will sometimes knock at their hearts, and protest against their murderous speculations. But they have a means of compounding with their nature. Their humanity is not dissolved. They only give it a long prorogation. They are ready to declare, that they do not think two thousand years too long a period for the good that they pursue. It is remarkable, that they never see any way to their projected good but by the road of some evil. Their imagination is not fatigued with the contemplation of human suffering through the wild waste of centuries added to centuries of misery and desolation. Their humanity is at their horizon—and, like the horizon, it always flies before them. The geometricians, and the chemists, bring, the one from the dry bones of their diagrams, and the other from the soot of their furnaces, dispositions that make them worse than indifferent about those feelings and habitudes, which are the support of the moral world. Ambition is come upon them suddenly; they are intoxicated with it, and it has rendered them fearless of the danger, which may from thence arise to others or to themselves. These philosophers consider men in their experiments, no more than they do mice in an air pump, or in a recipient of mephitic gas. Whatever his Grace may think of himself, they look upon him, and everything that belongs to him, with no more regard than they do upon the whiskers of that little long-tailed animal that has been long the game of the grave, demure, insidious, spring-nailed, velvet-pawed, green-eyed philosophers, whether going upon two legs, or upon four.

His Grace's landed possessions are irresistibly inviting to an *agrarian* experiment. They are a downright insult upon the rights of man. They are more extensive than the territory of many of the Grecian republics; and they are without comparison more fertile than most of them. There are now republics in Italy, in Germany, and in Switzerland, which do not possess anything like so fair and ample a domain. There is scope for seven philosophers to proceed in their analytical experiments, upon Harrington's seven different forms of republics, in the acres of this one duke. Hitherto they have been wholly unproductive to speculation; fitted for nothing but to fatten bullocks, and to produce grain for beer, still more to stupify the dull English understanding. Abbé Sieyès has whole nests of pigeon-holes full of constitutions ready made, ticketed, sorted, and numbered; suited to every person and every fancy; some with the top of the pattern at the bottom, and some with the bottom at the top; some plain, some flowered; some distinguished for their simplicity, others for their complexity; some of blood colour; some of *bouè de Paris;* some with directories, others without a direction; some with councils of elders, and councils of youngsters; some without any council at all. Some where the electors choose the representatives; others, where the representatives choose the electors. Some in long coats, and some in short cloaks; some with pantaloons; some without breeches. Some with five-shilling qualifications; some totally unqualified. So that no constitution-fancier may go unsuited from his shop, provided he loves a pattern of pillage, oppression, arbitrary imprisonment, confiscation, exile, revolutionary judgment, and legalized premeditated murder, in any shapes into which they can be put. What a pity it is, that the progress of experimental philosophy should be checked by his Grace's monopoly! Such are their sentiments, I assure him; such is their language, when they dare to speak; and such are their proceedings, when they have the means to act.

Their geographers and geometricians have been some time out of practice. It is some time since they have divided their own country into squares. That figure has lost the charms of its novelty. They want new lands for new trials. It is not only the geometricians of the republic that find him a good subject, the chemists have bespoken him after the geometricians have done with him. As the first set have an eye on his Grace's lands, the chemists are not less taken with his buildings. They consider mortar as a very anti-revolutionary invention in its present state; but properly employed, an admirable material for overturning all establishments. They have found that the gunpowder of *ruins* is far the fittest for making other *ruins,* and so *ad infinitum.* They have calculated what quantity of matter convertible into nitre is to be found in Bedford House, in Woburn Abbey, and in what his Grace and his trustees have still suffered to stand of that foolish royalist Inigo Jones, in Covent Garden. Churches, play-houses, coffee-houses, all alike are destined to be mingled, and equalized, and blended into one common rubbish; and, well sifted and lixiviated, to crystallize into true, democratic, explosive, insurrectionary nitre. Their academy del *Cimento* (per antiphrasin) with Morveau and Hassenfrats at its head, have computed that the brave sans culottes may make war on all the aristocracy of Europe for a twelve-month, out of the rubbish of the Duke of Bedford's buildings.[6]

While the Morveaux and Priestleys are proceeding with these experiments upon the Duke of Bedford's houses, the Sieyès, and the rest of the analytical legislators, and constitution-vendors, are quite as busy in their trade of decomposing organization, in forming his Grace's vassals into primary assemblies, national guards, first, second, and third requisitioners, committees of research, conductors of the travelling guillotine, judges of revolutionary tribunals, legislative hangmen, supervisors of domiciliary visitation, exactors of forced loans, and assessors of the maximum.

The din of all this smithery may some time or other possibly wake this noble Duke, and push him to an endeavour to save some little matter from their experimental philosophy. If he pleads his grants from the Crown, he is ruined at the outset. If he pleads he has

---

[6] There is nothing, on which the leaders of the republic, one and indivisible, value themselves, more than on the chemical operations, by which, through science, they convert the pride of aristocracy to an instrument of its own destruction—on the operations by which they reduce the magnificent, ancient country seats of the nobility, decorated with the *feudal* titles of Duke, Marquis, or Earl, into magazines of what they call *revolutionary* gunpowder. They tell us, that hitherto things "had not yet been properly and in a *revolutionary* manner explored."—"The strong *chateaus,* those *feudal* fortresses that *were ordered to be demolished,* attracted next the attention of your committee. *Nature* there had *secretly* regained her *rights,* and had produced saltpetre for the *purpose,* as it should seem, *of facilitating the execution of your decree by preparing the means of destruction.* From these *ruins,* which *still frown* on the liberties of the republic, we have extracted the means of producing good; and those piles, which have hitherto glutted the *pride of despots,* and covered the plots of La Vendée, will soon furnish wherewithal to tame the traitors, and to overwhelm the disaffected."—"The *rebellious cities,* also, have afforded a large quantity of saltpetre, *Commune Affranchie,* (that is, the noble city of Lyons reduced in many parts to a heap of ruins,) and Toulon, will pay a *second* tribute to our artillery." Report, 1st February, 1794.

received them from the pillage of superstitious corporations, this indeed will stagger them a little, because they are enemies to all corporations, and to all religion. However, they will soon recover themselves, and will tell his Grace, or his learned council, that all such property belongs to the *nation;* and that it would be more wise for him if he wishes to live the natural term of a *citizen,* (that is, according to Condorcet's calculation, six months on an average,) not to pass for an usurper upon the national property. This is what the *serjeants* at law of the rights of man will say to the puny *apprentices* of the common law of England.

Is the genius of philosophy not yet known? You may as well think the garden of the Tuileries was well protected with the cords of ribbon insultingly stretched by the National Assembly to keep the sovereign canaille from intruding on the retirement of the poor king of the French, as that such flimsy cobwebs will stand between the savages of the Revolution and their natural prey. Deep philosophers are no triflers; brave sans-culottes are no formalists. They will no more regard a Marquis of Tavistock than an Abbot of Tavistock; the Lord of Woburn will not be more respectable in their eyes than the Prior of Woburn; they will make no difference between the superior of a Covent Garden of nuns, and of a Covent Garden of another description. They will not care a rush whether his coat is long or short; whether the colour be purple or blue and buff. They will not trouble *their* heads, with what part of *his* head his hair is cut from; and they will look with equal respect on a tonsure and a crop. Their only question will be that of their *Legendre,* or some other of their legislative butchers, how he cuts up? how he tallows in the cawl, or on the kidneys?

Is it not a singular phenomenon, that whilst the sans-culotte carcass-butchers, and the philosophers of the shambles, are pricking their dotted lines upon his hide, and, like the print of the poor ox that we see in the shop-windows at Charing Cross, alive as he is, and thinking no harm in the world, he is divided into rumps, and sirloins, and briskets, into all sorts of pieces for roasting, boiling, and stewing, that all the while they are measuring *him,* his Grace is measuring *me;* is invidiously comparing the bounty of the Crown with the deserts of the defender of his order, and in the same moment fawning on those who have the knife half out of the sheath —poor innocent!

> "Pleas'd to the last, he crops the flow'ry food,
> And licks the hand just raised to shed his blood."

No man lives too long, who lives to do with spirit, and suffer with resignation, what Providence pleases to command, or inflict; but indeed they are sharp incommodities which beset old age. It was but the other day, that, on putting in order some things which had been brought here on my taking leave of London for ever, I looked over a number of fine portraits, most of them of persons now dead, but whose society, in my better days, made this a proud and happy place. Amongst these was the picture of Lord Keppel. It was painted by an artist worthy of the subject, the excellent friend of that excellent man from their earliest youth, and a common friend of us both, with whom we lived for many years without a moment of coldness, of peevishness, of jealousy, or of jar, to the day of our final separation.

I ever looked on Lord Keppel as one of the greatest and best men of his age; and I loved and cultivated him accordingly. He was much in my heart, and I believe I was in his to the very last beat. It was after his trial at Portsmouth that he gave me this picture. With what zeal and anxious affection I attended him through that his agony of glory, what part my son took in the early flush and enthusiasm of his virtue, and the pious passion with which he attached himself to all my connexions, with what prodigality we both squandered ourselves in courting almost every sort of enmity for his sake, I believe he felt, just as I should have felt such friendship on such an occasion. I partook indeed of this honour, with several of the first, and best, and ablest in the kingdom, but I was behindhand with none of them; and I am sure, that if to the eternal disgrace of this nation, and to the total annihilation of every trace of honour and virtue in it, things had taken a different turn from what they did, I should have attended him to the quarter-deck with no less good will and more pride, though with far other feelings, than I partook of the general flow of national joy that attended the justice that was done to his virtue.

Pardon, my Lord, the feeble garrulity of age, which loves to diffuse itself in discourse of the departed great. At my years we live in retrospect alone; and, wholly unfitted for the society of vigorous life, we enjoy the best balm to all wounds, the consolation of friendship, in those only whom we have lost for ever. Feeling the loss of Lord Keppel at all times, at no time did I feel it so much as on the first day when I was attacked in the House of Lords.

Had he lived, that reverend form would have risen in its place, and, with a mild, parental reprehension to his nephew the Duke of Bedford, he would have told him that the favour of that gracious Prince, who had honoured his virtues with the government of the navy of Great Britain, and with a seat in the hereditary great council of his kingdom, was not undeservedly shown to the friend of the best portion of his life, and his faithful companion and counsellor under his rudest trials. He would have told him, that to whomever else these reproaches might be becoming, they were not decorous in his near kindred. He would have told him, that when men in that rank lose decorum they lose everything.

On that day I had a loss in Lord Keppel; but the public loss of him in this awful crisis—! I speak from much knowledge of the person, he never would have listened to any compromise with the rabble rout of this sans-culotterie of France. His goodness of heart, his reason, his taste, his public duty, his principles, his prejudices, would have repelled him for ever from all connexion with that horrid medley of madness, vice, impiety, and crime.

Lord Keppel had two countries; one of descent, and one of birth. Their interest and their glory are the same; and his mind was capacious of both. His family was noble, and it was Dutch: that is, he was of the oldest and purest nobility that Europe can boast, among a people renowned above all others for love of their native land. Though it was never shown in insult to any human being, Lord Keppel was something high. It was a wild stock of pride, on which the tenderest of all hearts had grafted the milder virtues. He valued ancient nobility; and he was not disinclined to augment it with new honours. He valued the old nobility and the new, not as an excuse for inglorious sloth, but as an incitement to virtuous activity. He considered it as a sort of cure for selfishness and a narrow mind;

conceiving that a man born in an elevated place in himself was nothing, but everything in what went before and what was to come after him. Without much speculation, but by the sure instinct of ingenuous feelings, and by the dictates of plain unsophisticated, natural understanding, he felt, that no great commonwealth could by any possibility long subsist, without a body of some kind or other of nobility, decorated with honour, and fortified by privilege. This nobility forms the chain that connects the ages of a nation, which otherwise (with Mr. Paine) would soon be taught that no one generation can bind another. He felt that no political fabric could be well made without some such order of things as might, through a series of time, afford a rational hope of securing unity, coherence, consistency, and stability to the state. He felt that nothing else can protect it against the levity of courts, and the greater levity of the multitude. That to talk of hereditary monarchy, without anything else of hereditary reverence in the commonwealth, was a low-minded absurdity, fit only for those detestable "fools aspiring to be knaves," who began to forge in 1789 the false money of the French constitution—That it is one fatal objection to all *new* fancied and *new fabricated* republics, (among a people, who, once possessing such an advantage, have wickedly and insolently rejected it,) that the *prejudice* of an old nobility is a thing that *cannot* be made. It may be improved, it may be corrected, it may be replenished: men may be taken from it or aggregated to it, but the *thing itself* is matter of *inveterate* opinion, and therefore *cannot* be matter of mere positive institution. He felt that this nobility in fact does not exist in wrong of other orders of the state, but by them, and for them.

I knew the man I speak of: and, if we can divine the future, out of what we collect from the past, no person living would look with more scorn and horror on the impious parricide committed on all their ancestry, and on the desperate attainder passed on all their posterity, by the Orleans, and the Rochefoucaulds, and the Fayettes, and the Vicomtes de Noailles, and the false Perigords, and the long *et cætera* of the perfidious sans-culottes of the court, who like demoniacs, possessed with a spirit of fallen pride, and inverted ambition, abdicated their dignities, disowned their families, betrayed the most sacred of all trusts, and, by breaking to pieces a great link of society and all the cramps and holdings of the state, brought eternal confusion and desolation on their country. For the fate of the miscreant parricides themselves he would have had no pity. Compassion for the myriads of men, of whom the world was not worthy, who by their means have perished in prisons, or on scaffolds, or are pining in beggary and exile, would leave no room in his, or in any well-informed mind, for any such sensation. We are not made at once to pity the oppressor and the oppressed.

Looking to his Batavian descent, how could he bear to behold his kindred, the descendants of the brave nobility of Holland, whose blood, prodigally poured out, had, more than all the canals, meres, and inundations of their country, protected their independence, to behold them bowed in the basest servitude to the basest and vilest of the human race; in servitude to those who in no respect were superior in dignity, or could aspire to a better place than that of hangman to the tyrants, to whose sceptred pride they had opposed an elevation of soul, that surmounted, and overpowered, the loftiness of Castile, the haughtiness of Austria, and the overbearing arrogance of France?

Could he with patience bear, that the children of that nobility, who would have deluged their country and given it to the sea, rather than submit to Louis XIV., who was then in his meridian glory, when his arms were conducted by the Turennes, by the Luxembourgs, by the Boufflers; when his councils were directed by the Colberts, and the Louvois; when his tribunals were filled by the Lamoignons and the Daguessaus—that these should be given up to the cruel sport of the Pichegrus, the Jourdans, the Santerres, under the Rolands, the Brissots, and Gorfas, and Robespierres, the Reubels, the Carnots, and Talliens, and Dantons, and the whole tribe of regicides, robbers, and revolutionary judges, that, from the rotten carcass of their own murdered country, have poured out innumerable swarms of the lowest, and at once the most destructive, of the classes of animated nature, which, like columns of locusts, have laid waste the fairest part of the world?

Would Keppel have borne to see the ruin of the virtuous patricians, that happy union of the noble and the burgher, who, with signal prudence and integrity, had long governed the cities of the confederate republic, the cherishing fathers of their country, who, denying commerce to themselves, made it flourish in a manner unexampled under their protection? Could Keppel have borne that a vile faction should totally destroy this harmonious construction, in favour of a robbing democracy, founded on the spurious rights of man?

He was no great clerk, but he was perfectly well versed in the interests of Europe, and he could not have heard with patience, that the country of Grotius, the cradle of the law of nations, and one of the richest repositories of all law, should be taught a new code by the ignorant flippancy of Thomas Paine, the presumptuous foppery of La Fayette, with his stolen rights of man in his hand, the wild, profligate intrigue, and turbulency, of Marat, and the impious sophistry of Condorcet, in his insolent addresses to the Batavian republic.

Could Keppel, who idolized the house of Nassau, who was himself given to England along with the blessings of the British and Dutch revolutions; with revolutions of stability; with revolutions which consolidated and married the liberties and the interests of the two nations for ever, could he see the fountain of British liberty itself in servitude to France? Could he see with patience a Prince of Orange expelled as a sort of diminutive despot, with every kind of contumely, from the country, which that family of deliverers had so often rescued from slavery, and obliged to live in exile in another country, which owes its liberty to his house?

Would Keppel have heard with patience, that the conduct to be held on such occasions was to become short by the knees to the faction of the homicides, to entreat them quietly to retire? or, if the fortune of war should drive them from their first wicked and unprovoked invasion, that no security should be taken, no arrangement made, no barrier formed, no alliance entered into for the security of that, which under a foreign name is the most precious part of England? What would he have said, if it was even proposed that the Austrian Netherlands (which ought to be a barrier to Holland, and the tie of an alliance, to protect her against any species of rule that might be erected, or even be restored in France) should be formed into a republic under her influence, and dependent upon her power?

But above all, what would he have said, if he had heard it made a matter of accusation against me, by his nephew the Duke of Bedford, that I was the author of the war? Had I a mind to keep that high distinction to myself, as from pride I might, but from justice I dare not, he would have snatched his share of it from my hand, and held it with the grasp of a dying convulsion to his end.

It would be a most arrogant presumption in me to assume to myself the glory of what belongs to his Majesty, and to his ministers, and to his parliament, and to the far greater majority of his faithful people: but had I stood alone to counsel, and that all were determined to be guided by my advice, and to follow it implicitly—then I should have been the sole author of a war. But it should have been a war on my ideas and my principles. However, let his Grace think as he may of my demerits with regard to the war with regicide, he will find my guilt confined to that alone. He never shall, with the smallest colour of reason, accuse me of being the author of a peace with regicide. But that is high matter; and ought not to be mixed with anything of so little moment, as what may belong to me, or even to the Duke of Bedford.

I have the honour to be, &c.

EDMUND BURKE.